3/09
Brodar
19.95

W9-BYF-300

3 2802 00077 9083

Stop Foreclosure Now

346.7304
Segal

Segal, Lloyd M..

Stop foreclosure now

DUE DATE   19.95

Blauvelt Free Library
541 Western Hwy
Blauvelt, NY 10913

Stop Foreclosure Now

*The Complete Guide to Saving
Your Home and Your Credit*

Lloyd Segal

American Management Association

New York • Atlanta • Brussels • Chicago • Mexico City • San Francisco
Shanghai • Tokyo • Toronto • Washington, D.C

Blauvelt Free Library
541 Western Hwy
Blauvelt, NY 10913

Special discounts on bulk quantities of AMACOM books are
available to corporations, professional associations, and other
organizations. For details, contact Special Sales Department,
AMACOM, a division of American Management Association,
1601 Broadway, New York, NY 10019.
Tel.: 212-903-8316. Fax: 212-903-8083.
E-mail: specialsls@amanet.org
Website: www.amacombooks.org/go/specialsales
To view all AMACOM titles go to: www.amacombooks.org

This publication is designed to provide accurate and authoritative
information in regard to the subject matter covered. It is sold with the
understanding that the publisher is not engaged in rendering legal,
accounting, or other professional service. If legal advice or other expert
assistance is required, the services of a competent professional person
should be sought.

Library of Congress Cataloging-in-Publication Data

Segal, Lloyd M., 1948-
   Stop foreclosure now : save your house if you can, save your credit if you can't / Lloyd Segal.
      p. cm.
   ISBN 978-0-8144-1330-2
   1. Foreclosure—United States—Popular works.   I. Title.

KF697.F6S44   2008
346.7304'364—dc22

                                        2008020763

© 2007 by Lloyd Segal
All rights reserved.
Printed in the United States of America.

This publication may not be reproduced, stored in a retrieval system,
or transmitted in whole or in part, in any form or by any means, electronic,
mechanical, photocopying, recording, or otherwise, without the prior written
permission of AMACOM, a division of American Management Association,
1601 Broadway, New York, NY 10019.

Printing number

10 9 8 7 6 5 4 3 2

ACKNOWLEDGMENTS

I want to take this opportunity to especially thank those individuals who so graciously helped in compiling information, editing, and critiquing this book. Their suggestions and advice were warmly welcomed: William Godwin, Esq., John McGovern, David Stone, Foreclosure Trustee, Robert Sonnenblick, Karen Johnston-Tan, E. Jeffrey Smith, Robin Evans, Martin Garrick, Jimmy O'Loughlin, Sandy Duda, Jaime Jerugim, Accountant, Jonathan Kirsh, Esq., Stacey Kane, Patrick Tenore, Howard Gordon, Michael Scher, Dennis H. Johnston, Esq., Katy Blackwood, Deputy Hubert Bernat, Deidre Dickey, Chief of Loan Services for the Department of Veteran Affairs, Lt. Adam P. Feller, Naval Legal Services Office, Peter Fleming, agent extraordinaire, Ginger Atherton, Larry Johnson, HUD Mortgage Assistance Program, Department of Housing and Urban Affairs, Steve Maizes, mortgage broker to the stars, Jack Soussana, Yariv Asoulay, Ray Arthun, Susan Lipsett, editor, Lisa Goldoftas, editor, Steve Elias, Esq., editor, James C. Mills, "aspiring editor," Robbin Mills.

This book is dedicated to the loving memory of my mother, Seretta Segal (1928–2006), who encouraged me to achieve the impossible and educate others along the way.

Table of Contents

INTRODUCTION

A. What Is Foreclosure?..xi

B. When Will This Book Help You?..xii

C. What Types of Property Does This Book Cover?...xii

D. What Types of Foreclosures Does This Book Cover?...xii

E. Don't Panic xiii

F. Can You Really Do It Yourself? xiii

G. Will This Book Help You If You Do Have an Attorney? xiv

H. How to Use This Book xiv

CHAPTER 1

DEVELOP A PLAN TO STOP FORECLOSURE

A. Communicate With Your Lender 2

B. Get Organized 6

C. Learn the Clock 7

D. Decide Whether or Not to Keep Your Property 8

E. Develop a Plan of Action...14

CHAPTER 2

UNDERSTANDING THE DOCUMENTS UNDERLYING A FORECLOSURE

A. Promissory Note..18

B. Deed of Trust..27

C. Mortgages 36

D. Reviewing Your Deed of Trust or Mortgage..53

CHAPTER 3

NONJUDICIAL FORECLOSURES

A. Overview of Nonjudicial Foreclosure...60

B. Notice of Default and Election to Sell 61

C. The Reinstatement Period 68

D. Notice of Trustee's Sale 70

E. The Redemption Period 75

F. Trustee's Sale 78

CHAPTER 4

JUDICIAL FORECLOSURES

A. Why Lenders Choose Judicial Foreclosures...86

B. Overview of a Judicial Foreclosure 87

CHAPTER 5

NEGOTIATING WITH YOUR LENDER

A. Negotiating Strategies..112
B. Negotiating With an Institutional Lender...115
C. Negotiating With a Private Lender 121
D. Negotiating With HUD and the FHA 122
E. Negotiating With the U.S. Department of Veteran Affairs 126

CHAPTER 6

REFINANCING OUT OF FORECLOSURE

A. Deciding Whether to Refinance 132
B. Should You Use a Mortgage Broker?...134
C. Will You Qualify for Refinancing?...134
D. Overview of Refinancing 137
E. Kinds of Loans 138
F. How to Find a Lender to Refinance Your Property 145
G. Closing Costs 148

CHAPTER 7

USING YOUR MILITARY STATUS TO STOP FORECLOSURE

A. Are You Covered by the SSCRA? 152
B. How to Use the SSCRA to Reduce Your Interest Rate and Payments 155
C. How to Use the SSCRA to Stop a Nonjudicial Foreclosure 157
D. How to Use the SSCRA to Stop a Judicial Foreclosure 159

CHAPTER 8

USING THE COURTS TO STOP A NONJUDICIAL FORECLOSURE

A. Do You Have Grounds to Go to Court?...162
B. Overview of a Lawsuit to Enjoin Foreclosure..171
C. How to File a Lawsuit and Get a Temporary Restraining Order 174
D. How Your Case Proceeds After the TRO Hearing..................................187

CHAPTER 9

BANKRUPTCY

A. File for Bankruptcy and Stop the Foreclosure 189
B. How Bankruptcy Works..190
C. Which Bankruptcy Is Right for You? 203

D. Additional Resources 204

CHAPTER 10
HOW TO SELL YOUR PROPERTY QUICKLY TO STOP FORECLOSURE

A. Deciding Whether to Sell Your Property 206
B. Hire a Real Estate Agent 207
C. Implement a Plan to Sell Your Property 212
D. Prepare Your Property for Sale 214
E. Offers and Counter-Offers 215
F. Proceeding Through to Closing 217
G. Special Rules for Dealing With Equity Purchasers 218
H. Arranging a "Short Sale" With Your Lender 222

CHAPTER 11
GIVING YOUR LENDER A DEED IN LIEU OF FORECLOSURE

A. Reasons to Use a Deed in Lieu 228
B. Will Your Lender Accept a Deed in Lieu? 229
C. Negotiate Terms of the Deed in Lieu 231
D. How to Prepare a Deed in Lieu of Foreclosure 232

CHAPTER 12
HELP BEYOND THIS BOOK

A. Real Estate Lawyers 238
B. Using a Foreclosure Consultant 240
C. The Law Library, Internet, and Legal Research 243

APPENDIX
247

GLOSSARY
261

SUMMARY OF STATE FORECLOSURE LAWS
271

DEAR READER
339

ABOUT THE AUTHOR
341

INTRODUCTION

A. What Is Foreclosure? xi

B. When Will This Book Help You? xii

C. What Types of Property Does This Book Cover? xii

D. What Types of Foreclosures Does This Book Cover? xii

E. Don't Panic xiii

F. Can You Really Do It Yourself? xiii

G. Will This Book Help You If You Do Have an Attorney? xiv

H. How to Use This Book xiv

T he experience of falling behind on your loan payments and going into foreclosure can be painful, humiliating and stressful. And if you're like most people, your emotional distress is aggravated by a lack of knowledge as you are cast into unknown territory. But please be assured--you are not alone. Millions of people go into foreclosure every year throughout the United States.

To minimize your anxiety and maximize your understanding, this book provides a thorough discussion of what you will likely encounter once your property goes into foreclosure. But before we leap into the fray, there are several pointers that you should consider as you start your journey.

A. What Is Foreclosure?

Let's start with a clear definition of *"foreclosure."* In its simplest terms, your lender has the legal right to sell your property at a public auction if you fall behind on loan payments and don't bring your loan current within a specified period of time. This process, known as foreclosure, can be conducted though the court system (judicial foreclosure) or without going to court (nonjudicial foreclosure). Depending in which state your property is located, you will experience either judicial foreclosure or nonjudicial foreclosure. This book covers both.

Learning the lingo. If you're facing a foreclosure, you're going to run into a lot of unfamiliar legal terminology. Along the way, this book will try to explain the most common jargon in plain English. For a quick reference, you can also check the Glossary at the back of the book.

B. When Will This Book Help You?

If you are reading this book, there's a good chance your lender has already started foreclosure proceedings. This book will help you understand the foreclosure process and figure out what you can do to stop it. But this book will also be helpful if you've missed payments on a real estate loan and your lender is threatening to start foreclosure, or you are struggling to keep current on a real estate loan but expect that you won't be able to keep up the payments for much longer. In addition to learning about foreclosure methods, you'll find valuable information on how to negotiate with your lender or use other strategies to avoid a foreclosure.

Your goal should be to learn all you can about foreclosure so you can anticipate what might happen and develop a strategy to stop it. This book will also help you analyze whether or not to keep your property, by taking a long, hard look at your options and deciding which option(s) will ultimately be of benefit to you.

C. What Types of Property Does This Book Cover?

In this book, we use the generic word "property" to refer to all types of real estate. In other words, the information in this book applies to any real property, regardless of whether you own a single-family home, condominium, duplex, triplex, apartment building, shopping center, office building, commercial building, industrial park or raw land.

D. What Types of Foreclosures Does This Book Cover?

This book covers foreclosure by a lender who holds a written lien against your property (called a "mortgage" or "deed of trust") as security for repayment of its loan. This lender could be the financial institution that originally gave you a loan to purchase your property, or a lender who subsequently lent you additional money also backed by security in your property (such as a bank that granted you a home equity loan), or the lender that refinanced your property, or the seller of the property who accepted a portion of the sale's price in the form of a junior lien, or a company that subsequently purchased a loan from any of your original lenders.

Foreclosures not covered by this book. This book does not cover tax sales, court judgments, or mechanic's lien sales, which are not technically foreclosures. If you are involved with any of these forced sales, you should consult an attorney. Nevertheless, many of the strategies described in this book can be applied to these involuntary sales as well.

ICONS USED IN THIS BOOK

Throughout this book, we have included special icons to help organize the material and underscore particular points:

Legal or common sense tips to help you understand or comply with legal requirements.

A caution to slow down and consider potential problems.

A suggestion to seek the advice of a lawyer, tax advisor or other specialist.

An indication that you may be able to skip some material that does not apply to you.

A cross-reference to another section of this book, or a suggestion to consult another book or resource.

E. Don't Panic

Property owners in foreclosure are like deer caught in the headlights of an approaching automobile. Panicked, they freeze with inaction. Misunderstanding the process, they often use the word "foreclosed" in the past tense as though they have already lost their property. Or worse, some people assume their properties are already lost and move out without even putting up a fight. Don't let this happen to you!

Although easier said than done, it is important not to panic simply because a foreclosure has started. As you will learn in this book, foreclosure is a lengthy process--not a single event. The process takes a minimum of three months in some states (nonjudicial foreclosures), and as long as one to two years in other states (judicial foreclosures). Additionally, in a judicial foreclosure, you may have the right to buy back ("redeem") your property for an additional period after the foreclosure sale depending on the laws in your state.

So, whatever you do, don't think all is lost and give up without a fight. You still have time to develop and implement a plan to stop the foreclosure, and this book will help you.

F. Can You Really Do It Yourself?

Unless your foreclosure is unusually complex, the answer is yes--a resounding yes! You simply need to use your common sense, the willingness to learn about foreclosure procedures, and the commitment to deal with your lender. In other words, your everyday life experiences are the foundation of what you need to know.

For the most part, the techniques described in this book do not require legal knowledge. Forget the notion that you have to act or sound like an experienced lawyer to be successful in dealing with lenders. As you will discover, the vast majority of people you'll deal with during the foreclosure will not be lawyers.

Realize that no matter how many times you read this book and how carefully you prepare, you will probably be nervous when you first approach your lender, trustee or sheriff. But, rest assured, you're not the only one feeling uneasy. Most people (including lawyers) feel anxious when they begin a new task.

So take a deep breath and gather up your courage. As long as you combine your common sense with the principles and techniques described in this book, and are not afraid to ask people questions if you need help, you should be able to represent yourself competently and effectively.

G. Will This Book Help You If You Do Have an Attorney?

Finally, if an attorney already represents you, this book can still help you. Keep in mind that your property belongs to you--not your lawyer. Based upon this simple fact, no lawyer will ever be able to give as much attention to stopping your foreclosure as you can. But, a good lawyer can do a better job of representing you if you are informed and knowledgeable about the foreclosure process and can participate in making critical decisions.

H. How to Use This Book

This book is designed to increase your overall understanding of the foreclosure process (including procedures and strategies that may initially seem peculiar or foreign), and to provide specific techniques you can use to stop the foreclosure. Here's the best way to use this book.

Step 1. Read Chapter 1 and Decide Whether or Not to Keep Your Property

Chapter 1 orients you to the world of foreclosure law and helps you decide whether to keep your property. Based on your decision, you'll begin to develop a plan to stop foreclosure in Chapter 1, Section E.

If you're in the midst of a foreclosure. If you do not have the time to read large portions of this book, read Chapter 1, then proceed to those method(s) of dealing with foreclosure that apply to your particular situation.

Step 2. Learn About the Legal Documents Underlying a Foreclosure

Chapter 2 explains the underlying documents in a foreclosure: the promissory note and deed of trust, or the mortgage. Understanding these documents, which you signed when you obtained your loan, is fundamental to dealing with foreclosure.

Step 3. Read About the Kind of Foreclosure You're Facing

There are two kinds of foreclosures:
- **judicial**--where the lender files a lawsuit in court to foreclose a mortgage.
- **nonjudicial**--where the lender uses a trustee to follow an out-of-court procedure to foreclose on a deed of trust.

Each type of foreclosure follows different procedures, and you need to be concerned only with those procedures that apply to your particular state. If lenders in your state use mortgages to secure real estate loans, then most likely the foreclosure will be judicial, covered in Chapter 4. If, on the other hand, lenders in your state use deeds of trust to secure real estate loans, then most likely the foreclosure will be nonjudicial, covered in Chapter 3. (If you don't know which kind of foreclosure applies to you, look up your state in the Appendix in the back of this book.)

Step 4. Pursue Strategies to Stop Foreclosure

Depending on whether you've decided to keep or give up your property, you need only read those chapters with strategies that interest you. Chapter 1, Section E, summarizes your options and refers you to the appropriate chapters. (Chapters 5 through 9 describe strategies to keep your property. Chapters 10 and 11 cover strategies to get rid of your property.)

Step 5. Seek Additional Help If You Need It

In Chapter 12, you'll learn how to find a lawyer or foreclosure consultant to help you. Chapter 12 also gives helpful information on doing your own legal research.

FORECLOSURE BASICS—BY STATE

State	Security Instrument	Foreclosure Type	Initial Step	# of Months	Redemption	Deficiency
Alabama	Mortgage	Nonjudicial	Publication	1	12 months	Allowed
Alaska	Trust Deed	Nonjudicial	Notice of Default	3	None	Allowed
Arizona	Trust Deed	Nonjudicial	Notice of Sale	3	None	Allowed
Arkansas	Mortgage	Judicial	Complaint	4	None	Allowed
California	Trust Deed	Nonjudicial	Notice of Default	4	None	Prohibited
Colorado	Trust Deed	Nonjudicial	Notice of Default	2	75 Days	Allowed
Connecticut	Mortgage	Strict	Complaint	5	None	Allowed
Delaware	Mortgage	Judicial	Complaint	3	None	Allowed
Dist. of Col.	Trust Deed	Nonjudicial	Notice of Default	2	None	Allowed
Florida	Mortgage	Judicial	Complaint	5	None	Allowed
Georgia	Security Deed	Nonjudicial	Publication	2	None	Allowed
Hawaii	Mortgage	Nonjudicial	Publication	3	None	Allowed
Idaho	Trust Deed	Nonjudicial	Notice of Default	5	None	Allowed
Illinois	Mortgage	Judicial	Complaint	7	None	Allowed
Indiana	Mortgage	Judicial	Complaint	5	3 months	Allowed
Iowa	Mortgage	Judicial	Petition	5	6 months	Allowed
Kansas	Mortgage	Judicial	Complaint	4	6–12 months	Allowed
Kentucky	Mortgage	Judicial	Complaint	6	None	Allowed
Louisiana	Mortgage	Exec. Process	Petition	2	None	Allowed
Maine	Mortgage	Judicial	Complaint	6	None	Allowed
Maryland	Trust Deed	Nonjudicial	Notice	2	None	Allowed
Massachusetts	Mortgage	Judicial	Complaint	3	None	Allowed
Michigan	Mortgage	Nonjudicial	Publication	2	6 months	Allowed
Minnesota	Mortgage	Nonjudicial	Publication	2	6 months	Prohibited
Mississippi	Trust Deed	Nonjudicial	Publication	2	None	Prohibited
Missouri	Trust Deed	Nonjudicial	Publication	2	None	Allowed
Montana	Trust Deed	Nonjudicial	Notice	5	None	Prohibited
Nebraska	Mortgage	Judicial	Petition	5	None	Allowed
Nevada	Trust Deed	Nonjudicial	Notice of Default	4	None	Allowed

State	Security Instrument	Foreclosure Type	Initial Step	# of Months	Redemption	Deficiency
New Hampshire	Mortgage	Nonjudicial	Notice of Sale	2	None	Allowed
New Jersey	Mortgage	Judicial	Complaint	3	10 Days	Allowed
New Mexico	Mortgage	Judicial	Complaint	4	None	Allowed
New York	Mortgage	Judicial	Complaint	4	None	Allowed
North Carolina	Trust Deed	Nonjudicial	Notice Hearing	2	None	Allowed
North Dakota	Mortgage	Judicial	Complaint	3	60 Days	Prohibited
Ohio	Mortgage	Judicial	Complaint	5	None	Allowed
Oklahoma	Mortgage	Judicial	Complaint	4	None	Allowed
Oregon	Trust Deed	Nonjudicial	Notice of Default	5	None	Allowed
Pennsylvania	Mortgage	Judicial	Complaint	3	None	Allowed
Rhode Island	Mortgage	Nonjudicial	Publication	2	None	Allowed
South Carolina	Mortgage	Judicial	Complaint	6	None	Allowed
South Dakota	Mortgage	Judicial	Complaint	3	180 days	Allowed
Tennessee	Trust Deed	Nonjudicial	Publication	2	None	Allowed
Texas	Trust Deed	Nonjudicial	Publication	2	None	Allowed
Utah	Trust Deed	Nonjudicial	Notice of Default	4	None	Allowed
Vermont	Mortgage	Judicial	Complaint	7	None	Allowed
Virginia	Trust Deed	Nonjudicial	Publication	2	None	Allowed
Washington	Trust Deed	Nonjudicial	Notice of Default	4	None	Allowed
West Virginia	Trust Deed	Nonjudicial	Publication	2	None	Prohibited
Wisconsin	Mortgage	Judicial	Complaint	Varies	None	Allowed
Wyoming	Mortgage	Nonjudicial	Publication	2	3 months	Allowed

1

DEVELOP A PLAN TO STOP FORECLOSURE

A. Communicate With Your Lender 2

    1. Keep a Log of Contacts (Communications Chart) 3
    2. How to Respond to Lender's Initial Contacts 5
    3. Find Someone With Authority to Stop the Foreclosure................. 6

B. Get Organized 6

C. Learn the Clock 7

D. Decide Whether or Not to Keep Your Property 8

    1. Is There Any Equity in the Property?.. 8
    2. Does the Property Have Economic Value Apart From the Equity?.......11
    3. Are You Emotionally Attached to the Property?...........................11
    4. Other Considerations.. 12
    5. Tax Effects of Giving Up or Selling Your Property..................... 12

E. Develop a Plan of Action..14

    1. Options to Keep Your Property...15
    2. Options to Get Rid of Your Property 16

Most people believe that foreclosure laws are designed to hurt rather than help them. Not so. The truth is, foreclosure laws have evolved to protect the borrower--not the lender. The foreclosure process gives you, the borrower, specific periods of time in which to:

- bring your loan current by making up the missed payments (known as "reinstatement"), or

- pay off your loan in its entirety (called "redemption").

If neither of these options is feasible, you will still have time to prevent your property from being sold at a public auction (the foreclosure sale).

You will get the most benefit out of the foreclosure process if you envision it as a "window of opportunity" to resolve your financial problems. During this period, you have time to learn about the foreclosure process and implement a strategy to stop the foreclosure.

Another basic misconception about foreclosure is that lenders want to foreclose. Nothing could be further from the truth! Lenders are in the business of loaning money--not owning real estate. Lenders are also reluctant to incur the costs of a foreclosure. For example, if your lender is forced to foreclose, it will not only lose your back payments, but it will also incur foreclosure expenses, taxes, insurance, wear and tear while you (or your tenant) live in the property, rehabilitation expenses to refurbish the property for sale, and a real estate agent's commission once the property is sold. As a result, many lenders will go out of their way to work out a resolution-- short of actually foreclosing--if given the opportunity to avoid paying these costs.

A. Communicate With Your Lender

At the heart of stopping your foreclosure is communicating with your lender. Don't shy away because you've missed payments, concerned that you will miss some payments in the future, or that your property has already gone into foreclosure. Whether you communicate by telephone, letter, email, fax, or in person, you will have a much easier time stopping (or at the very least, delaying) the foreclosure if you talk to your lender rather than adopting a code of silence.

The first step is to determine who your lender actually is. (This is no small feat these days with lenders selling their loans to other lenders like hot potatoes.) If your property has already gone into foreclosure, the first person you will be dealing with either the foreclosing trustee, or the attorney for the lender. The trustee is responsible for handling the foreclosure process if it is nonjudicial. (For more on the trustee, read Chapter 2 Section B). If it is a judicial foreclosure, you will most likely be contacted by a process server, sent by the lender's attorney. But the problem is that you need to communicate with your lender, not the trustee or the attorney. So you should request from the trustee or the attorney, the name, telephone number, and address of the foreclosing lender. In the unlikely event that they refuse to disclose the name of your lender, you can look on the Notice of Default, or the summons and complaint, or telephone the customer service department of a local title insurance company.

Another situation may occur where you discover the name of your lender, but it turns out to be a servicing agent rather than the party that actually holds the deed of trust or mortgage. A servicing agent is a company (sometimes it can be a bank, mortgage company, or private corporation) that is hired by the actual lender to "service" the loan, including the collection of payments, issuing of payment coupons and late notices, monitoring the impounding of insurance and tax payments, and handling foreclosures if necessary. Fortunately, most servicing agents will disclose the name of the lender. If they won't, you may be forced to negotiate with the servicing agent. In either event, follow the guidelines in this book to communicate and negotiate with them.

Do not under any circumstance ignore your lender's contacts. Your goal should be to respond to every phone call or letter. Difficult as it may be to talk about your financial problems, be polite and cooperative. Follow up all telephone calls with a letter to the person you spoke to, confirming what was said. If you're not in when a call comes, return it as soon as you can.

When you receive a letter from your lender (always keep the original), immediately write a letter in response. It is important to establish a paper trail so you can prove to your lender (or a court, if necessary) that you have been cooperative, especially during the initial stages of the foreclosure process.

It is also important to send copies of all of your letters to:
- the lender's CEO
- the branch manager (if applicable)
- the loan officer who helped you obtain your loan, and
- any other person you know by name at your lender's office.

1. Keep a Log of Contacts (Communications Chart)

Catalog all communications on a

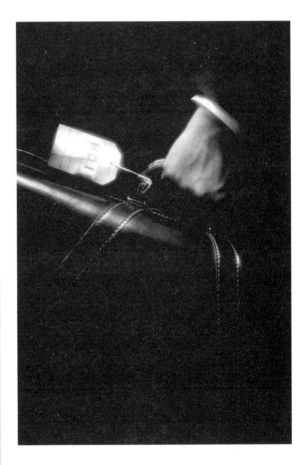

CONTACTING PEOPLE YOU KNOW AT THE LENDER'S OFFICE

Make sure your letter indicates you are sending copies by typing "cc:" and the name of the person(s) below your signature. Please don't be hesitant to send copies of your letters to these individuals, as they can't do anything to help you if they aren't aware of your predicament. At the very least, the person you sent the letter to won't be able to ignore your letter because he or she knows that supervisors have received copies.

Communications Chart (a sort of log), including the date and time of the communication, the method (by letter, telephone call, email, fax, or meeting), the name of the person you

spoke to, what she said, and what you said in response. A self-explanatory Communications Chart you can use appears on the next page. A tear-out copy of this form is also included in the Appendix.

COMMUNICATIONS CHART

Date of contact: Time:

[] Telephone [] Letter   [] Fax   [] Email [] Meeting/location

Name of contact person:

Who initiated communication?

What we discussed:

Agreements we reached, if any:

Date of contact: Time:

[] Telephone [] Letter   [] Fax   [] Email [] Meeting/location

Name of contact person:

Who initiated communication?

What we discussed:

Agreements we reached, if any:

Date of contact: Time:

[] Telephone [] Letter   [] Fax   [] Email [] Meeting/location

Name of contact person:

Who initiated communication?

What we discussed:

Agreements we reached, if any:

2. How to Respond to Lender's Initial Contacts

Typically, in their initial letters and telephone calls, your lender will state that they have not received your payment(s) and inquire innocently whether you have mailed a payment. What you say in response to your lender's inquiry is another matter. If you already mailed your payment, give your lender the date. If you have not, tell the truth. Your lender in turn will want to know why you haven't paid, and what date you will be sending a payment. Acknowledge that you are having temporary financial problems and that you won't be able to make the payments for the next couple of months. Provide a good explanation of your financial difficulties (i.e. layoff, medical emergency, death in the family, loss of business, divorce). Contrary to popular misconceptions, sharing this information will not speed up the foreclosure process. Each lender has its own foreclosure timetable. Nevertheless, what you say may make the lender more sympathetic to your situation and foster a positive atmosphere for negotiations later in the process. (For more on negotiating with your lender. see Chapter 5.)

Your lender may warn you that if payments are not made, your loan will go into default. It may also threaten

to start foreclosure proceedings unless you bring all of your payments current immediately. But don't be intimidated. Stay calm and understand that the person you're dealing with is simply doing his job. At this point, write a letter explaining your financial problem and requesting an appointment with a senior loan officer to discuss your loan. See the sample letter below.

September 6, 200X

William Blackman
Acme Savings Bank
1000 First Street
Syracuse, New York

Re: 1234 Highland Avenue,
    Syracuse, N.Y.

Loan No. 15400

Dear Mr. Blackman:

I own the property listed above. On September 5, you threatened to start a foreclosure against my property because I missed several loan payments.

I am having severe financial problems that will not be resolved for several months. Although several collection representatives of your bank have called me, they are not authorized to help me resolve my loan. Accordingly, I would like to schedule an appointment with an authorized officer of your bank who can discuss my options and assist me during this temporary crisis.

Please have a representative contact me as soon as possible. I am eager to resolve this problem and bring my loan current.

Sincerely,

David Stone

cc: Leslie Bernton, Bank President

3. Find Someone With Authority to Stop the Foreclosure

As you develop a strategy to stop your foreclosure, you will want to be in close touch with someone at your lender's office who has authority to stop the foreclosure. Don't waste your time dealing with a lower-level collection person who has little interest in your hardship or the reasons you are not making the monthly payments. All she wants to know is when you are going to pay. Collection personnel have no authority to negotiate with you or stop your foreclosure.

RESOURCES FOR HELP WITH FINANCIAL PROBLEMS

If your financial problems go beyond just one loan in foreclosure, you may want to read *Money Troubles: Legal Strategies to Cope With Your Debts*, by Robin Leonard (Nolo Press). Essential for anyone who is feeling overwhelmed by debts, this Book shows you how to deal with credit bureaus, creditors, challenge wage attachments, decide whether to file for bankruptcy and rebuild your credit.

If you're confronting a tax debt, *Stand Up to the IRS*, by Fred Daily (Nolo Press), provides excellent information for surviving a tax audit and resolving your tax problems.

If a collection person calls, politely say goodbye and hang up. Then call the main office of your lender. Ask for the names of the branch manager and the senior loan officer. When you get the information, thank the person you're speaking to, and hang up again.

Wait one hour, call back and ask for the branch manager or senior loan officer by name. Once you are connected, request an appointment.

If you can't get through and no one returns your call, send a letter such as the one on the previous page. Be sure you send a copy to the president of your lender. Wait several days and call again. Sooner or later, you'll reach someone with authority. This is the person you will want to meet with. (For more information on negotiating with your lender, see Chapter 5.)

B. Get Organized

It is important to gather together all the documents that relate to your property and your loan. In a typical real estate transaction, you signed a purchase contract, escrow instructions, a mortgage, or a promissory note and a deed of trust. Organize and review as many of these documents as you can in order to understand how the foreclosure process applies to you. Here's what you should get:

- Copies of the promissory note and deed of trust, or the mortgage.

- Copies of any documents and letters in your escrow (contact the escrow company or title company that handled the purchase of your property to get copies).

- A *"property profile"* which contains information on all documents recorded against your property. You can obtain a free copy of a property profile from the title insurance company that originally insured your purchase of the property. Also ask the company for copies of all documents recorded against your property in the county recorder's office.

• Your Communications Chart (see Section A above).

• Copies of all letters you sent to and received from your lender, along with the envelopes the letters from your lender came in, if you have them.

• Copies of your mortgage statements, loan payment stubs, or any other billing and payment information.

• Copies of all foreclosure documents you've received, if any. Also save the envelopes of documents you've received, if available.

Label one file folder for each group of documents and put them in the folders in chronological order. You will refer to these documents again and again as you read this book and fight your foreclosure.

C. Learn the Clock

Foreclosure involves very specific timetables in which notices must be carefully served, mailed, recorded, posted and published before your lender can legally foreclose. For example, in a nonjudicial foreclosure, a Notice of Default will be posted on your property and mailed to you. After several months (depending on your state), a Notice of Sale will be issued. Several weeks thereafter (depending on your state), a trustee's sale may be conducted. As you can see, a nonjudicial foreclosure will take two to four months depending on the state your property is located (See your state's timetable in the Appendix in the back of this book). With respect

UNDERSTAND THE DIFFERENCE BETWEEN JUDICIAL AND NONJUDICIAL FORECLOSURES

Foreclosures can be conducted either judicially or nonjudicially, depending on your state. Each kind of foreclosure has its own procedural rules, so you need to know whether you are facing a nonjudicial or judicial foreclosure. Here are the particulars:

Judicial foreclosure. This kind of foreclosure starts when your lender files a lawsuit in the court to foreclose a mortgage. You must be served (provided with) with a copy of the Summons and Complaint for foreclosure. A judicial foreclosure can take anywhere from one to two years. If you are involved in a judicial foreclosure, read Chapter 4.

Nonjudicial foreclosure. Most foreclosures of deeds of trust are nonjudicial. Your lender avoids the court system entirely by having a trustee (a third party who conducts the foreclosure) follow a specific series of notice procedures, then sells your property at a public auction. If you are involved in a nonjudicial foreclosure, read Chapter 3.

to a judicial foreclosure, it could take 1-2 years.

Knowing the foreclosure clock is crucial to successfully using the strategies in this book to stop your foreclosure. Chapters 3 and 4 explain the timetables in detail. Once you understand the time constraints within which you are working, you can customize a strategy that fits your particular situation. For example, if you have two to three months until the foreclosure sale, you have some time to bring your loan current, negotiate with your lender or refinance your property. On the other hand, if only days remain before the sale, your only option to stop the sale may be to file for bankruptcy.

Remember, these time periods are for your benefit--not your lender's. This is your opportunity to apply a strategy that can most effectively stop the foreclosure.

D. Decide Whether or Not to Keep Your Property

Before you can settle on a strategy to stop foreclosure, you should clearly and wisely assess whether you really want, and can afford, to keep your property. This may be the most difficult and important decision you'll make.

This is a critical decision because you don't want to spend your precious time and money saving a property that you really can't afford, or that may only cause you more financial headaches in the future. Although it may be difficult to accept, you simply may have to cut your losses and move on.

Rather than fighting the foreclosure to the bitter end, the wiser approach might be to apply one of the strategies described in this book to get rid of the property (quick sale, short sale, or deed in lieu of foreclosure) and buy (or rent) another less expensive property, with more affordable monthly payments. Of course, this is a decision only you can make. For most people, this decision rests on four important questions:

• Is there any equity in the property?
• Does the property have economic value apart from the equity?

• Are you emotionally attached to the property?
• Are there any other factors that may affect your decision?

Let's look at each of these questions in detail.

1. Is There Any Equity in the Property?

From an economic standpoint, you may think your property is worth keeping. It may therefore come as a surprise to find that the cost to stop the foreclosure and keep your property may outweigh the benefits. Whether or not you try to keep your property should be based on a realistic assessment of the amount of equity (or lack of equity) you have in your property. This is often a very painful task, especially if the value of your property has dropped significantly. But it must be done.

For starters, understand that "equity" refers to the market value of your property less (a) the balance owed on all of the liens (legal claims) against it and (b) the costs of sale. If you have equity in your property, then it is economically worth saving.

a. Changes in Property Values

If property values in your area have appreciated over the past years, the equity in your property has probably increased. In contrast, if property values in your area have gone down over the past several years, your equity may have decreased. As a result, you may have less equity in your property than you believe, even if you have dutifully made payments to your lender on time. This knowledge may hurt, but you are not alone.

Example: Steve and Karen purchased their Pittsburgh home for $200,000, making a down payment of $40,000 and financing $160,000. Eight years later, property values in their area have declined by 20%. Their home now has a present market value of $160,000. They have made approximately $120,000 in interest payments and $20,000 in principal payments, and incorrectly assume that the total equity in their property is $60,000 (down payment $40,000 + principal paid $20,000). But due to the decline in property values, they have only $20,000 in equity, and this is before deducting costs of selling their property.

b. Calculate Your Equity Using the Equity Worksheet

Use the following Equity Worksheet and accompanying instructions to figure out if you have equity in your property. You'll find much of the information requested in the worksheet on your loan documents and any foreclosure notices you may have received.

1. *Estimated sales price.* You need a reasonable estimate of how much your property would sell for on the open market. The basic methods are to ask a real estate agent, hire an appraiser, or look at comparable properties in your area. For now, just use a good ballpark figure. (For a more detailed discussion on how to estimate the fair market value of your property, see Chapter 10, How to Sell Your Property Quickly to Stop Foreclosure.)

2. *Estimated costs of sale.* Next, you need to estimate the costs of selling your property.

- *Real estate agent's commission.* If you decide to use a real estate agent (almost always advisable in foreclosure situations), she will charge a commission of approximately 6% of the sales price. Even if you think you won't use an agent, it is prudent to include this cost at this point.

- *Closing costs.* Closing costs include such expenses as the title insurance policy, escrow fees, document fees, transfer tax, termite inspection, tax prorations and loan payments. You can use a rough estimate of 2% of the estimated sales price.

- *Outstanding liens and taxes.* Next, you'll list the outstanding balances on your mortgage(s), deed(s)s of trust, as well as back payments owed, and any late fees. To determine what these fees will be, you can contact your lender directly and ask; they should have no problem giving you this information. Also list the amount of any other liens recorded against your property, such as judgment liens, tax liens and mechanic's liens.

- *Foreclosure costs.* If any foreclosure costs have already been incurred, these must be paid regardless of whether your property actually sells in a foreclosure sale. The foreclosure trustee (nonjudicial foreclosure) or attorney (judicial foreclosure) will have an estimate of these costs, but they are generally about 1-2% of the balance of the foreclosing mortgage or deed of trust.

3. *Total estimated costs of sale.* Add up the costs of sale above and fill in this amount.

4. *Your equity.* Finally, deduct all of the estimated costs of sale from the

EQUITY WORKSHEET

1. Estimated sales price: _____

2. List estimated costs of sale: _____

      a.   Real estate agent's commission (6% of sales price): _____

      b.   Closing costs (2% of estimated sales price): _____

      c.   Balance due on first mortgage or deed of trust: _____

      d.   Balance due on junior lienholders: _____

      e.   Balance due on any other loans: _____

      f.   Missed payments on first loan: _____

      g.   Missed payments and late fees on junior lienholders: _____

      h.   Any other liens: _____

      i.   Unpaid property taxes: _____

      j.   Foreclosure costs: _____

3. Total estimated costs of sale: _____

4. Your equity (1–3): _____

estimated sales price (1-3). The result is the estimated equity in your property.

c. How Much Equity Is Worth Saving?

After completing the Equity Worksheet, you will be able to determine how much equity you realistically have in your property. The next question is how much equity is worth saving?

Example: Let's continue with Steve and Karen, who you'll remember have only $20,000 of estimated equity remaining in their property. They decide to sell their property to avoid foreclosure. If they sell *their house for $165,000, here's what they'll pocket:*

Estimated sales price	$165,000
First mortgage	140,000
Back payments on first (4 at $ 2,200/month)	4,800
Foreclosure costs	1,500
Commission (6%)	9,900
Closing costs (2%)	-3,300
Total costs of sale	159,500
Seller's equity	$ 5,500

On the other hand, if you have no equity, your lender may require you to pay money at the closing before allowing you to sell. If this sounds unbelievable, consider the following example.

Example: If Steve and Karen sell their property for $150,000 to avoid foreclosure, they will actually lose money on the sale:

Estimated sales price	*$150,000*
First deed of trust	*-140,000*
Back payments on first	
(4 months at $1,200/month)	*- 4,800*
Foreclosure costs	*- 1,500*
Commission (6%)	*- 9,000*
Closing costs (2%)	*- 3,000*
Total costs of sale	*$158,300*
Seller's equity	*<8,300>*

In the above example, not only did Steve and Karen lose all of their equity, but they also had out-of-pocket costs of $8,300 to sell their property! While this may be hard to believe, it can occur in depressed real estate markets.

Unfortunately, there is no simple answer to the question: How much equity is worth saving? As difficult as it may seem, you'll need to take a good hard look at your property and the accuracy of your financial calculations. As a general rule, if your equity equals at least 8% of the value of your property it is probably worth saving. On the other hand, if your equity is under 8% of your property's value, all else being equal, consider letting go of it. But if the thought of giving up your property is just too painful to accept, the next section may address your predicament.

2. Does the Property Have Economic Value Apart From the Equity?

Even though you don't have any equity, your property may still be worth keeping if it has "economic value." Economic value can best defined as collateral for junior liens. For example, if your property is foreclosed upon by the senior lienholder, you may still be liable for repayment of the junior liens. On the other hand, if you stop the foreclosure, you can sell or refinance your property to pay off the junior liens. This economic value is an important reason to stop the foreclosure before you lose the property.

For example, let's say you own a property worth approximately $500,000. Your property is encumbered with a first mortgage for $450,000, a second mortgage for $65,000 and a tax lien for $15,000. In this example, although you don't have any equity in your property, it nevertheless has economic value worth saving. If you lose the property in foreclosure to the holder of the first mortgage, you will still be liable to the second mortgage ($65,000) and the taxing authority ($15,000). In contrast, if you stop the foreclosure and sell (or refinance) your property, you will be able to use its economic value to pay off the second mortgage and tax lien.

3. Are You Emotionally Attached to the Property?

Even if you have no equity in your property, strong emotional ties may make the thought of losing it unbearable. For instance, if you've lived in your home for many years, your children were born and raised in the home, or you've made significant renovations and customized improvements, your property may be worth the sacrifice it will take to save it. On the other hand, if you own income-producing investment property, such as a rental house, apartment building or commercial building, it probably has no sentimental value to you. In that case, you have no reason to fight for property in which you have no equity, no economic value, and no sentimental value.

As you can see, this decision is very personal. If you decide your property has value to you that money cannot replace, and if you're willing to put in the time and energy it will take to save your property, pursue the strategies in this book.

4. Other Considerations

Other considerations may affect your decision to stop the foreclosure. For example, if you believe your financial situation will improve in the next few months, you may want to fight to keep your property. Or if you need additional time to sell your property, it is worth stopping the foreclosure. On the other hand, if your financial future looks bleak, spending your time and money to fight foreclosure may not be prudent. You don't want to fight to keep your property now, only to lose it eventually because you can't really afford the loan payments.

Carefully consider the extent of your other debts and their effect on your financial situation. Perhaps you can trim your budget, sell a car or come up with other ways to bring your loan current, and meet your ongoing expenses. Or maybe your other unpaid bills could be eliminated in bankruptcy, leaving you with enough cash each month to easily afford the payments on your property. (See Chapter 9 for a detailed discussion of bankruptcy.)

Another important consideration may be your credit score. Although your credit report may already indicate missed or late payments to your lender (and possibly other creditors), this may not be so bad because you can usually explain why you missed payments. However, most people want to avoid a foreclosure - or bankruptcy - appearing on their credit reports because most creditors will not give credit when they see these more serious blemishes.

5. Tax Effects of Giving Up or Selling Your Property

It may come as shock to discover that by giving up your property in foreclosure, or selling it, you could actually incur a personal income tax obligation. This section gives you a general overview of income tax liability issues to watch out for, and suggests some ways you may be able to get out of such a predicament.

Get advice before you give up your property. No area of the law experiences more revisions and invites more questions than the tax code. Check with an accountant, tax attorney or other tax specialist to learn more about whether taxes will be due in your particular circumstance.

a. Tax Liability If You Sell Your Property

What if you sell your property during the foreclosure to pay off your foreclosing lender? If you pay taxes, it depends on whether you make a profit (called "capital gain") or suffer a loss (called "capital loss").

If the sales price exceeded the "adjusted cost basis" of your property, you have capital gains, which will be taxable by the Internal Revenue Service. Adjusted cost basis is defined as the price you paid for your property plus any capital improvements you put into it over the years (such as replacing the roof or adding a bathroom), plus costs of sale, minus any depreciation, casualty losses and postponement of gain from a previous sale. If the sales price is greater than the adjusted cost basis, you have a capital gain which is taxed by the IRS.

Example: Jean purchased a $400,000 home in Seattle, Washington, which she financed with a $300,000 loan with Olympia Federal Savings Bank. Over the years, Jean improved the home with a $20,000 swimming pool and jacuzzi, which adjusted her cost basis from $400,000 to $420,000. When Jean could no longer afford the payments, Olympia started foreclosure proceedings. To avert foreclosure, Jean sold her residence for $450,000, its current market value. The difference between $450,000 (sale price) and $420,000 (adjusted cost basis) is $30,000, which is her taxable gain.

However, you will not have to pay income taxes on your capital gains if the property is your personal residence and if, within 24 months of the sale, you purchase and occupy a new residence that costs at least as much as the old residence. Also, if you are over 55, you may qualify for a one-time $125,000 exclusion.

If you have a loss on the sale of your property, you can deduct the capital loss from any capital gains in order to reduce your tax liability, but only if the property is a rental or income-producing property. If it is your personal residence, your capital loss is not deductible.

b. Tax Liability If You Lose Your Property in Foreclosure

The IRS treats a foreclosure like any other sale of your property. In other words, if you lose your property in a foreclosure sale, you will be liable to the IRS for taxes if the adjusted cost basis of your property is less than the sales price at the foreclosure sale.

Example: Merv and Kathy own a property in Tampa, Florida, which they purchased many years ago for $500,000 with a $460,000 loan. Today, the loan balance is down to $400,000. When they defaulted on the loan payments, their lender foreclosed selling the property for $400,000. As a result, Merv and Kathy will have a capital gain of $60,000 (the difference between the original loan balance of $460,000 and the sale price of $400,000), which is taxable.

On the other hand, if their property had depreciated to $375,000, there would have been taxable ordinary income of $25,000 from the foreclosure sale (the difference between the sales price of $400,000 and the $375,000 depreciated value), which Merv and Kathy could offset against other ordinary losses provided the property was not their personal residence.

You may even face a tax bill for capital gains if your lender forecloses and sells your property for more than you originally paid (plus capital improvements), even if you don't get a penny back.

Example: Yvette bought a $180,000 summer home in the mountains of Colorado, making a $30,000 down payment and taking a $150,000 loan. The house significantly increased in value (although Yvette made no improvements to the property) and she took out a home equity loan for $75,000. Several years later, property values dropped drastically and Yvette lost her job. Her lender foreclosed, selling the property at a trustee's sale for $195,000. Yvette owed her first lender $140,000 and her second lender $65,000--a total of $205,000--so she received nothing from the sale. Unfortunately for Yvette, the IR5 rules that she has "discharge of debt" taxable income of $25,000 (the difference between the loans in the amount $205,000 and the original purchase price of $180,000).

c. Tax Liability If You Sell Your Property in a Short Sale

As an alternative to foreclosure, some property owners reach agreement with the foreclosing lender to sell the property in a "short sale" (for less than the balance of the loan). When your lender releases you from paying the deficiency, it is known as "discharge of debt" and is considered taxable income by the IRS. In fact, your lender will submit a Form 1099A to the IRS which will reflect the amount of the discharge.

Example: Mark and Theresa own a property in Milwaukee, Wisconsin encumbered with a $325,000 mortgage held by Unity Mortgage Company. In recent years, the market value of the property has fallen from $350,000 to $300,000. Mark and Theresa are able to convince Unity Mortgage to accept $300,000 as payment in full as part of a short sale. When the property is sold, although Mark and Theresa are forgiven for repaying the $25,000, it is considered "discharge of debt" income by the 1RS and taxable.

d. Income Tax Liability Exceptions

Several IRS exceptions may relieve you of tax liability for a discharge of debt:

- *Bankruptcy exception.* Under the Internal Revenue Code, any amount unpaid on a property loan (discharge of debt) is not recognized as taxable income if you are in bankruptcy. (IRS § lO8(a)(1)(A).)
- *Insolvency exception.* Should your secured and unsecured debt exceed the value of your assets at the time the discharge of debt occurs, the discharge of debt income may not be taxable (known as the "balance sheet test"). You will need to file documents with the IRS (Form 982) substantiating your insolvency.
- *Business losses.* Any property that isn't your primary residence is considered investment property--a summer cottage, rental house, retail store or apartment building. If you have investment property, you can offset discharge of debt income with business losses.
- *Senior exception.* If you are over 55, you may qualify for a one-time $125,000 exclusion, which means that up to $125,000 of the profit will be exempt from taxation as capital gains income ($250,000 if you are married).

E. Develop a Plan of Action

As you read this book and decide which strategies are most suitable to your situation, you can develop a concrete plan of action. The various approaches described in this book are not mutually exclusive, and like most people, you'll probably want to pursue more than one strategy at the same time. For example, if you want to keep your property, you may try to refinance your loan at the same time you negotiate with your lender (Chapter 5), or file a lawsuit to enjoin the foreclosure (Chapter 8).

Similarly, if you decide to get rid of your property, you may try to sell it while simultaneously preparing to give your lender a deed in lieu of foreclosure if you can't sell it (Chapter 11).

1. Options to Keep Your Property

After reading Section D, above, if you decide to keep your property, you can pursue the options listed below:

a. Negotiate With Your Lender (Chapter 5)

Your first strategy should always be to negotiate with your lender. Chapter 5 explains the basic rules for negotiating and suggests common solutions to resolve a defaulted loan. Chapter 5 also explains the special programs available to you if your loan is insured by the Federal Housing Association (FHA), or the Dept. of Veteran Affairs (VA). You'll also find information on how to negotiate with a private mortgage insurance company (PMI).

b. Refinance Your Property (Chapter 6)

Another important strategy is to refinance your property so you can either bring your loan current, or pay off your foreclosing lender, before the foreclosure sale. Chapter 6 covers sources of refinancing and distinguishes among various kinds of lenders. Chapter 6 also discusses the advantages and disadvantages of using a mortgage broker to obtain a new loan, rather than searching for potential lenders.

c. Use Your Military Connection (Chapter 7)

You may not realize it, but if you are in the military (or dependent on someone in the military), you may have the automatic right under the Soldiers and Sailors Civil Relief Act to stop the foreclosure. Chapter 7 explains who qualifies for military relief, who can provide military relief, and what you must ask for to obtain assistance. You'll also learn when you may qualify for a reduction in your interest rate.

d. File a Lawsuit to Stop a Nonjudicial Foreclosure (Chapter 8)

If you have grounds to do so, you can file a lawsuit to stop (enjoin) a pending nonjudicial foreclosure. Chapters 3 and 8 explain how to spot common procedural errors that occur during the nonjudicial foreclosure process as well as the most frequent mistakes lenders make when granting loans, which can be grounds for stopping the foreclosure. You'll also get a brief overview of the ins and outs of filing a lawsuit, and instructions on how to obtain an order from the court to stop the foreclosure, called a "temporary restraining order" in most states. (Of course, if you are facing a judicial foreclosure, you will have the opportunity to respond in court without initiating the lawsuit yourself. We explain judicial foreclosures in Chapter 4.)

e. File for Bankruptcy (Chapter 9)

If all else fails, bankruptcy may be your most viable option. Chapter 9 discusses the advantages and disadvantages of the different types of bankruptcy. You'll find out how bankruptcy automatically stops foreclosure (at least temporarily), and how to use bankruptcy to resolve the impasse with your lender and keep your property.

2. Options to Get Rid of Your Property

If you decide to get rid of your property, but want to do it on your own to stop the foreclosure, here are your options:

a. Sell Your Property (Chapter 10)

The most expedient strategy is to sell your property as quickly as possible. Chapter 10 discusses how to use a real estate agent, prepare your property for sale, price your property for a quick sale, market your property, negotiate offers and counter-offers, and remove contingencies so that the sale closes in time to beat the foreclosure. You'll also learn how to structure a "short sale," where your lender accepts less than the amount of your outstanding loan as payment in full. Finally, if you can't find a buyer willing to pay market value for your property in time to avoid the foreclosure sale, Chapter 10 covers sales to equity purchasers--individuals who pay you a fraction of your equity to get title to your property--and the pitfalls you need to guard against.

b. Give Your Lender a Deed in Lieu of Foreclosure (Chapter 11)

Another strategy is to deed your property to your lender in exchange for ending the foreclosure. Giving a deed in lieu of foreclosure maybe the most efficient method of giving up your property, although it also has pitfalls you need to guard against. For example, many lenders will refuse to accept a deed in lieu if there are junior liens on your property. Chapter 11 helps you assess the advantages and disadvantages of a "deed in lieu" (as it's called) and how to negotiate with your lender to accept one.

Chapter

2

UNDERSTANDING THE DOCUMENTS UNDERLYING A FORECLOSURE

A. Promissory Note 18

    1. Parties to a Promissory Note 18
    2. Reviewing Your Promissory Note.......................................18
    3. Understanding the Promissory Note................................. 20
    4. Types of Promissory Notes 26

B. Deed of Trust.. 27

    1. Parties to a Deed of Trust 28

C. Mortgages 36

    1. Parties to a Mortgage 36

D. Reviewing Your Deed of Trust or Mortgage...................................37

Real estate transactions rely heavily on paperwork. Think back to your own closing day--you probably felt like you were signing an endless stream of documents and that you should have brought a suitcase to carry them all home.

The loan documents you will need to review to learn how to stop the foreclosure are the promissory note, and either deed of trust or the mortgage (depending on which documents your state uses). These documents describe the rights and responsibilities of you and your lender. When you fail to adhere to your responsibilities, these documents provide the mechanism for your lender to foreclose. They also provide a basis for you to stop a foreclosure if there are any inconsistencies between your loan documents and the foreclosure documents.

➡️ *If you understand the significance of these documents and the provisions they contain.* Skip this chapter and proceed to either Chapter 3 (if yours is a nonjudicial foreclosure) or Chapter 4 (if yours is a judicial foreclosure).

A. Promissory Note

The first loan document you signed was a promissory note. The promissory note is the document in which you promised to repay the money that was loaned to you. The note sets forth the amount you borrowed, the interest rate and the particulars of how the loan is to be repaid. Typically no more than one to three pages in length, a promissory note is relatively easy to understand.

1. Parties to a Promissory Note

There are two parties to a promissory note:

a. Borrower

The borrower is the person who borrowed the money. The borrower is sometimes referred to as the "payor" or "obligor." This includes you and anyone who co-signed the loan, such as a spouse, non-marital partner, or business partner.

b. Lender

The lender is the financial institution that originally loaned you money and any financial institution (or investor) to whom your original lender subsequently sold your note. The lender is sometimes referred to as the "payee," "oblige," or "holder." When you borrowed money to purchase or refinance your property, the lender was probably a bank, savings bank, mortgage company, credit union, insurance company, family member or friend, or perhaps, the seller of the property. The current lender may be a company or investor that specializes in buying loans from the original lenders.

2. Reviewing Your Promissory Note

To stop the foreclosure, you'll need to understand the terms and conditions of your particular promissory note. You will also need to determine:

- the amount you have already paid on the note

- the amount you are in arrears, and

- the balance of your loan.

If the foreclosure documents recorded against your property are inaccurate, you'll probably have a basis to stop the foreclosure.

When you purchased or refinanced your property, your original lender (or the escrow officer) had you sign a promissory note and gave you a copy. If you don't have a copy of your signed note, get one as soon as possible. Your current lender should have a copy. However, if you don't want to ask your current lender, or aren't sure who they are, you can request a copy from the escrow company. If the escrow company can't help you, send a written request to your original lender similar to the sample letter set out below. Before sending the letter, telephone the lender's office and get the name of an officer that you can specifically send the letter to. Make sure you keep a copy of the letter.

January 10, 200X

Mr. Neal Brown
Branch Manager
Pacific Hills Bank
1234 Hill Street
Las Vegas, Nevada

Re: Loan No. 34-44356

To Whom It May Concern:

I own the property located at 245 Pacific Drive, in the City of Las Vegas, Nevada. In July of 200X, I borrowed $155,000 from your bank. The original promissory note securing my property was given to you. However, I don't have a copy. Could you please provide me with a photocopy of my promissory note? I will call and arrange to pick up the document at your office.

Thank you in advance for your anticipated cooperation.

Sincerely,

Michael Scher

Carefully review your note.

Promissory Note Breakdown:

1. Amount of indebtedness: The principal-actual--amount of money you borrowed.

2. Location of execution: The city where you signed the note.

3. Date of execution: The date the promissory note was signed.

4. Name of lender: The name of the person or company that lent you the money.

5. Address of lender: The mailing address of your lender.

6. Amount of indebtedness: The principal amount of money you borrowed is repeated here.

7. Interest effective date: The date when interest began to accrue on the principal.

8. Interest rate: The amount charged by your lender for loaning the money. The interest rate will be expressed as either fixed (interest rate remains the same during the entire term of your loan) or adjustable (interest rate will fluctuate on an annual basis).

9. Installment amounts: For a fixed-rate loan, the payment amount typically is shown in both written and numeric form. (If you have an adjustable interest rate, the installment amount will not be shown on the note, but will typically appear on your mortgage statements.)

10. Installment due date: The date of the monty that each payment is due (the vast majority of notes are paid monthly and due on the first of the month).

11. Commencement date: The date your first payment on the promissory note is due.

12. Final payment date: The date the final payment on your promissory note is due.

13. Signature of borrower: You and your co-borrowers signed the note here. Your lender does not sign the note.

A sample Promissory Note Worksheet appears below, and a blank tear-out copy is included in the Appendix. Use it to record the relevant terms and conditions and compare with your deed of trust or mortgage.

3. Understanding the Promissory Note

There are seven basic components in every promissory note:
- principal
- interest
- term
- payment
- security
- acceleration, and
- negotiability.

The first four are financial components. If you disagree with the amount your lender is claiming you owe (as set out in the foreclosure documents) it may become important for you to figure out whether your lender has calculated correctly the financial information, particularly the default amount ("arrears"). You will need to add up your missed payments, late fees, and penalties to determine your arrears. If you are unable to make these calculations, you may need to hire an accountant or bookkeeper. As we point out in Chapter 8, *Using the Courts to Stop a Nonjudicial Foreclosure*, lenders frequently make mistakes, especially if the note has an adjustable interest rate or unusual terms. A sample promissory note appears on pages 22-23. An explanation of its important terms follows.

PROMISSORY NOTE WORKSHEET

Date note is signed:

Borrower(s):

Lender:

Principal amount borrowed:

Interest rate:

Term (number of months, years or other arrangement):

Payment frequency (monthly or other arrangement):

Commencement data (date payments begin):

Payment amount:

Is there a reference in the note to the deed of trust or mortgage?

a. Principal

The principal is the amount of money you borrowed from your lender. This amount does not include any interest, points, or other fees. If you refinanced your loan, it is the amount of the refinanced loan, not the amount of your first loan.

b. Interest

Interest is the fee a lender charges to loan money. Interest is calculated as a percentage of the unpaid principal, on a yearly (per annum) basis. The interest rate will be computed on a 365-day year, unless otherwise specified in the promissory note. The interest rate can be either:

* "fixed", meaning your interest rate will remain the same during the entire term of your loan, or
* "adjustable", meaning that your interest rate will fluctuate on an annual basis as described in your promissory note. Lenders add a "margin" (profit) to a pre-selected index to determine the adjusted interest loan. (See the box below.)

c. Term

Term refers to the period of time in which you have to repay the loan. The term can range anywhere from 1 to 30 years, and some newer loans have terms as long as 40 years.

d. Payment

Payment is the amount of interest and/or principal that you promised to repay on a monthly basis. Your promissory note will specify the date when payments

ADJUSTABLE RATE INDEXES

The most common indexes used by lenders are:

* *Prime Rate* based upon the discount rate established periodically by the Federal Reserve Open Market Committee. The prime is the interest rate charged by banks for short-term loans to its most creditworthy customers.
* *District Cost of Funds ("COFI")*, reflects the weighted-average interest rate paid by Federal Home Loan Bank Board District savings institutions for savings and checking accounts.
* *London Interbank Offered Rate ("LIBOR")*, is an average of the interest rates on deposits (Eurodollars) traded between banks in London. It is an international index that follows world economic conditions.
* *Ten-year treasury notes*, which fluctuate daily based upon market forces in the economy, and is the standard for most 30-year mortgages.
* *Six-month certificates of deposit ("CODI")*, which fluctuate daily based upon market forces in the economy.
* *Twelve-month Treasury Averages ("MTA")* is the 12 month average yields of U.S. Treasury securities, as posted by the Federal Reserve.

are to start, the amount of each payment and the repayment schedule (usually monthly). Some loans call for you to make monthly payments for several years and then a lump sum payment at the end. This lump sum is called

Blauvelt Free Library
541 Western Hwy
Blauvelt, NY 10913

a "balloon payment." Foreclosures are often precipitated by a borrower's inability to make a balloon payment.

e. Security

Promissory notes are either *secured* or *unsecured*. A secured note simply means that you pledged your property as collateral for payment of the note (security). A secured note gives your lender the right to sell your property to pay off the loan if you default. This involuntary sale of your real property is called foreclosure. Secured notes usually use the word "secured" in the title and in the description ("this note is secured") so that the parties to the note, or subsequent purchasers, know that the note is secured by property. (See "Negotiability" below.) Assuming the note is secured, the lender can foreclose on the security (property) if the borrower defaults in the terms of the promissory note.

By way of comparison, an unsecured note does not have property as security for its repayment. In that situation, if the borrower fails to pay the note, the lender can't foreclose, but instead is required to file a lawsuit in court to collect the note.

f. Acceleration

An acceleration clause states that in the event you miss a payment (default), your lender has the right to declare the entire balance of principal and accrued interest due and payable. The purpose of an acceleration clause is to relieve your lender of the burden of having to sue you for each late payment one by one until the end of the loan. All promissory notes have an acceleration clause. [However, notwithstanding the acceleration clause, once the foreclosure starts, there is still a period of time (called the "reinstatement period") in which you can still stop the foreclosure by simply paying the amount that is in arrears.]

g. Negotiability

Negotiability refers to your lender's right to sell your promissory note to a third party, such as private or institutional investors. Investors typically purchase these loans in quantity and at a discount. This industry is called the "secondary market." The three largest purchasers of loans secured by real property in the secondary market are:

- Federal National Mortgage Association, also known as "FNMA" or "Fannie Mae" (www.fanniemae.com)
- Federal Home Loan Mortgage Corporation, also known as "FHLMC" or "Freddie Mac" (www.freddiemac.com), and
- Government National Mortgage Association, also known as "GNMA" or "Ginnie Mae" (www.ginniemae.gov).

Once your loan is sold, the third party acquires all the rights and obligations of your original lender under the promissory note. This means that even though your original lender's name may appear on your note, someone else may actually own the note and the right to receive your payments. Knowing who owns your note is vital to negotiating and using other strategies in this book. Although the holder may not be your original lender, we use the term

INITIAL INTEREST^{SM} NOTE

_____, _____   _____, _____
[Date]   [City]   [State]

_____
[Property Address]

1. BORROWER'S PROMISE TO PAY

In return for a loan that I have received, I promise to pay U.S. $_____ (this amount is called "Principal"), plus interest, to the order of the Lender. The Lender is _____ _____. I will make all payments under this Note in the form of cash, check or money order.

I understand that the Lender may transfer this Note. The Lender or anyone who takes this Note by transfer and who is entitled to receive payments under this Note is called the "Note Holder."

2. INTEREST

Interest will be charged on unpaid principal until the full amount of Principal has been paid. I will pay interest at a yearly rate of _____%.

The interest rate required by this Section 2 is the rate I will pay both before and after any default described in Section 6(B) of this Note.

3. PAYMENTS

(A) Time and Place of Payments

I will make a payment every month on the first day of the month beginning on _____, _____. Before the first fully amortizing principal and interest payment due date, my monthly payments will be only for the interest due on the unpaid principal of this Note. The due date of my first payment including fully amortizing principal and interest is the first day of _____, _____. I will make payments every month until I have paid all of the principal and interest and any other charges described below that I may owe under this Note. Each monthly payment will be applied as of its scheduled due date and if the payment includes both principal and interest, it will be applied to interest before Principal. If, on _____, _____, I still owe amounts under this Note, I will pay those amounts in full on that date, which is called the "Maturity Date."

I will make my monthly payments at

_____ or at a different place if required by the Note Holder.

(B) Amount of Monthly Payments

My monthly payment will be in the amount of U.S. $_____ until the due date of the first fully amortizing principal and interest payment. Beginning with the first fully amortizing principal and interest payment, my payment will be in the amount of U.S. $_____.

The Note Holder will notify me prior to the date of any change in the amount of my monthly payment in accordance with Section 7 of this Note. The Note Holder will provide the title and telephone number of a person who will answer any questions I may have regarding the notice.

4. BORROWER'S RIGHT TO PREPAY

I have the right to make payments of Principal at any time before they are due. A payment of Principal only is known as a "Prepayment." When I make a Prepayment, I will tell the Note Holder in writing that I am doing so. I may not designate a payment as a Prepayment if I have not made all the monthly payments due under this Note.

I may make a full Prepayment or partial Prepayments without paying a Prepayment charge. The Note Holder will use my Prepayments to reduce the amount of Principal that I owe under this Note. However, the Note Holder may apply my Prepayment to the accrued and unpaid interest on the Prepayment amount, before applying my Prepayment to reduce the Principal amount of the Note. If I make a partial Prepayment, there will be no changes in the due date of my monthly payment unless the Note Holder agrees in writing to the changes. If I make a partial Prepayment during the period ending with the due date of my last interest only monthly payment, the partial Prepayment will reduce the amount of my monthly payment. If I make a partial Prepayment after the due date of my last interest only payment, the amount of my monthly payment will not change unless the Note Holder agrees in writing to that change.

5.   LOAN CHARGES

If a law, which applies to this loan and which sets maximum loan charges, is finally interpreted so that the interest or other loan charges collected or to be collected in connection with this loan exceed the permitted limits, then: (a) any such loan charge shall be reduced by the amount necessary to reduce the charge to the permitted limit; and (b) any sums already collected from me which exceeded permitted limits will be refunded to me. The Note Holder may choose to make this refund by reducing the Principal I owe under this Note or by making a direct payment to me. If a refund reduces Principal, the reduction will be treated as a partial Prepayment.

6.   BORROWER'S FAILURE TO PAY AS REQUIRED

(A)   Late Charge for Overdue Payments

If the Note Holder has not received the full amount of any monthly payment by the end of _____ calendar days after the date it is due, I will pay a late charge to the Note Holder. The amount of the charge will be _____% of the overdue payment of interest during the period when my payment is interest only, and of principal and interest after that. I will pay this late charge promptly but only once on each late payment.

(B)   Default

If I do not pay the full amount of each monthly payment on the date it is due, I will be in default.

(C)   Notice of Default

If I am in default, the Note Holder may send me a written notice telling me that if I do not pay the overdue amount by a certain date, the Note Holder may require me to pay immediately the full amount of Principal which has not been paid and all the interest that I owe on that amount. That date must be at least 30 days after the date on which the notice is mailed to me or delivered by other means.

(D)   No Waiver By Note Holder

Even if, at a time when I am in default, the Note Holder does not require me to pay immediately in full as described above, the Note Holder will still have the right to do so if I am in default at a later time.

(E)   Payment of Note Holder's Costs and Expenses

If the Note Holder has required me to pay immediately in full as described above, the Note Holder will have the right to be paid back by me for all of its costs and expenses in enforcing this Note to the extent not prohibited by applicable law. Those expenses include, for example, reasonable attorneys' fees.

7.   GIVING OF NOTICES

Unless applicable law requires a different method, any notice that must be given to me under this Note will be given by delivering it or by mailing it by first class mail to me at the Property Address above or at a different address if I give the Note Holder a notice of my different address.

Any notice that must be given to the Note Holder under this Note will be given by delivering it or by mailing it by first class mail to the Note Holder at the address stated in Section 3(A) above or at a different address if I am given a notice of that different address.

8.   OBLIGATIONS OF PERSONS UNDER THIS NOTE

If more than one person signs this Note, each person is fully and personally obligated to keep all of the promises made in this Note, including the promise to pay the full amount owed. Any person who is a guarantor, surety or endorser of this Note is also obligated to do these things. Any person who takes over these obligations, including the obligations of a guarantor, surety or endorser of this Note, is also obligated to keep all of the promises made in this Note. The Note Holder may enforce its rights under this Note against each person individually or against all of us together. This means that any one of us may be required to pay all of the amounts owed under this Note.

9.   WAIVERS

I and any other person who has obligations under this Note waive the rights of Presentment and Notice of Dishonor. "Presentment" means the right to require the Note Holder to demand payment of amounts due. "Notice of Dishonor" means the right to require the Note Holder to give notice to other persons that amounts due have not been paid.

10.   UNIFORM SECURED NOTE

This Note is a uniform instrument with limited variations in some jurisdictions. In addition to the

MULTISTATE INITIAL INTEREST FIXED RATE NOTE--Single Family-- **Freddie Mac UNIFORM INSTRUMENT**   **Form 5206**   5/04

(page 2 of 3 pages)

protections given to the Note Holder under this Note, a Mortgage, Deed of Trust, or Security Deed (the "Security Instrument"), dated the same date as this Note, protects the Note Holder from possible losses which might result if I do not keep the promises which I make in this Note. That Security Instrument describes how and under what conditions I may be required to make immediate payment in full of all amounts I owe under this Note. Some of those conditions are described as follows:

Transfer of the Property or a Beneficial Interest in Borrower. As used in this Section 18, "Interest in the Property" means any legal or beneficial interest in the Property, including, but not limited to, those beneficial interests transferred in a bond for deed, contract for deed, installment sales contract or escrow agreement, the intent of which is the transfer of title by Borrower at a future date to a purchaser.

If all or any part of the Property or any Interest in the Property is sold or transferred (or if Borrower is not a natural person and a beneficial interest in Borrower is sold or transferred) without Lender's prior written consent, Lender may require immediate payment in full of all sums secured by this Security Instrument. However, this option shall not be exercised by Lender if such exercise is prohibited by Applicable Law.

If Lender exercises this option, Lender shall give Borrower notice of acceleration. The notice shall provide a period of not less than 30 days from the date the notice is given in accordance with Section 15 within which Borrower must pay all sums secured by this Security Instrument. If Borrower fails to pay these sums prior to the expiration of this period, Lender may invoke any remedies permitted by this Security Instrument without further notice or demand on Borrower.

WITNESS THE HAND(S) AND SEAL(S) OF THE UNDERSIGNED

_____ (Seal)
- Borrower

_____ (Seal)
- Borrower

_____ (Seal)
- Borrower

[Sign Original Only]

"lender" to refer to whoever actually holds your note today.

A promissory note will typically contain a paragraph describing its negotiability or assignability, or simply state "or order" after the name of the lender, which accomplishes the same purpose.

4. Types of Promissory Notes

There are three basic types of promissory notes, each of which has endless variations and permutations. This information is important if there is a dispute with your lender over the amount owed. The three basic types are:

• amortized (or installment) notes

IF YOU AREN'T SURE WHETHER YOUR LOAN WAS SOLD

Lenders usually send out an Assignment of Beneficial Interest or some other written document to borrowers to notify them that the loan has been sold. If you didn't receive written notification, but are nevertheless suspicious that your loan may have been sold, contact your initial lender and ask them whether they still own the loan. If it has been sold, get the name, address, and telephone number of the current holder of the loan. Or, you can contact a title insurance company and ask them to search the title to your property in the county's recorder's office and determine whether the loan has been sold. (Unfortunately, you probably won't be able to gain any leverage in the foreclosure process by claiming you didn't receive notice of the assignment.)

• interest-only notes, and
• straight notes.

a. Amortized (Installment) Notes

An amortized promissory note (also referred to as an installment note) calls for regular payments - typically monthly, but occasionally bi-weekly, quarterly, semi-annually or yearly. With a fixed interest rate, these payments are equal amounts. With an adjustable interest rate, payment amounts are generally adjusted annually.

Amortized notes are the most common type of notes used for single family home purchases. Over the term of an amortized note, you make a set number of payments. For example, with a typical 30-year loan, you would make 360 monthly payments. Every month payment would be identical. A portion of each payment would be attributed to interest and the other part to principal (as determined by amortization tables). At the end of the term, you will have paid back the entire loan.

Example 1: Douglas borrows $400,000 from First Federal Bank to purchase a new home in Phoenix, Arizona. The interest rate is fixed at 7% per year. The loan is to be repaid with monthly payments of $2,661.21, fully amortized over 30 years.

Example 2: Judy borrows $400,000 from her Credit Union to purchase a new home in Cleveland, Ohio. Judy chooses an adjustable rate loan because the interest rate is less than a fixed rate. The annual rate starts at 6.25%, but adjusts annually based on the LIBOR index each year. The loan is for 30 years. Her first year payments will be $2,462.87 per month, but will adjust after the first year and will continue to adjust (up or down) each year thereafter.

b. Interest-Only Notes

As its name implies, with an interest-only note you make scheduled interest payments, usually monthly. But you do not make any principal payments. Thus, at the end of the term of your loan, you must repay the entire principal balance in a single (balloon) payment.

Example: Kathy borrows $385,000 from Grass River Mortgage Company to refinance her home. The interest rate is fixed at 7% per year. The promissory note calls for interest-only monthly payments of $2,246 for ten years, with a lump-sum payment of $385,000 (original principal balance) at the end of the ten years.

Typically, an interest-only note is used when a borrower cannot afford high payments of principal and interest. The risk, however, is that when the note matures, the borrower will not be able to afford the balloon payment (which is a common cause of foreclosure). To avoid default, most property owners arrange to sell or refinance their property prior to when the balloon payment comes due.

c. Straight Notes

A straight note requires the borrower to repay the entire principal amount, plus interest, in one payment when the term of the note expires. Typically, these notes are for relatively short periods and small amounts. Straight notes are frequently used when an owner remodels or fixes his or her property, or uses it as security for a personal loan.

Example: Benjamin borrows $25,000 from First National Bank to remodel his kitchen. The annual interest rate is 8.25%. The promissory note calls for a single payment of $27,062.50 ($25,000 principal plus $2,062.50 interest) at the end of one year.

B. Deed of Trust

➡ If you signed a mortgage, you can skip this section and proceed to Section C, describing mortgages.

In a perfect world, borrowers would pay back their loans in full and on time. Lenders know, however, that some borrowers are either unable or unwilling to pay their debts on time. For this reason, lenders require that borrowers pledge property as security (collateral) for their loans. In that way, if the borrower defaults, the lender can force the sale of the property to recover the money owed. But as a practical matter, real property cannot be deposited at the bank pending repayment of the loan. Thus, the deed of trust was developed as a substitute for the impossibility of physically delivering property to a lender.

When you signed a promissory note to borrow money from your lender to purchase or refinance your property, you also signed a deed of trust. A deed of trust is evidence of your lender's security interest in your property. To be valid, the deed of trust is recorded in the recorder's office in the county where the property is located.

The deed of trust creates a lien (legal claim) against your property, which remains in force until you repay your loan or your lender forecloses. Although there is no standard form for a deed of trust, these documents have become relatively standardized across the country.

Unlike a mortgage, a deed of trust has a "power of sale" clause, which gives your lender the right to foreclose against your property without first suing you in court. This is known as a nonjudicial foreclosure (covered in Chapter 3).

A sample deed of trust is shown on the next page. An explanation of the important terms follows.

1. Parties to a Deed of Trust

As mentioned, there are three parties involved in a deed of trust: the trustor (the borrower), the beneficiary (the lender) and the trustee (an individual or company authorized to foreclose if the borrower defaults).

a. Trustor (You)

The trustor is the person, or persons, who own the property, signed the promissory note, and pledged the property as security for the loan. The trustor is almost always the borrower, especially where a single-family residence is involved. (Although rare, a trustor could agree to use his property as security for someone else's loan.)

b. Beneficiary

The beneficiary is the bank or financial institution that loaned you money to purchase or refinance your property. If the original beneficiary (your original lender) sells your loan, the new holder of the loan becomes the beneficiary.

c. Trustee

You probably didn't realize it at the time, but when you signed the deed of trust, you transferred legal title of your property to the trustee. The purpose of the transfer is for the trustee to hold title as security for your repayment of the loan. But don't worry, the trustee isn't going to move in or interfere with your enjoyment of your home. The trustee's

DEED OF TRUST VS MORTGAGE

Deeds of trust are similar to mortgages in that they both document real property as security for a loan. However, a mortgage is a two-party document (mortgagor and mortgagee), while a deed of trust is a three-party document (trustor, trustee and beneficiary). The significant difference is that a deed of trust contains a power-of-sale clause, while a mortgage does not. Thus, if you default on a mortgage, your lender must file a lawsuit in court to foreclose. In contrast, if you default on a deed of trust, your lender can invoke the power-of-sale clause (to avoid the courts entirely), and file a nonjudicial foreclosure. Mortgages are used primarily in states east of the Mississippi River. Deeds of trust are used primarily in states west of the Mississippi River. As to which document is used in your state, please refer to the Appendix in the back of this book.

involvement only exists on paper. The trustee serves two practical functions:

• to conduct a foreclosure of your property if you default on your loan, or

• to return the deed of trust to you when you repay your loan in full (called "reconveyance").

To conduct a foreclosure or to reconvey (return) a deed of trust, a trustee will not act on his own. A trustee will become involved only upon the request of the beneficiary--your lender. Institutional lenders, such as banks or savings banks, typically name their own subsidiary corporations as trustees in their deeds of trust. Private lenders often have title companies or independent foreclosure companies act as their trustees.

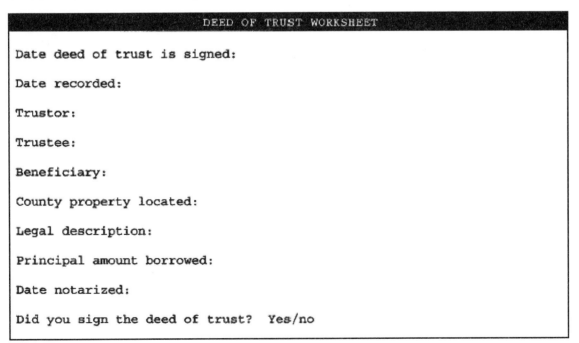

DEED OF TRUST WORKSHEET

Date deed of trust is signed:

Date recorded:

Trustor:

Trustee:

Beneficiary:

County property located:

Legal description:

Principal amount borrowed:

Date notarized:

Did you sign the deed of trust? Yes/no

DEED OF TRUST

THIS DEED OF TRUST ("Security Instrument") is made on
The trustor is

("Borrower"). The trustee is
("Trustee"). The beneficiary is

which is organized and existing under the
laws of   and whose address is
("Lender"). Borrower

owes Lender the principal sum of
Dollars (U S $). This debt is evidenced by Borrower's note dated
the same date as this Security Instrument ("Note"), which provides for monthly payments, with the full debt, if not
paid earlier, due and payable on   . This Security Instrument
secures to Lender : (a) the repayment of the debt evidenced by the Note, with interest, and all renewals, extensions
and modifications of the Note; (b) the payment of all other sums, with interest, advanced under paragraph 7 to protect
the security of this Security Instrument; and (c) the performance of Borrower's covenants and agreements under this
Security Instrument and the Note. For this pupose, Borrower irrevocably grants and conveys to Trustee, in trust, with
power of sale, the following described property located in
County, California:

which has the address of

                                  [Street]   *[City]*

California   ("Property Address");
             [Zip Code]

    TOGETHER WITH all the improvements now or hereafter erected on the property, and all easements, appurtenances,
and fixtures now or hereafter a part of the property. All replacements and additions shall also be covered by this Security
Instrument. All of the foregoing is referred to in this Security Instrument as the "Property."

    BORROWER COVENANTS that Borrower is lawfully seised of the estate hereby conveyed and has the right to grant
and convey the Property and that the Property is unencumbered, except for the encumberances of record. Borrower
warrants and will defend generally the title to the Property against all claims and demands, subject to any encumbrances
of record.

CALIFORNIA---Single Family---**Fannie Mae/Freddie Mac** UNIFORM INSTURMENT   FORM 3005 9/90 *(page 1 of 6 pages)*

THIS SECURITY INSTRUMENT combines uniform covenants for national use and non-uniform covenants with limited variations by jurisdiction to constitute a uniform security instrument covering real property.

UNIFORM COVENANTS. Borrowers and Lender covenant and agree as follows:

1. Payment of Principal and Interest: Prepayment and Late Charges. Borrower shall promptly pay when due the principal of and interest on the debt evidenced by the Note and any prepayment and late charges due under the Note.

2. Funds for Taxes and Insurance. Subject to applicable law or to a written waiver by Lender, Borrower shall pay to Lender on the day monthly payments are due under the Note, until the Note is paid in full, a sum ("Funds") for: (a) yearly taxes and assessments which may attain priority over this Security Instrument as a lien on the Property; (b) yearly leasehold payments or ground rents on the Property, if any; (c) yearly hazard or property insurance premiums; (d) yearly flood insurance premiums, if any; (e) yearly mortgage insurance premiums, if any; and (f) any sums payable by Borrower to Lender, in accordance with the provisions of paragraph 8, in lieu of the payment of mortgage insurance premiums. These items are called "Escrow Items." Lender may, at any time, collect and hold Funds in an amount not to exceed the maximum amount a Lender for a federally related mortgage loan may require for Borrower's escrow account under the federal Real Estate Settlement Procedures Act of 1974 as amended from time to time, 12 U.S.C. § 2601 et seq. ("RESPA"), unless another law that applies to the Funds sets a lesser amount. If so, Lender may, at any time, collect and hold Funds in an amount not to exceed the lesser amount. Lender may estimate the amount of Funds due on the basis of current data and reasonable estimates of expenditures of future Escrow Items or otherwise in accordance with applicable law.

The Funds shall be held in an institution whose deposits are insured by a federal agency, instrumentality, or entity (including Lender, if Lender is such an institution) or in any Federal Home Loan Bank. Lender shall apply the Funds to pay the Escrow Items. Lender may not charge Borrower for holding and applying the Funds, annually analyzing the escrow account or verifying the Escrow Items, unless Lender pays Borrower interest on the Funds and applicable law permits Lender to make such a charge. However, Lender may require Borrower to pay a one-time charge for an independent real estate tax reporting service used by Lender in connection with this loan, unless applicable law provides otherwise. Unless an agreement is made or applicable law requires interest to be paid, Lender shall not be required to pay Borrower any interest or earnings on the Funds. Borrower and Lender may agree in writing, however, that interest shall be paid on the Funds. Lender shall give to Borrower, without charge, an annual accounting of the Funds, showing credits and debits to the Funds and the purpose for which each debit to the Funds was made. The Funds are pledged as additional security for all sums secured by this Security Instrument.

If the Funds held by Lender exceed the amounts permitted to be held by applicable law, Lender shall account to Borrower for the excess Funds in accordance with the requirements of applicable law. If the amount of the Funds held by Lender at any time is not sufficient to pay the Escrow Items when due, Lender may so notify Borrower in writing, and, in such case Borrower shall pay to Lender the amount necessary to make up the deficiency. Borrower shall make up the deficiency in no more than twelve monthly payments, at Lender's sole discretion.

Upon payment in full of all sums secured by this Security Instrument, Lender shall promptly refund to Borrower any Funds held by Lender. If, under paragraph 21, Lender shall acquire or sell the Property, Lender, prior to the acquisition or sale of the Property, shall apply any Funds held by Lender at the time of acquisition or sale as a credit against the sums secured by this Security Instrument.

3. Application of Payments. Unless applicable law provides otherwise, all payments received by Lender under paragraphs 1 and 2 shall be applied: first, to any prepayment charges due under the Note; second, to amounts payable under pagraph 2; third, to interest due; fourth, to principal due; and last, to any late charges due under the Note.

4. Charges; Liens. Borrower shall pay all taxes, assessments, charges, fines and impositions attributable to the Property which may attain priority over this Security Instrument, and leasehold payments or ground rents, if any. Borrower shall pay these obligations in the manner provided in paragraph 2, or if not paid in that manner, Borrower shall pay them on time directly to the person owed payment. Borrower shall promptly furnish to Lender all notices of amounts to be paid under this paragraph. If Borrower makes these payments directly, Borrower shall promptly furnish to Lender receipts evidencing the payments.

Borrower shall promptly discharge any lien which has priority over this Security Instrument unless Borrower: (a) agrees in writing to the payment of the obligation secured by the lien in a manner acceptable to Lender; (b) contests in good faith the lien by, or defends against enforcement of the lien in, legal proceedings which in the Lender's opinion operate to prevent the enforcement of the lien; or (c) secures from the holder of the lien an agreement satisfactory to Lender subordinating the lien to this Security Instrument. If Lender determines that any part of the Property is subject to a lien which may attain priority over this Security Instrument, Lender may give Borrower a notice identifying the lien. Borrower shall satisfy the lien or take one or more of the actions set forth above within 10 days of the giving of notice.

5. Hazard or Property Insurance. Borrower shall keep the improvements now existing or hereafter erected on the Property insured against loss by fire, hazards included within the term "extended coverage" and any other hazards, including floods or flooding, for which Lender requires insurance. This insurance shall be maintained in the amounts and for the periods that Lender requires. The insurance carrier providing the insurance shall be chosen by Borrower subject to Lender's approval which shall not be unreasonably withheld. If Borrower fails to maintain coverage described above, Lender may, at Lender's option, obtain coverage to protect Lender's rights in the Property in accordance with paragraph 7.

All insurance policies and renewals shall be acceptable to Lender and shall include a standard mortgage clause. Lender shall have the right to hold the policies and renewals. If Lender requires, Borrower shall promptly give to Lender all receipts of paid premiums and renewal notices. In the event of loss, Borrower shall give prompt notice to the insurance carrier and Lender. Lender may make proof of loss if not made promptly by Borrower.

Unless Lender and Borrower otherwise agree in writing, insurance proceeds shall be applied to restoration or repair "of the Property damaged, if the restoration or repair is economically feasible and Lender's security is not lessened. If the restoration or repair is not economically feasible or Lender's security would be lessened, the insurance proceeds shall be applied to the sums secured by this Security Instrument, whether or not then due, with any excess paid to Borrower. If Borrower abandons the Property, or does not answer within 30 days a notice from Lender that the insurance carrier has offered to settle a claim, then Lender may collect the insurance proceeds. Lender may use the proceeds to repair or restore the Property or to pay sums secured by this Security Instrument, whether or not then due. The 30-day period will begin when the notice is given.

Unless Lender and Borrower otherwise agree in writing, any application of proceeds to principal shall not extend or postpone the due date of the monthly payments referred to in paragraphs 1 and 2 or change the amount of the payments. If under paragraph 21 the Property is acquired by Lender, Borrower's right to any insurance policies and proceeds resulting from damage to the Property prior to the acquisition shall pass to Lender to the extent of the sums secured by this Security Instrument immediately prior to the acquisition.

6. Occupancy, Preservation, Maintenance and Protection of the Property; Borrower's Loan Application; Leaseholds. Borrower shall occupy, establish, and use the Property as Borrower's principal residence within sixty days after the execution of this Security Instrument and shall continue to occupy the Property as Borrower's principal residence for at least one year after the date of occupancy, unless Lender otherwise agrees in writing, which consent shall not be unreasonably withheld, or unless extenuating circumstances exist which are beyond Borrower's control. Borrower shall be in default if any forfeiture action or proceeding, whether civil or criminal, is begun that in Lender's good faith judgment could result in forfeiture of the Property or otherwise materially impair the lien created by this Security Instrument or Lender's security interest. Borrower may cure such a default and reinstate, as provided in paragraph 18, by causing the action or proceeding to be dismissed with a ruling that, in Lender's good faith determination, precludes forfeiture of the Borrower's interest in the Property or other material impairment of the lien created by this Security Instrument or Lender's security interest. Borrower shall also be in default if Borrower, during the loan application process, gave materially false or inaccurate information or statements to Lender (or failed to provide Lender with any material information) in connection with the loan evidenced by the Note, including, but not limited to, representations concerning Borrower's occupancy of the Property as a principal residence. If this Security Instrument is on a leasehold, Borrower shall comply with all the provisions of the lease. If Borrower acquires fee title to the Property, the leasehold and the fee title shall not merge unless Lender agrees to the merger in writing.

7. Protection of Lender's Rights in the Property. If Borrower fails to perform the covenants and agreements contained in this Security Instrument, or there is a legal proceeding that may significantly affect Lender's rights in the Property (such as a proceeding in bankruptcy, probate, for condemnation or forfeiture or to enforce laws or regulations), then Lender may do and pay for whatever is necessary to protect the value of the Property and Lender's rights in the Property. Lender's actions may include paying any sums secured by a lien which has priority over this Security Instrument, appearing in court, paying reasonble attorneys' fees and entering on the Property to make repairs. Although Lender may take action under this paragraph 7, Lender does not have to do so.

Any amounts disbursed by Lender under this paragraph 7 shall become additional debt of Borrower secured by this Security Instrument. Unless Borrower and Lender agree to other terms of payment, these amounts shall bear interest from the date of disbursement at the Note rate and shall be payable, with interest, upon notice from Lender to Borrower requesting payment.

8. Mortgage Insurance. If Lender required mortgage insurance as a condition of making the loan secured by this Security Instrument, Borrower shall pay the premiums required to maintain the mortgage insurance in effect. If, for any reason, the mortgage insurance coverage required by Lender lapses or ceases to be in effect, Borrower shall pay the premiums required to obtain coverage substantially equivalent to the mortgage insurance previously in effect, at a cost substantially equivalent to the cost to Borrower of the mortgage insurance previously in effect from an alternate mortgage insurer approved by Lender. If substantially equivalent mortgage insurance coverage is not available, Borrower shall pay to Lender each month a sum equal to one-twelfth of the yearly mortgage insurance premium being paid by Borrower when the insurance coverage lapsed or ceased to be in effect. Lender will accept, use and retain these payments as a loss reserve in lieu of mortgage insurance. Loss reserve payments may no longer be required, at the option of Lender, if mortgage insurance coverage (in the amount and for the period that Lender requires) provided by an insurer approved by Lender again becomes available and is obtained. Borrower shall pay the premiums required to maintain mortgage insurance in effect, or to provide a loss reserve, until the requirement for mortgage insurance ends in accordance with any written agreement between Borrower and Lender or applicable law.

9. Inspection. Lender or its agent may make reasonable entries upon and inspections of the Property. Lender shall give Borrower notice at the time of or prior to an inspection specifying reasonable cause for the inspection.

10. Condemnation. The proceeds of any award or claim for damages, direct or consequential, in connection with any condemnation or other taking of any part of the Property, or for conveyance in lieu of condemnation, are hereby assigned and shall be paid to Lender.

In the event of a total taking of the Property, the proceeds shall be applied to the sums secured by this Security Instrument, whether or not then due, with any excess paid to Borrower. In the event of a partial taking of the Property in which the fair market value of the Property immediately before the taking is equal to or greater than the amount of the sums secured by this Security Instrument immediately before the taking, unless Borrower and Lender otherwise agree in writing, the sums secured by this Security Instrument shall be reduced by the amount of the proceeds multiplied by the following fraction: (a) the total amount of the sums secured immediately before the taking, divided by (b) the fair market value of the Property immediately before the taking. Any balance shall be paid to Borrower. In the event of a partial taking of the Property in which the fair market value of the Property immediately before the taking is less than the amount of the sums secured immediately before the taking, unless Borrower and Lender otherwise agree in writing or unless applicable law otherwise provides, the proceeds shall be applied to the sums secured by this Security Instrument whether or not the sums are then due.

If the Property is abandoned by Borrower, or if, after notice by Lender to Borrower that the condemnor offers to make an award or settle a claim for damage, Borrower fails to respond to Lender within 30 days after the date the notice is given, Lender is authorized to collect and apply the proceeds, at its option, either to restoration or repair of the Property or to the sums secured by this Security Instrument, whether or not then due.

Unless Lender and Borrower otherwise agree in writing, any application of proceeds to principal shall not extend or postpone the due date of the monthly payments referred to in paragraphs 1 and 2 or change the amount of such payments.

11. Borrower Not Released: Forbearance By Lender Not a Waiver. Extension of the time for payment or modification of amortization of the sums secured by this Security Instrument granted by Lender to any successor in interest of Borrower shall not operate to release the liability of the original Borrower or Borrower's successors in interest. Lender shall not be required to commence proceedings against any successor in interest or refuse to extend time for payment or otherwise modify amortization of the sums secured by this Security Instrument by reason of any demand made by the original Borrower or Borrower's successors in interest. Any forbearance by Lender in exercising any right or remedy shall not be a waiver of or preclude the exercise of any right or remedy.

12. Successors and Assigns Bound; Joint and Several Liability; Co-signers. The covenants and agreements of this Security Instrument shall bind and benefit the successors and assigns of Lender and Borrower, subject to the provisions of paragraph 17. Borrower's covenants and agreements shall be joint and several. Any Borrower who co-signs this Security Instrument but does not execute the Note: (a) is co-signing this Security Instrument only to mortgage, grant and convey that Borrower's interest in the Property under the terms of this Security Instrument; (b) is not personally obligated to pay the sums secured by this Security Instrument; and (c) agrees that Lender and any other Borrower may agree to extend, modify, forbear or make any accommodations with regard to the terms of this Security Instrument or the Note without that Borrower's consent.

13. Loan Charges. If the loan secured by this Security Instrument is subject to a law which sets maximum loan charges, and that law is finally interpreted so that the interest or other loan charges collected or to be collected in connection with the loan exceed the permitted limits, then: (a) any such loan charge shall be reduced by the amount necessary to reduce the charge to the permitted limit; and (b) any sums already collected from Borrower which exceeded permitted limits will be refunded to Borrower. Lender may choose to make this refund by reducing the principal owed under the Note or by making a direct payment to Borrower. If a refund reduces principal, the reduction will be treated as a partial prepayment without any prepayment charge under the Note.

14. Notices. Any notice to Borrower provided for in this Security Instrument shall be given by delivering it or by mailing it by first class mail unless applicable law requires use of another method. The notice shall be directed to the Property Address or any other address Borrower designates by notice to Lender. Any notice to Lender shall be given by first class mail to Lender's address stated herein or any other address Lender designates by notice to Borrower. Any notice provided for in this Security Instrument shall be deemed to have been given to Borrower or Lender when given as provided in this paragraph.

15. Governing Law; Severability. This Security Instrument shall be governed by federal law and the law of the jurisdiction in which the Property is located. In the event that any provision or clause of this Security Instrument or the Note conflicts with applicable law, such conflict shall not affect other provisions of this Security Instrument or the Note which can be given effect without the conflicting provision. To this end the provisions of this Security Instrument and the Note are declared to be severable.

16. Borrower's Copy. Borrower shall be given one conformed copy of the Note and of this Security Instrument.

17. Transfer of the Property or a Beneficial Interest in Borrower. If all or any part of the Property or any interest in it is sold or transferred (or if a beneficial interest in Borrower is sold or transferred and Borrower is not a natural person) without Lender's prior written consent, Lender may, at its option, require immediate payment in full of all sums secured by this Security Instrument. However, this option shall not be exercised by Lender if exercise is prohibited by federal law as of the date of this Security Instrument.

If Lender exercises this option, Lender shall give Borrower notice of acceleration. The notice shall provide a period of not less than 30 days from the date the notice is delivered or mailed within which Borrower must pay all sums secured by this Security Instrument. If Borrower fails to pay these sums prior to the expiration of this period, Lender may invoke any remedies permitted by this Security Instrument without further notice or demand on Borrower.

18. Borrower's Right to Reinstate. If Borrower meets certain conditions, Borrower shall have the right to have enforcement of this Security Instrument discontinued at any time prior to the earlier of: (a) 5 days (or such other period as applicable law may specify for reinstatement) before sale of the Property pursuant to any power of sale contained in this Security Instrument; or (b) entry of a judgment enforcing this Security Instrument. Those conditions are that Borrower: (a) pays Lender all sums, which then would be due under this Security Instrument and the Note as if no acceleration had occurred; (b) cures any default of any other covenants or agreements; (c) pays all expenses incurred in enforcing this Security Instrument, including, but not limited to, reasonable attorneys' fees; and (d) takes such action as Lender may reasonably require to assure that the lien of this Security Instrument, Lender's rights in the Property and Borrower's obligation to pay the sums secured by this Security Instrument shall continue unchanged. Upon reinstatement by Borrower, this Security Instrument and the obligations secured hereby shall remain fully effective as if no acceleration had occurred. However, this right to reinstate shall not apply in the case of acceleration under paragraph 17.

19. Sale of Note; Change of Loan Servicer. The Note or a partial interest in the Note (together with this Security Instrument) may be sold one or more times without prior notice to Borrower. A sale may result in a change in the entity (known as the "Loan Servicer") that collects monthly payments due under the Note and this Security Instrument. There also may be one or more changes of the Loan Servicer unrelated to a sale of the Note. If there is a change of the Loan Servicer, Borrower will be given written notice of the change in accordance with paragraph 14 above and applicable law. The notice will state the name and address of the new Loan Servicer and the address to which payments should be made. The notice will also contain any other information required by applicable law.

20. Hazardous Substances. Borrower shall not cause or permit the presence, use, disposal, storage, or release of any Hazardous Substances on or in the Property. Borrower shall not do, nor allow anyone else to do, anything affecting the Property that is in violation of any Environmental Law. The preceding two sentences shall not apply to the presence, use, or storage on the Property of small quantities of Hazardous Substances that are generally recognized to be appropriate to normal residential uses and to maintenance of the Property.

Borrower shall promptly give Lender written notice of any investigation, claim, demand, lawsuit or other action by any governmental or regulatory agency or private party involving the Property and any Hazardous Substance or Environmental Law of which Borrower has actual knowledge. If Borrower learns, or is notified by any governmental or regulatory authority, that any removal or other remediation of any Hazardous Substance affecting the Property is necessary, Borrower shall promptly take all necessary remedial actions in accordance with Environmental Law.

As used in this paragraph 20, "Hazardous Substances" are those substances defined as toxic or hazardous substances by Environmental Law and the following substances: gasoline, kerosene, other flammable or toxic petroleum products, toxic pesticides and herbicides, volatile solvents, materials containing asbestos or formaldehyde, and radioactive materials. As used in this paragraph 20, "Environmental Law" means federal laws and laws of the jurisdiction where the Property is located that relate to health, safety or environmental protection.

NON-UNIFORM COVENANTS. Borrower and Lender further covenant and agree as follows:

21. Acceleration; Remedies. Lender shall give notice to Borrower prior to acceleration following Borrower's breach of any covenant or agreement in this Security Instrument (but not prior to acceleration under paragraph 17 unless applicable law provides otherwise). The notice shall specify: (a) the default; (b) the action required to cure the default; (c) a date, not less than 30 days from the date the notice is given to Borrower, by which the default must be cured; and (d) that failure to cure the default on or before the date specified in the notice may result in acceleration of the sums secured by this Security Instrument and sale of the Property. The notice shall further inform Borrower of the right to reinstate after acceleration and the right to bring a court action to assert the non-existence of a default or any other defense of Borrower to acceleration and sale. If the default is not cured on or before the date specified in the notice, Lender at its option may require immediate payment in full of all sums secured by this Security Instrument without further demand and may invoke the power of sale and any other remedies permitted by applicable law. Lender shall be entitled to collect all expenses incurred in pursuing the remedies provided in this paragraph 21, including, but not limited to, reasonable attorneys' fees and costs of title evidence.

If Lender invokes the power of sale, Lender shall execute or cause Trustee to execute a written notice of the occurrence of an event of default and of Lender's election to cause the Property to be sold. Trustee shall cause this notice to be recorded in each county in which any part of the Property is located. Lender or Trustee shall mail copies of the notice as prescribed by applicable law to Borrower and to the other persons prescribed by applicable law. Trustee shall give public notice of sale to the persons and in the manner prescribed by applicable law. After the time required by applicable law, Trustee, without demand on Borrower, shall sell the Property at public auction to the highest bidder at the time and place and under the terms designated in the notice of sale in one or more parcels and in any order Trustee determines. Trustee may postpone sale of all or any parcel of the Property by public announcement at the time and place of any previously scheduled sale. Lender or its designee may purchase the Property at any sale.

Trustee shall deliver to the purchaser Trustee's deed conveying the Property without any covenant or warranty, expressed or implied. The recitals in the Trustee's deed shall be prima facie evidence of the truth of the statements made therein. Trustee shall apply the proceeds of the sale in the following order: (a) to all expenses of the sale, including, but not limited to, reasonable Trustee's and attorneys' fees; (b) to all sums secured by this Security Instrument; and (c) any excess to the person or persons legally entitled to it.

22. Reconveyance. Upon payment of all sums secured by this Security Instrument, Lender shall request Trustee to reconvey the Property and shall surrender this Security Instrument and all notes evidencing debt secured by this Security Instrument to Trustee. Trustee shall reconvey the Property without warranty and without charge to the person or persons legally entitled to it. Such person or persons shall pay any recordation costs.

23. Substitute Trustee. Lender, at its option, may from time to time appoint a successor trustee to any Trustee appointed hereunder by an instrument executed and acknowledged by Lender and recorded in the office of the Recorder of the county in which the Property is located. The instrument shall contain the name of the original Lender, Trustee and Borrower, the book and page where this Security Instrument is recorded and the name and address of the successor trustee. Without conveyance of the Property, the successor trustee shall succeed to all the title, powers and duties conferred upon the Trustee herein and by applicable law. This procedure for substitution of trustee shall govern to the exclusion of all other provisions for substitution.

24. Request for Notices. Borrower request that copies of the notices of default and sale be sent to Borrower's address which is the Property Address.

25. Statement of Obligation Fee. Lender may collect a fee not to exceed the maximum amount permitted by law for furnishing the statement of obligation as provided by Section 2943 of the Civil Code of California.

26. Riders to this Security Instrument. If one or more riders are executed by Borrower and recorded together with this Security Instrument, the covenants and agreements of each such rider shall be incorporated into and shall amend and supplement the covenants and agreements of this Security Instrument as if the rider(s) were a part of this Security Instrument. [Check applicable box(es)]

☐ Adjustable Rate Rider   ☐ Condominium Rider   ☐ 1–4 Family Rider
☐ Graduated Payment Rider   ☐ Planned Unit Development Rider   ☐ Biweekly Payment Rider
☐ Balloon Rider   ☐ Rate Improvement Rider   ☐ Second Home Rider
☐ Other(s) [specify]

BY SIGNING BELOW, Borrower accepts and agrees to the terms and covenants contained in this Security Instrument and in any rider(s) executed by Borrower and recorded with it.

_____ (Seal)
                                                Borrower

_____ (Seal)
                                                Borrower

_____ (Seal)
                                                Borrower

_____ (Seal)
                                                Borrower

——————————————————— [Space Below This Line For Acknowledgment] ———————————————————

State of California,   **County ss:**
        On   , before me,
personally appeared

known to me (or proved to me on the basis of satisfactory evidence) to be the person(s) whose name(s) is/are subscribed to the within instrument and acknowledged to me that he/she/they executed the same in his/her/their authorized capacity(ies), and that by his/her/their signature(s) on the instrument the person(s), or the entity upon behalf of which the person(s) acted, executed the instrument.

WITNESS my hand and official seal.

Signature _____   (Seal)

                                                        _____
My commission expires   Name (typed or printed)

REQUEST FOR RECONVEYANCE

TO TRUSTEE:
    The undersigned is the holder of the note or notes secured by this Deed of Trust. Said note or notes, together with all other indebtedness secured by this Deed of Trust, have been paid in full. You are hereby directed to cancel said note or notes and this Deed of Trust, which are delivered hereby, and to reconvey, without warranty, all the estate now held by you under this Deed of Trust to the person or persons legally entitled thereto.

    Dated: _____

Form 3005   9/90 (page 6 of 6 pages)

C. Mortgages

➡️ If you signed a deed of trust when you obtained your loan, then you can skip this section and read Section B (deeds of trust).

If you are in a mortgage state, the loan document you signed was a mortgage. Your mortgage is the document in which you promised to repay the money that was loaned to you. The mortgage sets forth the amount you borrowed, and the particulars of how the loan is to be repaid. Typically several pages long, a mortgage is similar to a deed of trust.

When you signed a mortgage to borrow money from your lender to purchase or refinance your property, it became evidence of your lender's security interest in your property. To be valid, the mortgage is recorded in the recorder's office in the county where the property is located.

The mortgage creates a lien (legal claim) against your property, which remains in force until you repay your loan or your lender forecloses. Although there is no standard form for a mortgage, these documents have become relatively standardized across the country. A sample of a typical FNMA mortgage used in most states is provided on the next page.

But unlike a deed of trust, mortgages do not have a "power of sale" clause. This means that your lender does not have the right to conduct a nonjudicial foreclosure. As a consequence, your lender must file a lawsuit in court in order to foreclose your property, which is a slower and more cumbersome procedure. Judicial foreclosures are covered in Chapter 4). An explanation of the important terms in a mortgage follows.

1. Parties to a Mortgage

There are two parties to a mortgage:

a. Mortgager (you)

The mortgager is the person or persons who borrowed the money. The borrower is sometimes referred to as the "mortgagor." This includes you and anyone who co-signed the loan, such as a spouse, non-marital partner, or business partner.

b. Mortgagee

The Mortgagee is the financial institution that originally loaned you money, or the financial institution (or investor) to whom your original lender sold your mortgage. The lender is sometimes referred to as the "mortgagee." When you borrowed money to purchase or refinance your property, the lender was probably a bank, savings bank, mortgage company, credit union, insurance company, family member, friend, or perhaps, the seller of the property. The current lender may be a company or person that specializes in buying loans from the original lenders.

A sample Mortgage Worksheet appears below, and a blank tear-out copy is included in the Appendix. Use it to record the relevant terms and conditions in your mortgage.

After Recording Return To:

_____

_____

_____

_____

_____**[Space Above This Line For Recording Data]**_____

MORTGAGE

DEFINITIONS

Words used in multiple sections of this document are defined below and other words are defined in Sections 3, 11, 13, 18, 20 and 21. Certain rules regarding the usage of words used in this document are also provided in Section 16.

(A)   **"Security Instrument"** means this document, which is dated _____, _____, together with all Riders to this document.

(B)   **"Borrower"** is _____.
Borrower is the mortgagor under this Security Instrument.

(C)   **"Lender"** is _____.
Lender is a _____ organized and existing under the laws of _____. Lender's address is _____ _____.   Lender is the mortgagee under this Security Instrument.

(D)   **"Note"** means the promissory note signed by Borrower and dated _____, _____. The Note states that Borrower owes Lender _____ Dollars (U.S. $_____) plus interest. Borrower has promised to pay this debt in regular Periodic Payments and to pay the debt in full not later than _____.

(E)   **"Property"** means the property that is described below under the heading "Transfer of Rights in the Property."

(F)   **"Loan"** means the debt evidenced by the Note, plus interest, any prepayment charges and late charges due under the Note, and all sums due under this Security Instrument, plus interest.

(G) **"Riders"** means all Riders to this Security Instrument that are executed by Borrower. The following Riders are to be executed by Borrower [check box as applicable]:

☐ Adjustable Rate Rider	☐ Condominium Rider	☐ Second Home Rider
☐ Balloon Rider	☐ Planned Unit Development Rider	☐ Other(s) [specify]
☐ 1-4 Family Rider	☐ Biweekly Payment Rider	

(H) **"Applicable Law"** means all controlling applicable federal, state and local statutes, regulations, ordinances and administrative rules and orders (that have the effect of law) as well as all applicable final, non-appealable judicial opinions.

(I) **"Community Association Dues, Fees, and Assessments"** means all dues, fees, assessments and other charges that are imposed on Borrower or the Property by a condominium association, homeowners association or similar organization.

(J) **"Electronic Funds Transfer"** means any transfer of funds, other than a transaction originated by check, draft, or similar paper instrument, which is initiated through an electronic terminal, telephonic instrument, computer, or magnetic tape so as to order, instruct, or authorize a financial institution to debit or credit an account. Such term includes, but is not limited to, point-of-sale transfers, automated teller machine transactions, transfers initiated by telephone, wire transfers, and automated clearinghouse transfers.

(K) **"Escrow Items"** means those items that are described in Section 3.

(L) **"Miscellaneous Proceeds"** means any compensation, settlement, award of damages, or proceeds paid by any third party (other than insurance proceeds paid under the coverages described in Section 5) for: (i) damage to, or destruction of, the Property; (ii) condemnation or other taking of all or any part of the Property; (iii) conveyance in lieu of condemnation; or (iv) misrepresentations of, or omissions as to, the value and/or condition of the Property.

(M) **"Mortgage Insurance"** means insurance protecting Lender against the nonpayment of, or default on, the Loan.

(N) **"Periodic Payment"** means the regularly scheduled amount due for (i) principal and interest under the Note, plus (ii) any amounts under Section 3 of this Security Instrument.

(O) **"RESPA"** means the Real Estate Settlement Procedures Act (12 U.S.C. §2601 et seq.) and its implementing regulation, Regulation X (24 C.F.R. Part 3500), as they might be amended from time to time, or any additional or successor legislation or regulation that governs the same subject matter. As used in this Security Instrument, "RESPA" refers to all requirements and restrictions that are imposed in regard to a "federally related mortgage loan" even if the Loan does not qualify as a "federally related mortgage loan" under RESPA.

(P) **"Successor in Interest of Borrower"** means any party that has taken title to the Property, whether or not that party has assumed Borrower's obligations under the Note and/or this Security Instrument.

TRANSFER OF RIGHTS IN THE PROPERTY

This Security Instrument secures to Lender: (i) the repayment of the Loan, and all renewals, extensions and modifications of the Note; and (ii) the performance of Borrower's covenants and agreements under this Security Instrument and the Note. For this purpose, Borrower does hereby mortgage, grant and convey to Lender and Lender's successors and assigns the following described property located in the _____

[Type of Recording Jurisdiction]

of _____ :

[Name of Recording Jurisdiction]

which currently has the address of _____

[Street]

_____ , Illinois _____ ("Property Address"):

[City]   [Zip Code]

TOGETHER WITH all the improvements now or hereafter erected on the property, and all easements, appurtenances, and fixtures now or hereafter a part of the property. All replacements and additions shall also be covered by this Security Instrument. All of the foregoing is referred to in this Security Instrument as the "Property."

BORROWER COVENANTS that Borrower is lawfully seised of the estate hereby conveyed and has the right to mortgage, grant and convey the Property and that the Property is unencumbered, except for encumbrances of record. Borrower warrants and will defend generally the title to the Property against all claims and demands, subject to any encumbrances of record.

THIS SECURITY INSTRUMENT combines uniform covenants for national use and non-uniform covenants with limited variations by jurisdiction to constitute a uniform security instrument covering real property.

UNIFORM COVENANTS. Borrower and Lender covenant and agree as follows:
  1. **Payment of Principal, Interest, Escrow Items, Prepayment Charges, and Late Charges.** Borrower shall pay when due the principal of, and interest on, the debt evidenced by the Note and any prepayment charges and late charges due under the Note. Borrower shall also pay funds for Escrow Items pursuant to Section 3. Payments due under the Note and this Security Instrument shall be made in U.S. currency. However, if any check or other instrument received by Lender as payment under the Note or this Security Instrument is returned to Lender unpaid, Lender may require that any or all subsequent payments due under

the Note and this Security Instrument be made in one or more of the following forms, as selected by Lender: (a) cash; (b) money order; (c) certified check, bank check, treasurer's check or cashier's check, provided any such check is drawn upon an institution whose deposits are insured by a federal agency, instrumentality, or entity; or (d) Electronic Funds Transfer.

Payments are deemed received by Lender when received at the location designated in the Note or at such other location as may be designated by Lender in accordance with the notice provisions in Section 15. Lender may return any payment or partial payment if the payment or partial payments are insufficient to bring the Loan current. Lender may accept any payment or partial payment insufficient to bring the Loan current, without waiver of any rights hereunder or prejudice to its rights to refuse such payment or partial payments in the future, but Lender is not obligated to apply such payments at the time such payments are accepted. If each Periodic Payment is applied as of its scheduled due date, then Lender need not pay interest on unapplied funds. Lender may hold such unapplied funds until Borrower makes payment to bring the Loan current. If Borrower does not do so within a reasonable period of time, Lender shall either apply such funds or return them to Borrower. If not applied earlier, such funds will be applied to the outstanding principal balance under the Note immediately prior to foreclosure. No offset or claim which Borrower might have now or in the future against Lender shall relieve Borrower from making payments due under the Note and this Security Instrument or performing the covenants and agreements secured by this Security Instrument.

2. **Application of Payments or Proceeds.** Except as otherwise described in this Section 2, all payments accepted and applied by Lender shall be applied in the following order of priority: (a) interest due under the Note; (b) principal due under the Note; (c) amounts due under Section 3. Such payments shall be applied to each Periodic Payment in the order in which it became due. Any remaining amounts shall be applied first to late charges, second to any other amounts due under this Security Instrument, and then to reduce the principal balance of the Note.

If Lender receives a payment from Borrower for a delinquent Periodic Payment which includes a sufficient amount to pay any late charge due, the payment may be applied to the delinquent payment and the late charge. If more than one Periodic Payment is outstanding, Lender may apply any payment received from Borrower to the repayment of the Periodic Payments if, and to the extent that, each payment can be paid in full. To the extent that any excess exists after the payment is applied to the full payment of one or more Periodic Payments, such excess may be applied to any late charges due. Voluntary prepayments shall be applied first to any prepayment charges and then as described in the Note.

Any application of payments, insurance proceeds, or Miscellaneous Proceeds to principal due under the Note shall not extend or postpone the due date, or change the amount, of the Periodic Payments.

3. **Funds for Escrow Items.** Borrower shall pay to Lender on the day Periodic Payments are due under the Note, until the Note is paid in full, a sum (the "Funds") to provide for payment of amounts due for: (a) taxes and assessments and other items which can attain priority over this Security Instrument as a lien or encumbrance on the Property; (b) leasehold payments or ground rents on the Property, if any; (c) premiums for any and all insurance required by Lender under Section 5; and (d) Mortgage Insurance premiums, if any, or any sums payable by Borrower to Lender in lieu of the payment of Mortgage Insurance premiums in accordance with the provisions of Section 10. These items are called "Escrow Items." At origination or at any time during the term of the Loan, Lender may require that Community Association Dues, Fees, and Assessments, if any, be escrowed by Borrower, and such dues, fees

and assessments shall be an Escrow Item. Borrower shall promptly furnish to Lender all notices of amounts to be paid under this Section. Borrower shall pay Lender the Funds for Escrow Items unless Lender waives Borrower's obligation to pay the Funds for any or all Escrow Items. Lender may waive Borrower's obligation to pay to Lender Funds for any or all Escrow Items at any time. Any such waiver may only be in writing. In the event of such waiver, Borrower shall pay directly, when and where payable, the amounts due for any Escrow Items for which payment of Funds has been waived by Lender and, if Lender requires, shall furnish to Lender receipts evidencing such payment within such time period as Lender may require. Borrower's obligation to make such payments and to provide receipts shall for all purposes be deemed to be a covenant and agreement contained in this Security Instrument, as the phrase "covenant and agreement" is used in Section 9. If Borrower is obligated to pay Escrow Items directly, pursuant to a waiver, and Borrower fails to pay the amount due for an Escrow Item, Lender may exercise its rights under Section 9 and pay such amount and Borrower shall then be obligated under Section 9 to repay to Lender any such amount. Lender may revoke the waiver as to any or all Escrow Items at any time by a notice given in accordance with Section 15 and, upon such revocation, Borrower shall pay to Lender all Funds, and in such amounts, that are then required under this Section 3.

Lender may, at any time, collect and hold Funds in an amount (a) sufficient to permit Lender to apply the Funds at the time specified under RESPA, and (b) not to exceed the maximum amount a lender can require under RESPA. Lender shall estimate the amount of Funds due on the basis of current data and reasonable estimates of expenditures of future Escrow Items or otherwise in accordance with Applicable Law.

The Funds shall be held in an institution whose deposits are insured by a federal agency, instrumentality, or entity (including Lender, if Lender is an institution whose deposits are so insured) or in any Federal Home Loan Bank. Lender shall apply the Funds to pay the Escrow Items no later than the time specified under RESPA. Lender shall not charge Borrower for holding and applying the Funds, annually analyzing the escrow account, or verifying the Escrow Items, unless Lender pays Borrower interest on the Funds and Applicable Law permits Lender to make such a charge. Unless an agreement is made in writing or Applicable Law requires interest to be paid on the Funds, Lender shall not be required to pay Borrower any interest or earnings on the Funds. Borrower and Lender can agree in writing, however, that interest shall be paid on the Funds. Lender shall give to Borrower, without charge, an annual accounting of the Funds as required by RESPA.

If there is a surplus of Funds held in escrow, as defined under RESPA, Lender shall account to Borrower for the excess funds in accordance with RESPA. If there is a shortage of Funds held in escrow, as defined under RESPA, Lender shall notify Borrower as required by RESPA, and Borrower shall pay to Lender the amount necessary to make up the shortage in accordance with RESPA, but in no more than 12 monthly payments. If there is a deficiency of Funds held in escrow, as defined under RESPA, Lender shall notify Borrower as required by RESPA, and Borrower shall pay to Lender the amount necessary to make up the deficiency in accordance with RESPA, but in no more than 12 monthly payments.

Upon payment in full of all sums secured by this Security Instrument, Lender shall promptly refund to Borrower any Funds held by Lender.

4.   Charges; Liens. Borrower shall pay all taxes, assessments, charges, fines, and impositions attributable to the Property which can attain priority over this Security Instrument, leasehold payments or ground rents on the Property, if any, and Community Association Dues,

Fees, and Assessments, if any. To the extent that these items are Escrow Items, Borrower shall pay them in the manner provided in Section 3.

Borrower shall promptly discharge any lien which has priority over this Security Instrument unless Borrower: (a) agrees in writing to the payment of the obligation secured by the lien in a manner acceptable to Lender, but only so long as Borrower is performing such agreement; (b) contests the lien in good faith by, or defends against enforcement of the lien in, legal proceedings which in Lender's opinion operate to prevent the enforcement of the lien while those proceedings are pending, but only until such proceedings are concluded; or (c) secures from the holder of the lien an agreement satisfactory to Lender subordinating the lien to this Security Instrument. If Lender determines that any part of the Property is subject to a lien which can attain priority over this Security Instrument, Lender may give Borrower a notice identifying the lien. Within 10 days of the date on which that notice is given, Borrower shall satisfy the lien or take one or more of the actions set forth above in this Section 4.

Lender may require Borrower to pay a one-time charge for a real estate tax verification and/or reporting service used by Lender in connection with this Loan.

5. Property Insurance. Borrower shall keep the improvements now existing or hereafter erected on the Property insured against loss by fire, hazards included within the term "extended coverage;" and any other hazards including, but not limited to, earthquakes and floods, for which Lender requires insurance. This insurance shall be maintained in the amounts (including deductible levels) and for the periods that Lender requires. What Lender requires pursuant to the preceding sentences can change during the term of the Loan. The insurance carrier providing the insurance shall be chosen by Borrower subject to Lender's right to disapprove Borrower's choice, which right shall not be exercised unreasonably. Lender may require Borrower to pay, in connection with this Loan, either: (a) a one-time charge for flood zone determination, certification and tracking services; or (b) a one-time charge for flood zone determination and certification services and subsequent charges each time remappings or similar changes occur which reasonably might affect such determination or certification. Borrower shall also be responsible for the payment of any fees imposed by the Federal Emergency Management Agency in connection with the review of any flood zone determination resulting from an objection by Borrower.

If Borrower fails to maintain any of the coverages described above, Lender may obtain insurance coverage, at Lender's option and Borrower's expense. Lender is under no obligation to purchase any particular type or amount of coverage. Therefore, such coverage shall cover Lender, but might or might not protect Borrower, Borrower's equity in the Property, or the contents of the Property, against any risk, hazard or liability and might provide greater or lesser coverage than was previously in effect. Borrower acknowledges that the cost of the insurance coverage so obtained might significantly exceed the cost of insurance that Borrower could have obtained. Any amounts disbursed by Lender under this Section 5 shall become additional debt of Borrower secured by this Security Instrument. These amounts shall bear interest at the Note rate from the date of disbursement and shall be payable, with such interest, upon notice from Lender to Borrower requesting payment.

All insurance policies required by Lender and renewals of such policies shall be subject to Lender's right to disapprove such policies, shall include a standard mortgage clause, and shall name Lender as mortgagee and/or as an additional loss payee. Lender shall have the right to hold the policies and renewal certificates. If Lender requires, Borrower shall promptly give to Lender all receipts of paid premiums and renewal notices. If Borrower obtains any form of insurance coverage, not otherwise required by Lender, for damage to, or destruction of, the Property, such policy shall include a standard mortgage clause and shall name Lender as mortgagee and/or as an additional loss payee.

In the event of loss, Borrower shall give prompt notice to the insurance carrier and Lender. Lender may make proof of loss if not made promptly by Borrower. Unless Lender and Borrower otherwise agree in writing, any insurance proceeds, whether or not the underlying insurance was required by Lender, shall be applied to restoration or repair of the Property, if the restoration or repair is economically feasible and Lender's security is not lessened. During such repair and restoration period, Lender shall have the right to hold such insurance proceeds until Lender has had an opportunity to inspect such Property to ensure the work has been completed to Lender's satisfaction, provided that such inspection shall be undertaken promptly. Lender may disburse proceeds for the repairs and restoration in a single payment or in a series of progress payments as the work is completed. Unless an agreement is made in writing or Applicable Law requires interest to be paid on such insurance proceeds, Lender shall not be required to pay Borrower any interest or earnings on such proceeds. Fees for public adjusters, or other third parties, retained by Borrower shall not be paid out of the insurance proceeds and shall be the sole obligation of Borrower. If the restoration or repair is not economically feasible or Lender's security would be lessened, the insurance proceeds shall be applied to the sums secured by this Security Instrument, whether or not then due, with the excess, if any, paid to Borrower. Such insurance proceeds shall be applied in the order provided for in Section 2.

If Borrower abandons the Property, Lender may file, negotiate and settle any available insurance claim and related matters. If Borrower does not respond within 30 days to a notice from Lender that the insurance carrier has offered to settle a claim, then Lender may negotiate and settle the claim. The 30-day period will begin when the notice is given. In either event, or if Lender acquires the Property under Section 22 or otherwise, Borrower hereby assigns to Lender (a) Borrower's rights to any insurance proceeds in an amount not to exceed the amounts unpaid under the Note or this Security Instrument, and (b) any other of Borrower's rights (other than the right to any refund of unearned premiums paid by Borrower) under all insurance policies covering the Property, insofar as such rights are applicable to the coverage of the Property. Lender may use the insurance proceeds either to repair or restore the Property or to pay amounts unpaid under the Note or this Security Instrument, whether or not then due.

   6.   Occupancy.   Borrower shall occupy, establish, and use the Property as Borrower's principal residence within 60 days after the execution of this Security Instrument and shall continue to occupy the Property as Borrower's principal residence for at least one year after the date of occupancy, unless Lender otherwise agrees in writing, which consent shall not be unreasonably withheld, or unless extenuating circumstances exist which are beyond Borrower's control.

   7.   Preservation, Maintenance and Protection of the Property; Inspections. Borrower shall not destroy, damage or impair the Property, allow the Property to deteriorate or commit waste on the Property. Whether or not Borrower is residing in the Property, Borrower shall maintain the Property in order to prevent the Property from deteriorating or decreasing in value due to its condition. Unless it is determined pursuant to Section 5 that repair or restoration is not economically feasible, Borrower shall promptly repair the Property if damaged to avoid further deterioration or damage. If insurance or condemnation proceeds are paid in connection with damage to, or the taking of, the Property, Borrower shall be responsible for repairing or restoring the Property only if Lender has released proceeds for such purposes. Lender may

ILLINOIS--Single Family--**Fannie Mae/Freddie Mac UNIFORM INSTRUMENT**   Form 3014   1/01   *(page 7 of 16 pages)*

disburse proceeds for the repairs and restoration in a single payment or in a series of progress payments as the work is completed. If the insurance or condemnation proceeds are not sufficient to repair or restore the Property, Borrower is not relieved of Borrower's obligation for the completion of such repair or restoration.

Lender or its agent may make reasonable entries upon and inspections of the Property. If it has reasonable cause, Lender may inspect the interior of the improvements on the Property. Lender shall give Borrower notice at the time of or prior to such an interior inspection specifying such reasonable cause.

8.   Borrower's Loan Application.   Borrower shall be in default if, during the Loan application process, Borrower or any persons or entities acting at the direction of Borrower or with Borrower's knowledge or consent gave materially false, misleading, or inaccurate information or statements to Lender (or failed to provide Lender with material information) in connection with the Loan.   Material representations include, but are not limited to, representations concerning Borrower's occupancy of the Property as Borrower's principal residence.

9.   Protection of Lender's Interest in the Property and Rights Under this Security Instrument.   If (a) Borrower fails to perform the covenants and agreements contained in this Security Instrument, (b) there is a legal proceeding that might significantly affect Lender's interest in the Property and/or rights under this Security Instrument (such as a proceeding in bankruptcy, probate, for condemnation or forfeiture, for enforcement of a lien which may attain priority over this Security Instrument or to enforce laws or regulations), or (c) Borrower has abandoned the Property, then Lender may do and pay for whatever is reasonable or appropriate to protect Lender's interest in the Property and rights under this Security Instrument, including protecting and/or assessing the value of the Property, and securing and/or repairing the Property.   Lender's actions can include, but are not limited to: (a) paying any sums secured by a lien which has priority over this Security Instrument; (b) appearing in court; and (c) paying reasonable attorneys' fees to protect its interest in the Property and/or rights under this Security Instrument, including its secured position in a bankruptcy proceeding. Securing the Property includes, but is not limited to, entering the Property to make repairs, change locks, replace or board up doors and windows, drain water from pipes, eliminate building or other code violations or dangerous conditions, and have utilities turned on or off.   Although Lender may take action under this Section 9, Lender does not have to do so and is not under any duty or obligation to do so.   It is agreed that Lender incurs no liability for not taking any or all actions authorized under this Section 9.

Any amounts disbursed by Lender under this Section 9 shall become additional debt of Borrower secured by this Security Instrument.   These amounts shall bear interest at the Note rate from the date of disbursement and shall be payable, with such interest, upon notice from Lender to Borrower requesting payment.

If this Security Instrument is on a leasehold, Borrower shall comply with all the provisions of the lease.   If Borrower acquires fee title to the Property, the leasehold and the fee title shall not merge unless Lender agrees to the merger in writing.

10.   Mortgage Insurance.   If Lender required Mortgage Insurance as a condition of making the Loan, Borrower shall pay the premiums required to maintain the Mortgage Insurance in effect.   If, for any reason, the Mortgage Insurance coverage required by Lender ceases to be available from the mortgage insurer that previously provided such insurance and Borrower was required to make separately designated payments toward the premiums for Mortgage Insurance,

Borrower shall pay the premiums required to obtain coverage substantially equivalent to the Mortgage Insurance previously in effect, at a cost substantially equivalent to the cost to Borrower of the Mortgage Insurance previously in effect, from an alternate mortgage insurer selected by Lender. If substantially equivalent Mortgage Insurance coverage is not available, Borrower shall continue to pay to Lender the amount of the separately designated payments that were due when the insurance coverage ceased to be in effect. Lender will accept, use and retain these payments as a non-refundable loss reserve in lieu of Mortgage Insurance. Such loss reserve shall be non-refundable, notwithstanding the fact that the Loan is ultimately paid in full, and Lender shall not be required to pay Borrower any interest or earnings on such loss reserve. Lender can no longer require loss reserve payments if Mortgage Insurance coverage (in the amount and for the period that Lender requires) provided by an insurer selected by Lender again becomes available, is obtained, and Lender requires separately designated payments toward the premiums for Mortgage Insurance. If Lender required Mortgage Insurance as a condition of making the Loan and Borrower was required to make separately designated payments toward the premiums for Mortgage Insurance, Borrower shall pay the premiums required to maintain Mortgage Insurance in effect, or to provide a non-refundable loss reserve, until Lender's requirement for Mortgage Insurance ends in accordance with any written agreement between Borrower and Lender providing for such termination or until termination is required by Applicable Law. Nothing in this Section 10 affects Borrower's obligation to pay interest at the rate provided in the Note.

Mortgage Insurance reimburses Lender (or any entity that purchases the Note) for certain losses it may incur if Borrower does not repay the Loan as agreed. Borrower is not a party to the Mortgage Insurance.

Mortgage insurers evaluate their total risk on all such insurance in force from time to time, and may enter into agreements with other parties that share or modify their risk, or reduce losses. These agreements are on terms and conditions that are satisfactory to the mortgage insurer and the other party (or parties) to these agreements. These agreements may require the mortgage insurer to make payments using any source of funds that the mortgage insurer may have available (which may include funds obtained from Mortgage Insurance premiums).

As a result of these agreements, Lender, any purchaser of the Note, another insurer, any reinsurer, any other entity, or any affiliate of any of the foregoing, may receive (directly or indirectly) amounts that derive from (or might be characterized as) a portion of Borrower's payments for Mortgage Insurance, in exchange for sharing or modifying the mortgage insurer's risk, or reducing losses. If such agreement provides that an affiliate of Lender takes a share of the insurer's risk in exchange for a share of the premiums paid to the insurer, the arrangement is often termed "captive reinsurance." Further:

(a)   **Any such agreements will not affect the amounts that Borrower has agreed to pay for Mortgage Insurance, or any other terms of the Loan. Such agreements will not increase the amount Borrower will owe for Mortgage Insurance, and they will not entitle Borrower to any refund.**

(b)   **Any such agreements will not affect the rights Borrower has - if any - with respect to the Mortgage Insurance under the Homeowners Protection Act of 1998 or any other law. These rights may include the right to receive certain disclosures, to request and obtain cancellation of the Mortgage Insurance, to have the Mortgage Insurance terminated automatically, and/or to receive a refund of any Mortgage Insurance premiums that were unearned at the time of such cancellation or termination.**

11. Assignment of Miscellaneous Proceeds; Forfeiture.   All Miscellaneous Proceeds are hereby assigned to and shall be paid to Lender.

If the Property is damaged, such Miscellaneous Proceeds shall be applied to restoration or repair of the Property, if the restoration or repair is economically feasible and Lender's security is not lessened. During such repair and restoration period, Lender shall have the right to hold such Miscellaneous Proceeds until Lender has had an opportunity to inspect such Property to ensure the work has been completed to Lender's satisfaction, provided that such inspection shall be undertaken promptly. Lender may pay for the repairs and restoration in a single disbursement or in a series of progress payments as the work is completed. Unless an agreement is made in writing or Applicable Law requires interest to be paid on such Miscellaneous Proceeds, Lender shall not be required to pay Borrower any interest or earnings on such Miscellaneous Proceeds. If the restoration or repair is not economically feasible or Lender's security would be lessened, the Miscellaneous Proceeds shall be applied to the sums secured by this Security Instrument, whether or not then due, with the excess, if any, paid to Borrower. Such Miscellaneous Proceeds shall be applied in the order provided for in Section 2.

In the event of a total taking, destruction, or loss in value of the Property, the Miscellaneous Proceeds shall be applied to the sums secured by this Security Instrument, whether or not then due, with the excess, if any, paid to Borrower.

In the event of a partial taking, destruction, or loss in value of the Property in which the fair market value of the Property immediately before the partial taking, destruction, or loss in value is equal to or greater than the amount of the sums secured by this Security Instrument immediately before the partial taking, destruction, or loss in value, unless Borrower and Lender otherwise agree in writing, the sums secured by this Security Instrument shall be reduced by the amount of the Miscellaneous Proceeds multiplied by the following fraction: (a) the total amount of the sums secured immediately before the partial taking, destruction, or loss in value divided by (b) the fair market value of the Property immediately before the partial taking, destruction, or loss in value. Any balance shall be paid to Borrower.

In the event of a partial taking, destruction, or loss in value of the Property in which the fair market value of the Property immediately before the partial taking, destruction, or loss in value is less than the amount of the sums secured immediately before the partial taking, destruction, or loss in value, unless Borrower and Lender otherwise agree in writing, the Miscellaneous Proceeds shall be applied to the sums secured by this Security Instrument whether or not the sums are then due.

If the Property is abandoned by Borrower, or if, after notice by Lender to Borrower that the Opposing Party (as defined in the next sentence) offers to make an award to settle a claim for damages, Borrower fails to respond to Lender within 30 days after the date the notice is given, Lender is authorized to collect and apply the Miscellaneous Proceeds either to restoration or repair of the Property or to the sums secured by this Security Instrument, whether or not then due. "Opposing Party" means the third party that owes Borrower Miscellaneous Proceeds or the party against whom Borrower has a right of action in regard to Miscellaneous Proceeds.

Borrower shall be in default if any action or proceeding, whether civil or criminal, is begun that, in Lender's judgment, could result in forfeiture of the Property or other material impairment of Lender's interest in the Property or rights under this Security Instrument. Borrower can cure such a default and, if acceleration has occurred, reinstate as provided in Section 19, by causing the action or proceeding to be dismissed with a ruling that, in Lender's judgment, precludes forfeiture of the Property or other material impairment of Lender's interest in the Property or rights under this Security Instrument. The proceeds of any award or claim for damages that are attributable to the impairment of Lender's interest in the Property are hereby assigned and shall be paid to Lender.

All Miscellaneous Proceeds that are not applied to restoration or repair of the Property shall be applied in the order provided for in Section 2.

12.   Borrower Not Released; Forbearance By Lender Not a Waiver. Extension of the time for payment or modification of amortization of the sums secured by this Security Instrument granted by Lender to Borrower or any Successor in Interest of Borrower shall not operate to release the liability of Borrower or any Successors in Interest of Borrower. Lender shall not be required to commence proceedings against any Successor in Interest of Borrower or to refuse to extend time for payment or otherwise modify amortization of the sums secured by this Security Instrument by reason of any demand made by the original Borrower or any Successors in Interest of Borrower. Any forbearance by Lender in exercising any right or remedy including, without limitation, Lender's acceptance of payments from third persons, entities or Successors in Interest of Borrower or in amounts less than the amount then due, shall not be a waiver of or preclude the exercise of any right or remedy.

13.   Joint and Several Liability; Co-signers; Successors and Assigns Bound. Borrower covenants and agrees that Borrower's obligations and liability shall be joint and several. However, any Borrower who co-signs this Security Instrument but does not execute the Note (a "co-signer"): (a) is co-signing this Security Instrument only to mortgage, grant and convey the co-signer's interest in the Property under the terms of this Security Instrument; (b) is not personally obligated to pay the sums secured by this Security Instrument; and (c) agrees that Lender and any other Borrower can agree to extend, modify, forbear or make any accommodations with regard to the terms of this Security Instrument or the Note without the co-signer's consent.

Subject to the provisions of Section 18, any Successor in Interest of Borrower who assumes Borrower's obligations under this Security Instrument in writing, and is approved by Lender, shall obtain all of Borrower's rights and benefits under this Security Instrument. Borrower shall not be released from Borrower's obligations and liability under this Security Instrument unless Lender agrees to such release in writing. The covenants and agreements of this Security Instrument shall bind (except as provided in Section 20) and benefit the successors and assigns of Lender.

14.   Loan Charges. Lender may charge Borrower fees for services performed in connection with Borrower's default, for the purpose of protecting Lender's interest in the Property and rights under this Security Instrument, including, but not limited to, attorneys' fees, property inspection and valuation fees. In regard to any other fees, the absence of express authority in this Security Instrument to charge a specific fee to Borrower shall not be construed as a prohibition on the charging of such fee. Lender may not charge fees that are expressly prohibited by this Security Instrument or by Applicable Law.

If the Loan is subject to a law which sets maximum loan charges, and that law is finally interpreted so that the interest or other loan charges collected or to be collected in connection with the Loan exceed the permitted limits, then: (a) any such loan charge shall be reduced by the amount necessary to reduce the charge to the permitted limit; and (b) any sums already collected from Borrower which exceeded permitted limits will be refunded to Borrower. Lender may choose to make this refund by reducing the principal owed under the Note or by making a direct payment to Borrower. If a refund reduces principal, the reduction will be treated as a partial prepayment without any prepayment charge (whether or not a prepayment charge is provided for under the Note). Borrower's acceptance of any such refund made by direct payment to Borrower will constitute a waiver of any right of action Borrower might have arising out of such overcharge.

15.   Notices. All notices given by Borrower or Lender in connection with this Security Instrument must be in writing. Any notice to Borrower in connection with this Security Instrument shall be deemed to have been given to Borrower when mailed by first class mail or when actually delivered to Borrower's notice address if sent by other means. Notice to any one Borrower shall constitute notice to all Borrowers unless Applicable Law expressly requires otherwise. The notice address shall be the Property Address unless Borrower has designated a substitute notice address by notice to Lender. Borrower shall promptly notify Lender of Borrower's change of address. If Lender specifies a procedure for reporting Borrower's change of address, then Borrower shall only report a change of address through that specified procedure. There may be only one designated notice address under this Security Instrument at any one time. Any notice to Lender shall be given by delivering it or by mailing it by first class mail to Lender's address stated herein unless Lender has designated another address by notice to Borrower. Any notice in connection with this Security Instrument shall not be deemed to have been given to Lender until actually received by Lender. If any notice required by this Security Instrument is also required under Applicable Law, the Applicable Law requirement will satisfy the corresponding requirement under this Security Instrument.

16.   Governing Law; Severability; Rules of Construction. This Security Instrument shall be governed by federal law and the law of the jurisdiction in which the Property is located. All rights and obligations contained in this Security Instrument are subject to any requirements and limitations of Applicable Law. Applicable Law might explicitly or implicitly allow the parties to agree by contract or it might be silent, but such silence shall not be construed as a prohibition against agreement by contract. In the event that any provision or clause of this Security Instrument or the Note conflicts with Applicable Law, such conflict shall not affect other provisions of this Security Instrument or the Note which can be given effect without the conflicting provision.

As used in this Security Instrument: (a) words of the masculine gender shall mean and include corresponding neuter words or words of the feminine gender; (b) words in the singular shall mean and include the plural and vice versa; and (c) the word "may" gives sole discretion without any obligation to take any action.

17.   Borrower's Copy. Borrower shall be given one copy of the Note and of this Security Instrument.

18.   Transfer of the Property or a Beneficial Interest in Borrower. As used in this Section 18, "Interest in the Property" means any legal or beneficial interest in the Property, including, but not limited to, those beneficial interests transferred in a bond for deed, contract for deed, installment sales contract or escrow agreement, the intent of which is the transfer of title by Borrower at a future date to a purchaser.

If all or any part of the Property or any Interest in the Property is sold or transferred (or if Borrower is not a natural person and a beneficial interest in Borrower is sold or transferred) without Lender's prior written consent, Lender may require immediate payment in full of all sums secured by this Security Instrument. However, this option shall not be exercised by Lender if such exercise is prohibited by Applicable Law.

If Lender exercises this option, Lender shall give Borrower notice of acceleration. The notice shall provide a period of not less than 30 days from the date the notice is given in accordance with Section 15 within which Borrower must pay all sums secured by this Security Instrument. If Borrower fails to pay these sums prior to the expiration of this period, Lender may invoke any remedies permitted by this Security Instrument without further notice or demand on Borrower.

     19.   **Borrower's Right to Reinstate After Acceleration.** If Borrower meets certain conditions, Borrower shall have the right to have enforcement of this Security Instrument discontinued at any time prior to the earliest of: (a) five days before sale of the Property pursuant to Section 22 of this Security Instrument; (b) such other period as Applicable Law might specify for the termination of Borrower's right to reinstate; or (c) entry of a judgment enforcing this Security Instrument. Those conditions are that Borrower: (a) pays Lender all sums which then would be due under this Security Instrument and the Note as if no acceleration had occurred; (b) cures any default of any other covenants or agreements; (c) pays all expenses incurred in enforcing this Security Instrument, including, but not limited to, reasonable attorneys' fees, property inspection and valuation fees, and other fees incurred for the purpose of protecting Lender's interest in the Property and rights under this Security Instrument; and (d) takes such action as Lender may reasonably require to assure that Lender's interest in the Property and rights under this Security Instrument, and Borrower's obligation to pay the sums secured by this Security Instrument, shall continue unchanged unless as otherwise provided under Applicable Law. Lender may require that Borrower pay such reinstatement sums and expenses in one or more of the following forms, as selected by Lender: (a) cash; (b) money order; (c) certified check, bank check, treasurer's check or cashier's check, provided any such check is drawn upon an institution whose deposits are insured by a federal agency, instrumentality or entity; or (d) Electronic Funds Transfer. Upon reinstatement by Borrower, this Security Instrument and obligations secured hereby shall remain fully effective as if no acceleration had occurred. However, this right to reinstate shall not apply in the case of acceleration under Section 18.

     20.   **Sale of Note; Change of Loan Servicer; Notice of Grievance.** The Note or a partial interest in the Note (together with this Security Instrument) can be sold one or more times without prior notice to Borrower. A sale might result in a change in the entity (known as the "Loan Servicer") that collects Periodic Payments due under the Note and this Security Instrument and performs other mortgage loan servicing obligations under the Note, this Security Instrument, and Applicable Law. There also might be one or more changes of the Loan Servicer unrelated to a sale of the Note. If there is a change of the Loan Servicer, Borrower will be given written notice of the change which will state the name and address of the new Loan Servicer, the address to which payments should be made and any other information RESPA requires in connection with a notice of transfer of servicing. If the Note is sold and thereafter the Loan is serviced by a Loan Servicer other than the purchaser of the Note, the mortgage loan servicing obligations to Borrower will remain with the Loan Servicer or be transferred to a successor Loan Servicer and are not assumed by the Note purchaser unless otherwise provided by the Note purchaser.

     Neither Borrower nor Lender may commence, join, or be joined to any judicial action (as either an individual litigant or the member of a class) that arises from the other party's actions pursuant to this Security Instrument or that alleges that the other party has breached any provision of, or any duty owed by reason of, this Security Instrument, until such Borrower or Lender has notified the other party (with such notice given in compliance with the requirements of Section 15) of such alleged breach and afforded the other party hereto a reasonable period after the giving of such notice to take corrective action. If Applicable Law provides a time period which must elapse before certain action can be taken, that time period will be deemed to be reasonable for purposes of this paragraph. The notice of acceleration and opportunity to cure given to Borrower pursuant to Section 22 and the notice of acceleration given to Borrower pursuant to Section 18 shall be deemed to satisfy the notice and opportunity to take corrective action provisions of this Section 20.

    21.   **Hazardous Substances.** As used in this Section 21: (a) "Hazardous Substances" are those substances defined as toxic or hazardous substances, pollutants, or wastes by Environmental Law and the following substances: gasoline, kerosene, other flammable or toxic petroleum products, toxic pesticides and herbicides, volatile solvents, materials containing asbestos or formaldehyde, and radioactive materials; (b) "Environmental Law" means federal laws and laws of the jurisdiction where the Property is located that relate to health, safety or environmental protection; (c) "Environmental Cleanup" includes any response action, remedial action, or removal action, as defined in Environmental Law; and (d) an "Environmental Condition" means a condition that can cause, contribute to, or otherwise trigger an Environmental Cleanup.

    Borrower shall not cause or permit the presence, use, disposal, storage, or release of any Hazardous Substances, or threaten to release any Hazardous Substances, on or in the Property. Borrower shall not do, nor allow anyone else to do, anything affecting the Property (a) that is in violation of any Environmental Law, (b) which creates an Environmental Condition, or (c) which, due to the presence, use, or release of a Hazardous Substance, creates a condition that adversely affects the value of the Property. The preceding two sentences shall not apply to the presence, use, or storage on the Property of small quantities of Hazardous Substances that are generally recognized to be appropriate to normal residential uses and to maintenance of the Property (including, but not limited to, hazardous substances in consumer products).

    Borrower shall promptly give Lender written notice of (a) any investigation, claim, demand, lawsuit or other action by any governmental or regulatory agency or private party involving the Property and any Hazardous Substance or Environmental Law of which Borrower has actual knowledge, (b) any Environmental Condition, including but not limited to, any spilling, leaking, discharge, release or threat of release of any Hazardous Substance, and (c) any condition caused by the presence, use or release of a Hazardous Substance which adversely affects the value of the Property. If Borrower learns, or is notified by any governmental or regulatory authority, or any private party, that any removal or other remediation of any Hazardous Substance affecting the Property is necessary, Borrower shall promptly take all necessary remedial actions in accordance with Environmental Law. Nothing herein shall create any obligation on Lender for an Environmental Cleanup.

    NON-UNIFORM COVENANTS. Borrower and Lender further covenant and agree as follows:

    22.   **Acceleration; Remedies.** **Lender shall give notice to Borrower prior to acceleration following Borrower's breach of any covenant or agreement in this Security Instrument (but not prior to acceleration under Section 18 unless Applicable Law provides otherwise). The notice shall specify: (a) the default; (b) the action required to cure the default; (c) a date, not less than 30 days from the date the notice is given to Borrower, by which the default must be cured; and (d) that failure to cure the default on or before the**

date specified in the notice may result in acceleration of the sums secured by this Security Instrument, foreclosure by judicial proceeding and sale of the Property. The notice shall further inform Borrower of the right to reinstate after acceleration and the right to assert in the foreclosure proceeding the non-existence of a default or any other defense of Borrower to acceleration and foreclosure. If the default is not cured on or before the date specified in the notice, Lender at its option may require immediate payment in full of all sums secured by this Security Instrument without further demand and may foreclose this Security Instrument by judicial proceeding. Lender shall be entitled to collect all expenses incurred in pursuing the remedies provided in this Section 22, including, but not limited to, reasonable attorneys' fees and costs of title evidence.

23.   **Release.** Upon payment of all sums secured by this Security Instrument, Lender shall release this Security Instrument. Borrower shall pay any recordation costs. Lender may charge Borrower a fee for releasing this Security Instrument, but only if the fee is paid to a third party for services rendered and the charging of the fee is permitted under Applicable Law.

24.   **Waiver of Homestead.** In accordance with Illinois law, the Borrower hereby releases and waives all rights under and by virtue of the Illinois homestead exemption laws.

25.   **Placement of Collateral Protection Insurance**. Unless Borrower provides Lender with evidence of the insurance coverage required by Borrower's agreement with Lender, Lender may purchase insurance at Borrower's expense to protect Lender's interests in Borrower's collateral. This insurance may, but need not, protect Borrower's interests. The coverage that Lender purchases may not pay any claim that Borrower makes or any claim that is made against Borrower in connection with the collateral. Borrower may later cancel any insurance purchased by Lender, but only after providing Lender with evidence that Borrower has obtained insurance as required by Borrower's and Lender's agreement. If Lender purchases insurance for the collateral, Borrower will be responsible for the costs of that insurance, including interest and any other charges Lender may impose in connection with the placement of the insurance, until the effective date of the cancellation or expiration of the insurance. The costs of the insurance may be added to Borrower's total outstanding balance or obligation. The costs of the insurance may be more than the cost of insurance Borrower may be able to obtain on its own.

BY SIGNING BELOW, Borrower accepts and agrees to the terms and covenants contained in this Security Instrument and in any Rider executed by Borrower and recorded with it.

Witnesses:

_____ _____ (Seal)

                           - Borrower

_____ _____ (Seal)

                           - Borrower

_____**[Space Below This Line For Acknowledgment]**_____

D. Reviewing Your Deed of Trust or Mortgage

If you do not have a copy of the recorded deed of trust or mortgage, request one from your lender, the foreclosing trustee, or the lender's attorney. If none of them has a copy readily available, call a local title insurance company and request a copy. If you can't afford the fee or are in a do-it-yourself mood, visit the county recorder's office in the county where your property is located. You can obtain a copy of the deed of trust or mortgage for a nominal fee.

Breakdown of the terms and conditions

1. *Lender's name and address*: The lender's name, street address, city and state are entered here so that the recorded document is returned to the lender.

2. *County recorder identification*: This area contains the county recorder's stamp, which reflects the time and date the document was recorded and the fee paid to have it recorded. If this is

blank, you probably have a copy of the document before it was recorded. It is possible the document was never recorded, but unlikely.

3. *Date of execution*: This is the date you signed the document.

4. *Trustor(s) or mortgagor(s) name*: This blank contains the name(s) of the borrower(s).

5. *Trustor's or mortgagor's address*: This is where your address goes. If you move, it is your responsibility to notify your lender of your new address.

6. *Trustee*: If it is a deed of trust, the name of the trustee. If it is a mortgage, there will not be a trustee.

7. *Lender*: If it is a deed of trust, the name of your beneficiary. If it is a mortgage, the name of the lender would be the mortgagee.

8. *Location of real property security*: The county in which your property is located.

9. *Legal description of your property*: The full legal description of your property typically includes the lot, block and tract, metes and bounds, or a government survey description.

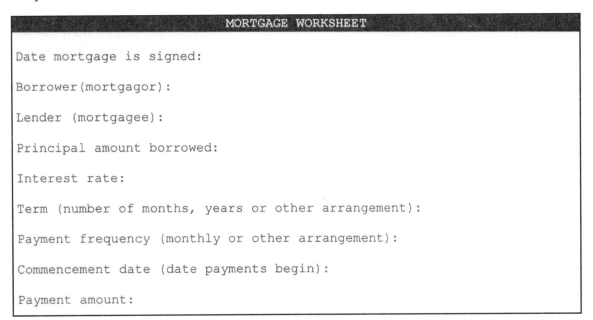

```
MORTGAGE WORKSHEET

Date mortgage is signed:

Borrower(mortgagor):

Lender (mortgagee):

Principal amount borrowed:

Interest rate:

Term (number of months, years or other arrangement):

Payment frequency (monthly or other arrangement):

Commencement date (date payments begin):

Payment amount:
```

10. *Principal amount of loan*: This is the principal amount you borrowed.

11. *Acknowledgment*: A formal written declaration, before a notary public, that you signed the document willfully.

12. *Signature(s) of trustor(s)or mortgagor*: Your signature (and that of any co-property owners) is here.

13. *Boilerplate language*: Every deed of trust and mortgage refers to the amount it secures and the location in each county (book and page number) of a document of legal requirements you must adhere to.

Sample Deed of Trust and Mortgage Worksheets appears in this chapter and tear-out copies are included in the Appendix. Use them to record the relevant terms and conditions in your deed of trust or mortgage.

1. Mortgages and Deeds of Trust Are Recorded

Each county in every state in the United States has a recorder's office, which keeps files on all real property in that county. The recorder's office tracks who owns property, who claims any interest in a property (such as an easement-- a claim of a right to use a portion of someone's property), and what liens (including mortgages and deeds of trust) have been recorded against a property. Any property that has one or more liens recorded against it is said to be "encumbered." The recorder's office is open to the public and you can review the county records with respect to your property at no cost (photocopies will cost you, however). To get started, the only information you will need is your street address. If you have difficulty, there are clerks available to help you. If you don't want to bother with the recorder's office, you can contact a local title insurance company that will do it for you for free or a small fee.

2. Multiple Lienholders

More than one deed of trust or mortgage can encumber your property. In fact, it is not unusual to see several liens recorded against a single property. The lender holding the first lien is considered the "senior lienholder" and has the first right to be paid in a foreclosure sale or if you sell or refinance your property. All other lenders holding subsequently recorded mortgages or deeds of trust (or any other type of lien) are called "junior lienholders."

Example: John owns a house in Boston, Massachusetts. Two mortgages encumber his property. The first is held by New England Savings Bank, which originally loaned John the money to purchase the house. The junior lienholder is Second Home Loan Company, which loaned money to John to remodel his kitchen. If John defaults on his payments and New England Savings conducts a foreclosure sale, New England Savings Bank will be paid first as the senior lienholder. Any excess proceeds from the sale will go towards paying off Second Home Loan, the junior lienholder.

3. Your Obligations Under a Mortgage or Deed of Trust

When you signed the mortgage or deed of trust, you agreed to undertake five obligations. If you default on any of these, the property may legally be foreclosed upon. The five requirements are to:
- pay the loan according to its terms
- insure the property and keep insurance payments current

- maintain and keep the property in good repair
- pay property taxes assessed against the property, and
- notify the lender when selling the property.

a. Paying the Deed of trust or Mortgage

A deed of trust and mortgage requires that you repay your loan according to its terms. Most importantly, you must make your payments on time. Late or missed payments are the most common causes of foreclosure.

Reality check. In most situations, one late payment will not cause your lender to initiate foreclosure. More likely, your lender wil1 send you a threatening letter and report the late payments to the three major credit reporting agencies (credit bureaus). Typically, lenders wait until payments are at least three to four months in arrears before initiating foreclosure. Nevertheless, a single late payment provides your lender with the legal right to start a foreclosure.

b. Maintaining and Repairing the Property

Most property owners diligently maintain their property and keep it in good repair no matter what their loan documents require. As long as you are current on your payments, if your lender becomes aware of some deterioration, you would probably receive a phone call or letter demanding that you maintain your property as you agreed to in the mortgage or deed of trust. But people who do not maintain their property also tend to default on payments, which would inevitably lead to foreclosure.

c. Paying Property Taxes

Your mortgage or deed of trust requires you to promptly pay all taxes and related charges assessed against your property. Here's why lenders include this provision.

The most common taxes are property taxes (assessed by the county) and special tax liens (assessed by cities, counties, water districts and other government bodies). These property and special tax liens always take priority over mortgages and deeds of trusts, regardless of when the tax liens were recorded. If you don't pay these taxes and your property is foreclosed on, or you sell or refinance, the taxing authority will be paid before your lender. So if the sale proceeds don't cover both the tax lien and what you owe on your loan, your lender won't receive all that they are owed.

To avoid this problem, lenders will typically pay your past due taxes if your property is already in foreclosure. Once that occurs, the amount you need to bring your loan current will increase and now include the amount of taxes your lender paid on your behalf.

d. Insuring Your Property

Your obligation to keep your property insured protects your lender in the event you abandon your property--perhaps after a fire or flood. Without insurance in such a situation, your lender would have a worthless piece of property and could collect only by suing you. With insurance, if you abandon the property, your lender can use the proceeds to either pay off the loan or rebuild the structure.

For this reason, virtually all mortgages and deeds of trust require that you maintain hazard insurance for at least the amount of your loan, to protect against damage to your property caused by fire or other destruction. Check your documents for other requirements. Institutional lenders generally require fire and extended coverage insurance, which covers most damage to your property except flood and earthquakes. Few lenders require earthquake insurance because of the high cost, unless you live in an earthquake-prone area. Similarly,

---

IF YOU AREN'T SURE WHETHER YOUR MORTGAGE WAS SOLD

Although not required to do so, lenders usually send out an Assignment of Beneficial Interest or some other written document to borrowers to notify them that their mortgage has been sold. If you didn't receive written notification, but are nevertheless suspicious that your mortgage may have been sold, contact your initial lender and ask them whether they still own the loan. If it has been sold, get the name, address, and telephone number of the new holder of the mortgage. Or, you can contact a title insurance company and ask them to search the title to your property in the county's recorder's office and determine whether the mortgage has been sold. (Unfortunately, you probably won't be able to gain any leverage in the foreclosure process by claiming you didn't receive notice of the assignment.)

---

lenders rarely require flood insurance unless your property is located in a designated flood-hazard zone.

Lenders will typically purchase insurance for your property if they discover it is not insured during the foreclosure. They'll then add the insurance cost to the amount you need to cure the default.

e. Selling Your Property With Notification to Your Lender

Almost all mortgages and deeds of trust include what is known as a "due-on-sale" clause. The due-on-sale clause requires that you notify your lender when you sell your property. The lender can't prohibit the sale; they can only require that the homeowner pay off the loan or if the new buyer assume the loan. In most situations, this problem resolves itself because a buyer typically obtains a new loan to pay off your existing lender. However, there may be a problem if you sell your property without your lender's knowledge. This is because the due-on-sale clause allows your lender to declare the entire balance immediately due and payable even though you may have years left on your loan.

Keep in mind that a due-on-sale clause does not prohibit you from selling your property. It simply requires that you either pay off your existing loan or have the new buyer assume the loan when you sell your property. If you don't, your lender has the right to foreclose.

Due-on-sale clauses are used by lenders to protect themselves in case interest rates rise after the loan is taken out. By forcing you to notify your lender when you sell your property, your lender can have the old lower interest loan paid off, or demand that the buyer assume the existing loan at the current (presumably higher) market rate of interest. In addition, by using a due-on-sale clause, the lender can earn additional fees for processing the assumption paperwork or a new loan for the buyer.

Example: Shirley and Edward own a single-family residence in Detroit, Michigan. Overstreet Bank holds the first mortgage, which secures a $375,000 loan at 5.5% interest. The mortgage has a due-on-sale clause. Without notifying Overstreet Bank, Shirley and Edward sell their property to Henry, who agrees to purchase the property subject to the existing low interest rate loan. Although Henry will make the payments, Shirley and Edward remain liable on the loan. Several months later, Overstreet Bank discovers the sale and immediately notifies Shirley and Edward that it has accelerated their loan because they violated the due-on-sale clause. If Shirley and Edward do not pay-off the loan within 30 days, Overstreet Bank threatens to begin foreclosure proceedings. Henry must immediately refinance the property with another lender and pay-off Overstreet Bank, or risk losing the property in foreclosure.

Chapter

3

NONJUDICIAL FORECLOSURES

A. Overview of Nonjudicial Foreclosure.. 60
    1. Nonjudicial Foreclosures Can Be Stopped 60
    2. The Nonjudicial Foreclosure Timetable... 61

B. Notice of Default and Election to Sell... 61
    1. Contents of the Notice of Default.. 61
    2. Notice Requirements for Notice of Default.. 61
    3. Complete a Notice of Default Worksheet 65
    4. Request Beneficiary Statement From Your Lender 67

C. The Reinstatement Period 68
    1. Contact the Trustee 68
    2. Partial Payments During the Reinstatement Period 69
    3. Extending the Reinstatement Period 69

D. Notice of Trustee's Sale 70
    1. Contents of the Notice of Trustee's Sale 70
    2. Notice Requirements for Notice of Sale.. 71
    3. Complete Notice of Trustee's Sale Worksheet.. 74
    4. If the Trustee Made a Mistake 74

E. The Redemption Period 75

F. Trustee's Sale 78
    1. Attend the Trustee's Sale 78
    2. Trustee's Sale May Be Postponed 79
    3. Overview of the Auction 80
    4. Trustee Finalizes Sale and Disburses Proceeds...................................... 81
    5. What Happens to Liens After Trustee's Sale 82
    6. Buyer May Take Possession of Your Property 84

➡️ If your foreclosure is judicial, then you should skip this chapter and read Chapter 4. If you're not sure, look-up your state in the Appendix in the back of this book and it will tell you whether foreclosures in your state are judicial or nonjudicial.

A nonjudicial foreclosure is a procedure in which your lender has your property sold to recover money you owe after you've defaulted on your loan. The conditions under which your lender may institute a nonjudicial foreclosure are addressed in your deed of trust. (Refer back to Chapter 2, Section B, for information on the deed of trust.)

Every state has slightly different nonjudicial rules. For sake of simplicity, this chapter will follow California's nonjudicial procedures. Most deed of trust states have similar procedures. For specific procedures in your state, look in the back of this book.

A. Overview of Nonjudicial Foreclosure

The main feature of a nonjudicial foreclosure is that your lender can have your property auctioned without going to court. Because courts do not oversee the foreclosure process, state law requires the trustee--the person authorized by your lender to conduct the foreclosure-- follow strict procedures before selling your property. But the good news is that if the trustee

sells your property for less than the full amount of the loan, your lender cannot (in most states) pursue you for the difference (which is called a "deficiency").

➡️ *Judicial foreclosures are covered in Chapter 4.* Another type of foreclosure, called a judicial foreclosure, is used most frequently in eastern and midwestern states. Judicial foreclosures use the court system and allow deficiency judgments (the lender may collect the balance due on the loan if the sale doesn't cover it). In most Western states, lenders only use judicial foreclosures for commercial and multi-residential properties, and nonjudicial foreclosures for single-family residences.

1. Nonjudicial Foreclosures Can Be Stopped

Property owners often misunderstand the nonjudicial foreclosure process. Many believe once it begins, it can't be stopped and that it happens quickly. However, a nonjudicial foreclosure takes at least two to four months (depending on your state), and frequently longer. During this period, you have the right to stop the foreclosure and save your property. You must receive adequate and timely notice of the upcoming foreclosure sale. And if the trustee does not properly conduct the procedures, you have grounds to stop the foreclosure by filing a lawsuit in court and enjoining it. (See Chapter 8 for more on injunctions and temporary restraining orders.)

What is crucial for you to understand at this point is that even after a nonjudicial foreclosure has already begun, you still have a period of time to stop it. Rather than throwing in the towel, you should envision this time period as a "window of opportunity" to either save your property or sell it! In this chapter, you will learn various strategies you can use to accomplish these goals while the foreclosure is pending.

2. The Nonjudicial Foreclosure Timetable

A nonjudicial foreclosure consists of five basic steps, summarized below in the *Nonjudicial Foreclosure Timeline* and covered in detail in the rest of this chapter. Once you learn each of the steps, you will better understand how and when to utilize the strategies described in this book.

B. Notice of Default and Election to Sell

A nonjudicial foreclosure begins when the trustee issues a document typically called a Notice of Default and Election to Sell (or simply a "Notice of Default"). The Notice of Default, which must be mailed to you, notifies you that because you have defaulted on your loan a nonjudicial foreclosure has started to sell your property to pay off your loan. The trustee prepares the Notice of Default only upon the request of your lender.

1. Contents of the Notice of Default

Although the Notice of Default may be one to two pages long, you are primarily interested in the following important information:

- your name (you're the trustor)

- the book and page number in the county recorder's office where your deed of trust was recorded
- a statement that your promissory note or deed of trust is in default
- a cursory description of your defaults, such as missed payments, delinquent property taxes and unpaid insurance, and

- a statement that your lender has elected to sell your property to satisfy the debt.

A sample Notice of Default and Election to Sell appears on the next page. Each paragraph in this sample is followed with an explanation. Use this information to review any Notice of Default you receive.

2. Notice Requirements for Notice of Default

The trustee must follow strict time formalities for recording, mailing, posting, and publishing the Notice of Default to ensure that you receive adequate legal notice of the pending foreclosure. If the trustee fails to follow any of these procedures, you will probably have a legal basis to stop the foreclosure.

Ironically, there's no requirement that you receive "actual" notice of the foreclosure. The foreclosure remains valid as long as the trustee carried out the notification procedures properly as described below. It doesn't matter if you were out of the country, in the hospital, or for some other reason didn't actually receive a copy of the Notice of Default.

DOC # 2006-0698880
09/21/2006 08:00A Fee:12.00
Page 1 of 2
Recorded in Official Records
County of Riverside
Larry W. Ward
Assessor, County Clerk & Recorder

RECORDING REQUESTED BY

T.D. SERVICE COMPANY

and when recorded mail to

T.D. SERVICE COMPANY
1820 E. FIRST ST., SUITE 210
P.O. BOX 11988
SANTA ANA, CA 92711-1988

S	R	U	PAGE	SIZE	DA	MISC	LONG	RFD	COPY
			2						
M	A	L	465	426	PCOR	NCOR	SMF	NCHG	EXAM 010

_____ SPACE ABOVE THIS LIN

NOTICE OF DEFAULT AND ELECTION TO SELL UNDER DEED OF TRUST

"IMPORTANT NOTICE"

T.S. No: A339144 CA   Unit Code: A   Loan No: 1947233/LEE
AP #1: 052-034-419-0
Property Address: '   ' CAVALRY CIRCLE, CORONA, CA 92880

IF YOUR PROPERTY IS IN FORECLOSURE BECAUSE YOU ARE BEHIND IN YOUR PAYMENTS, IT MAY BE SOLD WITHOUT ANY COURT ACTION, and you may have the legal right to bring your account in good standing by paying all of your past due payments plus permitted costs and expenses within the time permitted by law for reinstatement of your account, which is normally five business days prior to the date set for the sale of your property. No sale date may be set until three months from the date this notice of default may be recorded (which date of recordation appears on this notice).

This amount is $14,137.28, As of September 27, 2006

and will increase until your account becomes current.

While your property is in foreclosure, you still must pay other obligations (such as insurance and taxes) required by your note and deed of trust or mortgage. If you fail to make future payments on the loan, pay taxes on the property, provide insurance on the property, or pay other obligations as required in the note and deed of trust or mortgage, the beneficiary or mortgagee may insist that you do so in order to reinstate your account in good standing. In addition, the beneficiary or mortgagee may require as a condition to reinstatement that you provide reliable written evidence that you paid all senior liens, property taxes, and hazard insurance premiums.

Upon your written request, the beneficiary or mortgagee will give you a written itemization of the entire amount you must pay. You may not have to pay the entire unpaid portion of your account, even though full payment was demanded, but you must pay all amounts in default at the time payment is made. However, you and your beneficiary or mortgagee may mutually agree in writing prior to the time the notice of sale is posted (which may not be earlier than the end of the three-month period stated above) to, among other things, (1) provide additional time in which to cure the default by transfer of the property or otherwise; or (2) establish a schedule of payments in order to cure your default; or both (1) and (2).

Page 2

NOTICE OF DEFAULT AND ELECTION TO SELL UNDER DEED OF TRUST

T.S. No: A339144 CA   Unit Code: A   Loan No: 1947233/LEE
AP #1: 052-034-419-0

Following the expiration of the time period referred to in the first paragraph of this notice, unless the obligation being foreclosed upon or a separate written agreement between you and your creditor permits a longer period, you have only the legal right to stop the sale of your property by paying the entire amount demanded by your creditor.

To find out the amount you must pay, or to arrange for payment to stop the foreclosure, or if your property is in foreclosure for any other reason, contact:

LASALLE BANK, N.A. AS TRUSTEE FOR THE MLMI TRUST SERIES
2006-HE2
Devon Kortz
Fidelity National Foreclosure
and Bankruptcy Solutions
1720 Northland Drive
Suite 200
Mendota Heights, MN 55120
(651) 234-3500

If you have any questions, you should contact a lawyer or the government agency which may have insured your loan. Notwithstanding the fact that your property is in foreclosure, you may offer your property for sale, provided the sale is concluded prior to the conclusion of the foreclosure. Remember, **YOU MAY LOSE LEGAL RIGHTS IF YOU DO NOT TAKE PROMPT ACTION**

NOTICE IS HEREBY GIVEN THAT: T.D. SERVICE COMPANY is duly appointed Trustee under the following described Deed of Trust:

Trustor: .

Recorded November 23, 2005 as Instr. No. 2005-0975866 in Book --- Page --- of Official Records in the office of the Recorder of RIVERSIDE County; CALIFORNIA

Said Deed of Trust secures certain obligations including one Note for the sum of **$486,864.00**

That the Beneficial interest under such Deed of Trust and the obligations secured thereby are presently held by the Beneficiary; That a breach of, and default in, the obligations for which such Deed of Trust is security has occurred in that payment has not been made of:
THE INSTALLMENT OF PRINCIPAL AND INTEREST WHICH BECAME DUE JUNE 1, 2006 AND ALL SUBSEQUENT INSTALLMENTS OF PRINCIPAL AND INTEREST. PLUS LATE CHARGE(S). LESS CREDIT IN THE AMOUNT OF $150.68. PLUS MISCELLANEOUS FEE(S) IN THE AMOUNT OF $181.50.

That by reason thereof, the present Beneficiary under such Deed of Trust has executed and delivered to said duly appointed Trustee, a written Declaration of Default and Demand for Sale, and has deposited with said duly appointed Trustee, such Deed of Trust and all documents evidencing obligations secured thereby, and has declared and does hereby declare all sums secured thereby immediately due and payable and has elected and does hereby elect to cause the trust property to be sold to satisfy the obligations secured thereby.
DATED 09/20/06

T.D. SERVICE COMPANY, BY Fidelity National Title Insurance Company, as Agent for the Trustee

BY ___Dana Futh_____ BY _____

We are assisting the Beneficiary to collect a debt and any information we obtain will be used for that purpose whether received orally or in writing.

a. Recording Notice of Default

The trustee must record the Notice of Default in the recorder's office for the county in which your property is located. Occasionally, a trustee will forget to record the Notice of Default, or mistakenly record it against the wrong property, or in the wrong county. You need to be alert to these types of clerical errors.

You can find out if the Notice of Default was properly recorded by searching the property records at the recorder's office or asking the customer service department of a local title insurance company for assistance.

If the Notice of Default was not recorded or was improperly recorded, the foreclosure is invalid. In that case, you can demand that it be stopped until the trustee starts the foreclosure all over again from the beginning by issuing a new Notice of Default. To do this, send a letter to the trustee advising her of the failure to properly record the Notice of Default and demanding that she start over.

Some property owners wait until late in the foreclosure process before advising the trustee of her mistake. Since the trustee will have to reissue the Notice of Default, which requires that a whole new period elapse before the Notice of Trustee's Sale can be issued, the property owner will have that much more time to navigate the situation.

b. Mailing Notice of Default to You

After recording the Notice of Default, the trustee must mail you copies--one copy by registered or certified mail and the other copy by regular first-class mail. They will be sent to your address listed in your original deed of trust, or to your last known address, if it is different.

If the trustee sends the Notices to the wrong address, and you are certain you gave the lender your current address, the trustee must start over.

Example: Trudy owns a rental home in Las Vegas, Nevada. Trudy's old address appears on the recorded deed of trust. Trudy moved and notified her lender, Nevada Savings Bank, of her new address. When Trudy missed several monthly loan payments, Nevada Savings instructed its trustee to start a nonjudicial foreclosure. The trustee mailed a copy of the Notice of Default to Trudy at the address listed in the deed of trust, but didn't send a copy to her new address. When Trudy's tenant revealed that a foreclosure had been started, Trudy wrote a letter to the trustee demanding that the foreclosure be stopped. The trustee had no choice but to comply and start the foreclosure process over.

Make sure your lender has your current address. This is particularly important if you don't live in or receive mail at the property that is in foreclosure. The trustee is only obligated to send a Notice of Default to the address listed in the deed of trust or the last address you gave your lender. If the trustee doesn't have your current address, she can simply mail the Notice of Default to the address on the deed of trust and publish a copy of the Notice of Default in a local newspaper. In this event, there's a good chance you'll never see the notice.

c. Mailing Notice of Default to Others Affected

Simultaneous with recording, the trustee must also mail, by first-class and certified mail, a Notice of Default to:

- tenants living on your property
- any creditors who hold a deed of trust on your property junior to your foreclosing lender
- anyone claiming an interest in your property (by recording a lien, such as mechanic's lien, tax lien, or judgment lien in the county recorder's office), and
- anyone else who would be affected by the foreclosure, including people who purchased your property from you (if you're still liable to pay the promissory note, as explained m Chapter 2, Section B) and people who are under contract to buy your property.

d. Publishing Notice of Default

In most states, the trustee is required to publish the Notice of Default, particularly if the certified copy is returned by the post office. It must be published in a newspaper of general circulation in the county where your property is located. Typically it is published once a week or as required by your state. The publication must commence within days after the recording of the Notice of Default and must be published weekly until the sale.

e. Posting Notice of Default Is Optional

Trustees also frequently post a copy of the Notice of Default on the front door or another conspicuous place on the property. Such posting often takes place even before you receive the Notice of Default in the mail.

3. Complete a Notice of Default Worksheet

Assemble your promissory note, deed of trust, and Notice of Default. Then use the following self-explanatory Notice of Default Worksheet to make sure the trustee complies with all notice and mailing requirements. Remember, if the trustee makes a mistake along the way, you have grounds to stop the foreclosure. A tear-out copy of the worksheet is also included in the Appendix.

NOTICE OF DEFAULT WORKSHEET (NONJUDICIAL FORECLOSURE)

ARE THE FOLLOWING CORRECT ON THE NOTICE OF DEFAULT, AND CONSISTENT WITH
INFORMATION ON YOUR PROMISSORY NOTE AND/OR DEED OF TRUST?

Name of trustor (you and any co-signers)? [] No [] Yes   Name: _____

Name of beneficiary (lender)?   [] No [] Yes   Name: _____

Name of trustee?   [] No [] Yes   Name: _____

Information about recording
of deed of trust?   [] No [] Yes   Date: _____

Legal description of the property? Document No.: Book/Page No.: _____

Amount of original indebtedness? _____

Amount in default? [] No [] Yes Amount: _____

RECORDING REQUIREMENTS

Was the Notice of Default recorded in the recorder's
office for the county in which your property is located? [] No [] Yes

MAILING REQUIREMENTS

Was a copy of the Notice of Default mailed to you by
certified or registered mail within ten business days
of recording? [] No [] Yes When: _____

Was a copy of the Notice of Default mailed to you by
first-class mail within ten business days of recording? [] No [] Yes

Within 30 days of recording, was a copy of the Notice
mailed by first-class mail to everyone entitled to receive the
Notice--including tenants, junior beneficiaries and anyone
who recorded a Request for Notice? (You will need to
call them and ask them if they received the Notice.) [] No [] Yes When:

PUBLICATION REQUIREMENTS

If the trustee did not have your correct address, was the
Notice of Default published in a newspaper of general
circulation? (You have the right to ask the trustee to see its
Affidavit of Publication and copies of the newspapers.) [] No [] Yes

1st Date: _____
2nd Date: _____
3rd Date: _____
4th Date: _____

4. Request Beneficiary Statement From Your Lender

You have the legal right to get information from your lender about your defaulted loan. In legal jargon, this is known as your right to receive a beneficiary statement. As soon as you receive a Notice of Default, write to the foreclosing lender (also send a copy to the trustee) and request a beneficiary statement. Follow the guidelines of the sample letter below.

This request will demonstrate to your lender that you are serious about avoiding foreclosure and saving your property. In addition, the information will help you confirm the accuracy of the Notice of Default and other documents you receive during the foreclosure process. Your lender must respond to your written request for a beneficiary statement within months after the Notice of Default was filed and within several weeks of your written request (check your state's rules in the back of this book).

September 10, 200X

Foreclosure Department
Submarine Savings and Loan
21 May Avenue
Portland, Oregon

Loan Number: 645-567

Property: 3434 Laurel Street
Portland, Oregon

To whom it may concern:

Your company holds a deed of trust recorded against my property securing a promissory note in the original amount of $325,000. On September 1, I received a Notice of Default from your trustee.

Pursuant to Oregon law, please send me a beneficiary statement, including the following information, as soon as possible:

(1) Copy of my promissory note.
(2) Copy of recorded deed of trust.
(3) Unpaid balance of my loan.
(4) Current fixed or variable interest rate.
(5) Total amount of all overdue installments of principal and interest.
(6) The end of the term of the loan.
(7) Date through which real estate taxes and assessments have been paid by you, if any.
(8) Amount of hazard insurance and the premium you paid, if any.
(9) Balance of any tax or insurance impound accounts in your possession.
(10) Amount of any additional costs and expenses you have paid, including trustee's expenses.
(11) Whether or not I can transfer the loan to a new borrower (that is, whether or not the loan is assumable).

Please send me this information as soon as possible. If you have any questions, please call me at 544-8787.

Very truly yours,

Susan Young

cc. Trustee

C. The Reinstatement Period

The reinstatement period starts as soon as the Notice of Default is issued and ends prior to the trustee's sale depending on state law. During the reinstatement period, you can stop the foreclosure by simply bringing your loan current by paying the following:

- the amount of overdue principal, interest and late fees stated in the Notice of Default

- monthly payments that come due after the Notice of Default was recorded

- attorney fees incurred by your lender to collect your payments

- any tax or insurance payments advanced by your lender, and

- trustee's fees (the cost to process the nonjudicial foreclosure, including expenses to record, mail, publish and post notices).

As the foreclosure continues, the amount needed to reinstate your loan will increase daily as interest accrues and the trustee incurs additional expenses.

Example: Albert owns a condominium in Salt Lake City, Utah, and makes monthly payments of $1,996 on his $350,000 promissory note. Albert missed three monthly payments before First Fidelity started a nonjudicial foreclosure by having its trustee record a Notice of Default on April 1. The Notice of Default states that Albert owes $275,200. He is behind $4,200 in payments and late fees, and has incurred $1,000 in foreclosure fees, for a total of $5,200 as of April 1. Albert wants to stop the foreclosure by bringing his loan current. However, the longer he waits, the more he will have to pay to reinstate his loan as it continues to accrue interest and the trustee incurs more costs:

Date	Payment	Trustee Fees	Reinstate
May 1	*$1,996*	*$250*	*7,446*
June 1	*1,996*	*250*	*9,692*
July 1	*1,996*	*250*	*11,938*

1. Contact the Trustee

If you can reinstate your loan, your first step is to contact the trustee. Find out exactly how much you'll need to reinstate your loan as of a certain date.

The trustee is required to give you this information.

If you agree with the trustee's figures, purchase a cashier's check for that amount. If you disagree with the amount, you may need to contact your lender to get the correct payoff or file a lawsuit to determine the correct amount. (See Chapter 8 for more about filing a lawsuit to stop the foreclosure.)

Once you purchase a cashier's check, take it to the trustee's office and exchange it for a receipt. If the trustee's office is located out of town, send the cashier's check by certified or registered mail.

Assuming it is for the right amount, the trustee <u>must</u> accept your payment and stop the foreclosure. If the trustee refuses to accept, you have grounds for asking a judge to enjoin the foreclosure (see Chapter 8).

Once the trustee accepts your payment, request that he record a Notice of Rescission in the county recorder's office (which officially withdraws the Notice of Default and terminates the foreclosure) and mail a copy of the recorded notice to you.

2. Partial Payments During the Reinstatement Period

In general, lenders will not accept partial payments during the reinstatement period. If a lender accepts a partial payment, it becomes susceptible to later claims that you paid because your lender agreed to delay or stop the foreclosure. Courts tend to view with suspicion a lender that accepts a partial payment and then continues with foreclosure.

With that said, some lenders will accept partial payments and agree to temporarily postpone the foreclosure. You will, however, need to convince your lender that you can bring the loan current within a reasonable period of time. Of course, you won't know whether your lender is open to this suggestion until you ask. (See Chapter 5 for more on negotiating with your lender.)

If your lender agrees to accept a partial payment during the reinstatement period, keep in mind that it will not extend the reinstatement period, or stop the foreclosure unless the lender specifically agrees in writing to do so. If you convince your lender to postpone the foreclosure to give you extra time to bring your loan current, you must document the agreement in a letter similar to the sample below.

3. Extending the Reinstatement Period

Depending on state law, you may reinstate your loan up until the scheduled foreclosure sale. (For example, in California, it is five business days before the date of the trustee's sale, whereas, in most states, the reinstatement period continues only until the Notice of Sale is issued.) However, if the sale is postponed for any reason--for example, your lender agrees to a postponement or you file a lawsuit enjoining the foreclosure--the reinstatement period extends to the new sale date.

Example: Lisa falls behind on her monthly house payments to First National Bank, which starts a nonjudicial foreclosure proceeding. After receiving the Notice of Default, Lisa meets with representatives of First National and explains that she is expecting payment of a substantial commission within three months, and will be able to reinstate the loan. First National agrees in writing to postpone the sale for 110 days. Because of the postponement, the reinstatement period is extended until the new sale date.

February 9, 200X

Advanced Savings Bank
2345 Main Street
Sacramento, California

Loan: 45289M

Re: 21 Hill Street
      Sacramento, California

Dear Mr. Sanchez:

As you know, a foreclosure is currently pending against my property. The total amount to bring my loan current is approximately $31,300. As I previously explained to you, I cannot afford to pay the full amount at this time. You have agreed to accept a partial payment in the amount of $12,000 (enclosed with this letter) and postpone the foreclosure sale for 90 days. I understand that if I fail to bring my loan current by May 9, you will conduct a foreclosure sale.

If this letter accurately reflects our agreement, please sign in the space below and return one copy of this letter to me. If this letter is not accurate, please advise me immediately in writing and return my check.

Very truly yours,

Henry Gold
906-669-4354

AGREED AS TO FORM AND CONTENT:
ADVANCED SAVINGS BANK

By: _____
Authorized Officer

D. Notice of Trustee's Sale

If you do not bring your loan current within a specified period of time after the Notice of Default was issued (see your state's laws), the trustee will issue a Notice of Trustee's Sale, or simply a Notice of Sale. The purpose of the Notice of Sale is to announce the date, time and location of the foreclosure sale of your property.

The foreclosure sale must be scheduled a specified period of days after the Notice of Sale was issued pursuant to state law. Because of this, trustee's sales are typically scheduled three to four weeks after the Notice of Sale is issued to avoid the sale date falling on a weekend or holiday.

In most states, the reinstatement period continues after the Notice of Trustee's Sale is issued. In other words, the issuance of the Notice of Trustee's Sale has no effect on the reinstatement period. The reinstatement period continues to run until the foreclosure sale.

1. Contents of the Notice of Trustee's Sale

When you receive a Notice of Trustee's Sale, you may be inclined to put it aside, or worse, tear it up. Don't! Take the time to read it carefully. If you discover any inaccuracies in the Notice of Sale, you can buy yourself some time by demanding that the trustee correct the misinformation and record a new Notice of Sale. Any time a trustee records a corrected Notice of Sale, she must reschedule the trustee's sale, which will delay the foreclosure for at least an additional three to four weeks.

Carefully check the following on the Notice of Sale:

- that the date of the sale is more than 20 calendar days after issuance of the Notice of Sale (not the date you received the notice)
- that it names a specific location where the sale will be conducted, and
- the description of your property is the same as in your note, deed of trust, and Notice of Default (your street address need not be provided).

On the following page is an example of a Notice of Trustee's Sale, with explanations for each paragraph.

2. Notice Requirements for Notice of Sale

Because the foreclosure is not court supervised, the trustee must comply with strict procedural requirements for the Notice of Sale to be valid. If the trustee fails to follow the required mailing, recording, publishing and posting procedures, you can demand that she record a new Notice of Sale. If she refuses, you have the right to file a lawsuit in the courthouse to have the foreclosure enjoined. (See Chapter 8).

There's no requirement that you receive "actual" notice of the trustee's sale. The trustee's sale remains valid as long as the trustee carried out the notification process properly. It doesn't matter if you were out of the country, in the hospital, or for some other reason didn't get a copy of the Notice.

a. Mailing Notice of Sale to You

Depending on your states, the Notice of Sale must be mailed to you by certified or registered mail, as well as by first-class mail, several weeks before the scheduled sale date.

b. Mailing Notice of Sale to Others Affected

Copies must also be sent by certified (or registered) mail and by first-class mail to anyone else entitled to receive the Notice of Default, such as junior lienholders and tenants leasing your property.

RECORDING REQUESTED BY

T.D. SERVICE COMPANY

And when recorded mail to

T.D. SERVICE COMPANY
1820 E. FIRST ST., SUITE 210
P.O. BOX 11988
SANTA ANA , CA 92711-1988

___669170Z___ Space above this

DOC # 2006-0954421
12/29/2006 08:00A Fee:10.00
Page 1 of 2
Recorded in Official Records
County of Riverside
Larry W. Ward
Assessor, County Clerk & Recorder

S	R	U	PAGE	SIZE	DA	MISC	LONG	RFD	COPY
1			2						
M	A	L	465	426	PCOR	NCOR	SMF	NCHG	EXAM
									029

10   [T / 029]

NOTICE OF TRUSTEE'S SALE

T.S. No: A339144 CA   Unit Code: A   Loan No: 1947233/LEE
AP #1: 144-313-012-9

T.D. SERVICE COMPANY, as duly appointed Trustee under the following described Deed of Trust WILL SELL AT PUBLIC AUCTION TO THE HIGHEST BIDDER FOR CASH (in the forms which are lawful tender in the United States) and/or the cashier's, certified or other checks specified in Civil Code Section 2924h (payable in full at the time of sale to T.D. Service Company) all right, title and interest conveyed to and now held by it under said Deed of Trust in the property hereinafter described:

Trustor:

Recorded November 23, 2005 as Instr. No. 2005-0975866 in Book --- Page --- of Official Records in the office of the Recorder of RIVERSIDE County; CALIFORNIA , pursuant to the Notice of Default and Election to Sell thereunder recorded September 21, 2006 as Instr. No. 0698880 in Book --- Page --- of Official Records in the office of the Recorder of RIVERSIDE County CALIFORNIA.

YOU ARE IN DEFAULT UNDER A DEED OF TRUST DATED NOVEMBER 11, 2005. UNLESS YOU TAKE ACTION TO PROTECT YOUR PROPERTY, IT MAY BE SOLD AT A PUBLIC SALE. IF YOU NEED AN EXPLANATION OF THE NATURE OF THE PROCEEDING AGAINST YOU, YOU SHOULD CONTACT A LAWYER.

14197 CAVALRY CIRCLE, CORONA, CA 92880
"(If a street address or common designation of property is shown above, no warranty is given as to its completeness or correctness)."

Said Sale of property will be made in "as is" condition without covenant or warranty, express or implied, regarding title possession, or encumbrances, to pay the remaining principal sum of the note(s) secured by said Deed of Trust, with interest as in said note provided, advances, if any, under the terms of said Deed of Trust, fees, charges and expenses of the Trustee and of the trusts created by said Deed of Trust.

Said sale will be held on:
JANUARY 22, 2007, AT 3:30 P.M. *AT THE MAIN ENTRANCE TO THE COUNTY COURTHOUSE, 4050 MAIN STREET, RIVERSIDE, CA

At the time of the initial publication of this notice, the total amount of the unpaid balance of the obligation secured by the above described Deed of Trust and estimated costs, expenses, and advances is $508,417.55. It is possible that at the time of sale the opening bid may be less than the total indebtedness due.

Page 2
T.S. No: A339144 CA   Unit Code: A   Loan No: 1947233/LEE

Date: December 22, 2006

T.D. SERVICE COMPANY as said Trustee,

BY _____
FRANCES DEPALMA, ASSISTANT SECRETARY
T.D. SERVICE COMPANY
1820 E. FIRST ST., SUITE 210, P.O. BOX 11988
SANTA ANA, CA 92711-1988
(714) 543-8372

We are assisting the Beneficiary to collect a debt and any information we obtain will be used for that purpose whether received orally or in writing.

If the Trustee is unable to convey title for any reason, the successful bidder's sole and exclusive remedy shall be the return of monies paid to the Trustee, and the successful bidder shall have no further recourse.

If available, the expected opening bid and/or postponement information may be obtained by calling the following telephone number(s) on the day before the sale: (714) 480-5690 or you may access sales information at www.ascentex.com/websales.

c. Recording Notice of Sale

The Notice of Sale must be recorded several weeks before the sale date, although it may be recorded earlier.

Don't confuse deadlines. Borrowers sometimes mix up requirements for Notices of Default and Notices of Sale and incorrectly think a foreclosure may be voided because the trustee didn't record the Notice of Sale on time. Remember, each state has different requirements for when its Notice of Default (if at all) and Notice of Sale must be recorded. Check your particular state's requirements in the back of this book.

d. Publishing Notice of Sale

The Notice of Sale must be published in a newspaper of general circulation in the city, county, or judicial district where your property is located. Typically, publication must take place at least three times between the date the trustee issues the Notice of Sale and the date of the trustee's sale. You can find out if the trustee correctly followed this requirement by asking the trustee for its Affidavit of Publication. Then get copies of the newspapers from those dates and see if the Notice of Sale was indeed published. If the trustee refuses, you have grounds to file a lawsuit to stop the foreclosure. (See Chapter 8 on filing a lawsuit to enjoin the foreclosure.)

e. Posting Notice of Sale

The Notice of Sale must be posted--that is, displayed in a conspicuous location so that you (and any tenants), and the public can be made aware of the pending sale--several weeks prior to the sale date. Posting is usually required in two locations:

- a public place, such as a courthouse or city hall (which have special bulletin boards for such purposes), and/or

- on your property.

The Notice of Sale will be posted on your front door, or, if that is not possible, in another conspicuous place on your property. If your property is undeveloped land, the notice will probably be attached to a post or stake driven into the ground. Trustees take pictures of the posted notice, and you have the right to ask the trustee to show you the pictures.

3. Complete Notice of Trustee's Sale Worksheet

Use the following worksheet to make sure the trustee complies with all notice and mailing requirements for the Notice of Sale. A tear-out copy is in the Appendix. Remember, if the trustee makes a mistake along the way, you have grounds to stop the foreclosure by demanding that the trustee start the process all over again from the beginning.

4. If the Trustee Made a Mistake

If the trustee failed to comply with any of the requirements shown on your worksheet, send the trustee a letter, such as the sample below, demanding that a new Notice of Sale be issued using proper procedures. Be sure to send a copy of the letter to your lender so that they are also put on notice of the trustee's mistake.

When should you send the letter? You can send it immediately or wait until the last week or so before the scheduled sale. But if you wait, don't miss the deadline or neglect to leave yourself enough time to file a lawsuit if the trustee ignores your request. You may even want to hand deliver the letter or send it by overnight mail. If you send the letter by U.S. mail, send it certified, return receipt requested. If the trustee ignores your request, you have the right to file a lawsuit to stop the sale. (We give instructions in Chapter 8.)

Example: Thomas fell several months behind on payments for his condominium in Houston, Texas. His bank had its trustee start a nonjudicial foreclosure. The Notice of Sale was defective because it scheduled the sale for less than 20 days before the date of the Notice of Sale. Thomas wrote to the trustee and demanded that the Notice of Sale

be canceled and the foreclosure stopped. The trustee agreed, canceled the defective Notice of Sale and issued a new one, which delayed the sale for almost a month. If the trustee had ignored Thomas's request, he would have had to quickly file a lawsuit in the Court to stop the foreclosure.

E. The Redemption Period

Assuming you haven't brought your loan current before the expiration of the reinstatement period, the redemption period begins. Depending on state law, the redemption period consists of the last days before the trustee's sale. The redemption period ends the moment bidding starts at the trustee's sale.

During the redemption period, you no longer have the right to reinstate your loan by simply bringing it current. You can, however, "redeem" your property (which will stop the foreclosure) by paying off the entire unpaid balance of your loan, plus late fees, penalties, attorney fees and the trustee's costs.

If you have the funds to pay off your loan in full---perhaps through refinancing, a loan from friend or family, or some other method--call the trustee and ask them to calculate the total amount due. Make an appointment to meet with the trustee as soon as possible. Take a cashier's check for the correct amount and exchange it for a signed Full Reconveyance document, which is then recorded. The Full Reconveyance cancels the deed of trust and terminates the foreclosure.

NOTICE OF SALE WORKSHEET (NON-JUDICIAL FORECLOSURE)

ARE THE FOLLOWING CORRECT ON THE NOTICE OF TRUSTEE'S SALE, AND
CONSISTENT WITH INFORMATION ON YOUR NOTICE OF DEFAULT, PROMISSORY NOTE
AND DEED OF TRUST?

Name of trustor (you and any co-signers)?   [] No [] Yes   Name:

Name of beneficiary (lender)?   [] No [] Yes   Name:

Name of trustee?   [] No [] Yes   Name:

Information about recording of deed of trust?   [] No [] Yes   Date:
        Document Number:
        Book/Page Number:

Description of the property?   [] No [] Yes

Total amount of outstanding indebtedness?   [] No [] Yes   Amount:

Date, time and location of sale   [] No [] Yes   Date:
        Time:
        Location:

Is the date of sale at least 20 calendar days from
date the Notice of Sale was issued?   [] No [] Yes

MAILING REQUIREMENTS

Did the trustee wait several months
after recording a Notice of Default before
mailing you a Notice of Sale?   [] No [] Yes   When?

Was a copy of the Notice of Sale mailed to you by
registered or certified mail several weeks
before the scheduled sale date?   [] No [] Yes   When?

Was a copy of the Notice of Sale sent to you by
first-class mail before scheduled sale date?   [] No [] Yes   When?

Prior to the scheduled sale date,
was a copy of the Notice of Sale sent by
registered or certified mail to everyone
entitled to receive notice--including tenants,
junior beneficiaries and anyone
who recorded a Request for Notice?
(Ask the trustee for proof.)   [] No [] Yes   When?

Worksheet continued:

___

RECORDING REQUIREMENTS

Was the Notice of Sale recorded in the county
recorder's office where your property is located
weeks before the scheduled date?   [] No [] Yes When?

PUBLICATION REQUIREMENTS

Before the sale date, was the Notice of Sale
published in a newspaper of general circulation
in the county where the property is located
several times before the sale?
(As the trustee for proof.)   [] No [] Yes
                                                     1st Date:
                                                     2nd Date:
                                                     3rd Date:

___

POSTING REQUIREMENTS

Was a copy of the Notice of Sale posted in
a public place?   [] No [] Yes

Where?

Was a copy of the Notice of Sale posted
On your property?   [] No [] Yes

Trustee Service Corporation
25 Heaven Highway
Albuquerque, New Mexico

By certified mail, return receipt requested

Re: 453 Summa Lane
        Albuquerque, NM

Dear Trustee:

I own the above-referenced property, on which you are conducting a non-judicial foreclosure as trustee for National Mortgage Company.

You recorded a Notice of Default on January 20 and recorded a Notice of Sale on April 15. I noticed that the Notice of Sale is defective because you did not wait a full three months after issuing the Notice of Default before issuing the Notice of Sale.

As a result, I respectfully request that you immediately rescind the defective Notice of Sale and issue a new one. If you refuse and proceed with this illegal foreclosure, I will have no choice but to file a lawsuit in Court to enjoin your foreclosure. In such event, I may be allowed to collect my costs plus punitive damages against Trustee Service Corporation.

Please advise me on or before May 8, 200X in writing or telephone of your response.

Very truly yours,

John Heacock

cc: National Mortgage Company

Some lenders will let you reinstate your loan during the redemption period. Although your legal right to reinstate your loan ends at the redemption period, lenders are sometimes amenable to accepting payment of the arrears during the redemption period. Be forewarned, however--this is unpredictable territory. Once the redemption period kicks in, get any agreement to reinstate your loan in writing from your lender.

F. Trustee's Sale

The last step in the nonjudicial foreclosure process is the actual trustee's sale of your property.

If you haven't reinstated or redeemed your loan by the date scheduled for the trustee's sale, the trustee will conduct a public auction of your property. The sale must be conducted on a weekday between 9 a.m. and 5 p.m. in the county where your property is located. The sale normally will be conducted in front of the county courthouse or another government building.

1. Attend the Trustee's Sale

It might cross your mind to avoid the public auction as a way to preserve dignity in the face of foreclosure, but you have other priorities at this juncture. Although it may be humiliating to attend a trustee's sale of your own property, you should nevertheless make an effort to attend. There is always the possibility that the trustee (or auctioneer) may conduct the auction improperly or something else may occur that would give you grounds to file an action to set aside (overturn) the trustee's sale.

At the sale, you need to be an eagle-eyed observer. Take a friend along, if possible, to help you keep track of the sale and help you through the rough spots. Be prepared to take copious notes of everything that occurs. Later, you may need a good record of events that occurred during the sale if you wish to file a lawsuit to set it aside. (If you need to set aside a trustee's sale that has already occurred, you will need to consult an attorney.)

2. Trustee's Sale May Be Postponed

Trustee's sales may be postponed for a variety of reasons. For example, your lender may agree to postpone the sale if you are negotiating with them to cure your loan. Or the trustee may postpone the sale if he belatedly discovers that one of the notices was defective or was not mailed to everyone entitled to get notice. Or if no one bids on the property at the trustee's sale, the trustee may postpone and reschedule it.

At the time and place of the scheduled sale, the trustee must show up and announce that the sale has been postponed and why. He must also give the new sale date. If the trustee doesn't show up and disclose the new sale date, the Notice of Sale will be automatically canceled and the trustee will be required to issue a new Notice of Sale. That, of course, would temporarily stop the foreclosure and give you at least several more weeks before the next trustee's sale.

The trustee's sale may also be postponed by court order, such as a state court injunction, temporary restraining order, or because you filed for bankruptcy (which automatically prohibits the sale from occurring without the bankruptcy court's permission). Further, once the order or bankruptcy stay terminates, the trustee must wait at least seven more days before conducting the trustee's sale. (Injunctions and temporary restraining orders are covered in Chapter 8 and bankruptcy is discussed in Chapter 9.)

a. Promises to Postpone Sale Must Be in Writing

As a number of unfortunate property owners have discovered, a trustee may proceed with a properly noticed sale regardless of what the lender or trustee verbally promised. Accordingly, get any agreement with your lender or the trustee in writing because only a written agreement for postponement is enforceable. The agreement must clearly state that the trustee's sale has been postponed to a specific date in the future.

b. New Notice of Sale After Three Postponements

After several postponements of a scheduled trustee's sale in most states, the trustee must mail, record, publish and post a new Notice of Sale, following the rules discussed in Section D2, above. Note, however, that the following kinds of postponements do not count towards the total:

- postponements by court order, such as an automatic stay issued by a bankruptcy court or a temporary restraining order issued by a state court

- postponements by mutual agreement between you and the lender or trustee, and

- postponements caused by the required seven-day waiting period after an injunction, restraining order or stay has terminated.

3. Overview of the Auction

Anyone may bid at the foreclosure sale. In other words, you, your lender, junior lienholders and perfect strangers all may bid. Even the trustee may bid on his own behalf, although this is extremely unlikely. So, if you suddenly have the money and want to save your property, you can always bid at the sale.

To begin the sale, the trustee (or a hired professional auctioneer) will announce that your property is for sale. He will describe the terms of sale (such as all bids must be cash or cashier's check) and say that the condition and title of the property is being sold "as is," without any "warranties or representations." This means that the trustee makes no promises about your property's physical condition or title status (whether it has senior or tax liens encumbering it).

a. Foreclosing Lender's Opening Bid

The auctioneer will give the foreclosing lender the opportunity to make the opening bid. Your lender always bids first because they hold the deed of trust that is being foreclosed and want to protect their interest up to the value of their deed of trust.

Your lender is not required to bring cash to back its bid, as it would make little sense for your lender, to whom you already owe money, to produce cash at the sale to pay itself. Instead, the lender can "credit bid" up to the outstanding balance of their loan.

Example: A representative of Bank of America attends a trustee's sale of a house in Phoenix, Arizona, on which the Bank holds a first deed of trust. Several potential bidders are present. Bank of America starts the bidding by credit bidding $225,000, the outstanding balance of its loan. All subsequent bidders must have cash (or cashier's checks) for the amount of their bids.

b. Bidding Procedures

After the opening bid, the trustee will solicit bidding from the group of people assembled. Each bid constitutes an irrevocable offer to purchase your property at the named price. A bid is automatically canceled by the next higher bid. In most states, if the bidder does not have the money in cash or cashier's checks, his or her bid is automatically canceled. (In order to avoid problems, auctioneers generally inspect bidders before starting the auction to determine how high each person can bid.)

The trustee is expected to keep the sale fair and equitable between the various bidders. If there is anything improper in the bidding, you may have grounds to set aside the trustee's sale. For instance, if one person tries to prevent another person from bidding, the trustee will stop the bidding until everyone who wants to bid is given an opportunity to do so. In the end, your property will be sold to the highest bidder, even if the bid is below the property's fair market value.

You'll want to pay attention to any irregularities in the bidding process. For example, under no circumstances may bidders at a trustee's sale:

- accept money in exchange for not bidding

- offer to pay money to another bidder for not bidding or to withdraw from bidding

- fix bidding, or

- restrain bidding in any way.

Any of these acts would defraud you of your right to a "public" auction of your property at the highest price.

Maybe you're wondering why you should care about the sales price of property you're losing. First of all, if you have any junior lienholders, you'll continue to be personally liable to them after the sale, unless there are sufficient sale proceeds to cover debts owed to them. Second, there is the rare possibility that your property could

sell for more than you owe to all of the lienholders, meaning that you could actually receive the excess sale proceeds after everyone else is paid.

If you can prove that the trustee's sale was illegally conducted, the wrongdoer can be fined, imprisoned, or both. In addition, the sale can be set aside (canceled) and the trustee forced to conduct a new sale. For these reasons, it pays to be alert and observant during the entire auction. Situations like the following have been known to happen.

Example: Robert attends the trustee's sale of his 4-unit apartment building in Dallas, Texas, which has a current market value of $400,000. Five people attend the sale. Robert observes one man quietly handing money to each of the other potential bidders. When the sale begins, National City Savings, his lender, credit bids $275,000, the amount due on the loan. The man who paid off the other potential buyers bids only $1,000 more, $276,000. When no one makes a higher bid, the trustee declares this man to be the purchaser of the property for $276,000. Because of the obvious irregularity in the bidding process and disparity in the sale price, Robert may have grounds to set aside the trustee's sale.

4. Trustee Finalizes Sale and Disburses Proceeds

The trustee will give the highest bidder a Trustee's Deed Upon Sale document, also known in some states as a Trustee's Deed. This deed is then recorded in the county recorder's office. The Trustee's Deed officially transfers title to your property to the new owner.

The Trustee's Deed also conveys title free and clear of the foreclosing deed of trust and all junior liens. Because the proceeds of the trustee's sale are used to satisfy the foreclosing lien, the foreclosing deed of trust is extinguished after the sale, even if the sale proceeds do not satisfy the total claim.

Example: Bianca owes $650,000 on her home. The trustee's sale takes in $440,000. Bianca is no longer liable for the $440,000 loan or for the $210,000 shortage (deficiency). Because the trustee's sale extinguishes the note and deed of trust, the lender cannot subsequently sue Bianca for the deficiency.

Within a week of the trustee's sale, the trustee will disburse the sale proceeds in the following order, until the money is exhausted:

- The trustee is reimbursed for his costs and expenses to conduct the foreclosure.

- The foreclosing lender receives the sale proceeds up to the balance of their promissory note, plus costs.

- If there are any funds remaining, they are disbursed to any junior lienholders in order of priority.

- Finally, the owner (you) receive any surplus funds remaining. (But don't hold your breath because this is extremely unlikely.)

The trustee prepares a settlement sheet that describes how the sale proceeds were distributed. As soon as possible, call or write the trustee and ask for a copy of the trustee's settlement sheet. If you find errors in the calculations, you can write to the trustee (and send a copy to your lender), describing the mistake and demanding

that the trustee rectify the problem within 30 days. Of course, you should only go this far if you believe that you (or one of your junior lienholders) will receive a portion of the sale proceeds if they are redistributed. If the trustee ignores your letter, you have the right to file a lawsuit in Court to have the sale proceeds redistributed. (This would require further research or a lawyer's help. See Chapter 12.)

5. What Happens to Liens After Trustee's Sale

When the trustee gives a Trustee's Deed to the buyer at the trustee's sale, it grants title to your property as of the date you signed the deed of trust--not the date of the trustee's sale. This is legally important because only those liens that were recorded before the foreclosing lienholder's deed of trust continue to encumber the property after the trustee's sale. For example, if a senior lienholder forecloses, all junior liens would be eliminated because they were recorded after the date the foreclosing lienholder recorded its deed of trust. In contrast, if a junior lienholder forecloses, the new owner acquires the property subject to the senior lien.

Example: Ted owns a single-family home in Minneapolis, Minnesota. There are two loans encumbering the property. First National Bank holds a first deed of trust and Second Mortgage Company holds a second deed of trust. While remaining current with First National, Ted defaults on his monthly payments to Second Mortgage. Second Mortgage initiates a nonjudicial foreclosure and sells Ted's house at a trustee's sale. First National is unaffected by Second Mortgage's foreclosure. The end result is that the new purchaser owns property that is still encumbered by a first deed of trust in favor of First National.

a. Junior Lienholders

All deeds of trust, abstracts of judgments and judicial liens that were recorded after the date the foreclosing lender recorded their deed of trust are eliminated ("wiped out") by the trustee's sale. In other words, the successful bidder at the trustee's sale takes title to your property free of junior liens.

Even though their deeds of trust are extinguished by the foreclosure, you are still liable to pay those junior lienholders what you owe them (provided they are not purchase money loans). Because a junior lienholder's interest in the property is now unsecured, the junior lienholder must now file a lawsuit to recover the unpaid debt, obtain a judgment, and then record a judgment lien against your other property.

Example: Telly owns a triplex in Oklahoma City, Oklahoma. There are two loans encumbering his property: First National Bank holds a first deed of trust, and Second Credit Union holds a second deed of trust. Telly fell behind on both of his loans and First National filed a foreclosure and sold the property for less than the amount due on the loan. Second Credit Union's deed of trust was wiped out by the trustee's sale because it was junior to First National's deed of trust. Nevertheless, Telly continues to be liable to Second Credit Union for the full balance of the loan. But Second Credit Union can no longer foreclose because its deed of trust was extinguished. Second Credit Union can only sue Telly in Court if he doesn't pay.

b. Special Lien Situations

Certain liens on your property are unaffected by a trustee's sale, regardless of when they were recorded. The new owner will receive title to your property subject to these remaining liens and you will continue to remain liable. Here are the particulars.

- *Property tax liens*: Liens for real property taxes cannot be eliminated by a foreclosure sale. For example, if you owe the county property taxes for your home, the taxes become a senior lien against your property, regardless of when the lien was recorded. Although you will remain liable, the tax liens will remain on the property even if you don't own it anymore, unless they are paid off at the trustee's sale (which is what most frequently happens).

IRS and state tax liens. These liens are considered to be personal in nature. As such, even though you continue to remain personally liable, they are automatically removed from the property after a foreclosure sale.

- *Mechanic's liens*: Mechanic's liens are liens recorded against your property by persons who worked on your property and did not get paid (plumbers, contractors and the like). Mechanic's liens are eliminated by a trustee's sale only if the date on which the work commenced--not the date the lien was recorded--was before the date the foreclosing lender recorded its deed of trust. Even if the mechanic's lien is eliminated, you are still liable to the workers for the amount of the lien.

6. Buyer May Take Possession of Your Property

Although it may seem severe and unfair, once the new owner receive a Trustee's Deed, he or she is entitled to take possession of your property and you are expected to immediately move out. Of course, some lenders or buyers have no intention of moving into the newly purchased property and may consider leasing it to you if you want to live there. If you are interested in leasing the property after the trustee's sale, get the name and phone number of the new owner from the trustee and contact the owner immediately.

If you refuse to leave the premises voluntary, the new owner may serve you with a Notice to Quit, which states that you must move out within three days. If you still don't move out, the new owner has the right to file an eviction action (called an unlawful detainer) against you in court. You may defend an unlawful detainer by challenging the purchaser's title and/or the validity of the trustee's sale. However, with the foreclosure completed, it will be very difficult to win.

If you have tenants on your property, you won't be able to collect rents after the trustee's sale. From that date forward, the tenants will be required to pay rent directly to the new owner.

chapter

4

JUDICIAL FORECLOSURES

A. Why Lenders Choose Judicial Foreclosures... 86
    1. The Borrower signed a Mortgage.. 86
    2. Lender May Want Rental Income From the Property 87

B. Overview of a Judicial Foreclosure 87
    1. Lender Files Complaint... 87
    2. Lender Records Lis Pendens 93
    3. Answer the Complaint Within 30 Days... 93
    4. The Reinstatement Period 97
    5. Discovery... 98
    6. Foreclosure Trial 99
    7. Equity of Redemption Period 99
    8. Writ of Sale 100
    9. Notice of Sale 100
    10. Foreclosure Sale 104
    11. Deficiency Judgment 106
    12. Post-Sale Redemption Period 108

If you default on the terms of your mortgage (covered in Chapter 2), your lender may foreclose on your property. Depending on the laws in your state, your lender may initiate a judicial foreclosure, which is covered in this chapter.

With a judicial foreclosure, your lender files a lawsuit in county courthouse seeking the sale of your property to payoff your loan. Although the thought of being involved in a lawsuit may at first intimidate you, you'll have plenty of time to get your bearings, respond to the lawsuit, and explore ways to bring your loan current.

Only if you can't work things out with your lender will a judge allow the county sheriff to conduct a foreclosure sale. The problem with a judicial foreclosure (unlike a nonjudicial foreclosure) is that if the sale doesn't produce enough cash to pay off your debt, you may owe your lender the "deficiency" --the difference between the balance of your loan and the amount received at the foreclosure sale. The entire process, from the initiation of the lawsuit to the actual sale, may take one to two years.

You may sensibly ask yourself, "What should I be doing during the judicial foreclosure process?" The answer to that question is simple. Develop a plan to stop the foreclosure, as discussed in Chapter 1. This is your "window of opportunity" to apply various strategies to stop the pending foreclosure, covered in Chapters 5 through 11 of this book.

Judicial foreclosures are complex and lengthy. This chapter shows you how to respond to a lawsuit and summarizes the judicial foreclosure process. Because we cannot provide comprehensive step-by-step instructions on all phases of court lawsuits (an in-depth analysis would take up an entire book!), you should probably hire a lawyer. If you cannot afford an attorney, try contacting a local legal-aid services organization for assistance or referrals. Look in your local yellow pages, search the internet, or contact your city's bar association.

 Nonjudicial foreclosures are covered in Chapter 3. The other type of foreclosure is nonjudicial, in which a trustee conducts the foreclosure procedures without the involvement of the court. Nonjudicial foreclosures do not allow a deficiency judgment and there generally is no post-sale redemption rights.

A. Why Lenders Choose Judicial Foreclosures

The majority of foreclosures of single-family residences are nonjudicial, which bypass the court system entirely (sec Chapter 3.) Lenders usually prefer nonjudicial foreclosure because they are quicker (approximately three to four months), less expensive (no attorney fees, and trustee fees are limited by law), and the property owner will not have the right to redeem (buy back) the property after the trustee's sale. Nevertheless, there are two distinctive situations in which lenders may opt to foreclose judicially.

1. The Borrower signed a Mortgage

If you signed a mortgage to secure your loan, there is no power-of-sale clause in the document. Accordingly, the lender has no choice but to file a judicial foreclosure in court. And although the process is longer, the lender has the ability to obtain a "deficiency judgment" against you if your property sells for less than the balance you owe. Only a judicial foreclosure enables a lender to obtain a court judgment for the deficiency. Remember, the "deficiency" is the difference between the unpaid balance of your loan and the amount received at the foreclosure sale.

Fortunately, however, for a lender to get a deficiency judgment, it must show all of the following to be true:

• The debt was secured by your property.

• You signed a mortgage as security for the debt.

• The mortgage provides that you are personally liable to repay the loan (known as "recourse").

2. Lender May Want Rental Income From the Property

Even if the lender cannot obtain a deficiency judgment against you, your lender may still file a judicial foreclosure (regardless of whether you signed a mortgage or a deed of trust) if your property is income-producing (multi-residential or commercial). This is because your lender can ask the judge to appoint a receiver--someone who is legally empowered to take over management of your property and collect the rents.

In some states, don't be surprised if your lender files both judicial and nonjudicial foreclosures if you have a multi-residential or commercial property. That way, a court-appointed receiver will manage your property and collect the rents while the nonjudicial foreclosure is pending. Using this strategy, once the nonjudicial trustee's sale is completed, your lender will dismiss (cancel) the judicial foreclosure.

B. Overview of a Judicial Foreclosure

A judicial foreclosure is a lengthy, court-supervised procedure that consists of 12 basic steps, summarized in the Judicial Foreclosure Timeline below and covered in detail in the rest of this chapter.

1. Lender Files Complaint

Your lender starts a judicial foreclosure by filing a Complaint (a written document) seeking foreclosure of your property in the Court in the county in which your property is located. Your lender is known as the plaintiff--the party filing the action. The complaint must list all defendants-the party or parties defending against the lawsuit. Your lender will name as defendants you and everyone who has any interest in your property, including any and all present owners, tenants, senior and junior lienholders (including any former owner that holds a mortgage), taxing authorities, and guarantors.

The Complaint will claim that you signed (executed) a mortgage naming your lender as the mortgagee. Your lender will state that the documents were delivered to your lender and recorded in the county recorder's office. Most importantly, the complaint will allege that you have defaulted under the terms of your mortgage.

Your lender will ask the court to order that: 1) your property be sold to satisfy your debt, and 2) your lender receive a money judgment for any deficiency remaining after the sale proceeds are applied to your debt. (If no deficiency judgment is sought, your lender will insert a statement in the Complaint waiving a deficiency judgment.) See the sample Complaint for Judicial Foreclosure on the next page.

Your lender will have copies of the Complaint, together with a document called a Summons (announcement of lawsuit), personally served upon (delivered) you and each of the other defendants. If a process server cannot serve you personally, a copy of the Summons and Complaint will be left with an adult at your residence (or place of business) and copies will be mailed to you.

JUDICIAL FORECLOSURE TIMELINE

ACTION	WHEN	PURPOSE
Lender files Complaint in court	Sometime after loan has gone into default—usually several months	Starts the lawsuit for judicial foreclosure
Lender records lis pendens with county recorder	Soon after lawsuit is filed	Gives public notice of lawsuit; effectively prevents property from being sold or refinanced
Borrower files an answer to Complaint	Within 30 days after borrower is served with (personally given) copy of Complaint	Prevents lender from obtaining default judgment and immediately proceeding with foreclosure sale
Reinstatement period	From date lawsuit is filed until entry of judgment after trial	Gives borrower opportunity to bring loan current by paying arrears and lender's costs and expenses of filing lawsuit
Discovery	From date borrower answers Complaint until case goes to trial	Borrower and lender collect evidence in the case: exchange documents, take depositions and follow other procedures
Trial	About two to three years after lawsuit was filed	Resolves lawsuit—judgment is entered; ends reinstatement period

NOTE: IF LAWSUIT IS RESOLVED IN BORROWER'S FAVOR, THE CASE IS DISMISSED AND THE REST OF THIS CHART DOES NOT APPLY.

Redemption period	Runs from end of trial (entry of judgment) to foreclosure sale	Borrower may stop foreclosure by paying off entire balance of loan plus foreclosure costs
Writ of Sale and Notice of Levy	Starts clock running as to date of foreclosure sale	Gives written notice that sale of property is permitted
Notice of Sale	At least 20 days before foreclosure sale if lender seeks deficiency judgment. Otherwise, a minimum of 120 days after Notice of Levy was issued	Informs borrower when property will be sold
Foreclosure sale	Date listed on Notice of Sale	Sheriff sells property at a public auction, gives buyer a Certificate of Sale and distributes proceeds within a week
Deficiency judgment	Within three months of foreclosure sale	Lender must file application with court that heard trial and get deficiency judgment from the court
Post-sale redemption period	Starts the day of the sale and continues for either one year (if lender seeks deficiency judgment) or three months (if no deficiency judgment)	Borrower may get property back by paying foreclosure sales price plus foreclosure costs

1   *[Complaint for Judicial Foreclosure]*

2

  LAW OFFICES OF FAWN AND GREEN

3   2525 Main Street
  Newark, New Jersey, California

4   862-333-6666

5   Attorney for Plaintiff
  Old Federal Bank

6

7

8

9   COURT OF THE STATE OF NEW JERSEY

10   COUNTY OF ESSEX

11   Old Federal Bank,   )
)   Case No: 00000

12   Plaintiff,   )
  v.   )   COMPLAINT FOR

13   )   JUDICIAL FORECLOSURE
  Betty Bush, Does 1 to 10, Inclusive,)

14   )
            Defendant.   )

15   _____)

16

      Plaintiff, Old Federal Bank ("Bank") complains and alleges as follows:

17   VENUE

18   1. Venue in the Court for the County of Essex is proper under the laws of

19   the State of New Jersey because the property subject to this action is located
  within Essex County.

20   THE PARTIES

21   2. Bank is, and at all times mentioned herein was, a New Jersey bank,

22   chartered by the Federal Deposit Insurance Corporation, and doing business in
  the State of New Jersey.

23   3. Bank is informed and believes, and thereon alleges that Defendant Betty

24   Bush ("Borrower" or "Defendant") is, and at all relevant times herein was, an
  individual residing in the State of New Jersey.

25   4. Bank is ignorant of the true names and capacities of the defendants

26   sued herein as DOES 1 through 10, inclusive, and therefore sues these defendants
  by such fictitious names. Bank will amend the Complaint to allege their true

27   names and capacities when the DOE defendants have been ascertained. Bank is
  informed and believes and on that basis alleges that DOE 1 through DOE 10,

28   inclusive, are creditors of Defendant or others, and are named as beneficiaries
  or assignees of the beneficiaries in mortgages recorded against the Property.
  Said defendants are creditors junior, subsequent and subject to Bank liens as

previously described, and each of them is responsible in some manner for the events, occurrences, and obligations herein alleged and for the losses incurred by Bank as a result of the nonpayment of the loan obligations.

<u>THE LOAN DOCUMENTS</u>

5. On or about April 8, 200X, Borrower, for valuable consideration, made, executed and delivered to Bank a promissory note ("Note") in the amount of $200,000, a true and correct copy of which is attached hereto as Exhibit "A" and incorporated by this reference with the same force and effect as if set forth in full herein. Under the terms of the Note, Borrower agreed to make monthly payments of $1,330.60, comprised of principal and interest. The interest was calculated at the initial rate of 7% per year, payable the first day of each month. The Note provided that upon default the holder could declare all monies payable thereunder immediately due, owing and payable. The Note also provided for a default interest rate at 4% plus the contract rate.

6. B On or about April 8, 200X, Borrower, for valuable consideration, made, executed and delivered to Bank a Mortgage ("Mortgage") in the amount of $200,000, a true and correct copy of which is attached hereto as Exhibit "B" and incorporated by this reference with the same force and effect as if set forth in full herein. By the terms of the Mortgage, Borrower as Mortgagor, irrevocably granted, transferred and assigned to Mortgagee, all of its right, title and interest in that certain single family residence located at 8500 Foothill Blvd., Newark, New Jersey, and legally known by the description set forth in the Mortgage as recorded with the Essex County Recorder (hereinafter, the "Property"). The Mortgage was duly acknowledged and recorded in the Official Records of the County Recorder on or about April 11, 200X, as Instrument No. XX-345634.

7. Bank complied with all of its contractual obligations under the Note and Mortgage by disbursing the monies as required.

<u>LOAN DEFAULTS</u>

8. Borrower defaulted in its performance of the Note when the May 1, 200X payment was not made. All monies payable under the Note have been declared and are now immediately due and payable, with interest thereon from May 1, 200X.

9. Prior to the commencement of this action, demand was made on Borrower for the balance due on the Mortgage, but no part of said balance has been paid. There remains due, owing and unpaid as of May 1, 200X, the principal sum of $185,423 plus accrued interest from January 1, 200X to May 1, 200X in the amount of $6,394.10 and late charges of $319.71. The total amount owing is approximately $192,136.81 as of May 1, 200X. Interest continues to accrue at the daily rate of $38.36 from May 1, 200X.

10. Under the terms of the Mortgage, Borrower is obligated to pay costs, reasonable attorneys' fees and expenses incurred in the collection of the Note.

<u>FIRST CAUSE OF ACTION</u>
(for Judicial Foreclosure of Mortgage)

11. Bank hereby realleges and incorporates by reference the allegations contained m paragraphs 1 through 10, inclusive, as though fully set forth herein.

12. Bank is informed and believes, and thereon alleges, that the defendants sued fictitiously herein as DOE 1 through DOE 10, inclusive, are creditors of defendant or others, and claim interest in the Property as judgment creditors, lienholders, mechanic's lienholders, holders of tax liens and/or claim to be creditors and have filed lawsuits and notices of pendency of actions to this effect and/or recorded attachments on the Property. Said defendants are creditors junior, subsequent and subject to the lien of Bank as previously described.

13. Bank is the lawful holder of the Mortgage and the lawful owner of the beneficial interest under the Mortgage encumbering the Property.

14. The Note and Mortgage provide that upon default in monthly payments, or in the performance of any obligation, covenant, promise or agreement, Bank may, at its election, declare the entire amount of the principal and unpaid interest to be immediately due and payable. Such election and declaration of acceleration has theretofore been made by Bank as a result of the defaults described herein.

15. Bank is informed and believes, and thereon alleges that Defendants are unwilling and/or unable to cure the defaults described herein.

16. By reason of the defaults as described herein, pursuant to New Jersey statute, Bank is entitled to a judgment that:

(i) the rights, claims, ownership, liens, titles and demand of Defendants and all persons or entities claiming under any of them are subject to the Mortgage;

(ii) the Mortgage is foreclosed and the Property shall be sold according to law by a commissioner or a representative appointed by the Court, and when the time for redemption lapsed, the commissioner or representative shall execute and deliver a deed to the purchaser(s) of the Property at the foreclosure sale and that said purchaser(s) be put into possession of the Property upon delivery of said Deed; and

(iii) a judgment against Defendant for any amount of the above obligation left unsatisfied after the foreclosure and sale of the Property in the amount of such deficiency.

18. Due to the Defendant's default, Bank has been forced to employ attorneys and incur other expenses and costs, no part of which have been paid by Defendant. Under the terms of the Mortgage, Defendant is obligated to pay the reasonable attorneys' fees, expenses, and costs incurred by Bank in exercising its powers to protect the security interest.

WHEREFORE, Bank prays for judgment as follows:

1. For judgment that the rights, claims, ownership, liens, title and demands of Defendants are subject to the Mortgage;

2. That all defendants sued herein and each of them, and all persons claiming under them, subsequent to the execution of the Mortgage, either as lien claimants, judgment creditors, claimants under a junior mortgage or trustee, purchasers, encumbrances, or otherwise, be barred and foreclosed from all

rights, claims, interests or equity in redemption of the property, if any, in every part of the Property, when time for redemption, if any, has elapsed;

3. That Bank have judgment and execution against Defendants for any amount of the obligation identified in the Mortgage which is left unsatisfied after the foreclosure sale of the Property in the amount of such deficiency, plus any additional amount to which Bank is entitled for any misappropriation of rental income, security deposit, insurance proceeds or condemnation awards and waste or damage caused to the Property by Defendants that may remain after applying all the proceeds of the sale of the Property;

4. For an order adjudging that the Mortgage be foreclosed, and that judgment be made for the foreclosure sale of the Property, according to law, by a Sheriff appointed by the Court;

5. For an order permitting Bank, or any other parties to this action, to become a purchaser at the foreclosure sale;

6. For an order declaring that Defendants are liable for a deficiency, if there shall be one, after the sale of the property;

7. That when the time for redemption has elapsed, the Sheriff execute a deed to the party who purchases the Property at the foreclosure sale, and that the Purchaser be put into possession of the Property upon production of said deed;

8. For all costs, charges and expenses incurred in connection with Bank's sale and foreclosure;

9. For such other and further relief as the Court may deem just and proper.

DATED May __, 200X   FAWN & GREEN

                                      By: _____
                                          Joseph Fawn
                                          Attorneys for Old Federal Bank

2. Lender Records Lis Pendens

Immediately after your lender files a Complaint, they will record a "Lis Pendens" (this is a Latin term meaning "Notice of Pending Action") in the recorder's office in the county in which your property is located. A Lis Pendens states that a lawsuit for judicial foreclosure of your property has been filed in the county's courthouse. Your lender doesn't have to attach a copy of the Complaint to the Lis Pendens. Your lender must then mail a copy of the Lis Pendens to you and each of the other defendants. Once properly prepared, recorded and mailed, a Lis Pendens gives public notice of the foreclosure action. In that way, anyone considering purchasing or refinancing your property will check with the county records and discover that there is a judicial foreclosure pending. The net result is that you won't be able to sell or refinance your property until the judicial foreclosure is resolved and your lender is brought current or paid off. (Of course, the purpose of selling or refinancing your property would be to pay off the foreclosing lender.)

3. Answer the Complaint Within 30 Days

In most states, you have 30 days from the date you received the Complaint for judicial foreclosure to file an Answer (written response) to your lender's Complaint with the court. The filing fee varies from state to state, and from county to county, but averages $100 to $200 per defendant. You'll also need to have copies of your Answer mailed to your lender and their attorney.

If you don't file a written Answer within the 30 days, your lender will be able to obtain an immediate default judgment (ruling in its favor) and proceed with the foreclosure sale. In that event, there won't be a trial. So you should always file an answer as promptly as possible!

Your Answer should admit each of the lender's allegations (statements) in the Complaint that are true and deny each allegation that is false. Although this may sound complicated, it really isn't. For example, you can admit as true the allegations that you own the property that is being foreclosed, that you borrowed the money from the lender, and that you signed the mortgage. However, if you do not owe the exact amount your lender states in the Complaint, you would deny that allegation.

1 [*Answer to Complaint for Judicial Foreclosure*]

2 Betty Bush
   8500 Foothill Blvd.
3 Newark, New Jersey
   201-333-7777

4
   Defendant In Pro Per
5

6

7

8   COURT OF THE STATE OF NEW JERSEY

9   COUNTY OF Essex

10 Old Federal Bank,   )
)   Case No: 00000
)
11   Plaintiff,   )
    v.   )   ANSWER TO COMPLAINT FOR
12   )   JUDICIAL FORECLOSURE
   Betty Bush, Does 1 to 10, Inclusive,)
13   )
                Defendant.   )
14 _____)

15
        Defendant, Betty Bush, answering the complaint for herself and no other,
16 hereby responds as follows:

17   VENUE

18   1. Defendant admits that venue in the Court for the County of Essex is
   proper under the laws of the State of New Jersey because the property subject to
19 this action is located within Essex County.

20   THE PARTIES

21   2. Defendant lacks sufficient information and belief with which to respond
   to the allegations contained in this paragraph, and on that basis only,
22 generally and specifically denies each and every allegation contained therein.

23   3. Defendant admits that she is, and at all relevant times herein was, an
   individual residing in the State of New Jersey.
24
        4. Defendant lacks sufficient information and belief with which to respond
25 to the allegations contained in this paragraph, and on that basis only,
   generally and specifically denies each and every allegation contained therein.

26

27

28

THE LOAN DOCUMENTS

5. Defendant denies each and every allegation contained therein and the whole thereof.

6. Defendant denies each and every allegation contained therein and the whole thereof.

7. Defendant denies each and every allegation contained therein and the whole thereof.

LOAN DEFAULTS

8. Defendant denies each and every allegation contained therein and the whole thereof.

9. Defendant denies each and every allegation contained therein and the whole thereof.

10. Defendant denies each and every allegation contained therein and the whole thereof.

FIRST CAUSE OF ACTION
(for Judicial Foreclosure of Mortgage)

11. Defendant realleges and incorporates by reference her responses contained in paragraphs 1 through 10, inclusive, as though fully set forth herein.

12. Defendant denies each and every allegation contained therein and the whole thereof.

13. Defendant denies each and every allegation contained therein and the whole thereof.

14. Defendant denies each and every allegation contained therein and the whole thereof.

15. Defendant denies each and every allegation contained therein and the whole thereof.

16. Defendant denies each and every allegation contained therein and the whole thereof.

17. Defendant denies each and every allegation contained therein and the whole thereof.

1   WHEREFORE, Defendant prays for judgment as follows:

2   1. That plaintiff take nothing by their complaint;

3   2. That Defendant be awarded her costs of suit, including reasonable
attorney's fees;

4
        3. That Defendant be awarded such other and further relief as the Court
5   may deem just and proper.

6
DATED May __, 200X   _____
7   Betty Bush
                                            Defendant In Pro Per
8

9

10

11

12

13

14

15

16

17

18

19

20

21

22

23

24

25

26

27

28

It is important for your Answer to include affirmative defenses--brief explanations of why you believe your lender's judicial foreclosure action is improper. For example, if the terms in your mortgage are wrong, you should raise these issues as affirmative defenses. Or, if your mortgage is not secured by your property, or the mortgage was never properly recorded against your property, you'd make those points as affirmative defenses.

4. The Reinstatement Period

The reinstatement period is a time during which you may stop the judicial foreclosure by bringing your loan current. During the reinstatement period, your lender must accept the amount due and dismiss the lawsuit.

The reinstatement period starts when your lender files a Complaint in court and runs until the trial ends and a judge decides the case ("judgment"). It can take one to two years for a case to go to trial, depending on the court's calendar of cases.

To reinstate your loan, you must pay your lender:
- the amount of payments you have missed (arrears), plus

- foreclosure costs and expenses incurred by your lender, including attorney fees.

The amount needed to reinstate your loan will increase daily as interest keeps accruing. As the lawsuit proceeds, your lender will also incur more legal fees and costs. For these reasons, if you are able, reinstate your loan as soon as possible.

a. Contact Your Lender

If you can come up with the funds to reinstate your loan, contact your lender (or lender's attorney) and determine the exact amount as of the date you anticipate paying the lender. (If you disagree with the amount, ask your lender for details. If all else fails, you have the right to file a motion in court to order an accounting of your lender's books and records to determine the correct amount owed.)

You'll need to purchase a cashier's check for the reinstatement amount and take it to your lender's office. Don't forget to ask for a receipt for the payment. As mentioned earlier, your lender must accept your payment and stop the foreclosure. Request that your lender file a Request for Dismissal with the Court and record a Notice of Withdrawal of Lis Pendens in the county recorder's office. Ask your lender to mail you copies of these two documents as soon as they are processed.

b. Partial Payments During the Reinstatement Period

Most lenders will not accept partial payment of the arrears during the reinstatement period. Nevertheless, don't discount your ability to negotiate with your lender. If you can convince your lender that you can bring the loan current within a reasonable period of time, your lender may agree to accept a partial payment and temporarily postpone the foreclosure. (See Chapter 5 for tips on negotiating with your lender.)

Lenders that do accept partial payments will typically have you sign a letter acknowledging that the partial payment does not waive your default or extend the reinstatement period. Even if your lender doesn't require anything in writing, you should document your understanding with a letter, such as the sample below.

5. Discovery

Because most court systems are backlogged, it can take anywhere from one to two years for your lender's case to come to trial. During this time, you and your lender are expected to conduct discovery--the process in which the parties gather the evidence to prove their case.

The most common types of discovery include:

- *interrogatories*: written answers to a series of questions

- *depositions*: cross-examination by the opposing attorney in front of a court reporter

- *requests for admissions*: series of written questions that require you to admit or deny specific facts, and

- *requests for production of documents*: the turnover of relevant documents.

Discovery resource. The various types of discovery available to you and the timing of these procedures are beyond the scope of this book. But, *Represent Yourself in Court*, by Paul Bergman and Sara Berman-Barrett (Nolo Press), gives an excellent explanation of discovery and the procedures leading up to trial.

January 10, 200X

Hugh Powell
Best Savings Bank
346 Second Street
Tampa, Florida

Loan: 528977

Dear Mr. Powell:

On December 6, 200X, you filed a Complaint for Judicial Foreclosure in the county courthouse to sell my property. The total amount to bring my loan current is approximately $33,345. As I have explained to you, I cannot afford to pay the full arrears at this time.

Nevertheless, you have agreed to accept a partial payment in the amount of $13,000 (enclosed with this letter) and agreed to suspend the judicial foreclosure for four months. I understand that if I fail to bring my loan current by May 10, you will resume the foreclosure.

If this letter accurately reflects our agreement, please sign in the space provided below and return this letter to me. Otherwise, please advise me immediately in writing and return my check.

Sincerely,

Harold Brown

AGREED AS TO FORM AND CONTENT:

BEST SAVINGS BANK

By:_____
Authorized Officer

6. Foreclosure Trial

If your case goes to trial, your lender must present evidence that proves all of the following facts:

- You executed (signed) and delivered to your lender a mortgage as security for the loan.

- A copy of the mortgage was recorded in the county recorder's office.

- You defaulted on the terms of the mortgage.

- Under the terms contained in the mortgage and state law, your property may be sold to satisfy the unpaid debt.

- Your lender is entitled to (or waives its right to) a judgment for any deficiency that may result after applying the proceeds from the foreclosure sale to your unpaid debt.

To win the case, you must demonstrate with witnesses and documents that your lender failed to prove at least one of the previous points and that at least one of your affirmative defenses is true.

The trial could last anywhere from several hours to a few weeks, depending on the complexity of the case. At the end of the trial, the judge will either rule immediately or take it under submission for several days to think over the decision. You will receive a copy of the judgment in the mail.

If the judge rules in your favor, the judicial foreclosure will be dismissed. If, on the other hand, the court finds that your lender proved their case, it will enter a judgment of foreclosure and order the sale of your property by the sheriff to satisfy the debt. Finally, the judgment will specify whether you (or anyone else named in the Complaint) will be personally liable for a deficiency if your property is sold for less than the amount of the judgment.

7. Equity of Redemption Period

From the time the judge enters a court judgment in your lender's favor until the actual foreclosure sale, you are in what's known as the equity of redemption period--or redemption period. This period can range anywhere from several weeks to several months, depending on your state. (See the specific time periods your state uses in the back of this book.)

During the redemption period, you can no longer simply bring your loan current. The only way you can stop the foreclosure is to redeem your property, which consists of paying off the entire unpaid balance of your loan, plus foreclosure costs (including attorneys' fees, interest and whatever other expenses your lender incurred in prosecuting the foreclosure). For various strategies to deal with redemption, read Chapter 5 (*Negotiating With Your Lender*), Chapter 6 (*Refinancing out of Foreclosure*), and Chapter 10 (*How to Sell Your Property Quickly to Stop Foreclosure*).

If you can raise the funds to pay off your entire loan, call the sheriff and find out the total amount to redeem. Make an appointment to meet with the sheriff and bring a cashier's check for the correct amount. In exchange for payment, the sheriff will give you a document called a Certificate of Redemption.

Lenders sometimes allow reinstatement during the redemption period. Although your lender is not obligated to accept your late payments during the redemption period, some lenders will still consider reinstatement if they do not want your property. Be forewarned, however, that this is unpredictable territory, and most lenders will only accept full payment of your loan. (See Chapter 5 for more on negotiating with your lender.)

8. Writ of Sale

In most states, assuming you haven't redeemed your property, your lender will obtain a Writ of Sale from the court and deliver it to the county sheriff. A Writ of Sale orders the sheriff to sell your property according to the instructions in the judgment. In other states, the court automatically delivers the judgment to the sheriff or whoever else is responsible for the sale of the property.

   If the sheriff fails to properly follow these procedures, you can file a motion in the court demanding that the foreclosure be stopped until the sheriff completes the proper procedure.

9. Notice of Sale

The next document you will receive in this blizzard of paperwork is the Notice of Sale. The Notice of Sale is issued by the sheriff and advises you (and any junior lienholders) that your property will be sold on a specific date. It gives the actual date, time and location of the foreclosure sale. The sale is typically

scheduled one to three months after the notice is issued, depending on your state. (Please refer to your specific state's timetable in the back of this book.)

a. Notification Requirements for the Notice of Sale

Depending on your state, the sheriff must follow strict notice requirements for the Notice of Sale to be valid. Here are the rules:

- *Service.* The sheriff must serve the Notice of Sale on you personally, or leave a copy of the notice with an adult at your residence or place of business.

- *Mailing.* Several weeks before the sale date, the sheriff must send the Notice of Sale by first-class mail to you and everyone entitled to receive notice, including any junior lienholders and tenants.

- *Publishing.* The Notice of Sale must be published several times between the time the Notice of Sale is issued and the sale date. The publishing must be in a newspaper of general circulation in the city, county, or judicial district where your property is located.

- *Posting.* The Notice of Sale must be posted both in a public place, such as a courthouse or city hall, and on your property in a conspicuous location.

- *Recording.* Depending on the state, sheriffs usually record a copy of the Notice of Sale in the county recorder's office to assure that there has been adequate public notice of the foreclosure sale.

3229.4-1 Rev. (12/04)

STATE OF ILLINOIS   **UNITED STATES OF AMERICA**   **COUNTY OF DU PAGE**
IN THE CIRCUIT COURT OF THE EIGHTEENTH JUDICIAL CIRCUIT

CASE NUMBER

PLAINTIFF

VS.

DEFENDANT

FILE STAMP HERE

NOTICE OF JUDICIAL SALE
OF REAL ESTATE MORTGAGE FORECLOSURE

NOTICE IS HEREBY GIVEN that pursuant to a judgment heretofore entered by the said Court in the above entitled cause, **JOHN E. ZARUBA,** Sheriff of DuPage County, Illinois will on (day of week) _____

the _____ day of _____ at the hour of _____ M.
at the west entrance of the DuPage County Sheriff's office, located at 501 North County Farm Road, in the City of Wheaton, Illinois sell at public auction to the highest bidder for cash, all and singular, the following described premises and real estate in the said judgment mentioned, situated in the County of DuPage, State of Illinois, or so much thereof as shall be sufficient to satisfy said judgment to wit:

Said property is commonly known as: _____

The person to contact for information regarding the property is: _____

_____

The terms of sale are: **Ten percent (10%) due by cash or certified funds at the time of the sale and balance is due within 24 hours of the sale. The subject property is subject to real estate taxes, special assessments or special taxes levied against said real estate and is offered for sale without any representation as to quality or quantity of title and without recourse to plaintiff and in "as is" condition. The sale is further subject to confirmation by the court.**

The property is improved by_____

Property may be inspected prior to sale _____

Together with all buildings and improvements thereon, and the tenements, hereditaments and appurtenants thereunto belonging.

CHRIS KACHIROUBAS, CLERK OF THE 18TH JUDICIAL CIRCUIT COURT ©
WHEATON, ILLINOIS 60189-0707

American LegalNet, Inc. www.USCourtForms.com

PUBLICATION NOTICE FOR JUDICIAL SALE   3229.4-2 Rev. (02/04)

WITNESS: **CHRIS KACHIROUBAS,** Clerk of the Eighteenth
                                   Judicial Circuit Court, and the seal thereof, at
                                   Wheaton, Illinois.

                                   _____

                                   _____
                                            Clerk of the Circuit Court

Name:_____ ☐ PRO SE

DuPage Attorney Number: _____

Attorney for:_____

Address:_____

City/State/Zip:_____

Telephone: _____

Published in _____ on _____

NOTICE TO NEWSPAPER
The following notice must be published in the same issues as the above legal notice
in the section of the newspaper that contains Real Estate Listings.

NOTICE OF PUBLIC AUCTION OF REAL ESTATE

Case No._____

On _____ 20__ certain real estate commonly known as

Street Address: _____

_____

will be sold at public auction to the highest bidder for cash:

The property consists of _____

_____

_____

_____

_____

CONTACT: _____ at _____

Formal Notice of this Judicial Sale of Real Estate will be found in the Legal Notices section of this newspaper
with the above case number.

NOTICE OF SALE WORKSHEET (JUDICIAL FORECLOSURE)

DID THE NOTICE OF SALE INCLUDE

Date of sale?   ☐ No   ☐ Yes   Date:

Time of sale?   ☐ No   ☐ Yes   Time:

Specific location of sale?   ☐ No   ☐ Yes   Location:

Correct legal description of the property,
including the street address?   ☐ No   ☐ Yes

Correct name and address of lender?   ☐ No   ☐ Yes

SERVICE AND MAILING REQUIREMENTS

How many days was the Notice of Sale mailed
to you by first-class mail before the scheduled
sale date?   ☐ No   ☐ Yes   When?

Was the Notice of Sale personally served on you?   ☐ No   ☐ Yes   When?

Was the Notice of Sale mailed by first-class
mail to everyone entitled to receive notice
(including tenants and junior lienholders)?   ☐ No   ☐ Yes   When?

PUBLICATION REQUIREMENTS

Was the Notice of Sale published once a week
over several weeks before the sale date?   ☐ No   ☐ Yes   1st Date:
                                           ☐ No   ☐ Yes   2nd Date:
                      ☐ No   ☐ Yes   3rd Date:

Was the Notice of Sale published in a newspaper
in the county where your property is located?   ☐ No   ☐ Yes

POSTING REQUIREMENTS

Was Notice of Sale posted in a public place?   ☐ No   ☐ Yes   Where?

Was the Notice of Sale posted on your front
door or another conspicuous place?   ☐ No   ☐ Yes   Where?

May 22, 200X

Sheriff of the County
Civil Division
23 State Street
Baltimore, Maryland

Re: Case No. 23456

Sheriff's File No. 612

Dear Sheriff:

Your office is conducting a judicial foreclosure of my property, located at 56 Grande Drive in the city of Baltimore.

You issued and recorded a Notice of Sale on May 15, 200X. However, the Notice of Sale was defective because you did not wait the required number of days.

As a result, I respectfully request that you immediately cancel the pending foreclosure sale and issue a new Notice of Sale. If you refuse and proceed with an illegal sale, I will have no alternative but to file a motion in Court to enjoin the foreclosure sale. In that event, you may be held liable for punitive damages for ignoring my request.

Please advise me immediately in writing of your response.

Very truly yours,

John Freidman

cc: First Credit Union

b. Notice of Sale Worksheet

The accompanying Notice of Sale Worksheet will help you determine if the sheriff has made any mistakes in issuing a Notice of Sale. Fill in the worksheet with information from your mortgage,

judgment, and Notice of Sale, and compare the information to your state's procedures in the back of the book.

c. What to Do If Notice Was Not Properly Given

Sheriffs have been known to make mistakes, so it is wise to closely monitor the sheriffs activities. You may have grounds to stop the foreclosure sale and force the sheriff to start the procedures all over again if he doesn't comply with the notice rules described in Section D2, above.

If the sheriff makes a mistake, immediately write him a letter, such as the sample below. Send it by certified or registered mail, with a copy to your lender.) Demand that the sale either be postponed or rescheduled using proper procedures. If the sheriff ignores your request, you may file a motion in court to enjoin (stop) the foreclosure. (See Chapter 12 for information on hiring a lawyer or doing your own legal research.)

10. Foreclosure Sale

The next step in the judicial foreclosure process is the actual foreclosure sale. If you can't pay off your loan by the date scheduled for the foreclosure sale, the sheriff will conduct a public auction of your property. Depending on your state, the sale will typically be conducted on a weekday between the hours of 9 a.m. and 5 p.m. The sale normally will be conducted in front of the county courthouse or another government building in the county where your property is located.

a. Attend the Foreclosure Sale

It might cross your mind to avoid the public auction as a way of avoiding embarrassment and preserving your dignity. But if you are reading this book, you already appreciate that you have other priorities at this juncture-- namely, to stop the foreclosure if at all possible.

There is always the possibility that the sheriff may conduct the auction improperly or something else may occur to invalidate the sale. For this reason, you should attend the sale and observe the procedures closely. Follow the descriptions below to see if the sheriff violates any of the procedural rules. You need to be an eagle-eyed observer. If possible, take a friend along to help you keep track of the sale and give you moral support. Take detailed notes of everything that occurs. At some later point, you may need a good record of events during the sale if you wish to challenge the sale in court. (See Chapter 8.)

b. The Bidding Process

Because the sheriff will advertise the sale, and the Notice of Sale is recorded and posted, there should be plenty of potential buyers present. (See Chapter 3, Section G, for what to watch out for at a foreclosure sale.)

Anyone but the sheriff may bid at the foreclosure sale, including you, your lender and any junior lienholders. With the exception of the foreclosing lender, all bids must be backed by cash or cashier's checks for a portion of the bid.

The sheriff will start the auction by inviting your lender to make the opening bid. Your lender is in a unique position at the sale, because it can give the sheriff a copy of the court judgment and receive a credit up to the amount of the judgment.

Example: Malik defaulted on a loan secured by an apartment building in Atlanta, Georgia. Guardian Savings Bank, which holds the first mortgage, obtained a $385,000 judgment for foreclosure. Accordingly, at the foreclosure sale, a representative of Guardian Savings credit bids $385,000.

The sheriff then invites higher bids from those assembled. If no one else bids, your lender becomes the owner of the property. If the sheriff receives higher bids, each bid constitutes an irrevocable offer to purchase your property at a specific price, and automatically cancels the previous high bid. When the bidding is exhausted, the highest bidder is the new owner of your property.

c. Sheriff Finalizes Sale and Distributes Proceeds

Within a week after the foreclosure sale is completed, the sheriff will distribute the proceeds as directed by the court judgment. The costs of sale, including the sheriff's fees, will be paid first. Next, your lender will be repaid up to the amount of its judgment. If there is any surplus--and there seldom is--it will go to any junior lienholders. The remainder, if any (don't hold your breath), will be paid to you.

If your lender sought a deficiency judgment, the sheriff will give the purchaser a Certificate of Sale document. The Certificate of Sale states that the property was sold subject to your right to repurchase (redeem) it by paying the foreclosure sales price.

(See Section B12 below on post-sale redemption rights.)

In the event that your lender did not ask for a deficiency judgment, the sheriff will give the purchaser a Deed of Sale or Sheriff's Deed. This document contains the title of the court in which the judgment was entered, date of the entry of judgment, name and address of the foreclosing lender, your last known address, a description of your property and the date of sale. At this point, you can no longer redeem the property.

d. What Happens to Liens After the Foreclosure Sale

All liens that are junior (recorded subsequent) to the foreclosing lender's mortgage, such as a second mortgage, mechanic's liens, abstract of judgment, writs of attachment, or similar liens, are extinguished by the foreclosure sale. However, property tax liens will continue to encumber the property (regardless of when they were recorded) unless they were paid off at the foreclosure sale.

Although junior liens may disappear, the underlying debts remain intact. In other words, those "wiped out" junior lienholders now are required to sue you directly to recover their debt.

Further, creditors holding mechanic's liens, tax liens, writs of attachments or judgment liens have the right to record those liens on other property you own or later buy.

11. Deficiency Judgment

Not all lenders seek deficiency judgments. If your lender's complaint did not seek

a deficiency judgment against you, or subsequently waived it, you can skip this section and go to Section B12 below.

Your lender won't recover the full amount of your unpaid debt from the foreclosure sale if your property sells for less than the unpaid balance of your mortgage, plus costs and attorney fees. This shortage is called a "deficiency." A court-ordered deficiency judgment entered against you for this shortage allows your lender to recoup its loss. (Of course, if your property sells for more than the amount of your lender's judgment, you won't be liable for a deficiency, and may even receive some of those sale proceeds.)

To obtain a deficiency judgment, your lender must request it in the original Complaint and file an application for a deficiency judgment with the Court (that conducted the foreclosure trial) within a specific time period (depending on your state) after the foreclosure sale. Your lender must mail you a copy of the application. If your lender doesn't file an application on time, they may lose the right to get a deficiency judgment.

a. "Fair Value" Hearing

If you believe your property was sold for fair value, skip this section and proceed to Subsection b, below.

Let's say you believe that your property sold for substantially less than its current market value. In response to your lender's application for deficiency judgment, you have the right in most states to petition the court to conduct a hearing to determine the market value

of your property. This hearing is called a "fair value hearing."

The sole function of the hearing will be for the judge to determine the fair market value of your property on the date of the foreclosure sale. The judge will also determine whether your indebtedness (plus interest and costs of the levy and sale) exceeds the fair value of your property.

To prepare for this hearing, you should hire an appraiser to testify as to the market value of your property as of the date of the foreclosure sale. The appraiser will take about one to two weeks to appraise your property and charge anywhere from $250 to $1,000, depending on the value and size of the property.

The hearing will probably be conducted in front of the same judge who conducted the foreclosure trial, and should last approximately one to two hours. A representative of your lender will be present, and you should also attend, although it is unlikely that you will be required to testify. After listening to the appraisers you and your lender bring to court, the judge will decide the fair market value of your property on the date of the foreclosure sale.

After the fair market value of your property has been determined, the judge will enter its ruling. If the court determines that the fair market value of your property was greater than the price obtained at the foreclosure sale, it will adjust the deficiency judgment accordingly.

ANTI-DEFICIENCY LAWS: AN HISTORICAL PERSPECTIVE

During the depression of the 1930s, homeowners all across America suffered foreclosures in record numbers. To make matters worse, home prices spiraled downward, which meant that foreclosure sales inevitably brought prices less than the amount of the debt. Consequently, it became routine for defaulting homeowners first to lose their homes--bad enough in any economic context--and then find themselves liable for the deficiency.

Confronted with the economic ruin of millions of homeowners, lawmakers in several states passed legislation that severely restricts a lender's right to collect a deficiency judgment {"anti-deficiency legislation"). Today, only a minority of states continue to protect homeowners with anti-deficiency legislation.

Example: First Savings Bank forecloses Norma's property in Kansas City, Missouri, on which she owes $290,000, plus a total of $10,000 in foreclosure costs and attorney *fees. The property has a current market value of approximately $250,000 but sells for only $200,000 at the foreclosure sale. First Savings files an application with the court requesting a deficiency judgment against Norma for $100,000 ($300,000-$200,000). Norma objects and requests a fair value hearing. At the hearing, Norma presents an appraiser who testifies that the property had a value of $250,000, and First Savings presents an appraiser who testifies that the property had a value of only $225,000. The judge analyzes both appraisals, and finally agrees with Norma's appraiser. Accordingly, the judge reduces the deficiency judgment from $100,000 to $50,000 ($300,000-$250,000).*

b. Court Issues Deficiency Judgment

The deficiency judgment will consist of your unpaid debt, plus interest and costs, minus the fair value of the property (as determined at the hearing). It will also state that the amount of the deficiency-exclusive of interest and costs--may not exceed the difference between the entire amount of your indebtedness and the foreclosure sale price. The deficiency judgment will be issued by the Court that heard your case.

Once you receive the deficiency judgment, there is nothing more you can do--except, of course, pay the judgment if you can. If you cannot pay, your lender will be permitted to pursue all the various collection procedures allowed under state law, including wage garnishments, bank attachments, and seizing any of your valuable property. Remember, you always have the right to negotiate with your lender for a reduced lump-sum payment, or a payment

schedule, in full settlement. In addition, there are ways to prevent a creditor from seizing your assets. (See Chapter 5 on negotiating with your lender and Chapter 9 for more on bankruptcy options.)

For information on your rights and options as a judgment debtor, refer to *Money Troubles: Legal Strategies to Cope with Your Debts,* by Robin Leonard (Nolo Press). For the creditor's perspective, see *Collect Your Court Judgment,* by Gini Scott, Stephen Elias and Lisa Goldoftas (Nolo Press).

12. Post-Sale Redemption Period

After the foreclosure sale, the sheriff in most states will give you a Notice of the Right to Redemption. The notice states that you have the right to redeem your property by paying the full foreclosure sales price plus the sheriff's costs and expenses. (See the sidebar on the next page, *"How Much Will It Cost to Redeem Your Property?"* for details.) Only you, as the former owner of the property, may redeem after the foreclosure sale. Junior lienholders, guarantors, and tenants cannot redeem your property.

If you redeem your property by paying the redemption price, ownership of the property will be restored to you, with all junior liens wiped out. Ironically, even if you redeem your property, your lender may still have a deficiency judgment against you. In that event, you will find yourself in the precarious position of once again owning your property while simultaneously owing your lender.

Example: Jaimie's lender sells his property for $323,000 at a foreclosure sale and gets a deficiency judgment for $120,000 for the unpaid amount of his loan plus costs of the sale. Jaimie redeems the property for $328,000 (which includes costs incurred by the purchaser plus interest). Jaimie's lender still has a judgment against him for $120,000, and can pursue collection methods to get paid, including selling his property. And here we go again!

In most states, the only way your lender can block your redemption rights is to waive its deficiency claim against you before the foreclosure judgment is ordered by the judge.

How long you have to redeem your property depends on the sales price at the foreclosure sale or the price determined at the fair value hearing (if higher), and state law:

- If the sale did not bring in enough to satisfy the indebtedness (including interest and costs), there is a deficiency. If your lender seeks to recover this deficiency, you typically have one year from the date of sale to redeem. (Please refer to your state's time period in the back of this book.)
- If the sale proceeds satisfied your total indebtedness (including interest and costs), you typically have several months from the date of sale to redeem. (Please refer to your state's time period in the back of this book.)

You will not receive reminders of the redemption deadlines. You are expected to know the expiration date of your state's redemption period on your own.

Example: John loses his Baton Rouge, Louisiana property in a foreclosure sale, where a purchaser pays $250,000 for the property. A month later, John receives a hefty inheritance from his grandfather and decides to redeem the property. The sheriff gives John these figures:

Purchase price:	$250,000
Property taxes paid:	7,633
Fire and casualty insurance:	2,500
Property repairs and maintenance:	1,745
Interest on the above amount:	2,182
Subtotal:	$264,060
Minus rents purchaser received:	12,000
Total:	$252,060

HOW MUCH WILL IT COST TO REDEEM YOUR PROPERTY

To redeem your property, you pay the sheriff a total of the following, minus any rents and profits the purchaser received during the redemption period:

- the purchase price at the foreclosure sale (not necessarily the fair market value of your property)
- any assessments or taxes due
- reasonable amounts for fire insurance, maintenance, upkeep, repair or improvements on your property incurred by the purchaser during the redemption period
- any amounts the purchaser paid to senior lienholders during the redemption period, and
- interest on all amounts specified above from the date paid until the dare you deposit the redemption price with the sheriff.

a. You Retain Possession of Property During the Redemption Period

It may be hard to believe, but during the redemption period, you are permitted to retain possession of your property. That means you can live there or rent it out as you wish. During this period, however, the purchaser is entitled to receive:

- the fair rental value of your use and occupancy of the property if you live there, or

- any rents from your property, if you have tenants.

If you fail to pay either of these items, the purchaser has the right to go to court and file an action to recover this lost income.

b. Certificate of Redemption

Once you have deposited the required amount to redeem your property, the sheriff will turn over the funds to the purchaser of your property (who is not necessarily your lender). The purchaser must accept the money and must give up ownership (and possession, if applicable) of your property.

In most states, the sheriff will then cancel the previously issued Certificate of Sale, issue a Certificate of Redemption, record the Certificate in the county recorder's office, and send you a certified copy by registered mail within several days. Once this Certificate is recorded, you will once again legally own your property.

What if the purchaser refuses to accept payment? If the sheriff notifies you that the purchaser disputes the amount needed to redeem your property, you can file a motion asking the court to resolve the redemption price. Usually, within several weeks of receiving your motion, the court will schedule a hearing to resolve the monetary dispute. Prior to the hearing, you'll need to deposit the undisputed portion of the redemption price with the sheriff or the court. At the hearing, each side will be required to present evidence to the judge as to what the redemption price should be. The judge will then determine the correct amount required to redeem the property.

c. After the Redemption Period Expires

If you don't redeem your property before the redemption period expires, the sheriff will record a Sheriff's Deed conveying title of your property to the purchaser at the foreclosure sale. The sheriff will deliver the deed directly to the purchaser. You will not receive a copy.

At this point, you (or your tenants) must vacate the property unless the purchaser allows you to stay. If you are interested in staying, you must contact the purchaser directly and negotiate an extended rental of the property. If you (or your tenants) don't leave when asked, the purchaser may serve you with a Notice to Quit. If you still refuse to move voluntarily, the purchaser will then file an unlawful detainer action (eviction) and evict you.

Chapter

5

<u>NEGOTIATING WITH YOUR LENDER</u>

A. Negotiating Strategies 112

    1. Act Immediately 112

    2. Respond to All Calls, Letters, and Emails 112

    3. Make Sure You Are Dealing With Your Current Lender 113

    4. Negotiate in a Spirit of Cooperation 113

    5. Talk Your Lender's Language, Not Yours 113

    6. Explain Reasons for the Non-Payment 114

    7. Know the Facts 114

    8. Don't Make Promises You Can't Keep 114

    9. Remind Your Lender of Its Foreclosure Costs 114

    10. Consider Working With a Foreclosure Consultant 115

    11. Learn About Your Lender 115

B. Negotiating With an Institutional Lender 115

    1. Goals of an Institutional Lender 115

    2. Contact Your Lender 116

    3. Main Issues in a Workout 117

    4. Submit a Written Version of Your Workout Proposal 119

    5. Getting Help From Your Private Mortgage Insurer 119

C. Negotiating With a Private Lender 121

D. Negotiating With HUD and the FHA 122

    1. Will You Qualify for the HUD Program? 123

    2. Overview of HUD Assignment Program 123

E. Negotiating With the U.S. Department of Veteran Affairs 126

    1. VA Servicing Procedures 126

    2. VA In-House Financial Counseling 128

    3. Delinquency Classifications 129

    4. Overview of VA Foreclosure Avoidance Program 129

Most people don't realize that one of the most effective ways to stop a foreclosure is to negotiate a solution directly with the foreclosing lender. Most lenders would prefer if you simply bring your loan current rather than having to foreclose. After all, they're in the business of loaning money, not owning properties. Only if you fail to work out a resolution of the default will your lender be forced to foreclose.

Your first course of action should always be to negotiate with your lender. You may be pleasantly surprised by the results. Property owners often miss this obvious starting point because they are intimidated by lenders or embarrassed by their predicament. This chapter is designed to take the mystery and fear out of contacting and negotiating with your lender.

⚠️

If your finances are still in shambles. Do not proceed with this chapter or negotiate with your lender unless you have your financial problems under control, have the ability to bring your loan current, and resume your monthly payments. If, after a realistic look at your situation, you conclude that you cannot afford the monthly payments, consider the other strategies described in this book, introduced in Chapter 1.

A. Negotiating Strategies

Good communication is the underlying basis of any successful negotiation. Unless you communicate directly with your lender and understand your lender's goals and priorities, you will have little chance of stopping foreclosure. To prepare for negotiations with your lender, consider the suggestions below.

1. Act Immediately

You may think that waiting to the last minute will buy you some extra time. You couldn't be more wrong. If you are interested in negotiating with your lender, don't wait! Lenders rarely cooperate with borrowers who contact them on the eve of a foreclosure sale.

Establish a dialogue as soon as possible. If the lender's office is local, request a face-to-face meeting with a representative of your lender at his or her earliest convenience. If the lender's office is out of town, you will have to do your negotiating by telephone, email, or correspondence.

Either way, be prepared to discuss specific proposals for restructuring your loan or bringing the arrears current ("workout"). It is your responsibility-not your lender's--to propose a manageable solution. If possible, bring several different proposals in writing to the meeting.

2. Respond to All Calls, Letters, and Emails

Respond to every communication you receive from your lender. Even if you have nothing to say, at least confirm in writing their calls or receipt of their letters. Further, request a meeting as soon as possible, and reiterate your determination to resolve the loan default.

Create a log that chronicles all telephone conversations, letters, and emails. Include the date, time, who you spoke to, what was discussed, and anything else noteworthy about the call or letter. (See the Communications Chart in Chapter 1, Section A.)

Resources on negotiating. Several books on negotiating may be helpful in your discussions with your lender, including *Getting to Yes: Negotiating Agreements Without Giving In*, by Roger Fisher and William Ury (Penguin Books), *Getting Past No: Negotiating Your Way from Confrontation to Cooperation*, by William Ury (Bantam Books) and the "Bible" on this subject, *You Can Negotiate Anything*, by Herb Cohen (Citadel Press).

3. Make Sure You Are Dealing With Your Current Lender

Although you may be receiving monthly statements, letters, and telephone calls from a certain company, they may not actually own your loan. The company may be acting merely as the loan "servicer"--a company (occasionally your former lender, if they sold the loan) that receives a fee for administering loans. A loan servicer may not be as willing to avoid a foreclosure as your current lender because the money is not theirs. They are only responsible for collecting the monthly payments. In contrast, the actual lender may be more accommodating as to how and when they will be paid back. So, it behooves you to go around the servicer and contact your current lender as soon as possible.

There are several ways to get the name of your current lender:

- call the institution that loaned you money and simply ask
- look at your billing statement and see if another name appears in addition to the name of your original lender
- contact the customer service department of a local title insurance company, or
- go to the county recorder's office and find out if an assignment of your mortgage or deed of trust has been recorded, and to whom.

Once you determine the name and address of your current lender, contact their loan workout or foreclosure department.

4. Negotiate in a Spirit of Cooperation

This is no time to be belligerent. Remember, your property is in, or soon may be in, foreclosure and your lender is already dubious that you are serious about paying your loan. Express your willingness to cooperate and your commitment to curing the default.

5. Talk Your Lender's Language, Not Yours

Obviously, you are preoccupied with stopping the foreclosure. But this is not your lender's primary concern. From the lender's viewpoint, foreclosure is an effective method to catch your undivided attention. It is their way to see that a delinquent loan is quickly brought current and monthly payments resume.

Accordingly, do not demand that the foreclosure be stopped. Rather, focus on solving your lender's problem first. Your lender may eventually agree to stop the foreclosure, but only after they are assured that you have the ability and intention to bring your loan current and resume making monthly payments.

6. Explain Reasons for the Non-Payment

Do not shy away from this issue. Anticipate your lender's inquiry and be prepared to concisely explain why you failed to make your loan payments. Regardless of whether the reason was a divorce, illness, death in the family, loss of job, business reversal, or other financial problem, be prepared to assure your lender that the cause of the default is being (or has been) resolved. Generally, a lender will need to feel comfortable that your problems are behind you before they will work out a solution to the defaulted loan.

7. Know the Facts

Do you know the date you took out your loan? How about the date you made your last payment? If a nonjudicial foreclosure, when was the Notice of Default recorded? If a judicial foreclosure, when the complaint was filed? When was the last date someone called from your lender's office regarding your loan?

All of these facts, and many more, are extremely relevant to the negotiations. Take the time to organize your documents (we give suggestions in Chapter 1, Section B), and write down the relevant facts about your property, loan, the amount of the default, the pending foreclosure, and any communications with your lender. Use the Notice of Default Worksheet in Chapter 3 if yours is a nonjudicial

foreclosure, or the Judicial Foreclosure Worksheet in Chapter 4 if it is a judicial foreclosure, to set up a chronology of events.

8. Don't Make Promises You Can't Keep

The worst thing you can do while negotiating with your lender is to make an unrealistic promise. Your credibility is already in question because you failed to make your payments as promised. As a result, your lender has gone to the trouble of starting foreclosure proceedings. Now that your lender has your undivided attention, do not offer or agree to a settlement you cannot adhere to. The temptation may be great and your intentions may be noble, but do not be seduced by the pressure. Only agree to what you can really afford.

You also need to appreciate the financial impact of your promises. You may end up with higher monthly payments or a balloon payment. In that event, if you temporarily stop the foreclosure, the actual dollars-and-cents impact to your pocketbook may be more disastrous in future years.

9. Remind Your Lender of Its Foreclosure Costs

You already know that it will cost you money if you lose your property in foreclosure. But did you realize that your lender would also lose money if they foreclose? For example, if your lender completes the foreclosure, they stand to lose back payments, foreclosure costs, wear and tear while you occupy the property, damage to the property when you (or your tenants) leave, loss of future payments until the property is sold, and marketing costs to resell the property. Don't forget to mention these costs when you talk with your lender. Your lenders may need to be frequently reminded that these costs can be avoided if they will negotiate a resolution of the default with you.

10. Consider Working With a Foreclosure Consultant

At some stage during the foreclosure process, you may be contacted by foreclosure consultants eager to help you resolve your foreclosure or negotiate with your lender. If you are considering working with a foreclosure consultant, read Chapter 12, Section B.

11. Learn About Your Lender

The approach you use to negotiate should depend on which kind of lender has instituted the foreclosure. Because different lenders have different criteria for resolving loans in foreclosure, your approach should depend on whom you are dealing with. You need to read only the section of this chapter that is geared to your particular lender:

- institutional lenders (Section B)

- private lenders (Section C)

- U.S. Department of Housing and Urban Development (HUD) (Section D)

- U.S. Department of Veteran Affairs (Section E)

B. Negotiating With an Institutional Lender

Banks, savings banks, credit unions, mortgage companies and pension funds are all "institutional lenders." An institutional lender is governed by state and federal regulations and recycles their loans on the secondary market. For purposes of this book, this category also includes secondary market investment groups, including the Federal National Mortgage Association ("FNMA" or as they are more commonly known "Fannie Mae"), the Federal Home Loan Mortgage Corporation ("FHLMC" or as they are more commonly known "Freddie Mac"), and the Government National Mortgage Association ("GNMA" or as they are more commonly known "Ginnie Mae").

1. Goals of an Institutional Lender

Before negotiating with an institutional lender, you should understand what they need to achieve. The goals of an institutional lender are twofold:

- To receive a steady cash flow. If your lender can count on you and their other borrowers to make regular loan payments, cash flow is steady. But when cash flow is interrupted, your lender is not getting the money they need to pay expenses. Usually, lenders maintain a delicate balance between cash flow and expenses. When expenses exceed cash flow, the institutional lender loses money and endangers its own continuing existence.

- To avoid a loss. Your lender wants to avoid a loss on their balance sheet.

A loss does not, however, come about by foreclosing. When your lender forecloses, it simply performs a bookkeeping entry. Instead of a mortgage or deed of trust owned as an asset, your lender's books will now show a property owned (known as "Real Estate Owned" or more commonly as "REO"). In both cases, this is an asset. A loss would show up on your lender's books only if the property sells for less than the balance of your loan.

Remember that if your lender ends up taking your property back, there will be additional costs (repairs, marketing costs, legal fees, escrow or closing charges, title insurance and the like). If your property's sale price won't cover the outstanding loan balance and these additional costs, your lender will suffer a loss. This explains why a lender should be highly motivated to resolve your defaulted loan.

2. Contact Your Lender

Call your lender and ask to speak to an officer in charge of your loan. Politely refuse to deal with the collection department or someone who calls you to find out why you haven't made your payments. They don't have the authority to negotiate with you. You dealt with an officer when you obtained the loan--surely you deserve the same respect when you are resolving the repayment of that loan.

How to track down a person with authority to solve your problem. Call the main office of your lender and ask for the name of the branch manager or supervisor. Then

hang up. Call back a while later and ask for that specific person by name. Once you are connected, request an appointment. If this person will not take your call (or does not call you back), send a letter chronicling these events and repeat your request for a meeting. Mail a copy of the letter to the president of your lender. Sooner or later, someone with authority will most certainly return your call!

Once you reach a manager, or someone else who has the authority to negotiate with you, request an appointment if they have a local office. An actual meeting will exponentially increase the odds of reaching an agreement. During the meeting, you'll need to convey that your default is a temporary problem and emphasize that you want to avoid foreclosure. You should also update your lender on the condition of your property. If there are problems, be sure to let your lender know. On the other hand, if you have made improvements and repairs, point them out also.

Ask your lender to explain the foreclosure process. Gently coach your lender into explaining what happens to REO ("real estate owned") properties your lender takes back in foreclosure. Ask if your lender has a large inventory of REO's or needs more. Initially, the manager may he reluctant to discuss these issues, but as he or she sees that you understand the ramifications of foreclosure (from your lender's perspective), the manager may be more willing to talk. These discussions are important because they may reveal how eager--or reluctant--your lender is to take your property back in foreclosure. Especially if the manager admits that they don't want another REO on their hands, you can proceed with concretely discussing alternatives.

Propose possible solutions, such as restructuring the loan, additional moratorium on payments, forbearance, or refinancing. As your lender considers various options, you will learn exactly how flexible they are towards solving your problem. Keep in mind that the options are as varied as the terms of your loan. For example, a restructuring of your loan could involve a modification of principal, interest, term and/or payment. The variations are limited only by the creativity and negotiating skills of you and your lender.

If you're unlucky and confront a recalcitrant supervisor who's set on taking your property back regardless of the outcome, your job is more difficult. Be prepared to discuss aspects of the foreclosure procedures that may have been conducted improperly (see Chapter 3 or 4). This should certainly grab his attention.

If all else fails, and your lender isn't budging, you may want to mention bankruptcy. Bankruptcy automatically stays (stops) all foreclosure activity, causing your property to be tied up for months or even years. During that period, your lender may not receive payments, would incur attorney fees and most importantly, lose time. Of course, your lender already knows these possibilities. What's important is that now your lender knows that you know them too!

After discussing the foreclosure procedural defects and/or bankruptcy, your lender may have a change of heart. During this stage in the meeting, it is important for you to remain calm and cordial. Don't be rude or make threats,

no matter how uncooperative your lender is. Be professional and eager to find a solution. Emphasize that you don't want to file bankruptcy, but unless you can work out an amicable solution to the foreclosure, you may be left with no other alternative.

3. Main Issues in a Workout

If your lender is willing to consider a workout (an arrangement to bring your loan current and stop the foreclosure), there are generally two main issues that must be addressed separately:

- past due payments (arrears), and

- future payments.

Your circumstances will dictate your approach. For example, you may be able to bring your loan current, but be unable to make future payments as they come due. On the other hand, you may be ready to resume monthly payments, but need time to bring the arrears current. Following are some guidelines on these two topics of negotiation.

a. Workouts for Future Monthly Payments

In general, lenders are more concerned that monthly payments resume immediately than how the arrearage is going to be paid. If, however, you can't resume your monthly payments in full, there are two alternatives:

- Delay making payments for a period of months (forbearance). As part of an overall loan workout, lenders will typically allow you to skip your monthly payments for three to six months, provided you have reasonable justification. You repay this amount over a period of months in addition to your regular payments.

Example: George owns a 4-unit apartment building in a small college town. Renters are hard to come by in the summer, and he misses several loan payments. His bank threatens foreclosure. George immediately contacts the bank, explains his financial situation, and negotiates a workout. The bank agrees that George can forebear from making payments for four more months. He then must repay the total arrears over 18 months while simultaneously resuming his monthly payments.

- Make reduced payments for a set time. Offer to make partial payments for several months until you are back on your feet. Typically, lenders will accept partial payments for six months to one year, provided you have an explanation for the missed payments, a reason for the partial payments, and a prognosis for when full payments can resume.

Example: Arthur owns a cattle ranch outside Topeka, Kansas. Rumors of a disease at his ranch have a devastating effect on business. While Arthur is successfully countering the negative PR (started by a competitor), he doesn't have enough funds to make his regular loan payments, and Southern Savings Bank starts foreclosure proceedings. Arthur immediately contacts Southern and negotiates a resolution of the defaulted loan. Because he cannot afford to resume payments, Arthur suggests that he make one-third payments for three months and then half payments for three more months. Beginning with the seventh month, Arthur will resume the monthly payments in

full. At the end of one year, Arthur will pay the balance of the arrears over 12 months. Southern agrees to the workout and stops the foreclosure.

b. Workouts for the Arrears

If you can't afford to pay the arrears (past due payments) all at once, you have three basic options, with endless variations:

- Add arrears to the principal loan balance and resume regular scheduled payments. Your loan will immediately return to current status, the principal balance will increase (by the amount of your arrears), and your monthly payment will increase minimally. Unfortunately, strict banking regulations make this option exceedingly difficult for some lenders. Nevertheless, it is worth proposing because it is the most effective workout for the financially strapped borrower.

Example: Henry and Susan run into financial problems and miss four monthly mortgage payments. After several meetings with an officer at their bank, they successfully negotiate a workout of their default. The bank agrees to stop the foreclosure and add the default amount ($6,000) to the loan balance ($350,000), provided Henry and Susan immediately resume making the monthly payments. Henry and Susan's monthly payments increase from $2,500 to $2,800 per month.

- Make partial payments until arrears are paid. Financial institutions will often agree to let you resume your regular monthly payments and pay a portion of the arrears over the course of six months to a year.

Example: John and Sally operate a small bed-and-breakfast in Santa Fe, New Mexico.

John has a serious injury and runs up a mountain of credit card bills. They miss four monthly payments of $1,425 on their home loan. They work out an arrangement with their bank to make six equal monthly payments of $950 plus their regular monthly payment of $1,425 until their loan is brought current. After paying $2,375 for six months, their payments will return to $1,425 per month.

- Make a balloon payment at a later date. You may agree to pay the arrears in total in one payment on a specific date. However, do not commit to this arrangement unless you believe you will be able to pay the balloon payment when it comes due.

  Example: Adriana owns a farm outside of Des Monies, Iowa. Times have been rough, and she's missed five loan payments ($6,250). Now she has a new crew working for her and a bumper crop on the way. Adriana convinces her bank that although she doesn't have the full $6,250 now, she will have it within six months. Her bank reviews her financial records, checks the farmer's almanac, and finally agrees to accept $6,250 within six months--provided that Adriana resumes her regular monthly payments immediately.

4. Submit a Written Version of Your Workout Proposal

Once you and your lender negotiate a resolution of your defaulted loan, you should sign a written agreement, commonly known as a "workout," "standstill" or "forbearance agreement." It behooves you to take the initiative to get your agreement in writing, which can be done by letter or email, such as the sample on the next page. If your lender submits an agreement, consider having an attorney review it to be sure it conforms with your understanding of the workout.

5. Getting Help From Your Private Mortgage Insurer

➡️ *If you don't have private mortgage insurance.* If your loan is not insured by a private mortgage insurer (check your loan coupons or ask your lender), skip this section.

Private mortgage insurance is required by institutional lenders (and paid by the borrower) whenever the loan is greater than 80% of the property's value. The purpose of the insurance is to insure a lender's loss in the event of foreclosure. Because most defaults occur early on, the private mortgage insurance ("PMI") typically insures only the first five years of a loan against default.

If your lender forecloses, the PMI must pay out a claim to your lender up to the limits of its coverage. To avert this potential liability, the PMI may want to

Without a signed agreement, you don't have a deal. Simply sending a letter or email to your lender doesn't count for anything unless it is signed and returned to you. Some lenders will respond by sending their own workout agreement.

SAMPLE WORKOUT LETTER:

April 17, 200X

Fourway National Bank
2700 Fourth Street
Columbia, South Carolina

Re: 1256 Magnolia Street
Columbia, South Carolina
Loan No.: 1 2345

Dear Mr. Plimpton:

As you know, your bank holds a mortgage encumbering my property as security for a loan in the amount of $335,000. Your bank initiated a judicial foreclosure after I missed three payments. On April 16, 200X, the bank agreed to stop the pending foreclosure, provided I make payments as follows:

DUE DATE:	AMOUNT:	FOR THE MONTH:
Aug 1, 200X	$600	50% of Jan, 200X pmt
Sep 1, 200X	$600	50% of Jan, 200X pmt
Oct 1, 200X	$600	50% of Feb, 200X pmt
Nov 1, 200X	$600	50% of Feb, 200X pmt
Dec 1, 200X	$600	50% of Mar, 200X pmt
Jan 1, 200X	$600	50% of Mar, 200X pmt
Feb 1, 200X	$600	50% of Apr, 200X pmt
Mar 1, 200X	$600	50% of Apr, 200X pmt
Apr 1, 200X	$600	50% of May, 200X pmt
May 1, 200X	$600	50% of May, 200X pmt
Jun 1, 200X	$600	50% of Jun, 200X pmt
Jul 1, 200X	$600	50% of Jun, 200X pmt
Aug 1, 200X	$600	50% of Jul, 200X pmt
Sep 1, 200X	$600	50% of Jul, 200X pmt

I understand that these payments are in addition to my monthly $1,200 payment, which will resume on August 1, 200X. Once all of the above payments are paid, the Bank has agreed to rescind the foreclosure.

If this letter accurately reflects our agreement, please sign in the space provided below and return a copy of this letter to me.

Sincerely,

Bill Smith

AGREED AND ACCEPTED TO:

_____
Authorized Officer on behalf
of Fourth National Bank

participate in workout negotiations to minimize its losses. A PMI won't necessarily hear about a foreclosure until a property has been sold and the lender makes a claim. You may need to alert the PMI to the pending foreclosure and your efforts to work out a resolution with your lender.

Only get the PMI involved if negotiations with your institutional lender are stalled--but don't wait too long in the foreclosure process. If you come to an impasse with your lender, write a letter to the PMI, request its assistance and ask to meet in person as soon as possible. At the meeting, explain your financial situation and your plans for resolving your defaulted loan, and request help in dealing with your lender.

If you and your lender have reached a deadlock, the PMI may be able to jump-start stalled negotiations. The PMI may have more influence and leverage with your lender than you. If you have no success in dealing with a stubborn lender, the PMI may come to the rescue, if you ask, After all, the PMI has nothing to lose and everything to gain!

As an alternative, you may request that the PMI help you out of foreclosure by fronting a portion of your delinquent payments for several months. You may wonder why a PMI would cover any portion of your arrearage. If your lender forecloses, the PMI will likely have to pay a claim to your lender. It may be more economical for the PMI to assist you now by covering your arrears than to pay a claim to your lender later. In return, you'll agree to reimburse the PMI.

But convincing a PMI that it makes good business sense to pay some of your delinquent payments (rather then the lender's eventual claim) is not usually an easy task. You will need to show that:

- you can afford to resume monthly payments to your lender immediately, and

- you will be able to reimburse the PMI for its advances within a reasonable period of time, usually a period of months.

C. Negotiating With a Private Lender

Private lenders are typically concerned with retirement income, taxes, or ways to defer income. Spend some time talking with your lender to get a handle on his/her financial objectives. You cannot be creative about a financial solution that benefits both of you until you understand your lender's fears and goals.

On the other hand, if your private lender is a family member or close friend, personal relationships may be at stake and patience may have worn thin. It's your responsibility to take charge of the situation and defuse problems before they get out of hand.

Most private lenders have never confronted the prospect of foreclosing and probably won't know exactly what's involved. Some private lenders won't use attorneys, preferring to handle it themselves. You may need to explain how a foreclosure works (a copy of this book may help) and point out that it is to neither party's advantage to proceed. Start by describing or reminding your lender about the high costs of foreclosure, including lost interest income and potential losses when reselling foreclosed property.

Private investors in real estate. Occasionally, private lenders are as sophisticated as institutional lenders (if not more so), and hold large portfolios of real estate loans. If that sounds like your lender, treat them as an institutional lender and refer back to Section B, above.

Here are several options for negotiating an end to the foreclosure with a private lender:

- You resume making your scheduled loan payments and agree that the arrears will be paid back as a balloon payment at a later date.

- You "rollover" your loan into a new longer-term loan, which is also secured by your property.

- If your monthly payments were consistently late, you can volunteer a late fee (if your mortgage or promissory note does not call for one) or a security deposit.

- Although not necessarily a good move, you could offer to increase the interest rate and/or the amount of the monthly payments.

- If your private lender is concerned with a large financial commitment (such as taxes or college tuition), you can propose to increase the monthly payments to cover her commitment.

- You can also utilize some of the methods described for institutional lenders in Section B3, above.

If all else fails, an emotional appeal may work. Most individuals (or their spouses) will go out of their way to spare a family from losing their home.

D. Negotiating With HUD and the FHA

The U.S. Department of Housing and Urban Development ("HUD") is a federal agency that runs various housing (predominately residential) programs for American citizens.

One of HUD's most popular programs is run by the Federal Housing Administration ("FHA"). The FHA insures mortgage loans that banks and other institutional lenders make for new and existing properties. The FHA funds itself by charging mortgage insurance each month, which is included in your monthly payments.

When the FHA insures a loan, it agrees to reimburse the lender if the borrower defaults on payments. Because of the FHA program, lenders can make loans that they would not otherwise risk. Over the past 70 years, millions of homes have been financed using FHA insurance.

When there are a lot of foreclosures, the FHA is overloaded with properties. Conceivably, it could take back tens of thousands of properties, but that would drain money from its fund. Therefore, HUD looks for alternatives to foreclosure and essentially offers homeowners a "second chance" to make good on a defaulted loan.

The "**HUD Home Mortgage Assignment Program**" is designed to prevent FHA-insured homeowners from losing their homes in foreclosure. You must take specific steps to participate in the program; it is not automatic. Under the program, your lender assigns (turns over) your mortgage or deed of trust to HUD instead of foreclosing on your property. HUD pays off your lender, and takes an assignment of your loan, and then works with you directly to structure a plan to cure your default.

The good news is that HUD is likely to be far more flexible than an institutional lender in negotiating a workout that fits your financial needs.

HUD DEED-IN-LIEU PROGRAM

If you don't want to keep your property: HUD also has a deed in lieu program for property owners that do not want to keep their property, but nevertheless want to avoid the foreclosure. More information on this program is available through the HUD hotline (see below). Chapter 11 also covers HUD's program for deeds-in-lieu of foreclosure.

1. Will You Qualify for the HUD Program?

You can only take advantage of the HUD assignment program if your loan is FHA-insured. If you don't know whether or not your loan is FHA-insured, either ask your lender or check your monthly payment loan coupon. If it includes a charge for FHA insurance, yours is an FHA loan. You may also contact HUD directly and ask if your loan is FHA-insured:

HUD Housing Hotline
  800-569-4287
  www.hud.gov/foreclosure

You must meet three criteria to qualify for HUD's assignment program:

- You must be behind at least three monthly payments.

- You must have a good reason, beyond your control, for missing payments--such as being laid off from work, becoming ill or suffering an injury. The reason must be temporary--for example, permanent illness or paralysis will not qualify.

- You must have a reasonable prospect of resuming monthly payments within a specific period of time, not to exceed 36 months.

Once HUD determines that these three criteria are met, it will contact your lender and have your loan assigned to HUD.

2. Overview of HUD Assignment Program

Below is an overview of the steps involved in HUD's Home Mortgage Assignment Program. Follow these steps carefully, because the procedures have strict compliance deadlines.

a. Lender Advises You of HUD Program

Your lender should send you a letter advising you of the pending foreclosure and the availability of HUD's Home Mortgage Assignment Program. Your lender's letter will probably state that you have 15 days to contact HUD before it will initiate foreclosure. If you don't receive a letter from your lender, call the HUD hotline directly and request that HUD contact your lender.

b. Ask Your Lender to Assign Your Loan to HUD

It is up to you to request that your lender assign your loan to HUD; your lender will not do it for you. You have 15 days from the date your lender mailed you a letter about the HUD program to furnish your lender with a completed HUD-92068F form (your lender has blank copies, if you need them, or you can download them from the HUD website). Your lender will forward this form to HUD.

If your lender won't provide you with the information and paperwork you need, send HUD a letter, such as the sample below, and request HUD's immediate involvement. You can get the address of your local HUD office by calling the HUD hotline, or go online. Send the letter by certified mail, return receipt requested, or overnight express.

c. Complete HUD Application

The self-explanatory HUD application form (HUD92068F) must include a statement of current income and expenses and potential sources of future income, and an explanation of events causing you to fall behind in payments. Your form must also include an explanation of future events that will allow you to resume full monthly payments within three years and a budget of future income and expenses.

Fill out and return your application to HUD within 15 days of receipt, along with copies of relevant documents (for safety's sake keep the originals in your personal files). Send everything by certified mail, return receipt requested, or overnight express.

September 12, 200X

HUD Home Mortgage Assignment Program
HUD Office Address
City, State, Zip Code

To whom it may concern:

I own property located at 2560 Main Street in Memphis, Tennessee. General Savings Bank holds the first deed of trust encumbering my property securing a loan in the amount of $450,000. The loan is insured by the FHA.

I am currently three months behind in my payments and General Savings has threatened foreclosure. General Savings has not responded to my request that my loan be assigned to HUD under your Home Mortgage Assignment Program. The purpose of this letter is to formally request such on assignment.

Please contact me at your earliest convenience so that we may submit whatever documents you need to accept the assignment.

Sincerely,

Jonathan Dutton
2560 Main Street
Memphis, Tennessee

cc: General Savings Bank

d. HUD Makes Preliminary Determination

A HUD field office will review your application for assignment and send you a letter with one of four responses:
- HUD will accept your application for assignment.

• HUD has referred your application to your lender for further handling.

• HUD needs more information to

determine whether you are eligible. In this case, promptly gather whatever additional documentation and supporting evidence may support your position (letters, receipts, bills and the like) and deliver copies to the HUD office.

• HUD has rejected your application.

e. What to Do If Application Is Rejected

If HUD initially rejects your application, don't be disheartened. It is only a *preliminary* decision. You still have 15 days from the date the rejection was issued to appeal. HUD will typically explain exactly why you do not appear to be eligible for assignment. Fortunately, HUD will also tell what additional information would change its preliminary determination.

Immediately telephone your local HUD office and request: 1) a reconsideration conference, which will be scheduled within 25 days of HUD's initial decision letter, and 2) copies of all documents in your file at HUD.

If you do not appeal within 15 days. HUD will send a letter to your lender authorizing foreclosure. At that point, there is nothing else HUD can do to assist you.

Your task is to prepare a written response (with documentation, if possible) to each of the requirements HUD contends you did not meet. Prepare a current detailed budget of your income and expenses as well as a projected budget for the next three years. In addition, explain in writing how you'll be able to resume your loan payments within three years.

At the conference, you should discuss why your loan qualifies for assignment to HUD. Be prepared to present all of your documents and respond to each of HUD's reasons why your loan may not qualify for assignment. You may bring an attorney or financial advisor to this conference, but it is not required.

f. HUD Makes a Final Decision

Within 30 to 90 days from the date you first requested an assignment, HUD will notify you and your lender of its decision. During this period, your lender is required to hold off the foreclosure and you are not required to make the monthly payments.

If HUD accepts the assignment, HUD will set up a meeting to discuss the terms of a workout plan. In the interim, HUD will work directly with your lender to handle the actual assignment documents. HUD will also advise your lender not to report your loan as a foreclosure to the credit reporting agencies--but check your credit report to make sure. After the assignment, only HUD (not your old lender) will be involved in your loan.

If HUD rejects the assignment of your loan, your only recourse is to appeal HUD's decision directly to the Federal Court. This is beyond the scope of this book and you will probably need a lawyer.

g. Meet With HUD to Finalize Workout

To finalize the assignment, you and a HUD representative will discuss and sign a loan workout agreement-- really a loan extension. Workouts are customized and will depend on your individual situation. They typically involve a payment of the arrears within a maximum of three years, as well as lower monthly payments and an extension of the loan. Once you sign the HUD agreement, you will make all future payments directly to HUD.

HUD may also refer you to a HUD- approved financial counseling agency, which provides advice and counseling to help you understanding the responsibilities of home ownership and financing.

E. Negotiating With the U.S. Department of Veteran Affairs

If you are a veteran, your loan may be guaranteed by the United States Department of Veteran Affairs ("VA'). The VA helps veterans obtain loans for owner-occupied single-family residences by providing loan guarantees (insurance) to lenders. The cost of the insurance is added to your monthly loan payment and is called a "funding fee."

VA loan guarantees are a benefit program bestowed upon U.S. veterans to repay them for serving our country. As an extension of those benefits, the VA *"Foreclosure Avoidance Program"* assists financially distressed veterans in foreclosure keep their homes.

To check whether your loan is VA- guaranteed and whether you qualify for their Foreclosure Avoidance Program, call the VA office nearest you or:

Veterans Affairs Hotline:
800-827-1000
www.va.gov

1. VA Servicing Procedures

Lenders must carefully follow proscribed VA guidelines, summarized below, before foreclosing or they risk losing their VA insurance. At the heart of the VA guidelines is an expectation that your lender will communicate with you and try to work out a mutually acceptable solution.

If your lender does not follow VA procedures or is uncooperative, immediately let the VA know. You can telephone your VA office, but it is more effective to write a letter, email, or personally visit your local VA office. If the VA office is unresponsive to your lender's indifference, you may want to write your local congressional representative or senator, with a copy to your VA office.

a. Telephone Calls

The VA expects lenders to telephone veterans who have missed monthly payments. Telephone calls are intended to establish personal communication and encourage a discussion of potential solutions.

VA guidelines prohibit your lender from insinuating that nothing can be done to stop your foreclosure. Your lender is required to explain the various VA programs that are available to avoid foreclosure and encourage you to contact your local VA office. Be sure to make a note of your lender's approach using the Communications Chart, Chapter 1, Section A.

b. Letters

Your lender must send you a personalized letter within 20 days from the date your monthly payment is late. The VA requires that the letter:

- advise you that your payment is late

- request immediate payment

- request a personal interview

- if you made only a partial payment, explain that your check is being returned because it's not the full amount

- confirm any agreements with you, your lender and/or the VA regarding the default

- remind you that you must keep your payments current, and

- address any issues that are relevant to your particular circumstances.

As always, keep copies of all letters you receive.

c. Field Visits

If your lender can't reach you by telephone or you don't respond to their letters or emails, a representative must meet with you and inspect your property, called a "field visit." A field visit will normally occur in the evening, when you are likely to be home, and will not necessarily be announced. As the VA Servicing Guidelines states:

> "...before the foreclosure decision is made, it is imperative that there be a meaningful, detailed interview with the borrower. The purpose of the analysis is to gain a thorough understanding of the nature and reasons for the default, the prospects of curing the default, both short-term and long-term, and to determine what action might avoid foreclosure. The pre-foreclosure analysis provides an opportunity to look at the borrower's attitude, willingness to cooperate, and motivation."

Although you may not appreciate having your lender show up unexpectedly at home to interview you, use the field visit as an opportunity to demonstrate your commitment to resolving your defaulted loan. It is also an excellent time to show the representative any physical conditions on the property that may be creating a problem (foundation, plumbing, electrical, roof, heating). Physical problems frequently contribute to a lender's newly discovered willingness to negotiate a workout plan rather than taking a troubled property back in foreclosure.

Keep a log of the field visit. On your Communications Chart (Chapter 1, Section A), write down the date and time of the visit, the name of the representative, what was inspected during the visit, what was discussed, and the representative's attitude. Keeping detailed records can be intimidating and may help pressure a sloppy lender to follow VA procedures.

After the visit, the representative must write a report and submit copies to your lender and the VA. If the report is positive, your lender is likely to forestall the foreclosure and be more willing to negotiate a workout with you than to proceed with the foreclosure. Obviously, your goal should be for your lender to write a good report.

If you miss payments for at least three months, your lender must give the VA notice of its intention to foreclose at least 30 days before commencing foreclosure. The VA will then send you a letter advising you of your lender's intention to foreclose.

2. VA In-House Financial Counseling

You don't have to wait for your lender to contact you; you can always contact the VA and ask for financial counseling to help resolve your financial difficulties before you lose your home in foreclosure. The VA can provide in-house counseling or can refer you to non-VA, federal, state, local or private organizations that provide low-cost or free financial counseling.

Keep in mind that financial counseling requires a face-to-face meeting with an interviewer to discuss your financial situation in detail. You should be prepared to talk about the following:

• *Reasons for the default.* Acceptable reasons for missing payments include illness, accident, unemployment, death or injury of family member and business reversals. An unwillingness or refusal to make the payments is not acceptable.

• *Your domestic situation.* Because divorce or separation often prompts a foreclosure, the VA interviewer must find out if you are single, married, separated or divorced. Are there marital problems that will affect your ability to repay the loan? Who is responsible for repaying the loan? Who has the ability to pay? Who lives in the property?

• *Employment.* Unemployment is also a frequent reason for foreclosure, so the interviewer will ask if you're employed, the name and address of your employer and your weekly income. She will also question you if you are self-employed. Is your income based upon a salary or commission? If your income has decreased, will it increase again soon? If unemployed, will you be able to get a new job in the near future?

• *Your financial situation.* The interviewer will ask questions about your regular income, expenditures, assets and liabilities. She will use this data when determining whether you can accomplish a workout of your defaulted loan.

3. Delinquency Classifications

After analyzing your situation, the VA will classify you in one of the following two categories:

- *Distressed delinquent.* This means you have reasonable excuses for the default, along with the ability and desire to cure it. The VA will request that your lender work out a repayment plan with you and see that you get financial counseling. It is to your advantage to be classified as a distressed delinquent.

- *Chronic delinquent.* If you're in this category, the VA believes you have no justified reason for missing loan payments and are habitually late. You cannot appeal this designation. The VA refers these cases back to the lenders, who may proceed with foreclosure.

4. Overview of VA Foreclosure Avoidance Program

The VA requires a series of procedural steps to help a borrower who's defaulted on a VA-guaranteed loan:

a. Your Lender Issues a VA Notice of Default

Once your lender files a Notice of Default, your lender must send the VA Form 26-6850a (VA Notice of Default)

between 60 to 105 days of your first uncured default.

b. Get Help From Your Leader or Seek Supplemental Servicing

Immediately contact your lender and ask for help. If your lender is uncooperative, contact the local VA office and request "supplemental servicing." With supplemental servicing, a VA representative is assigned to work directly with you to assure that you have every opportunity to avoid foreclosure. There is no cost for this service.

c. VA Intervenes

Your VA servicing representative will contact your lender and try to work out a solution to your foreclosure. He or she will try to resolve the default, work out a repayment plan, and minimize the VA's risk of paying a claim. Once the VA intervenes, your lender is required to stop, or at least delay, the foreclosure until an adequate resolution can be achieved. If you have any evidence that your lenders didn't follow VA procedures, bring it to the VA representative's attention.

d. Agree on a Workout Plan

If the VA determines that you can bring the default current within a reasonable period of time, the VA representative will negotiate a workout plan with your lender. There are several ways your delinquency may be resolved with your lender with the assistance of the VA:

- *Loan forbearance.* Your lender may agree to accept less than your regular monthly payment over a longer period than the term of your loan. Within 12 months of the date of the workout agreement, however, the delinquency must be cured by increased payments, payment of a lump sum or a sale of your property. Although VA-assisted, this type of relief does not need formal VA approval.

PARTIAL PAYMENTS

VA servicing guidelines encourage lenders to accept partial payments whenever possible rather than insisting on the full arrearage. Nevertheless, there are several circumstances in which VA-insured lenders are authorized to refuse partial payments:

- You are keeping rental income from your property instead of turning it over to your lender.
- Your partial payment is less than one full month's payment.
- Your payment is less than $100 or less than 50% of the total amount due, whichever is less.
- Your payment is made by personal check instead of cash or cashier's check, if previously requested by your lender.
- Any part of your payment is more than six months past due.
- A Notice of Default or Lis Pendens has been recorded

• *Loan modification.* Your lender may agree to change the terms of your mortgage or promissory note. For example, monthly payments can be reduced or increased by adjusting the interest rate, extending the loan term, or re-amortizing the loan. The

VA does not need to formally approve this type of relief.

• *Compromise sale agreement.* Typically, this occurs in a down market when you have no equity in your property and no foreseeable way to cure your loan. You will be allowed to sell your property at its current market value, presumably less than the amount of your loan. The VA will reimburse the lender for its loss. Although you may be required to sign a promissory note in the amount of the VA's loss, the VA rarely chases veterans in this predicament. Because of the VA's direct involvement, this type of agreement requires VA approval. The VA will only approve a compromise sale agreement if the loss will be no greater than the VA guaranty, unless your lender agrees to waive the difference.

• *VA "Refunding" program.* Under this program, you request that the VA purchase your loan from your lender. This process is called "refunding." The VA will purchase your loan only if it believes the VA has a reasonable chance of saving your property from foreclosure. The VA will agree to refunding if it is the only alternative to stopping foreclosure.

chapter

6

<u>REFINANCING OUT OF FORECLOSURE</u>

A. Deciding Whether to Refinance 132
    1. Other Ways to Raise Money...132
    2. Refinancing Considerations 133

B. Should You Use a Mortgage Broker?...134

C. Will You Qualify for Refinancing?...134
    1. Do You Have Sufficient Equity (Loan-to-Value Ratio)? 134
    2. Are You a Good Credit Risk? 136

D. Overview of Refinancing 137

E. Kinds of Loans 138
    1. Conventional Loans 139
    2. Home Equity Loans 140
    3. Hard Money Loans 142
    4. Loans From Friends or Family...145

F. How to Find a Lender to Refinance Your Property 145
    1. Commercial Banks...146
    2. Savings Banks 146
    3. Credit Unions 147
    4. Mortgage Brokers 147
    5. Life Insurance Companies 147
    6. Brokerage Firms..148
    7. Hard Money Lenders..148
    8. Individuals and Real Estate Investors..148

G. Closing Costs 148

Refinancing consists of obtaining a loan from a new lender to pay your existing lender. In a foreclosure context, you'll want a loan to either pay off your foreclosing lender entirely, or simply bring your foreclosing loan current.

The thought of refinancing property that is already in foreclosure may at first seem an impossible task. Granted, foreclosure will make it more difficult to obtain a loan, will require you to aggressively shop around, and will cost more. Nevertheless, it should be possible to refinance your property as long as either your credit is in reasonably good shape or you have some equity in your property. In fact, an entire industry of lenders caters to property owners in foreclosure. This chapter explores when and how refinancing can be a viable option to stop foreclosure.

➡️

Message to readers. If you have bad credit (credit score below 550) and no equity in your property, this chapter probably won't help you and you should skip ahead.

⚠️

If you've already received a Notice of Sale, you have limited time to refinance. In fact, in most states, you only have several weeks to get a loan before your property will be sold. Because of the time constraints, you should limit your loan options to home equity lenders (See Section E2), hard money lenders (See Section E3), or family and friends (See Section E4).

A. Deciding Whether to Refinance

Before you pursue refinancing, compare it to the other strategies described in this book.

1. Other Ways to Raise Money

Assuming that refinancing still looks like the best strategy, you should consider (especially if you're only behind a couple of thousand dollars) borrowing or raising the money to bring your loan current (reinstate the loan). You might seek an unsecured loan or sell some of your assets. For example, you could:

- borrow against the cash value in your insurance policy

- sell a major asset, such as a car, furniture or stocks

- sell your jewelry, electronic equipment or musical instruments at a pawnshop

- have a large yard or garage sale

- cash in an IRA, 401(k) plan, or tax-deferred account (and pay the resulting penalties)

- use a savings account earmarked for something else

- borrow from a local finance company and pledge an asset (other than your real estate) as collateral, or try for an unsecured consolidation loan

- contact the IRS's Problem Resolution Program

and ask to get your tax refund early

- get a short-term, unsecured loan from a friend, or

- take a cash advance from your credit cards.

Although each of these resources can provide cash in a hurry, watch out for exorbitant interest rates and another monthly payment that stretches you beyond your means.

2. Refinancing Considerations

If you pursue refinancing, keep these thoughts in mind:

- *Be clear about how much you need to borrow.* You need enough money to cover the costs of the new loan and pay off the foreclosing lender, including the foreclosure costs and accrued interest on the loan. (See Section G for more on the specific costs to refinance.)

- *Make sure you can afford ongoing payments.* Don't burden yourself unnecessarily. If refinancing isn't a long-term solution to your problem, it probably isn't worthwhile. Only agree to a loan if the lender's total cost for the loan (including points and additional fees) is affordable on an ongoing basis. Be especially wary of loans with balloon payments, such as interest-only loans ending with a large balloon payment that you may not be able to make.

- *Shop around.* Lenders have different guidelines for granting loans, and vary in their abilities to approve loans quickly. Because of the pressing foreclosure, you don't want to put all your eggs in one basket. You'll want to compare the different loan terms offered and get the best deal in the limited time available. If needed, you can even fill out several loan applications and then take the first loan that comes in.

- *Seek a loan with the lowest possible interest rate.* This concept may seem obvious, but it is crucial because interest is probably your most important consideration because of its cost over time. If you are confused about the variety of interest rates and points, don't be afraid to ask potential lenders to explain their charges. Then compare them to what other lenders charge.

- *Find out how long it will take to get the loan.* It may take your lender days, weeks or months to process your loan application, depending on the type of lender you deal with. Ask the lender pointedly when you can expect approval and how long it will be until your loan is "funded" (your foreclosing lender is paid off). Have your lender issue you a commitment letter. But, above all, don't risk losing your property by agreeing to a funding date that occurs too close to the foreclosure sale. If something goes wrong, you may not receive the new loan in time to stop the foreclosure.

- *Interest payments are tax-deductible.* The loans discussed in this chapter are tax deductible, which means that you can deduct the interest portion of your monthly payment from your income on your tax returns.

• *Be on the lookout for restructuring opportunities.* Refinancing should not be viewed as a final solution that must remain unchanged once you have completed the refinance. For example, you may have to take out a high interest-rate loan to get through this temporary difficulty. Nonetheless, the important concept to remember is that this isn't the end of the line; once your foreclosure is resolved, there will always be new opportunities to refinance or restructure your loan in the future to obtain better terms, either with your existing lender or some new lending source.

B. Should You Use a Mortgage Broker?

A mortgage broker is an individual (or company) that, for a fee, will help locate lenders that are willing to refinance your property. Mortgage brokers connect qualified borrowers with lenders, such as obscure banks and investors flush with cash to lend. But just like everything else in life, there are good mortgage brokers and bad mortgage brokers. A good mortgage broker can get a loan for just about anybody, including someone in foreclosure! In contrast, a bad mortgage broker is a waste of your precious time.

The advantage of a good mortgage broker is that he will have a pulse on the financial markets and know which lenders are giving loans to borrowers in foreclosure and on what terms. A

mortgage broker can comparison shop among many lenders--and a lot more quickly than you ever could. Good mortgage brokers do business with 50 to 100 different lenders. They can quickly tell you whether you qualify for a particular loan and help you fill out the loan application and necessary paperwork. They are usually very flexible, offering various refinancing packages depending on your individual circumstances.

On the other hand, some mortgage brokers tend to become too cozy with a handful of favorite lenders with whom they regularly do business. There is always a temptation for the broker to choose the loan that's best for his business, instead of the loan that's best for you. A mortgage broker doesn't work for free. He or she will receive a commission of approximately 1% to 2% ("points"), but it will be deducted out of the loan proceeds.

C. Will You Qualify for Refinancing?

Although refinancing is decided on a case-by-case basis, lenders will normally consider two overriding issues: the extent of your equity and your credit score.

1. Do You Have Sufficient Equity (Loan-to-Value Ratio)?

Equity is the surplus of value in property after deducting the outstanding balances of all mortgages, deeds of trust and/or liens that are recorded against it. For example, if your property has a value of $500,000 and there are two mortgages (or deeds of trust) recorded against it with balances totaling $400,000, you have $100,000 of equity in your property. Lenders will only loan money against property (regardless of whether it is in foreclosure) when there is sufficient equity to support the amount of the loan.

But lenders will only loan on a portion of the equity in your property. Lenders always leave an "equity cushion" to offset potential unforeseen costs in the event your property loses value (depreciates) and they need to foreclose. The loan-to-value ratio ("LTV") is the percentage of a property's appraised market value on which a lender will loan. From this amount, the lender will deduct the balances of any outstanding loans and liens, if any, to determine how much they will loan.

Every lender has its own LTV standards. LTVs can range from 100% on government-insured loans to as low as 65% for high-risk loans. Accordingly, it is advisable to ask a prospective lender about its LTV policy before submitting a loan application.

Example 1: A lender with an 80% LTV guideline is considering making a loan on a $400,000 house. The lender calculates the amount it is willing to loan, provided there are no liens or other claims against the property:

Property value:	$400,000
80% LTV:	*x 80%*
Lender will loan:	$320,000

Example 2: Let's use the same figures, but this time the borrower has a first mortgage encumbering the property. Here's is the result:

Property value:	$400,000
80% LTV:	*x 80%*
	$320,000
Amount due on mortgage:	-280,000
Lender will loan:	$ 40,000

As you can see, the amount a lender will loan changes dramatically if there are already underlying loans encumbering your property. But remember, all lenders have their own LTV guidelines, which vary according to the type of lender, its internal policies, the type of loans it gives, and financial conditions in the marketplace.

DIFFICULTY IN GETTING A GOOD DEAL UNDER FORECLOSURE CIRCUMSTANCES

Depending on the time remaining in your foreclosure and your ability to find a loan, a mortgage broker may be a welcome addition to your team. You can use the broker alone or in connection with your own efforts to track down a willing lender. Just check all loan terms carefully and don't be pressured into accepting a bad deal. Nevertheless, appreciate that your property is in foreclosure and that the deals offered to you may not be as favorable as you would receive under normal refinancing circumstances.

To locate a mortgage broker, look in your local yellow pages under "mortgage brokers" or "real estate loans," or search the internet for "mortgage brokers" in your area. Mortgage brokers also frequently run advertisements in the classified real estate section of the Sunday newspaper. And, of course, a referral from family, or friends is always effective.

To figure your property's equity, the lender will hire a licensed real estate appraiser to determine its current market value. Lenders charge the borrower for the appraisal, which can run from $300 to $1,000 depending on the size of the property. Some lenders will add this cost to the amount of your loan, while others will require you pay the appraisal fee upfront.

2. Are You a Good Credit Risk?

Although not all lenders place as much value on credit as equity, credit is still a significant criterion. The issue of credit really breaks down into two questions:

- *Do you have the financial resources to repay the loan*? You typically need to submit complete financial statements to demonstrate that notwithstanding the foreclosure, you will be able to make loan payments on the refinanced loan. You must include all income sources, including investments, non-job-related sources, assets and liabilities, including child support and alimony, dividends and royalties.
- *What is your credit score*? The lender will check out your creditworthiness by ordering your credit report from the three major credit-reporting agencies, Experian, Trans Union and Equifax (this is called a "tri-merged" credit report). Most lenders aren't fazed by one or two negative marks on your credit report. However, if you have a low credit score with several negative marks, you will need to explain your problems to your new lender. (For more on credit reports, credit scores, and how lenders interpret them, read *Your Credit Score*,

by Liz Pulliam Weston [Pearson Prentice Hall].)

CREDIT SCORES		
FICO	Credit	Rating
720+	AAA	Superior Credit
700-719	AA	Excellent Credit
680-699	A	Very Good Credit
660-679	A-	Good Credit
640-659	B+	Fine Credit
620-639	B	Fair Credit
600-619	C	Less Than Fair Credit
580-599	C-	Inferior Credit
520-579	D	Bad Credit
519-	F	Extremely Bad Credit

Credit scores range from a low of 350 to a high of 850. Here is the typical range:

The average score in the United States is 629. But you need to remember that your credit score is not permanent or static. It changes almost daily. It can go up or down as you use credit and pay your bills. But you must always monitor it and appreciate that increasing your score is like climbing a mountain; the higher you go, the harder it gets.

Check out your credit if you're planning to refinance. You should anticipate the credit issue and obtain a copy of your credit report from each of the three major credit bureaus:

Experian: www.experian.com
888-397-3742
Trans Union: www.transunion.com
800-888-4213
Equifax: www.equifax.com
800-685-1111

All three companies will supply a free credit report once a year, and if you were denied credit within the past 30 days.

D. Overview of Refinancing

To refinance your property in time to stop the foreclosure, you'll generally follow the steps set out below.

Step 1. Decide What Type of Refinancing To Seek

There are four different options for refinancing your property: conventional refinancing, home equity loans, hard money loans, and loans from family and friends. Guidelines for selecting the best kind of loan in your circumstances are described in Section F below.

Step 2. Compare Different Lenders

Every lender provides different kinds of loans, terms and services. To ensure that you make a wise consumer decision, check out and compare several different lenders.

Step 3. Apply for Loans

Most banks and lending institutions will require that you meet and fill out a loan application (called a "1003"). In contrast, a hard money lender (who specializes in high-risk loans with correspondingly high interest rates) has an "application" that consists of a series of questions asked over the telephone. And of course, family and friends are unlikely to require any kind of application.

Avoid the anxiety and aggravation of a delay in getting the loan approved. Before signing your application, ask for a "Good Faith Estimate," in writing, that addresses specifics about the kind of loan, term, interest rate, prepayment penalties, points, escrow (settlement), title insurance, and other costs. Make a condition of your application that the lender will approve or reject your application by a specific date. If you can't get such a written commitment, you have no choice but to go elsewhere.

Step 4. Lender May Check Your Credit

A conventional or home equity lender will check your credit report and credit score to be assured that you have a history of paying your bills on time. On the other hand, a hard money lender will probably ignore your credit report (assuming you have sufficient equity), and a friend or relative probably wouldn't think of it.

Step 5. Lender Checks Title and Has Property Appraised

Your lender will contact a title insurance company and request a title report. The title insurance company checks the county recorder's office and confirms that you hold title to (own) your property and the number of mortgages, deeds of trust, and/or liens recorded against it.

Your lender will also have your property appraised to determine its current market value. The lender will then subtract the outstanding balances of the mortgages, deeds of trust, and liens from the current market value to determine the amount of equity in your property and whether it is within their loan-to-value guidelines. If it is, your loan can be approved. Otherwise, the lender will deny your loan.

Step 6. Sign the Loan Documents

Assuming your loan goes through, you will receive a telephone call and/or email, and shortly thereafter, a formal letter announcing that your loan has been approved. The letter will include a form confirming that you agree to the terms of the loan and your formal request that the lender prepare the loan documents. If possible, to keep the ball roiling, deliver the letter in person rather than mailing it back to your lender.

When you deliver the form, your lender will schedule an appointment to sign the loan documents in front of a notary (the "closing"), assuming the lender is local. Request that the meeting be as soon as possible. (Whatever date the lender proposes, request a date sooner! You have a foreclosure swirling over your head and need these funds immediately.) If your lender is out of town, request that the documents be sent by overnight mail or emailed. Similarly, make sure you return all of the loan documents by overnight mail.

Most lenders will simply have you sign a mortgage or promissory note and deed of trust (see Chapter 2). However, depending on the size of the loan and its complexity, some lenders may also ask that you sign additional loan documents that spells out in detail (in contract form) the terms and conditions of your loan and other financial disclosures that are required pursuant to federal and state law. Either way, read these documents closely before signing. In addition, make absolutely sure that any promises or representations that your lender is making, such as the initial interest rate, or the terms of the loan, are included in the loan documents.

Step 7. Three-Day Rescission Period Begins

After you sign the loan documents, an institutional lender must tell you (pursuant to the federal Truth-in-Lending Act) that you are entitled to withdraw from the loan agreement any time during the next three days. This provision in the law, called the "rescission period," originated to protect consumers against fast talking door-to-door salespeople who signed people up at their front doors for short-term consumer loans before borrowers realized they were mortgaging their homes at exorbitant interest rates. Since then, these laws have been expanded to cover practically all real estate financing transactions.

Even though it is unlikely that you will cancel after all the trouble you went through to obtain a loan, this option is nevertheless available to you. It cannot be waived!

E. Kinds of Loans

As mentioned earlier, there are several alternative ways to refinance your property:

• conventional loans

• home equity line of credit ("HELOC")

• hard money loans, and

• loans from friends or family.

Let's explore each category of loans separately.

1. Conventional Loans

Conventional refinancing takes approximately two to four weeks to process. So if you've already received a Notice of Sale (or Notice of Trustee's Sale), don't waste your time on a conventional loan; they take too long to obtain. Instead, pursue the other refinance options described in this chapter.

A conventional loan is a single loan that you use to pay off and replace all of your underlying loans, including the foreclosing lender's. A conventional loan will typically be for 30 years. It can be either fully-amortized (paid off during the term of the loan), or interest-only. The loan will come from a new lender, not the lender that is foreclosing.

A conventional loan is the hardest loan to qualify for. You must have a good credit score and demonstrate an ability to make monthly payments. You will need to supply your tax returns for at least the last two years, as well as an income verification from your employer. If you are already in foreclosure, or have fallen behind in your payment schedule, there's a good chance that you won't qualify.

a. How Much Can You Refinance With a Conventional Loan?

The average loan-to-value ratio on a new conventional loan is typically 80%. For example, if your property has a current market value of approximately $400,000, most conventional lenders will not loan you more than $320,000. If you owe your foreclosing lender an amount more than 80% of your property's value (in principal, interest, late fees and foreclosure costs), a conventional loan is probably not a viable option.

b. Costs of a Conventional Loan

The typical costs associated with a new conventional loan will average approximately 2% to 3% of the amount borrowed, and will include points, title search, title insurance, escrow (settlement) fees, credit reports, attorney fees, processing fees, and other related costs. (We cover costs in detail in Section G below.)

Whether it is to your advantage to obtain a new conventional loan (rather than a home equity loan or hard money loan) will depend on your particular situation. Assuming all other criteria are equal, you need to do the math. Ask yourself whether the cost of a conventional refinance will be less than the combined payments of your existing first loan and a new second. If it is cheaper, and you qualify, it is to your advantage to seek a conventional loan.

c. Interest Rates on a Conventional Loan

Depending on current interest rates, the rate on a conventional loan will be typically lower than the combined average interest rates of two loans. This is because your lender will be in senior position to be paid with a first mortgage or deed of trust. In contrast, a lender with a lien in second (or junior position) is in a riskier position if there is a foreclosure. This is because there may not be sufficient proceeds from a foreclosure sale to pay the lender who is in the unfortunate position of being a junior lienholder. As a result, a lender in a junior position traditionally charges a higher interest rate (than the senior lienholder) because they are taking more risk.

Conventional lenders will charge either a fixed rate or an adjustable rate, depending upon which type of loan you prefer. With a new loan you may be able to lower your interest rate if rates have come down. But if rates have gone up, you will spend more. You may also obtain an advantage if you switch to an adjustable rate mortgage ("ARM"), which typically has a lower interest rate than a fixed rate loan. A lower interest rate will allow you to make lower payments, at least for a while, which should also help your financial situation. (Note, however, that the interest rate will be slightly higher if you don't live in the property, since this is considered a "non-owner occupied" property.)

2. Home Equity Loans

A home equity loan is nothing more than an old-fashioned second mortgage (or second deed of trust) with a fancy new marketing name. The loan is based on the available equity in your property after deducting the balances of any underlying mortgages, deeds of trust and/or liens. The new loan will be secured by a junior lien encumbering your property. Assuming you already have a first mortgage or deed of trust encumbering your property, your home equity loan will be in second position.

A home equity loan application (Form #1003) can be taken over the telephone in a matter of minutes, or you can fill out a relatively short application at your lender's office. Usually, you will receive an answer within 24 to 48 hours. Most lenders can then process a home equity loan and fund it within one to two weeks.

A home equity loan typically lasts for ten to fifteen years, depending on what you negotiate with your lender. And just like your senior lender, if you miss the payments on your home equity loan, the junior lender will have the right to initiate foreclosure proceedings.

a. Kinds of Home Equity Loans

There are two kinds of home equity loans, both of which are secured by a junior lien recorded against your property:

- *Closed-ended home equity loan.* This is a one-time loan that closes--or ends--once the loan is paid off. The advantage of a closed-ended equity loan is that you'll pay a fixed rate of interest on the amount you borrow (although slightly higher rate than you would initially pay on an home equity line of credit). The loans are typically amortized over 30 years, but due in 15 years. When the loan is paid off in full, it is retired. This is commonly referred to as a "stand-alone second."

- *Home equity line of credit (open-ended).* This is nothing more than a revolving line of credit that is secured by a junior mortgage or deed of trust recorded against your property. Although your loan is for a specific amount, you are not required to borrow (or repay) the entire amount all at once. This is commonly referred to as a "HELOC." The advantage of a HELOC is that you can pay interest-only. The disadvantage is that the loan is adjustable rather than fixed.

In contrast to a stand-alone second, a HELOC will be for the total amount the lender approves, even if you don't actually borrow the full amount. For example, if you are approved for $100,000 and you borrow only $60,000, your lender will still have you sign a mortgage or deed of trust for $100,000 and record the document. Of course, you can always borrow the balance if and when you need it. In addition, you can pay off the amount you borrowed without canceling the right to re-borrow on the HELOC later.

The interest rate on a closed-ended home equity loan is typically fixed for a period of time. The interest rate on a HELOC is usually adjustable, but you are charged interest only on the amount you actually borrow. For example, if you have an $80,000 HELOC, you might use $40,500 to bring your foreclosing lender current, but not borrow the rest. In that scenario, you will be charged interest only on the $40,500 that you actually borrowed.

At first glance, a HELOC may seem more attractive than a closed-ended loan. But consider this; if interest rates decrease, a HELOC will be to your advantage. On the other hand, if interest rates rise, the closed-end loan payments (with a fixed interest rate) will not change, while the HELOC payments (with an adjustable interest rate) will increase.

b. Eligibility for a Home Equity Loan

A home equity loan is difficult, but not impossible, to come by in a foreclosure situation. If you have missed only a few payments, you have some equity in your property, and your credit score is decent, you may qualify for a home equity loan. If on the other hand, you have already received a Notice of Sale and don't have good credit, your refinance opportunities are better with a hard money loan (covered in Section E3, below).

In contrast to a conventional loan, sufficient equity in your property is the most important criterion for a home equity loan, although credit score is also important to the lender. To qualify, you must provide evidence that you'll be able to afford monthly payments on a home equity loan as well as resuming payments to your foreclosing lender. Most home equity loans do not exceed a cumulative loan-to-value ratio ("CLTV") of 70% to 80%, minus any existing loans encumbering your property.

Example: Alice owns a home in San Antonio, Texas, that has a current market value of approximately $500,000. First National Bank holds a first deed of trust securing the loan, with an outstanding balance of $350,000. When her property goes into foreclosure, Alice approaches Second Street Bank about a home equity loan. Second Street has an CLTV limitation of 80% on home equity loans. In Alice's situation, 80% of $500,000 would be $400,000. However, because the balance of the first deed of trust with First National is $350,000, Second Street Bank will lend Alice only $50,000. Fortunately, that is all Alice needs to bring First National Bank current and pull herself out of foreclosure.

c. Interest Rates on a Home Equity Loan

Lenders that stand second in line to recover their money in foreclosures are taking a higher risk of loss than conventional lenders who are in first priority position. To protect themselves, home equity lenders charge higher interest than conventional lenders. Nevertheless, the lending business is highly competitive, so lenders charge interest rates that will attract business. Because of this economic reality, you need to spend time comparison-shopping among various lenders to find the best rates.

d. Costs of a Home Equity Loan

Because of intense competition in the financial marketplace, most home equity lenders will not require any money up front for processing your loan. Home equity lenders typically front the necessary processing costs, including appraisal costs, points, title fees and

escrow fees, and then add them to the loan balance at closing. If yours is an HELOC, your lender may also charge a maintenance fee (anywhere from $100 to $500, depending on the size of the loan) per year.

3. Hard Money Loans

A hard money loan can best be described as a loan to a borrower who is in foreclosure and has bad credit, but has some equity in her property. Hard money loans come from private investors, who (because of the risks involved) expect high yields on their investments. With a hard money loan, you usually make interest-only payments for a term of one to five years. At the end of the loan term, you make a balloon payment of the entire principal and any accrued interest! Now you know why it is called "hard money" – it is "hard" to pay back.

A hard money loan is probably the easiest to get, but it comes with the highest interest rate (usually 5% higher than a home equity loan), and 5 to 10 points (each point equals 1% of the loan). Nevertheless, when all else fails, it may be your one and only option if you are determined to refinance.

Example: Henry runs into financial problems and defaults on his monthly mortgage payments. He is determined to refinance and keep his property. Because of his poor credit and a pending foreclosure, Henry borrows $10,000 from Fast Cash, Inc., a hard-money lender to bring his senior loan current. Fast Cash charges 6 points ($600) plus closing costs of 2% ($200). The interest rate is 15% per year and payments are interest-only ($125) per month. At the end of three years, Henry will have paid

$4,500 in interest, $200 in closing costs and $600 in points-and he'll still owe a balloon payment of $10,000. In all, he'll pay a total of $5,300 to borrow $10,000.

Applications for hard money loans are typically taken over the telephone and can be processed within one to three days. (If it takes longer, there is a problem with the lender and you should move on.)

The danger with a hard money loan is that although you receive the money to bring your defaulted loan current and stop the pending foreclosure, you may end up in a more precarious financial position than when you started. You'll still have your previous loan(s) to pay, plus your new hard-money loan to pay, so your overall monthly loan payments will be substantially larger than before. Plus, at the end of the term of the hard money loan (just a few short years), you will be faced with a balloon payment that may be extremely difficult to pay. Because of this potential problem, it should come as no surprise that more hard money loans go into default and cause foreclosure then all other types of loan combined!

a. Eligibility for a Hard Money Loan

Quite simply, if you have equity in your property, you can obtain a hard money loan. You do not need a high credit score and you usually do not even need to provide tax returns or income verifications.

But the loan-to-value ratio of a hard money lender is usually much narrower than a conventional or a HELOC lender. A hard money lender will not typically loan in excess of 60% to 65% of your property's value, less amounts already

INTEREST RATES ON OPEN-ENDED HOME EQUITY LOANS

Home equity lines of credit almost always have adjustable interest rates. The variation is based on one of the many publicly advertised interest rate indexes (such as the prime rate or the District Cost of Funds). These indexes increase or decrease as the financial marketplace fluctuates.

Once your lender selects an appropriate index, it will add a small percentage ("margin"), ranging anywhere from 1% to 3% over the index. This margin is your lender's profit margin for giving you the loan. For example, if your lender charges a margin of 1 1/2% over the prime rate, and the prime rate increases to 7%, then your adjustable interest rate on your loan will be 8½%. On the other hand, if several months later the prime rate falls to 5%, your interest rate will likewise fall to 6½%. As you can see, while an adjustable rate may benefit you in a falling market, it can cause problems in a rising market.

Most lenders will agree to put a ceiling ("Cap") on the interest rate they can charge. This cap can range from 1% to 4% per year, and a lifetime cap of 10% to 15% maximum interest rate over the life of the loan. For instance, although your interest rate may be 3% over prime, your rate may be capped at 12% over the life of the loan regardless of how high the prime rate may rise.

owed against your property.

Example:
Market value of property: $500,000
Hard money lender's LTV: <u>x 65%</u>

                  328,445
Existing loans and liens: <u>300,000</u>
Available equity for hard
money loan: $28,445

b. Costs of a Hard Money Loan

As mentioned earlier, the costs of a hard money loan are much higher than conventional or home equity loans, especially the "points" charged by the lender. (Points are nothing more than pre-paid interest-another way for your lender to make an extra buck at your expense!) You may be charged anywhere from 5% to 10% of the principal loan amount as "points." So be prepared for these charges.

Similar to conventional loans and home equity loans, you will be charged closing costs (including title search, title insurance, escrow and/or settlement fees), which will equal roughly 2% of the principal loan amount. These costs will be deducted from the loan before you receive any money.

c. Watch Out for Unscrupulous Hard Money Lenders

Although the majority of hard money lenders are honest and reputable, some unscrupulous lenders spoil the pot with unethical and questionable business practices.

Hard money lenders have been known to wait until the last days before a foreclosure sale and then suddenly say that you don't qualify for a loan. They

then advise you that they can give you an emergency loan with less appealing terms than previously offered--for example, 10 points rather than 5 points, or 15% interest rate instead of 12%. Unfortunately, although these lending practices are unethical, they are not necessarily illegal. Besides, you don't have the time nor money to sue these lenders for breach of contract; you are in foreclosure and need new financing by a certain deadline.

The best methods to safeguard yourself against these tactics are:

- Negotiate with more than one hard money lender. Because most lenders will not require an up-front fee when they take your application, you can apply to several lenders and pick the first one that gives you a loan or the one that comes through with the best terms.

- Insist that the lender make a written commitment about the interest rate and points during negotiations, and give you a good faith estimate.
- Do not sign loan documents that state "subject to lender's approval," which would allow the lender to switch to a more expensive loan at the last minute.

When all is said and done, steer clear of hard money lenders that charge outrageous rates, fully expecting (and wanting) you to default so they can foreclose and take over your property. Afterall, there is no point digging deeper into trouble with a hard money lender that will eventually initiate their own foreclosure anyway.

4. Loans From Friends or Family

Many people believe this is the most "expensive" loan of all. Asking for money from a friend or family member almost always comes with unexpected baggage. But this may be your only viable financing option, particularly if your LTV and credit score are insufficient for normal lenders. If you go this route, it is your responsibility to make the business arrangement work out. In other words, don't borrow from your friends or family if you don't truthfully believe you can pay them back.

If you approach a friend or relative to request a loan to stop the foreclosure, offer them interest on their money even if they say it isn't necessary. Make an offer they can't refuse and one you can afford. Knowing what you now know about the range of lenders, you can offer a rate of interest that, while lower than what you would have been charged in the marketplace, would still be higher then what they would receive if they had invested their money in a certificate of deposit or money market fund.

Finally, formalize your agreement by filling-out a mortgage or promissory note, and deed of trust which contains all of the terms of the loan. In addition, record the mortgage (or a deed of trust) in the county recorder's office.

F. How to Find a Lender to Refinance Your Property

There are at least eight different categories of available lenders to consider for refinancing out of foreclosure:

• commercial banks

• savings banks (formerly savings and loan associations)

• mortgage companies

• credit unions

• life insurance companies

• stock brokerage houses

• hard money lenders, and

• individuals.

Lenders offer a wide variety of interest rates, terms, costs, conveniences, and services. Unfortunately, most borrowers don't spend the time necessary to shop different lenders. The tendency is to borrow from an institution that is conveniently located, recommended by someone you know, or that solicits your business. But now knowing that other lenders are also available will hopefully encourage you to shop around, even if it is only by telephone or on the internet. Just remember, the more lenders you talk to, the better equipped you will be to decide which lender suits your particular needs.

Check with a reputable real estate agent. A local real estate agent can be an excellent resource if you want to find the names of banks, mortgage brokers, and other institutions, that give conventional, home equity, and hard-money loans. Remember to pump them, politely, for the names of several lenders, not just one.

1. Commercial Banks

Increasingly, commercial banks have become major real estate-based lenders. More recently, they have actively encouraged home equity loans.

The range of a bank's real estate based loan programs will vary. With the exception of hard money loans, large metropolitan banks usually have all the loan products you will need: home equity loans and conventional loans. Smaller banks, on the other hand, may not write conventional loans.

Further, commercial banks are as interested in home equity loans as conventional loans, and will actively compete to get home equity loan business. A home equity loan is profitable to a commercial bank because of its low service costs--there is little for the bank to do after it sets up an equity loan. Banks eager to give home equity loans advertise their rates in the Sunday newspapers. You can also surf the internet, or shop-around by telephoning major banks in your area (check the yellow pages). Ask for their current interest rates, points, application fees, and other charges for conventional and home equity loans.

2. Savings Banks

Because of the 1980's debacle in the savings and loan industry (S&Ls were permitted to expand into many unrelated activities, and many of them met financial disaster), the vast majority of savings and loan associations have distanced themselves from that notoriety. They've achieved this by changing their names to "savings banks," the new buzzword in the industry. While you may be concerned about the financial strength of an institution when you are a saver, you personally need not worry as a borrower. After all, you have their money; they don't have yours.

Savings banks continue to write the majority of Americans' conventional home loans, so it is only natural that borrowers would also turn to these institutions when seeking home equity loans. The positive result is that savings banks process loans faster than commercial banks, regardless of whether it is a conventional loan or a home equity loan. Savings banks, being real estate specialists, tend to be more aggressive in going after conventional and home equity loans than commercial banks. Similar to commercial banks, savings banks do not provide hard money loans.

But in this era of deregulation in the lending industry, it has become virtually impossible to distinguish savings banks from commercial banks. So the decision really comes down to investigating which institution offers you the best rates and terms. Shop around before you decide.

3. Credit Unions

Credit unions are sleepers among real property lending possibilities because few people think of them as potential lending sources. Credit unions are financial institutions established for the benefit of their members, who open accounts and borrow money. In effect, the members borrow from each other. Being non-profit cooperative institutions, credit unions' interest rates tend to be one to two points below rates charged by commercial banks and savings banks. However, their services are available to members only. They generally don't advertise, which helps keep their costs down.

Credit unions are authorized to grant loans secured by real property. In fact, the conventional real estate loan business has become one of credit unions' largest activities. Credit unions have also expanded into home equity loans in recent years.

If you do not belong to a credit union, don't despair. There may still be time if the foreclosure clock has not ticked too far along. Check out whether you are eligible to join the credit union of some group with which you are already associated. Ask your employer, government bureau, educational institution, or cooperative association whether they are affiliated with a credit union. You can find a list of credit unions by searching the internet, or in your local yellow pages under "credit unions." Call them and ask about their eligibility requirements. You maybe pleasantly surprised how easy some of them are to join.

4. Mortgage Brokers

Mortgage brokers are agents that deal with many different lenders on a wholesale basis. They act as "money merchants," arranging loans for borrowers by scouring the country for the best loan programs and best interest rates.

Mortgage brokers can find you a loan quickly. Mortgage brokers provide a needed service to homeowners in foreclosure because they can find obscure lenders and loan programs that are more liberal in their guidelines, credit scores, and loan-to-value ratios. Another advantage of using a mortgage broker is that they can typically process loans faster, and push lenders to fund your loan as soon as possible. Another advantage is that mortgage brokers are in constant contact with various lenders and know which ones have money to lend people in foreclosure and the terms. Keep this in mind if the foreclosure clock is running out of time.

You can find local mortgage brokers by asking real estate agents, searching the internet, or looking in your local yellow pages.

5. Life Insurance Companies

Life insurance companies invest heavily in commercial real estate financing. So if you own commercial property in foreclosure, you should check with life insurance companies. A list of insurance companies is easy to locate on the internet, or in your local yellow pages under "life insurance."

In contrast, if you own residential property, either a single- family residence, condominium, or a 1-4 unit apartment building, contacting a life insurance company is probably a waste of your precious time. Life insurance companies rarely deal directly with homeowners.

6. Brokerage Firms

Deregulation has opened the "financial services" floodgates to stock brokerage firms to participate in real estate loans. Today, most full-service brokerage firms have a wide assortment of loan programs, including conventional loans and home equity loans. Although they are still small players in the refinancing field, there are currently several major brokerage firms in the United States (with local offices near you) as well as many small brokerage houses in your city that offer real estate loans. Search the internet or look in your local yellow pages under "stockbrokers."

7. Hard Money Lenders

Hard money lenders tend to be individuals or small companies that loan only on local properties that they can keep a close eye on. The easiest way to find hard money lenders is the Sunday classified real estate section of your local newspaper. Hard money lenders' advertisements will scream out at you: "no qualifying," "easy cash," "no credit required," "cash within days."

Then again, you may not need to find hard money lenders--they will find you! Hard money lenders typically subscribe to special foreclosure listing services that give them a daily list of properties in foreclosure. These lenders then send you a letter or promotional mailer advertising their loan services. In fact, if you've already been served with a complaint or received a Notice

of Default, you have probably been flooded with these advertisements. (<u>Hint</u>: proceed with caution, for reasons discussed in Section E3, above.)

8. Individuals and Real Estate Investors

The problem with individuals who loan money as a living (not family and friends) is that they tend to charge a higher rate of interest than commercial banks or savings banks. Nevertheless, these individuals may be an excellent sources of home equity loans, provided the interest rates and fees are acceptable to you.

It may be difficult to distinguish between an individual investor and a hard money lender, especially if the proposed interest rate is incredibly high. (If you are confronted with this dilemma, you can assume you are dealing with a hard money lender, regardless of whether it is an individual or a company.)

G. Closing Costs

If you go forward with a refinance, understand that closing costs will be deducted out of your loan proceeds. These costs are set out here so that you can not only anticipate them, but perhaps negotiate with your lender on how these costs can be waived or reduced:

- *Application fee*. Also called an "administration fee" or "processing fee." Some lenders charge a fee when you apply for the loan. The justification is that the lender needs to cover the cost of processing your application. Application fees may be a flat amount, such as $250, or they may be set as a percentage of the loan amount, such as 1% or 2%. Some lenders will refund the application fee if you don't qualify, while others will apply the fee towards your closing costs if your loan is funded. If, however, you qualify for a loan and choose not to take it, you often forfeit the application fee. Check a potential lender's policy before you plunk down any money.

- *Appraisal fee*. Because a lender must make sure that your property is worth enough to provide adequate collateral for the loan, it will hire a state-licensed appraiser to calculate your property's current market value. You pay the cost of the appraisal, which often ranges from $300 to $1,000, depending on the size of your property.

- *Title search*. Before your lender will consider giving you a loan secured by your property, it will have a title insurance company or an attorney (depending on your state) conduct a search of the county recorder's office. The purpose of the search is to determine the chain of title and what claims are recorded against your property, such as mortgages, deeds of trust, mechanic's liens, attachments, easements, liens and judgments. The fee can range anywhere from $500 to several thousand dollars depending on the value of your property. Once again, you will pay this fee out of the loan proceeds. You will not pay this fee if your loan is not funded.

- *Title insurance*. Your lender wants to be assured that you have clear and unimpeded title to your property

and that its lien (i.e. mortgage or deed of trust) will be recorded in the correct priority position. To avoid the possibility that someone else may claim title to your property or that another lien is senior to your lender's, your lender obtains insurance from a title insurance company. The cost is based on the value of your property, and can run anywhere from $500 to several thousand dollars. Like everything else in a refinance, this one-time insurance premium is deducted from your loan proceeds.

- *Credit report*. The cost of credit reports comes to about $15 to $60 per report. Some lenders will charge this expense upfront when you apply for the loan, while others will simply deduct the expense out of your loan when it is funded. If the loan is not funded, you are not responsible for the cost.

- *Impound account*. If you prefer, lenders will set up a special account (called an impound account), in which you pay your taxes and insurance on a monthly basis. Out of this account, your lender will pay your property taxes and property insurance premiums. Lender prefer to be responsible for these payments so they can verify that payments are made (and your property's value is protected). When the loan is funded, the lender will require that the escrow company withhold enough funds in an impound account to fund several months of tax and insurance payments.

- *Loan origination fee ("points")*. This is a fee you pay to your lender for obtaining a loan. The loan origination fee is often expressed in terms of "points," where each point represents 1% of the loan amount. Points are likely to be one of your biggest closing costs, and unfortunately they are rarely negotiable. Points are charged only if the loan is granted. They are deducted from the loan proceeds when funded.

• _Lock-in fee_. Some lenders charge a lock-in fee of 1% to 2% of the loan amount if you want them to guarantee in writing the interest rate the lender is be charging at the time you applied for the loan, regardless of whether interest rates subsequently go up (or down!).

• M_ortgage insurance ("MI")_. This insurance should really be called "loan default insurance" because it protects your lender if you default on your loan and the property is foreclosed. Although it would seem logical that a lender should pay for MI, no such luck. This cost is also pushed onto you. The good news is that lenders do not require mortgage insurance unless you are refinancing more than 80% of the value of your property. The cost is usually .03% to 1% of the loan amount.

• _Notary fee_. This fee covers the services of a notary public, a person licensed by the state to verify that people's signatures on legal documents are genuine. This is a one of the smallest fees you will pay, often $100 or less.

• _Recording fee_. All loan documents (i.e. mortgages or deeds of trust) are recorded in the recorder's office of the county where the property is located. The cost to record, between $25 to $100 depending on your county, is charged to you.

chapter

7

USING YOUR MILITARY STATUS
TO STOP FORECLOSURE

A. Are You Covered by the SSCRA? 152

    1. Are You on Active Duty?..153
    2. Are You a Servicemember Covered by the SSCRA?............................153
    3. Are You a Co-Signer for or a Dependent of a Servicemember on
       Active Duty?..153
    4. Was the Debt Incurred Before Active Duty Began?............................153
    5. Was the Servicemember "Materially Affected"?................................154

B. How to Use the SSCRA to Reduce Your Interest Rate and Payments.................155

    1. Send Your Lender a Letter..155
    2. What to Expect From Your Lender 156

C. How to Use the SSCRA to Stop a Nonjudicial Foreclosure 157

    1. Send a Letter to Your Lender 157
    2. What to Expect From Your Lender 157

D. How to Use the SSCRA to Stop a Judicial Foreclosure..159

    1. File Affidavit With the Court 159
    2. What Your Lender Will Do 159
    3. If You Don't Respond to the Lawsuit..160

If you don't have a military connection. Skip this entire chapter if you are not in the military, not the dependent of someone in the military, or did not co-sign a loan with someone in the military.

One of the primary benefits of the Soldiers' and Sailors' Civil of 1940 and the Service Members Civil Relief Act of 2003 (collectively the "SSCRA") is the protection of active military personnel and their families (and anyone who co-signed a loan with them) from foreclosure. Although the SSCRA will not relieve you of your obligation to repay your loan, it will allow for temporary suspension of collection actions (including foreclosure) while you are on active duty.

The SSCRA has far-reaching effects and may be used to:

- *stop a foreclosure.* If you are on active duty, you may get immediate relief from a pending foreclosure. (See Sections C and D.)

- *invalidate a foreclosure sale.* If your property was sold while you were on active duty, you may be able get your property back. (See Sections C and D), and

- *reduce your loan interest rate.* While you're on active military duty, you may be entitled to a lower than market interest rate on your property loan—even if you're not in foreclosure. This may significantly reduce your monthly payments. (See Section B, below.)

This chapter helps you assess whether or not you are eligible for protection under the SSCRA. You'll also find a helpful overview of how you can use the SSCRA to stop your foreclosure. This chapter does not, however, go into depth regarding the court documents or procedures you might need. At some point, you may need to consult with an attorney or your military commander. You can also research the military website, www.military.about.com, for specifics.

A. Are You Covered by the SSCRA?

To use the SSCRA as a "shield" to stop the foreclosure, you must be able to show a court that all of the following apply:

- You are on "active duty," or you are the dependent or co-signer of a servicemember on active military duty.

- The debt is secured by a mortgage or deed of trust against your property.

- You incurred the debt prior to your active duty in the military.

- You, or your dependents, still own the property.

- Your lender has started foreclosure proceedings.

- Your ability to meet your financial obligations has been "materially affected" by your military service (see Section A5 below). (For example, your in-service income is substantially below your pre-service income or you're stationed overseas.)

Courts have broad discretion in interpreting and applying the SSCRA to foreclosure situations. Courts are sympathetic with a servicemember unable to keep current on his or her loan payments. Courts are almost always compassionate to servicemembers (and their co-signers and dependents) attempting to stop foreclosures of their property.

1. Are You on Active Duty?

If you are on active duty in the armed forces, you are entitled to special protection under the SSCRA. Section 532 of the SSCRA helps active military personnel by temporarily suspending all foreclosure proceedings (both nonjudicial and judicial, covered in Chapters 3 and 4, respectively).

2. Are You a Servicemember Covered by the SSCRA?

The SSCRA protects members of the U.S. armed forces (army, navy, air force, marine corps, and coast guard), including reservists, who are on active duty. The U.S. armed forces defines "active duty" as full-time presence on a military base due to military assignment or full-time training prior to induction. The SSCRA also protects officers of the Public Health Service who are detailed for duty with any branch of the military.

Not all military personnel are covered. The SSCRA does not protect servicemembers who are not on active duty, are on unauthorized absence ("AWOL"), or are in a military prison.

3. Are You a Co-Signer for or a Dependent of a Servicemember on Active Duty?

Frequently, a spouse, friend or family member may have signed loan documents along with a service member. When a lender discovers that they cannot legally pursue the servicemember (because of his or her active duty status in the military), they may attempt to collect from a co-signer on the loan. In these circumstances, the SSCRA extends to everyone who co-signed with an active servicemember.

The SSCRA also covers a service member's dependents who didn't sign the loan, such as children or a spouse. In other words, a lender can't proceed against a servicemember's dependents while he or she is on active duty.

4. Was the Debt Incurred Before Active Duty Began?

The SSCRA applies only to debts incurred before you began active duty in the military.

Example: Five years ago, George purchased a farm outside of Bowling Green, Kentucky. He later enlisted in the U.S. Navy and was assigned to the Long Beach Naval Shipyard. Several months after George went on active duty, he defaulted on his loan payments and his lender started foreclosure proceedings. Because George purchased his property before going on active duty, he can invoke the SSCRA and demand that his lender temporarily stop the foreclosure.

The SSCRA does not, however, apply to loans entered into after beginning active military duty. If you borrowed money to purchase property while you were already on active military duty (or after you'd left the military), the SSCRA will not stop your foreclosure.

Example: Henry, a buddy of George's, is also stationed at the Long Beach Naval Shipyard. After being on duty for several months, Henry purchases a house in Long Beach. Almost immediately, he begins missing payments and his lender initiated foreclosure proceedings. Unfortunately for Henry, the SSCRA (and its protection against foreclosure), does not apply to him because he purchased his property after he was already on active duty.

5. Was the Servicemember "Materially Affected"?

To understand your rights under the Act, you'll need to learn a bit of

HISTORY OF THE SOLDIERS' AND SAILORS CIVIL RELIEF ACT (SSCRA)

In 1918, Congress formally recognized that servicemembers couldn't reasonably attend to their financial and legal commitments while serving during wartime. Finding it unfair for lawsuits to proceed to the detriment of someone who had volunteered in the armed forces or was drafted in time of war, Congress passed the Soldiers' and Sailors Civil Relief Act of 1918. The SSCRA was intended to boost morale and allow U.S. troops to devote their attention exclusively to the war effort, without concern for their financial obligations back home,

The present SSCRA statute was passed in 1940 during World War II and has subsequently gone through only minor modifications. For foreclosure purposes, you'll be primarily interested in Chapter 4, Section 532 of the SSCRA, which deals with promissory notes, deeds of trust, mortgages, and other liens.

legal jargon. The SSCRA only covers servicemembers who are "materially affected." A servicemember who cannot protect his or her legal rights or fulfill his or her financial obligations because of being on active duty is "materially

affected." Let's look more closely at these issues.

a. Inability to Protect Your Legal Rights

If a servicemember is sued for judicial foreclosure in court, and that servicemember cannot participate in the lawsuit because of active duty in another city, state or country, that servicemember may petition the court for a stay (postponement) until he or she can personally appear and participate. In that event, the court must determine whether military service materially affects the servicemember's ability to protect his or her rights.

Example: June purchased a triplex in Syracuse, New York, and took out a loan with Scarlet Credit Union. The next year, June volunteered for the Army and was assigned to a military base in Germany. When Scarlet starts a foreclosure, June disputes their legal right to foreclose because she is on active duty. Because June's ability to protect her legal rights in New York is materially affected by her military status in Germany, the SSCRA will apply and Scarlet will be prohibited from foreclosing (at least until June returns from active duty in Germany).

PERIOD OF COVERAGE

If you are in the military, the Act protects you the day you begin active duty. The coverage also extends for 90 days after the date your active military service is completed. This protection extends to co-signers and family members.

b. Servicemember's Inability to Meet Financial Obligations

If a servicemember defaults on a loan obligation because he or she can no longer afford the payments due to being on active duty, that servicemember can contend that the military's lower wages has "materially affected" his or her financial ability to pay debts as previously agreed. This issue arises because servicemembers typically receive substantially less income in the military than they received in private life, or they are in combat and unavailable to make loan payments.

In either circumstance, the servicemember (or a co-signer or dependent) must file papers with a court asking it to stop the foreclosure until the servicemember is off active duty.

Example: John borrows $250,000 from Ace Financial Corporation to purchase a house in Grand Rapids, Michigan. Several years later, John volunteers for the U.S. Navy and is assigned to Tampa, Florida, where he's paid $1,500 per month. When John defaults on his monthly payments, Ace starts foreclosure proceedings. Because John's active duty in Tampa materially affects his ability to meet his financial obligations to Ace, John may invoke the SSCRA to stop the foreclosure until he returns home.

You will be pleased to learn that in determining the meaning of "materially affects," courts have traditionally favored the servicemember. In fact, the Supreme Court has declared that the Act must be read with "an eye friendly to those who drop their affairs to answer their country's call." (LeMaistre v. Leffers, 333 U.S. 1, 6 (1943).)

B. How to Use the SSCRA to Reduce Your Interest Rate and Payments

Regardless of the interest rate stated in your loan documents, your lender must reduce your interest rate while you are on active duty, assuming that you qualify under the "materially affected" test. Your lender's obligation to lower your interest rate is not affected by whether you are in default or there is a pending foreclosure. (50 U.S.C. § 526.)

Your only obligation is to give your lender a written request to lower the interest rate. Your lender is not required to lower the interest rate automatically if you are on active duty.

Of course, if your interest rate is lowered, your monthly payments will be correspondingly lower.

Example: Sally borrowed $320,000 from Hightop Financial Services to purchase a home in Reno, Nevada. The promissory note provided for an annual interest rate of 10%, payable at $2,667 interest-only per month. Several months later, Sally was called up for active duty in the Air Force and stationed in Seattle. Sally, aware of the SSCRA, notified Hightop of her active duty in the Air Force and asked that her interest rate be reduced to 6% while she remained on active duty. Hightop agreed and her monthly payments dropped to $1,600.

1. Send Your Lender a Letter

To reduce your interest rate on a loan you obtained before entering active military duty, you'll need to send your lender a letter. Include a copy of your military orders. Mail the letter certified mail, return receipt requested, or by overnight mail, return receipt requested. You can use the sample letter below as a guide.

[SAMPLE LETTER ASKING LENDER TO REDUCE INTEREST RATE]

June 3, 200X

Mr. Peter London
Vice President
Baltor Mortgage Company
2343 Baltor Court
Cincinnati, Ohio

Re: Account No. 65-3421

Dear Mr. London:

I own the property located at 467 Briar Street, Cincinnati, Ohio. In 200X, I borrowed $355,000 from Baltor to purchase this property, which was secured by a mortgage against my property. The purpose of this letter is to advise you that I am now on active duty with the United States Army.

Because of my call-up, and for the duration of my active duty status, I will lose my civilian employment income. As a result, my ability to repay my mortgage has been materially affected by the temporary reduction in my income. I estimate that my period of active service will end in approximately July of 200X. I will notify you in writing upon my return.

I understand that the Soldiers' and Sailors' Civil Relief Act ("Act") limits the annual rate of interest on this debt while I am on active duty {50 U.S.C. § 526). As used in the Act, the term "interest" includes service charges, carrying charges, renewal charges, fees and any other charge (except bona fide insurance) added to my loan. I understand that my dependents and cosigners are also provided protection under the Act.

Upon receipt of this request, please adjust my account to reflect the statutory interest rate and notify me of the revised payment schedule. Thank you for your understanding and cooperation in this matter.

Sincerely,

Thomas Eagle
Private First Class
U.S. Army
Enclosure: copies of military orders

2. What to Expect From Your Lender

If your lender ignores the SSCRA and proceeds with the foreclosure, you have the right to bring a lawsuit to enforce the SSCRA (See Chapter 8). In that event, your lender can be sanctioned by the Court for ignoring the SSCRA after you advised them of your active duty. Because of this potential liability, most lenders will promptly respond to your request by lowering your interest rate. The lower interest rate will continue until your tour of active duty is completed.

Occasionally, a lender may prefer to go to court and demonstrate that your financial condition is not "materially affected" by active duty and that you can still afford the regular interest rate. (We discuss the meaning of "materially affected" in Section A above.) In that unlikely event, you must demonstrate to the court that you are making substantially less money during your active duty then you did in your previous civilian employment. (Needless to say, this should be fairly easy, given the low wages paid by the military.)

When you are discharged from the military, your lender has the right to automatically increase the interest rate to the rate provided in your loan documents. Fortunately for you, your lender can't retroactively charge you the interest it "lost" during your period of active duty.

Example: George borrowed $100,000 from Pismo Savings Bank, with an interest rate of 9% adjustable. When George was called to active duty in Navy, George notified the Bank and requested that the

interest rate on his loan be reduced to 6%
pursuant to the SSCRA. The bank agreed.
When George completed his active duty, the
Bank automatically increased his interest rate
to 9%. But George was not liable for the 3%
spread (9% in the loan documents versus the
6% while on active duty) that the Bank lost
during his tour of active duty.

C. How to Use the SSCRA to Stop a Nonjudicial Foreclosure

If your lender filed a judicial foreclosure, you
can skip this section and read Section D,
below. For a review of the nonjudicial
foreclosure process, read Chapter 3.
Judicial foreclosures are covered in
Chapter 4.

A lender cannot foreclose
nonjudicially once you inform them that
you are on active duty and are seeking
protection under the SSCRA. You can
stop it by simply advising your lender
of your active military status. Either
contact your lender before you leave
or after you arrive at the military base
where you are stationed. Once you
notify your lender that you are away
from home on a military assignment,
your lender has two choices:

- Your lender may stop the nonjudicial
foreclosure and wait for you to return
from active duty.

- Your lender may file an action in
court, asking permission to proceed
with the nonjudicial foreclosure.

Because most judges understand the
significance of your military duty, they
are unlikely to allow foreclosure. Thus,
you are likely to be protected for as long
as you are on active duty in the military.

1. Send a Letter to Your Lender

Write your lender a letter as soon as
you are called to active duty and mail it
certified mail, return receipt requested.
Your letter should advise your lender
that you have been called into the
military. Request that your lender stop
the foreclosure (or hold off initiating a
foreclosure) and lower the interest rate
during your active duty. You can use the
following sample letter as a guide.

2. What to Expect From Your Lender

Because the SSCEA allows the courts to
sanction lenders who pursue foreclosure
knowing that the borrower is in the
military, most lenders will stop the
foreclosure and lower your interest
rate to 6% per year during your active
military duty without further question.

Most lenders will comply with
your request and stop the foreclosure
immediately. In this case, your
lender will advise you that upon the
termination of your active duty, the
foreclosure will resume unless you cure
the default.

But if your lender ignores your
request and proceeds with a nonjudicial
foreclosure, you have the right to file a
lawsuit in court to enjoin the foreclosure
based upon the SSCRA. (See Chapter
8 on how to file a lawsuit to enjoin a
nonjudicial foreclosure.)

SAMPLE LETTER TO LENDER (NON JUDICIAL FORECLOSURE)

December 22, 200X

Ms. Karen Johnston
Vice President
Sanctity Savings Bank
25 Main Street
Duluth, Minnesota

Re: Loan No. 976555

Dear Ms. Johnston:

In 200X, I borrowed $325,000 from Sanctity Savings Bank to purchase property located at 6701 Third Avenue, Duluth, Minnesota. I signed a promissory note and a deed of trust, which was recorded against my property. On July 6, 200X, I received notice from Sanctity that it was initiating a nonjudicial foreclosure of my property.

I understand that the Soldiers' and Sailors' Civil Relief Act prohibits the foreclosure of my property for non-payment of any sum due under the loan during the period of my military service and for 90 days thereafter (50 U.S.C. § 532). The purpose of this letter is to advise you that I am on active duty with the United States Coast Guard. Because of my call-up, and for the duration of my active duty status, I will lose my civilian employment income. As a result, my ability to repay my loan according to the terms I previously agreed has been materially affected by the temporary reduction in my income.

Accordingly, I request that you stop the pending foreclosure until I return from active duty. I estimate that my period of active service will end in approximately July of 200X. I will notify you in writing upon my return.

I also understand that the Act limits the rate of interest on this debt to six percent

(6%) per year while I am on active duty (50 U.S.C. § 526). As used in the Act, the term "interest" includes service charges, carrying charges, renewal charges, fees, and any other charge (except bona fide insurance) related to the liability. I understand that my co-signers and dependents are also provided protection under the Act.

Upon receipt of this letter, please adjust my account to reflect the statutory 6% rate and notify me in writing of the revised schedule.

Thank you for your understanding and cooperation in this matter.

Sincerely,

John Overton
Seaman
U.S. Coast Guard Reserve

If the court finds that you have been materially affected by your active duty, it may take any or all of the following actions:

- stay (stop) the foreclosure until you return from active duty

- lower your monthly payments until you return from active duty

- if a trustee's sale has already occurred, set aside (invalidate) the sale and stay the foreclosure until you return from active duty, and

- sanction your lender if they knew you were in the military and proceeded with a foreclosure anyhow.

If your lender wants to go to court to prove that you will not be adversely affected by a foreclosure, it will file a judicial foreclosure. Guidelines on how to deal with a judicial foreclosure are in Section D, below.

D. How to Use the SSCRA to Stop a Judicial Foreclosure

If your lender filed a nonjudicial foreclosure, you can skip this section and read Section C, above. For a review of the judicial foreclosure process, read Chapter 4. Nonjudicial foreclosures are covered in Chapter 3.

If your lender flies a judicial foreclosure, you need to advise the court immediately that you are on active duty. This will allow the Court to determine whether you have the ability to defend the action or it should be stayed until you return from active duty.

1. File Affidavit With the Court

Write an affidavit (sworn statement under penalty of perjury) on legal paper and file it with the Court that is handling the foreclosure. You will need to include in your affidavit the court's name and address, the case number and other important information which you will find in the Summons and Complaint you received. There is no fee for filing an affidavit. A sample affidavit, in a form recommended by the military, follows on the next page. A blank piece of numbered legal paper is provided in the Appendix.

2. What Your Lender Will Do

Once you file an affidavit with the court, the court will order that your lender stop the judicial foreclosure until you return from active duty. Because your lender can be sanctioned by the court for pursuing a foreclosure in violation of the SSCRA, they will likely comply with the court order and wait until you return from active duty before proceeding with the lawsuit. It will also lower your interest rate during your active military duty. (By the way, you should not be surprised if your lender suddenly wants to negotiate new loan terms with you.)

Occasionally, a lender will try to convince the court that you will not be adversely affected if it is allowed to proceed with the judicial foreclosure. For example, that you are making more money in the military, or that your military activity is a rouse.

3. If You Don't Respond to the Lawsuit

Let's say you didn't get notice of the lawsuit, or you didn't file a formal affidavit (or answer) to your lender's Complaint. To prevent a lender from getting a default judgment against you while you're on active duty, your lender must file a statement, under penalty of perjury, that you are not in the military. In the statement, your lender must specify that they took reasonable steps to ascertain that you are not in the military. If there is any doubt of your military status, the court may order your lender to post a security deposit to protect you in the event you need to later set aside the default judgment. The security deposit will be used for damages you may suffer as a result of a default judgment incorrectly entered against you.

If a default judgment for foreclosure was entered by the court while you were on active duty, you have powerful rights under the SSCRA. Within 90 days from the date of your discharge, you should file an application with the court and mail a copy to your lender. Your application should request that the court set aside (invalidate) the default judgment, based upon the following:

- you were on active duty in the military when the default judgment was entered by the court

- you have suffered damages (you lost your property or a derogatory item was placed on your credit report), or your case is prejudiced because you could not properly present your side of the case, and

- you have a valid, legal defense you wish to present to the court.

In the unlikely event your lender obtains a default judgment of foreclosure by falsely stating on the court form that you were not in the military, you may ask the court to sanction your lender and nullify the default judgment.

If your lender gets a default judgment against you. If you find yourself in this predicament, you will probably need to hire an attorney to file an application with the court to set aside the default judgment. For more on finding an attorney, turn to Chapter 12.

chapter

USING THE COURTS TO STOP A NONJUDICIAL FORECLOSURE

A. Do You Have Grounds to Go to Court?...162

   1. Disputes With Trustee Over Foreclosure Procedures...........................163
   2. Disputes With Lender Over Amount Due or the Terms of
      Promissory Note or Deed of Trust..165

B. Overview of a Lawsuit to Enjoin Foreclosure...171

   1. Temporary Restraining Order (TRO)...171
   2. Preliminary Injunction 172
   3. Permanent Injunction 173

C. How to File a Lawsuit and Get a Temporary Restraining Order 174

   1. Decide When to File the Lawsuit 174
   2. Decide Where to File the Lawsuit 175
   3. Check Court Rules 175
   4. Prepare Court Documents 176
   5. Complete Summons and Civil Case Cover Sheet 183
   6. Photocopy and File Documents With Court...183
   7. Record Lis Pendens 183
   8. Provide Notice and Prepare Declaration...184
   9. Attend the TRO Hearing 184
  10. Judge Rules on the TRO...185
  11. Make Sure All Service Requirements Are Met 186

D. How Your Case Proceeds After the TRO Hearing..187

If your lender filed a judicial foreclosure. A judicial foreclosure uses the court system to conduct foreclosure proceedings. You will know that a judicial foreclosure has been filed because you will have been served with an official Summons and Complaint. You may present arguments against the foreclosure as part of your answer or by way of a Cross-Complaint. We cover judicial foreclosures in Chapter 4.

As you probably know by now, a nonjudicial foreclosure is conducted without any court involvement. (We cover the step-by-step nonjudicial foreclosure procedures in Chapter 3.) But fortunately, you can still use the court system to stop a nonjudicial foreclosure if you believe that either:

- your lender did not follow the correct foreclosure procedures required in your state, or

- your lender didn't have legal grounds to foreclose in the first place.

To use the court system you must file a lawsuit--in legal jargon, an "action to enjoin the trustee's sale"--that asks a judge to temporarily enjoin (prevent) the trustee's sale until your objections are resolved. If the judge rules in your favor, he or she will grant an "injunction"--a court order that staves off the foreclosure. Injunctions can last anywhere from several weeks to several years, depending upon the validity of your objections and the type of injunction issued.

This chapter gives an overview of how to use the courts to stop a nonjudicial foreclosure. You'll examine whether or not you have grounds for going to court and what an action to enjoin the trustee's sale will accomplish. You'll also find instructions on how

to file your lawsuit and get a type of injunction known in most nonjudicial states as a temporary restraining order ("TRO"). Most lenders will be anxious to negotiate if you succeed in obtaining a TRO. If, however, you need to proceed further with the lawsuit, you'll need to go beyond this book. We summarize the legal proceedings and give suggestions on where to go for help.

A. Do You Have Grounds to Go to Court?

Before you make up your mind to file a lawsuit, be sure you have a valid legal basis for stopping the foreclosure. Don't consider going to court if you simply missed payments and now are desperately searching for a way to delay the foreclosure. Personal problems such as illness, divorce, credit card, or job loss, while crucial to you, are not relevant to the basic legal issue of whether your lender has the right to foreclose.

The legal grounds for filing a lawsuit to enjoin (stop) the trustee's sale fall into two general categories:

- disputes over your state's foreclosure procedures, and

- disputes with your lender over the terms of your promissory note and/or deed of trust. (If you have a dispute over the terms of your mortgage, you are most likely in a judicial foreclosure already.)

Below, we examine these two categories in detail. If you find you have legal grounds to file a lawsuit, first read the rest of this chapter to get a sense of what is involved in an action to enjoin the trustee's sale.

1. Disputes With Trustee Over Foreclosure Procedures

Let's say your lender has the legal right to foreclose. That is, you are in default because you haven't made your payments. But, during the non-judicial process, the trustee violates the procedural requirements of your state. For example, there may be defects in the Notice of Default, or Notice of Sale, or an irregularity in how the trustee mailed the notices. A judge may order that the foreclosure be enjoined (stopped) until the trustee corrects the procedural mistake. But if the trustee only made a minor mistake, a judge is not likely to enjoin the trustee's sale for very long. More likely, the judge will order that the process start over at the point the trustee went astray. Nevertheless, even a minor delay may provide the additional time you need to utilize other strategies described in this book.

In the event a trustee makes several procedural mistakes, the judge will probably order the trustee to start the foreclosure process over again from the beginning. (If this should occur, don't be surprised to find a plethora of possibilities, not the least of which may be your lender's sudden willingness to negotiate.)

In Chapter 3, we examined each of the nonjudicial foreclosure steps in detail. Further, the specifics of your state's foreclosure procedures are in the Appendix. Below, we help you assess whether or not the trustee handled all these procedures correctly. The bottom line is this; if the nonjudicial foreclosure process wasn't conducted properly, you have grounds to file a lawsuit.

a. Notice of Default

In Chapter 3, Section B, we provide a worksheet to help you spot errors in the Notice of Default (assuming your state uses a Notice of Default). If you haven't already completed the Notice of Default Worksheet, and compared that information to your promissory note and deed of trust, turn to Chapter 3, Section B, and do so now. Specifically make sure the following are accurate in the Notice of Default:

- name of trustor (you)
- name of beneficiary (your lender)
- name of trustee
- legal description of your property
- amount of original indebtedness
- date deed of trust was recorded, and
- document number of the deed of trust.

Also double-check that the trustee followed the correct requirements of your state for mailing, publishing, posting and recording the Notice of Default. Again, refer to the Notice of Default Worksheet. If you don't have all of the information, you have the right to ask the trustee to provide written evidence that it mailed, published, recorded and posted the Notice of Default.

b. Reinstatement Period

As you may recall, the reinstatement period is the time period that runs from the date the Notice of Default is issued and ends prior to the trustee's sale. If, during the reinstatement period, any of the following occurred, you have grounds to stop the foreclosure:

• The trustee or your lender failed to respond to your written request for a beneficiary statement after the Notice of Default was filed. (We show you how to request a beneficiary statement in Chapter 3, Section B4.)

• The trustee or your lender sent you a beneficiary statement, but the statement did not fulfill the legal requirements because it didn't include a breakdown of your unpaid balance, the total arrears, the amount of your monthly payment, the date your loan is due, the amounts of any liens paid by your lender, the date through which taxes have been paid, the amount of insurance (if any), the amounts in any impound accounts, or a statement of whether your loan is assumable.

• If your loan was assigned to another lender, your lender failed to send you a notice of the assignment by mail, which included the name and address of your new lender (or servicer), the date of the transfer, and the due date for your next payment.

• You offered to pay the total arrears and trustee's fees during the reinstatement period, but the trustee or your lender refused to accept it (For more on the reinstatement period, see Chapter 3, Section C.)

c. Notice of Sale

The Notice of Sale (also called a "Notice of Trustee's Sale" in some states) must be consistent with the information in your promissory note, deed of trust and Notice of Default. Carefully scrutinize these documents for errors. If the information is inconsistent, you may have grounds to stop the foreclosure. We provide a Notice of Sale Worksheet in Chapter 3, Section D3, to help you with this process. We also review some of the common errors trustees make in Chapter 3, Section D4. Cross-check the following:

• name of trustor (you)

• name of beneficiary (your lender). If the name of the beneficiary is different, ask the trustee or a title insurance company whether the new lender has recorded a Notice of Assignment of Beneficial Interest.

• name of trustee. If the trustee is different that the trustee named on your deed of trust, ask a title insurance company to determine whether a Substitution of Trustee was recorded in the county recorder's office prior to the Notice of Default being recorded.

• legal description of your property

• amount of original indebtedness

• date deed of trust was recorded

• document number of the deed of trust

• were the mailing requirements properly followed pursuant to your state's laws? (See worksheet in Chapter 3, Section D3 for this and succeeding questions.) Were the publishing requirements properly followed pursuant to your state's laws? Were the posting requirements properly followed pursuant to your state's laws? Were the <u>recording</u> requirements properly followed pursuant to your state's laws?

- was the Notice of Sale recorded sufficiently after the Notice of Default was recorded?

- does the Notice of Sale state the date, time, location and terms of the trustee's sale?

- if an IRS or state Tax lien has been recorded, did the trustee send a copy of the Notice of Sale to the taxing agency a specific number of days prior to the scheduled sale date? If the trustee doesn't have or won't disclose this information, contact the customer service department of a local title insurance company to determine whether any tax liens are recorded against your property. Then, armed with this information, contact the particular taxing agency and inquire whether they received a copy of the Notice of Sale.)

- is the trustee's sale scheduled a specific number of days after the date of the Notice of Sale?

d. Redemption Period

The final calendar days before the trustee's sale are called the Redemption Period and is different in every state. During the Redemption Period, the trustee may have mishandled the foreclosure procedures. For example, if your lender refused to accept your payment even though you offered full payment of the amount you owed (including principal, unpaid interest,

costs, penalties, late fees and foreclosure costs).

IF THE TRUSTEE'S SALE HAS ALREADY HAPPENED

If your property was already sold at a trustee's sale, it's obviously too late to file a lawsuit to enjoin the trustee's sale. Nevertheless, if the trustee conducted the foreclosure procedures improperly, you may still have some recourse.

If your lender purchased the property, you may ask a court to invalidate the trustee's sale and return the property to you, known as a lawsuit to "set aside the trustee's sale." This lawsuit will be somewhat complicated by the fact that you must justify why you waited until after the trustee's sale before filing the lawsuit.

If your property was sold at the trustee's sale to a third party (rather than your lender), you cannot set aside the sale or get back your property. Instead, you're limited to filing a lawsuit for money damages against your lender or trustee.

Because filing a lawsuit after the trustee's sale is quite complex, you should see a lawyer if you want to proceed.

2. Disputes With Lender Over Amount Due or the Terms of Promissory Note or Deed of Trust

You have the right to challenge your lender's right to foreclose if:

- you dispute the amount your lender claims you owe

- Regulation Z requirements (federal disclosure laws designed to protect borrowers) were not followed

- there was fraud in the original transaction, or

- the promissory note or deed of trust is defective.

Let's explore each of these categories separately, starting with the most common problem and progressing to the least likely.

a. Disagreements Over the Amount Owed

Accounting disputes frequently arise over the amount that is in default or whether a payment was (or wasn't) made. If this should occur and you believe your lender is overcharging you to reinstate or redeem your property, you have the right to file a lawsuit to stop the foreclosure. If you can convince a judge that there is a legitimate dispute over the amount in default, the Judge will briefly enjoin the pending foreclosure until the correct amount owed can be determined. There tend

to be more disputes over adjustable-rate-mortgage (ARM) loans than fixed-interest-rate notes, primarily because ARMs are constantly fluctuating up and down and are more likely to contain mathematical errors.

At first glance, you may think that the chances of your loan being improperly calculated by your lender are improbable at best.

The fact is that the error rate is higher with adjustable rate loans as compared to fixed-rate loans. Why are errors so prevalent? More than 75% of the errors were caused by lenders using the wrong index value in determining the interest rate. Personnel who manage thousands of promissory notes on a daily basis usually are overworked and inadequately trained. They have been known to input incorrect dates, or rates, when it comes time to adjust the interest rate. Further, outmoded computer systems, and the sheer volume and variety of loans, also contribute to the problem.

Here are six separate warning signs of loan errors:

- *Your original lender sold your loan.* When loan data are transferred from one lender to another lender or servicer, there is an increased possibility that processing systems are incompatible or data was interpreted incorrectly.

- *Your loan is based on an uncommon index.* The one-year treasury bill is a common index. But less common indices, such as the cost of funds, cost of savings, or Libor rate, require ongoing research to ensure that current statistical information from the index is adjusted to determine the correct interest rate. If your lender is using an unusual index, their calculations are more likely to be wrong.

- *Your promissory note contained blank spaces.* If any spaces were left blank, your lender could have added terms you didn't agree to.

- *Your loan has complex or unusual terms.* Loans with short terms (three years or less), bi-weekly payments, or an unusual term or condition (such as graduated payments depending on irregular principal reductions), or negative amortization, leave more room for error because the figures cannot be plugged into a standard computer program.

- *Your lender can't answer your questions.* If you aren't satisfied with your lender's explanation about a problem, there's a good chance your lender is confused about it as well.

GETTING HELP

Companies that specialize in calculating the correct interest rates, payments, arrears, and outstanding balances on loans spring up and disappear quicker than you can say "My lender is cheating me!" Such companies can typically be found in your local yellow pages or on the internet. Nevertheless, the better approach, if you can afford it, is to hire a certified public accountant who has experience in auditing loans.

If even one warning sign applies, immediately write a letter to the lender and demand to have your CPA audit

your loan, at your expense, before the lender proceeds further with the foreclosure. Refer to the sample letter on the next page as a guide.

Don't be surprised if your lender is extremely responsive and temporarily postpones the foreclosure sale until your CPA can audit the loan. If your lender is not willing to cooperate, go ahead and file your lawsuit to enjoin the foreclosure. You are still in a better position than if you had not written the letter, as you now have additional "ammunition" to use in your lawsuit to demonstrate your lender's bad faith. Based on this evidence, a court would certainly order an audit before allowing your lender to proceed with a foreclosure. The only caution here is to avoid waiting too long for your lender to respond.

If you're running out of time. If a Notice of Sale has already been issued, file a lawsuit and request that the court enjoin the foreclosure until an audit can be conducted.

b. Failure to Comply With Truth-in-Lending (Regulation Z) Disclosures

The federal Truth-in-Lending Act provides a series of laws to protect consumers who are borrowing money to purchase or refinance real estate. For purposes of foreclosure, the most important section of the Act is called "Regulation Z."

Regulation Z applies to all lenders who loan money more than 25 times a year (or more than five times a year if the loans are secured by owner-occupied residences), which includes

August 12, 200X

Mr. Edgar Williams
Vice President
Toucan Mortgage Company
6666 Main Street
Salt Lake City, Utah

Re: Loan No. 3423464

Dear Mr. Williams:

In September of 200X, I borrowed $360,000 from Toucan Mortgage Company. This loan was secured by a deed of trust recorded against my property located at 234 Bird Street, Salt Lake City, Utah.

Last month, Toucan's trustee initiated a nonjudicial foreclosure by recording a Notice of Default in the county recorder's office. Upon close inspection of the Notice of Default, I saw that it states I owe $5,245 to reinstate my loan. This amount is incorrect. I believe I owe less than $2,930. I believe this mistake is caused by your incorrect calculation of the interest rate.

Under the circumstances, I request that my certified public accountant audit your books and records with respect to my loan. I will follow up this letter by telephoning your office on Wednesday morning to schedule an appointment for my CPA to conduct the audit. If you will not be available to accept my call, please designate someone to discuss the audit arrangements with me. In the interim, I request that the foreclosure be postponed until we can determine the correct amount owed.

Thank you in advance for your anticipated cooperation in this matter.

Sincerely,

Peter Berger

most institutional lenders. Private lenders who are not in the business of loaning money, such as the previous property owner who accepted a deed of trust or mortgage as a portion of the purchase price, ordinarily are not required to comply with Regulation Z.

Under Regulation Z, lenders must disclose the following information, in writing, to each borrower:

- total amount financed
- annual percentage interest rate charged (APR)
- amount of each payment
- total interest to be paid
- time schedule for payments
- total finance charge
- total of all payments during the term of loan
- any transaction or service charges
- loan fees
- premiums for private mortgage insurance, if applicable, and
- premiums for property insurance, if applicable.

If your lender didn't comply with Regulation Z, you may have the right to stop the foreclosure until your lender gives you all of the required disclosures, even if you took out the loan years ago. Even minor errors in the disclosures or calculations, especially in the interest rate, may be sufficient grounds to have a judge enjoin the foreclosure. Regulation Z also slaps penalties on lenders that make errors or fail to properly disclose financial information. Penalties may include a loss of interest due the lender and punitive damages up to three times the amount of the loan.

Most lenders provide a Truth-in-Lending Statement and Regulation Z form that contain all required information (at the top of the documents in a series of easy-to-understand boxes) and a Notice of Right to Cancel. A good lender will also have you sign or initial the forms so they have physical evidence that you received the required information. If, however, your lender never gave you a Truth-in-Lending Statement, or Regulation Z form, or a Notice of Right to Cancel, or neglected to disclose financial terms in writing, or incorrectly calculated the financial information on the form, you may have legitimate grounds for filing a lawsuit.

Start by locating your Truth-in-Lending Statement, Regulation Z form, and Notice of Right to Cancel (if you have it), and carefully check the accuracy of the financial information. If you have any problems analyzing the calculations, consider hiring a bookkeeper or an accountant to determine whether the disclosures are correct.

IF YOU CAN'T FIND YOUR REGULATION Z FORM

If you can't find copies of your Regulation Z forms, call the escrow, settlement agent, or title company that handled your loan and ask if there is a copy in their closed files. If you can't get a copy from them, call your lender and ask for the name of the President, Vice President, branch manager, or loan officer. Then write a letter to that person and request a copy of your Truth-in-Lending Statement, Regulation Z form,

and Notice of Right to Cancel. Because the foreclosure clock is ticking, you can't afford to lose any more time, so arrange to pick up the copies at their office. A sample letter requesting the Regulation Z forms appears on the next page.

July 10, 200X

Mr. John Smith
Vice President
Ocean Savings Bank
4545 Third Avenue
Tampa, Florida

Re: Loan No. 67-45654

Dear Mr. Smith:

My wife, Susan, and I obtained a loan with Ocean Savings Bank in August of 200X for $500,000. The loan was secured by a mortgage encumbering our property located at 234 Oak Street, Tampa, Florida.

As you may know, last month, Ocean initiated a judicial foreclosure. While preparing to resolve the foreclosure, we looked for a copy of our Truth-in-Lending Statement and Regulation Z form, but were unable to locate it. In fact, I do not recall ever receiving a Regulation Z form.

If you have a copy of these forms, please photocopy them for me. I will telephone you in the morning on Monday, July 15, to arrange to pick up the copies. Thank you for your prompt attention to my request.

Very truly yours,

John Sousa

If your lender doesn't respond within several days, immediately send a second letter. At the bottom, indicate that you're sending a copy to the United States

Office of Thrift Supervision ("OTS"), if the lender is a savings bank. The OTS is the department of the United States government responsible for regulating savings banks. The address of the OTS is located at 1700 G Street NW, Washington, D.C. 20552 If the lender is a commercial bank, send a copy of your letter to the Federal Deposit Insurance Corporation ("FDIC"). The address of the FDIC is 550 17th Street, Washington, D.C. 20429. You will be amazed at how quickly your lender may now respond when it sees that you sent a copy to the OTS or the FDIC.

If your lender won't give you a copy of your Truth-in-Lending Statement, Regulation Z form, or Notice of Right to Cancel. It's probably because your lender either didn't provide the forms to you in the first place, cannot find them, or doesn't want you to see your forms (because there are errors in them). Your lender's recalcitrance in turning over copies (if they even exist) will exemplify their bad faith and become further evidence that they failed to comply with Regulation Z. Proceed with your lawsuit to enjoin the foreclosure and attach your two letters, and any written response you receive from your lender, as exhibits.

c. Fraud in the Original Transaction

This category of disputes is a catch-all for any situation in which your lender may have acted improperly when they lent you money. If nothing comes to mind, it probably does not apply to you. On the other hand, if the words "fraud" and "misrepresentation" set off alarm bells in your head, and remind you that

there was something dishonest in the way your lender dealt with you, you may have grounds to ask a court to stop the foreclosure.

Following are some examples of fraud:

• When you signed the loan documents, your lender promised in writing (forget it if the promises were only oral) that you could extend the loan when it came due, or that they would gladly refinance your loan if you ever needed to. Now suddenly, that same lender is foreclosing and won't even return your telephone calls.

• You signed loan documents that contained onerous conditions, such as an extremely high (usurious) interest rate.

• After foreclosing on property you owned, your lender required that you sign a deed of trust or mortgage on another property.

• The party foreclosing is a foreclosure consultant you previously hired to help you with an earlier foreclosure, who (improperly) took back a mortgage or deed of trust as part of his or her compensation.

If any of these scenarios sound familiar to you. Consult an attorney immediately. This very technical area is beyond the scope of this book. A real estate lawyer can assist in filing a lawsuit based upon your lender's fraud in the original transaction.

d. Defects in the Mortgage or Deed of Trust

Although rare, there are occasionally defects in a mortgage, promissory note, or deed of trust, such as incorrect or inconsistent terms. Or the loan documents are not signed, never recorded, recorded against the wrong property, or contain incorrect or inconsistent terms. If you believe that your loan documents are invalid for any reason, you have grounds for filing a lawsuit to enjoin the foreclosure. You should contact a lawyer for assistance in preparing such a lawsuit. (See Chapter 2 for explanations of promissory notes, deeds of trust, and mortgages.)

MONITOR TRUSTEE'S ACTIVITIES

Even if you have an agreement with your Lender to temporarily postpone a nonjudicial foreclosure sale, you should still monitor the trustee's activities. If the trustee schedules a sale anyway, immediately advise the trustee and lender in writing. In most cases, your letter will stop the sale. If it doesn't, you'll need to file a lawsuit to enjoin the foreclosure based upon your lender's breach of the agreement. (See Section B below.)

B. Overview of a Lawsuit to Enjoin Foreclosure

If you file a lawsuit, you will ask the court for an injunction (court order), stopping the foreclosure until the issues raised in your complaint can be resolved. Different injunctions apply at various stages of your lawsuit, and each state has slightly different names for each injunction. Depending on your state, first you'll get a temporary restraining order ("TRO"), then a preliminary injunction, and finally, if the dispute is still going on, a permanent injunction.

1. Temporary Restraining Order (TRO)

In the foreclosure context, a temporary restraining order ("TRO") is an emergency interim court order that immediately stops all foreclosure activity. A judge can grant a TRO within a very short period of time, typically within 24 hours, and after a brief hearing in the courtroom. Depending on your state, a TRO will last approximately 7-14 days, or until the judge can schedule a preliminary hearing on the matter.

A TRO won't be granted automatically. Within a foreclosure context, you must file an application (or motion), and present evidence (your declaration and supporting documents) at a hearing and convince a judge of these three points:

1. *You will be "irreparably harmed" if the TRO is not granted.* If you are trying to protect your home, you are in an excellent position to argue that you will be "irreparably harmed" unless the TRO is granted. This is because a single-family, owner-occupied residence, is presumed "unique" because there is no real substitute. Because your home is unique and has special sentimental value to you, losing it in foreclosure would be unquestionably harmful. On the other hand, if your property is not your personal residence, you have a more difficult burden. For example, a multi-residential or commercial property is presumed to be an investment, the value of which can be recovered in

monetary damages in a regular lawsuit. So if the property being foreclosed is not in fact your residence, be prepared to argue that your property is nevertheless unique (because of its architectural attributes, historical significance, or some other special feature) and that you will be irreparably harmed if you lose it through foreclosure.

2. *Money damages are not adequate*. This test is easy to demonstrate. If you lose your residence through foreclosure, and then win your lawsuit, you would be entitled only to monetary damages. Judges understand and sympathize that money damages could never make up for the loss of your family residence. If, however, your property is nonresidential, money damages are presumed adequate unless you can prove otherwise.

3. *You are likely to win the case*. A judge will grant a TRO only if it appears from the documentation you submit that (a) there is a real question as to how much you owe, (b) your lender acted improperly, or (c) the trustee committed a procedural error while conducting the nonjudicial foreclosure. But, until all of the evidence and testimony have been presented-which won't happen until your case goes to trial in one to two years--the judge can't know for sure whether you will win. As a result, judges treat this requirement with less significance than the previous two, as long as your case looks good on paper.

If a judge decides the three issues in your favor, he or she will grant the TRO to stop the foreclosure. Otherwise, the judge will deny the TRO and allow the trustee to proceed with the foreclosure. Either way, the judge will schedule a hearing for a preliminary injunction (usually within 15 to 30 days),

and request that you and your lender prepare additional memoranda (legal briefs on the relevant legal issues) and present further evidence to support your respective positions.

When granting a TRO, judges sometimes require that you tender (pay) any arrears that you admittedly owe your lender. However, you may convince a judge to waive this requirement in situations where:

• the promissory note or deed of trust is defective

• there was fraud in the original transaction

• the amount you owe is in dispute and an audit must be conducted determine how much you owe

• payment might be construed as relinquishing your right to rescind (as for example in a Regulation Z violation. Where the lender has violated Regulation Z, if the borrower continues to make the payments, she is deemed to have waived the violation), or

• you can prove that nothing is due, or you have a claim against your lender, such as a setoff for an amount that exceeds the amount you owe your lender.

2. Preliminary Injunction

Depending on your state, approximately two to four weeks after the TRO hearing, you will attend another hearing and ask the judge for a preliminary injunction--an order enjoining (stopping)

BOND MAY BE REQUIRED

Depending on the facts of your case, don't be surprised if the Judge grants a TRO on the condition that you post a "bond" to protect your lender should the TRO turn out to be unwarranted. A bond is a written contract you enter into with a bonding company. Similar to insurance, you pay the bonding company a fee (typically 10% of the amount of the bond) and the bonding company agrees to reimburse your lender for its actual damages (such as lost interest and legal fees) in the event the TRO is subsequently terminated.

The amount of the bond is frequently the most contentious issue at a TRO hearing. Your lender will try to convince the Judge to set the bond as high as possible so that you won't be able to pay for it. In response, be prepared to argue that if there is adequate equity in the property {pre-lien equity}, the lender is protected because the deed of trust already protects your lender against defaults. In other words, the bond should protect your lender only against losses caused by delays in the foreclosure. You'll want to point out that if a bond is required at all, it should cover less than one month's payment, because the TRO will delay the foreclosure for only 2-4 weeks.

the foreclosure until the trial. Because the trial may not take place for one to two years, a preliminary injunction is a powerful weapon. Of course, if the TRO was denied and the trustee's sale occurred, you will no longer need a preliminary injunction. However, even without a preliminary injunction, your lawsuit against your lender will

still proceed. In that event, you will be limited to recovering monetary damages against your lender rather than an injunction of the foreclosure.

The same three issues the judge considered at the TRO hearing will apply at the preliminary hearing: you will be irreparably harmed if the injunction isn't granted, monetary damages are inadequate, and there is a reasonable likelihood that you will win at trial. The only difference now is that the judge will have heard your lender's version of the story and reviewed most of the evidence. The trustee typically will not attend these hearings unless there is a dispute over the trustee's handling of the foreclosure procedures.

If the judge grants a preliminary injunction, that order will replace the TRO. You will be allowed to keep the property while your case is wending its way to trial and the bond will stay in effect. At this point don't be surprised if your lender is suddenly eager to negotiate with you, because in essence you have neutralized the foreclosure.

If the judge denies the preliminary injunction, the TRO will be extinguished and the foreclosure will resume. You'll still have the right to try your case. However, you may decide against doing so because by the time your case goes to trial, you will no longer be the owner of the property. Further, you'll be limited to seeking monetary damages rather than your right to keep the property.

3. Permanent Injunction

As you can see above, most cases are settled early and never go to trial. If you get the TRO and preliminary injunction, lenders typically negotiate a settlement with you rather than waiting for trial. On the other hand, if you lose the injunction and the property is foreclosed, you probably won't have the impetus to pursue the lawsuit. Nevertheless, if your case does go to trial, a judge will make a final ruling on the foreclosure dispute (called a "judgment"). If the judgment is in your favor, the judge will issue a "permanent injunction," that permanently stops the foreclosure (and supersedes the preliminary injunction). On the other hand, if the judge rules in favor of your lender, the preliminary injunction will be terminated and your lender will resume its foreclosure.

Although legally possible, it is rare for either side to appeal to a higher court. An appeal would require a lawyer's help.

C. How to File a Lawsuit and Get a Temporary Restraining Order

Filing a lawsuit to enjoin a nonjudicial foreclosure is not an easy task. The lawsuit must be filed in the court in the county where your property is located (regardless of where you actually live) These courts notoriously have the trickiest rules and the least help for someone appearing without a lawyer. Accordingly, if you have the funds, or qualify for legal aid, a lawyer can be a valuable asset during the proceedings.

If you hire a lawyer. This chapter will help you understand the procedures and lexicon involved in a lawsuit to enjoin a foreclosure. In this way, you'll be better equipped to help your lawyer fight the foreclosure in court. Afterall, who knows your case better than you?

That being said, you may have difficulty finding an affordable lawyer or you may choose to forge ahead on your own. This section shows you how to file a lawsuit yourself (called "in pro per" in legalese) and get a temporary restraining order.

1. Decide When to File the Lawsuit

Here's your dilemma: If you file your lawsuit too soon after the Notice of Default is recorded, your lender (or the trustee) has plenty of opportunity to correct its errors and proceed with the foreclosure, or start the foreclosure over from the beginning. On the other hand, if you wait and file your lawsuit just days before the scheduled trustee's sale, a judge may interpret your timing as a bad-faith delay tactic (called "laches") and deny your request for a TRO.

We suggest you follow these guidelines, based on your reasons for going to court:

• If you dispute the foreclosure procedures, file your Complaint as soon as you receive a copy of the Notice of Sale, and know the actual date and time of the trustee's sale. (Section A1, above, discusses disputes over foreclosure procedures.)

• If your dispute is over how much is owed or concerns the terms of the promissory note or deed of trust, file your Complaint within 30 days after the Notice of Default is recorded (if possible). (Section A2, above, discusses these kinds of disputes.)

2. Decide Where to File the Lawsuit

A lawsuit to enjoin a trustee's sale must be filed in the Court of the county in which your property is located. Look in the phone book, search the internet, or call directory assistance to locate the court. If there are two or more branches of the Court in your county, use the one that is closest to your property. If you are unsure, go to one of the courts and ask in the clerk's office, which Court is appropriate for filing a lawsuit involving property located at your address.

3. Check Court Rules

Every court, in every county, in every state, has slightly different rules governing how to file a lawsuit and seek a temporary restraining order (TRO). There is nothing terribly difficult about the rules, but you may have to do a little digging to make sure you understand and follow them. Call or visit the court clerk's office and ask if you must follow special rules. In legal jargon (depending on your state), you will be bringing an "Ex Parte Application for a TRO"-- meaning you won't give formal advance written notice to the other side. The clerk should refer you to:

• the court's local rules, available from the court, your local law library, or on their website

• the statewide Rules of Court available in law libraries, some large public libraries, or on the state's website, or both.

Next, get answers to the following questions by reviewing the rules--and checking with the court clerk if you get stuck:

• When are Ex Parte Applications heard? Usually, they are heard either in the morning (at 8:30 a.m.), or in the afternoon (at 1:30 p.m.), before regularly scheduled hearings. You may need to contact the court directly to find out the correct times.

• How much does it cost to file a Complaint and Ex Parte Application? The filing fees vary from state to state, and among counties, and range from $100 to $400. (These may be waived if you qualify as indigent.)

• How many copies of the documents are required?

• Do the documents have to be submitted in a particular form? For example, some courts may require that documents be on recycled pleading paper, be two-hole punched at the top, or have blue paper stapled to the back of the documents.

4. Prepare Court Documents

If you think you have already seen a lot of paperwork, you'll need to steel yourself for a great deal more. Your lawsuit must be typed or word processed, double-spaced, on 8 x 11" pleading paper that is numbered and vertically lined. A piece of numbered lined paper is provided in the Appendix. You can either photocopy it in abundance or buy numbered lined paper from an office supply store. If you have access to a computer, most word processing programs (such as Word or Wordperfect) have pleading paper within their programs.)

On the first page of every document, fill in your name, address and telephone number at the top left corner. Starting on line 8, center the title of the court in capital letters. Place the caption (the name of plaintiff(s), defendant(s), case number and name of the document) several lines below. Fill in the title of the document. (See example on the following page.)

Depending on your state's rules, to file a lawsuit and get a TRO, you must prepare eight documents:
1. Complaint for Declaratory Relief and Injunctive Relief
2. Ex Parte Application for Temporary Restraining Order and
   preliminary injunction
3. Memorandum of Points and Authorities
4. Declaration(s) in Support of the Application
5. Proposed Temporary Restraining Order
6. Notice of Lis Pendens
7. Summons, and
8. Proof of Service.

Below, we describe these documents and, except for the Summons, provide samples you can use as templates to compose your own versions. (If you need more help preparing your court documents, check the resources described above in Section B or those described in Chapter 12.)

The idea of these documents is to tell what happened chronologically and ask for relief, not to use a bunch of legal jargon that you don't understand. If you have trouble with some of the language in the samples, and the book's glossary doesn't help, just do the best you can--in your own words.

Don't use our samples blindly. Every county in every state has different rules and different forms. The samples in this chapter are only intended as suggestions and guides, but should not be copied verbatim. You will need to substitute your own information that is unique to your case into the documents and delete material that doesn't apply in your case.

a. Complaint to Enjoin the Trustee' Sale

A Complaint is a document that states the facts of your case, the legal theories that you believe apply (called "causes of action"), and the relief you want from the court (for instance, a temporary restraining order). Depending on your circumstances, your complaint may request:

• Declaratory relief. (A request that the court decide whether your position or your lender's position is legally correct.)

• Injunctive relief. (A request that the court enjoin the scheduled trustee's sale until the court can determine if your allegations are correct.)

• An accounting. (A request that your lender make the relevant books and records available to your accountant, so he or she can audit your loan and determine the correct amount owed.)

• Fraud and misrepresentation. (A request that, based upon your lender's misrepresentations or misconduct, the court rule that there was fraud in the loan transaction causing the foreclosure to be improper.)

A sample Complaint, with several different causes of action begins on the following page. Use only the causes of action that specifically apply to your situation.

b. Ex Parte Application for Temporary Restraining Order

This document asks a judge to issue a court order temporarily enjoining (stopping) the pending trustee's sale. It is generally one or two pages and summarizes in a couple of sentences why the foreclosure should be enjoined.

The application is referred to as "ex parte" (without formal advance written notice to the other side) because the court will typically hear it within 24 to 48 hours, even if the defendants (your lender and the trustee) do not attend the hearing. You will need to justify why your application must be heard on less than the regular notice (usually 21 days). As shown in the sample beginning on the next page, you may simply state that

the trustee's sale is scheduled to occur on a specific date that doesn't allow for regular advance notice (which is typically 21 days away).

c. Memorandum of Points and Authorities

This document states the facts of your case, the issues you want the judge to consider in your favor ("points"), the applicable law on those points ("authorities"), and how the law applies to your facts. If the judge grants the TRO, it will be based upon the arguments in your memorandum.

Your most important job is to present the relevant facts correctly, preferably in chronological order. Refer to the specific documents that support the facts and, if possible, attach copies of those documents as exhibits to your declaration. (See subsection d, below for guidance on how to prepare exhibits.) In the sample beginning on the next page, we provide some model language and give legal citations to use in your memorandum.

d. Declaration in Support of the Application (With Documentary Evidence)

The declaration (also known as an "affidavit") is your written statement, under penalty of perjury, that substitutes for your live testimony (a judge rarely wants live testimony at the initial TRO hearing). The declaration should mirror the facts presented in your Memorandum of Points and Authorities.

All documents that confirm the facts of your case should be attached as exhibits to your declaration, to serve as documentary evidence. You should include copies of these documents as exhibits to your declaration (remember to keep the originals):

- deed to the property
- promissory note
- deed of trust
- relevant monthly statements
- relevant canceled checks
- Notice of Default
- Notice of Trustee's Sale
- Letters and notices received from lender and trustee, and
- letters you sent to your lender and trustee.

Organize copies of the documents in chronological order and label them as exhibits on the bottom of the first page of each document ("Exhibit A," "Exhibit B," and so on). Then staple them to your declaration. Make sure your declaration refers to each exhibit by document name and exhibit number--for example, "See Notice of Default, attached to this declaration as Exhibit A and incorporated herein by this reference." A sample declaration begins on the following page.

e. Proposed Court Order

If a judge grants your request for a TRO, she will sign a temporary restraining order, which puts the judge's decision into effect. But, the judge doesn't write the order; you will need to supply a proposed order to the judge for her signature. Follow the sample provided at the end of this chapter, modifying it to fit your situation. And don't worry, if the judge wants to make any modifications, she will handwrite the changes directly on the proposed order.

f. Lis Pendens

A Notice of Pending Action ("Lis Pendens") document states that you have filed a lawsuit contesting your lender's right to foreclose your property. You don't file the Lis Pendens with the court; instead, you record it in the recorder's office in the county where your property is located. It should be recorded immediately after you file your Complaint in the Court. (We give instructions on how to record the Lis Pendens in Section C5, below).

A Lis Pendens is often called the "poor's man injunction." That is because once you file your lawsuit, you have the automatic right to record a Lis Pendens; you don't need court approval. The recorded Lis Pendens gives notice to everyone investigating the title of your property that a lawsuit about the ownership is pending. When title companies or attorneys run a title search, or a purchaser obtains a preliminary title report, the Lis Pendens will appear as a cloud (defect) on title to your property. This will discourage anyone from buying the property until your lawsuit is resolved.

A Lis Pendens provides great incentive for your lender to settle the lawsuit. Until your lawsuit is resolved, or the Lis Pendens is removed by the court (called "expunged"), any purchaser would acquire your property subject to the Lis Pendens. In other words, if someone buys your property at a trustee's sale with a Lis Pendens recorded against it and you eventually win your lawsuit, the buyer will be forced to give the property back to you. This alone may scare off potential buyers and title insurance companies (which will refuse to give insurance because of your Lis Pendens). See the sample Lis Pendens at the end of this chapter.

[Sample of Complaint to Enjoin Trustee's Sale]

Herbert Shellford
453 Rialto Avenue
Sacramento, California
916-555-5555

Plaintiff In Pro Per

SUPERIOR COURT OF THE STATE OF CALIFORNIA

FOR THE COUNTY OF SACRAMENTO

HERBERT SHELLFORD,)	Case No: SC-734423
)	
Plaintiff,)	**Complaint for:**
)	1. Declaratory Relief
V.)	2. Injunctive Relief
)	3. Accounting
GOLDEN STATE SAVINGS BANK;)	
TRUSTEE SERVICE CORPORATION;)	
and DOES 1 to 5, inclusive,)	
)	
Defendants.)	
)	

_ _ _ _ _ _ _ _ _ _ _ _ _ _ _ _ _ _

Plaintiff HERBERT SHELLFORD ("Plaintiff") alleges:

FIRST CAUSE OF ACTION
(Declaratory Relief)

1. Plaintiff is a resident of the County of Sacramento, State of
California. Plaintiff is the owner of the real property located at 453
Rialto Avenue, Sacramento, California (the "Property").

2. Defendant, Golden Savings Bank ("Golden State"), a federally
chartered savings bank, is engaged in the banking business in California.

3. Defendant, Trustee Service Corporation ("TSC"), a California
corporation, is a trustee in the business of conducting non-judicial
foreclosures of real property.

4. Plaintiff is unaware of the true names and capacities of the
Defendants sued as Does 1 through 10 inclusive, and therefore sues these
Defendants as Does. Plaintiff is informed and believes that each of these
Doe Defendants is responsible in some manner for the acts alleged in

this Complaint and is responsible for the damages suffered by Plaintiff described in this Complaint. The Plaintiff will advise the Court of the true names and capacities of these Doe Defendants as soon as their identities are ascertained.

5. Plaintiff is informed and believes that some of the defendants are the agents, servants, and/or employees of the remaining Defendants, and in doing the things described in this Complaint were acting within the scope of their agency and/or employment.

6. On or about August 15, 200X, Plaintiff borrowed $360,000.00 from Defendant Golden State to purchase the Property. As evidence of the loan transaction, Plaintiff signed and delivered to Defendant Golden State a written promissory note. A copy of the promissory note is attached to this Complaint as Exhibit "A" and incorporated by this reference.

7. To secure payment of the promissory note, Plaintiff signed and delivered to Defendant Golden State a deed of trust dated August 15, 200X, in which Plaintiff (as trustor) conveyed to Defendant TSC (as trustee) an interest in the Property as security for payment of the promissory note to Defendant Golden State (as beneficiary).

8. On or about August 16, 200X, the deed of trust was recorded in the Official Records of Sacramento County, California. A copy of the deed of trust is attached to this Complaint as Exhibit "B" and incorporated by reference.

9. On or about February 10, 200X, Defendant TSC recorded a Notice of Default and Election to Sell in the Official Records of Sacramento County, California, alleging a default of the promissory note and deed of trust. A copy of the Notice of Default is attached to this Complaint as Exhibit "C" and incorporated by reference.

10. On or about May 6, 200X, Defendant TSC recorded a Notice of Trustee's Sale in the Official Records of Sacramento County, California, announcing that TSC will conduct a trustee's sale of the Property on May 29, 200X, at the hour of 10:00 a.m., in front of the County courthouse, located at 10 Elm Street, Sacramento, California. A copy of the Notice of Trustee's Sale is attached to this Complaint as Exhibit "D" and incorporated by reference.

11. Defendant TSC has failed to comply with the publishing and posting requirements of Civil Code Section 2924F in that TSC, as trustee, failed to wait three full months after issuing the Notice of Default before issuing the Notice of Trustee's Sale. As a result, an actual controversy exists between Plaintiff and Defendants as to their respective rights and duties with respect to the pending non-judicial foreclosure. Plaintiff contends that the trustee has failed to comply with Civil Code Section 2924f and Defendants TSC and Golden State dispute this contention and contend that the trustee acted in compliance with Section 2924 of the Civil Code.

12. The amount Defendant Golden State contends in the Notice of Default and Notice of Trustee's Sale that is in default is incorrect.

Accordingly, the Plaintiff is not in default under the terms of the promissory note and deed of trust. However, Defendant Golden State refuses to accept a partial payment until the amount in dispute is resolved. As a result, an actual controversy exists between Plaintiff and Defendant Golden State concerning their rights and duties with respect to the pending nonjudicial foreclosure in that Defendant Golden State contends that $6,432 is owed, and Plaintiff contends that less than $1,000 is owed.

13. Plaintiff desires a judicial determination and declaration of Plaintiff's and Defendants' respective rights and duties; specifically that Plaintiff did not breach the terms of the promissory note and deed of trust. Further, that the trustee failed to comply with state non-judicial foreclosure procedures. Such a judicial determination is appropriate at this time so that Plaintiff may determine his rights and duties before the Property is sold at a trustee's sale.

14. Plaintiff has incurred attorney fees in prosecuting this action in an amount that is not yet fully ascertained. The Plaintiff will provide the total amount of attorney fees as soon as they are determined.

SECOND CAUSE OF ACTION
(Injunctive Relief)

15. Plaintiff realleges and incorporates by reference the allegations contained in paragraphs 1 through 14 of the First Cause of Action.

16. Defendant TSC intends to sell, and unless restrained, will sell the Property on May 29, 200X, at 10:00 a.m., at the County Courthouse, located at 10 Elm Street, Sacramento, California, causing great and irreparable injury to the Plaintiff in that if the trustee's sale takes place as scheduled, Plaintiff, having no right to redeem the Property after the sale, will forfeit it.

17. The trustee's sale is wrongful and should be enjoined. Plaintiff has no other plain, speedy, or adequate remedy, and the injunctive relief requested for in this Complaint is necessary and appropriate at this time to prevent irreparable injury and loss of Plaintiff's Property.

THIRD CAUSE OF ACTION
(Accounting)

18. Plaintiff realleges and incorporates by reference the allegations contained in paragraphs 1 through 17 of the First and Second Causes of Action.

19. A controversy exists between Plaintiff and Defendant Golden State with respect to the correct amount of money that is actually owed by Plaintiff to Defendant Golden State. However, Defendant Golden State refuses to provide an accurate accounting or allow Plaintiff's representatives to audit Golden State's books and records as they relate to Plaintiff's loan.

20. As a result, the correct amount of money due and owing from Plaintiff to Defendant Golden State remains in dispute and cannot be determined without an accounting.

21. Plaintiff requires that Defendant Golden State make available its books and records (only as they relate to the Plaintiff's loan) in order that Plaintiff may have a certified public accountant, or similarly qualified representative, audit the books and records.

WHEREFORE, Plaintiff demands judgment as follows:

1. That the Court issue a declaration of the rights and duties of the parties; specifically that Defendant TSC has no right to conduct the trustee's sale because the trustee failed to properly follow the foreclosure procedures described in Civil Code Section 2924, and that the amount necessary to bring the loan current is in dispute.

2. That the court issue a temporary restraining order, preliminary injunction, and permanent injunction restraining the Defendants, their agents, attorneys and representatives, and all persons acting in concert or participation with them, from selling, attempting to sell, or causing to be sold the Property either under the power of sale clause contained in the deed of trust or by a judicial foreclosure action.

3. That the court order an accounting between Plaintiff and Defendant Golden State, determining the amount, if any, actually due and owing from Plaintiff to Defendant Golden State.

4. That Plaintiff recover his attorney fees and costs incurred in this action.

5. For the costs of suit incurred by the Plaintiff; and

6. For such other and further relief as the Court may deem just and proper.

Dated: May 10, 200X

_ _
HERBERT SHELLFORD
Plaintiff in pro per

5. Complete Summons and Civil Case Cover Sheet

There is one additional document you will need to prepare--the Summons. You can obtain a summons from the court clerk's office.

1. The Summons

To complete the summons:
a. Enter the names of the lender and the trustee (the parties you named in the Complaint as the defendants).
b. Enter the name and address of the Court (the Court you put on the Complaint).
c. Enter your address and telephone number in the indicated space (assuming you are representing yourself).
d. Leave the rest of the form blank for now.

6. Photocopy and File Documents With Court

Make at least three photocopies of all your documents (or more, if your local rules require it). At least one day before the day you scheduled the hearing (with the clerk's office), take all the documents, together with a check for filing fees, to the Court. The court clerk will file or "lodge" (temporarily place the documents in the court file pending the hearing) the original, and file stamp your copies. The clerk will give the judge the original documents and perhaps one set of copies. (If your court doesn't require the documents be filed in advance, you can simply bring them to the hearing.) The clerk will give you back the original Summons after signing it. Later, if necessary, you will fill out the bottom portion and the reverse side

(Proof of Service) and then file it with the court. After receiving the original Summons back from the clerk, make two copies and staple two copies to the front of two copies of the Complaint.

CHECKLIST OF DOCUMENTS

You should be filing the following documents (depending on your state's rules of court):

1. Complaint
2. Ex parte Application for Temporary Restraining Order and Preliminary Injunction
3. Memorandum of Points and Authorities
4. Declaration(s) in Support of the Application
5. Proposed Temporary Restraining Order
6. Summons

If you can't afford the filing fee. Most courts have fee waiver programs where you can pay the filing fee over a period of months. And if you are below the poverty line, you may not have to pay at all. If you need this service, ask the clerk for the fee waiver form to fill out when you file your documents.

7. Record Lis Pendens

After you file your lawsuit in the courthouse, you should immediately record a Notice of Pending Action (Lis Pendens) in the county recorder's office. You must record the lis pendens in the county where your property is located. You should take several copies of the Lis Pendens for recording. (The county recorder's Office will charge a small fee for recording the lis pendens, approximately $10 to $20).

Remember, all of these various fees will be recoverable if you win the lawsuit.

Don't neglect to record the Lis Pendens. If you don't record the Lis Pendens and for some reason the foreclosure sale goes through before you can get a court order enjoining it, you may lose your property, even if you eventually win in court. Unless the buyer is your lender or someone closely associated with your lender, it will be presumed that the buyer at the trustee's sale had no notice of your pending lawsuit (called a "bona fide purchaser for value") and thus will receive good title to your property. Even if you ultimately win your lawsuit, you will not be able to get your property back (although you may get money damages from your lender).

8. Provide Notice and Prepare Declaration

At least 24 hours before the scheduled hearing date, you must give both your lender and the trustee notice of the hearing on your Ex Parte Application (called "ex parte notice"). You may provide oral (verbal) notice by a polite telephone call telling them that an ex parte hearing will be held, and advising them of the date, time, and location of the hearing. It is a good idea to write a script with the pertinent information and stick to it. In that way, you can repeat the exact words in your Declaration of Telephonic Notice (see next page). Be sure to write down the name of each person you spoke to.

If the lender or trustee requests copies of the application. If the lender or trustee demand copies of the papers you have filed, politely explain that copies will be waiting for them at the entrance to the courtroom before the hearing. If they ask the basis of your application, state it in very general terms: "It involves a dispute over the actual amount I owe you," or "It involves a dispute over the trustee's procedures." Don't elaborate or try to justify your reasons for suing. You'll only get yourself in trouble, and may see your comments used by the other side during the hearing.

After making your phone calls, draft a Declaration of Ex Parte Telephonic Notice. Indicate the name of each person you spoke to, his or her telephone number, the date and time of the call, and the actual words you used regarding notice of the hearing on your ex parte application.

This document is extremely important. If you don't show up at the hearing with a Declaration of Telephonic Notice, signed under penalty of perjury, the judge probably will not consider your application unless the defendants also attend. A sample Declaration of Ex Parte Telephonic Notice appears on the next page.

9. Attend the TRO Hearing

On the day of the hearing, arrive at the courthouse early and bring at least three copies of all your documents. Give yourself plenty of time to find the courtroom where your ex parte application will be heard. Check in with the courtroom clerk or bailiff. (If the court doesn't have a clerk or bailiff, just sit quietly until your case is called.) Ask the clerk if the lender or foreclosure trustee or their attorneys have checked in. If not, request that the bailiff advise you when they arrive. Once the attorney for the lender or trustee checks in, introduce yourself and give him or her copies of all the documents you filed with the clerk. Don't forget to ask the attorney for copies of any pleadings they may have brought in opposition to your ex parte application. If you have time, review these documents carefully, because you will need to counter their arguments during the hearing.

While waiting for your case to be called, you'll want to observe your judge handling other cases, to the extent they're handled in open court. Some judges prefer handling ex parte matters informally in their chambers rather than in open court.

The judge will first read the motion and responding briefs (if any) and then call the parties to the front of the courtroom, or into her chambers to discuss the case. Occasionally, a judge might read all of the papers and then give her ruling from the bench without any oral arguments from either side, although this is rare.

When your case is called, if it is being handled in open court, step forward and introduce yourself as the plaintiff. Remember to always address the judge as "Your Honor," and to address all of your arguments directly to the judge, not to the lender's lawyer. Remember, always face the judge!

Some judges prefer to ask questions, while others will ask you to make a brief opening statement explaining why the foreclosure should be enjoined. If so, succinctly explain your request in your own words. Your lender's attorney, if one shows up, will be given an opportunity to respond. Never interrupt or speak directly to the other attorney!

During the hearing, the judge will probably ask you questions. Be sure to listen carefully to the judge's questions and answer them directly. Whatever you do, don't avoid or ignore the judge's question. If possible, "turn into the skid" by incorporating your answer to the judge's question into your arguments for enjoining the foreclosure. For example, if the judge asks why you waited until the last minute to file the lawsuit, explain that (if true) you wrote letters to your lender and tried to negotiate, but your letters were ignored, or the negotiations were going nowhere.

10. Judge Rules on the TRO

After the judge has heard arguments from you and your lender's attorney, she must make a ruling. The judge may make a decision on the spot or take the matter under "submission," which means she will decide later and send written notice of the decision to all parties.

If the judge agrees with your ex parte application, she will issue a TRO enjoining the trustee from proceeding with the foreclosure for approximately 7-14 days (depending on your state) and schedule a preliminary hearing. The judge will sign your proposed order, possibly with her own changes.

If the judge denies the TRO, the trustee will proceed with the foreclosure. Your lender may also recover money damages for defending against your ex parte application, including attorney fees and costs.

11. Make Sure All Service Requirements Are Met

Assuming that the lender or the trustee (or their lawyer) shows up for the hearing, you don't have to worry about serving the order or the other papers you filed. The fact that you handed them the papers when they arrived in court is good enough. Similarly, if the lender or trustee (or their attorney) is in court when the judge signs the order, they will receive a copy then and there, and service is unnecessary.

But what if nobody for the other side shows up? In that case, you will have to serve the Order (and the other papers) on the lender and the trustee. How to do this? Because time is usually very important in these situations, and because you'll want to be able to prove that the lender and trustee received the order before the sale, your best approach is to have the order personally served. And because you'll have to have the other papers you filed personally served to continue with your lawsuit, you can kill two birds with one stone by including in the package to be served all your papers, both those you filed and the order signed by the judge.

Papers can be personally served by anyone over the age of 18 who is not a plaintiff. In other words, you can't serve your own papers. So you can always get a friend or relative to do it for you, but we strongly recommend that you hire a professional process server to serve the papers. Although the sheriff's office will do it for less money, many of them are so overworked that there may be a significant delay. If you do decide to have the papers served by a friend or relative, make sure they understand that the papers must be personally delivered to a person who is authorized to accept service on behalf of the defendant being served. They should also understand that personal delivery means handing the papers to the person or, if the person refuses to take them, dropping them on the person's desk or at the person's feet.

Whoever serves the papers must then fill-in and file a Proof of Service for each party served. So, assuming personal service is made on the lender and on the trustee, separate proofs of service must be filled out.

If you are using a private process server, all you need to do is deliver the original summons to them. They will handle the rest. If, however, you are having a friend or relative carry out the service, you will need to have that person fill in the bottom part and back of the original summons and, if a second party is served, a second proof of service (in the Appendix).

To sum up:

- If a defendant appears in court, no additional service is necessary as long you hand them copies of the papers you filed and they are present when the judge signs the order.

- If no defendant appears, then you will need to have the papers and order (assuming the judge signs it) served on both defendants.

- Because this is such an important part of the case, we recommend that you have a professional process server carry out the service.

D. How Your Case Proceeds After the TRO Hearing

Most disputes involving lenders and trustees are resolved shortly after a TRO is granted. By now, the reasons should be obvious. If it looks like you are going to win, most lenders will settle rather than go through years of expensive litigation and uncertainty.

If your lender won't settle. We can't possibly cover all the intricacies of a full-blown court trial. If your case goes this far, we suggest you hire a lawyer or be prepared to use *Represent Yourself in Court,* by Paul Bergman and Sara J. Berman-Barrett (Nolo Press), as well as to become familiar with basic legal research techniques.

Barring your lender's willingness to settle, here's how your case will proceed. First, the court will schedule a preliminary injunction hearing usually within two weeks of the TRO being issued (regardless of who won) and request that you and the lender submit further pleadings and evidence to support your respective positions. If the court issues a preliminary injunction at or following that hearing, you will probably be able to settle quickly because your lender won't be able to foreclose until the case is resolved. On the other hand, if the court doesn't issue a preliminary injunction, you are still entitled to press ahead with the lawsuit, but your lender will be allowed to complete their foreclosure.

At the preliminary injunction hearing, the court may establish deadlines for discovery (written and oral questions of opposing witnesses and examination of documents). Finally, the case will go to trial. The few foreclosure lawsuits that go to trial usually involve serious allegations of lender fraud, where a lender is in danger of losing and incurring a large money judgment or punitive damages. Depending on the backlog in your county's Court calendar the trial will occur within one to two years after you filed suit. The preliminary injunction will enjoin the foreclosure until the trial date.

chapter

9

<u>BANKRUPTCY</u>

A. File for Bankruptcy and Stop the Foreclosure 189

B. How Bankruptcy Works 190

    1. How Bankruptcy Treats Debts 191
    2. Overview of Chapter 13 Bankruptcy...193
    3. Overview of Chapter 7 Bankruptcy...195
    4. Overview of Chapter 12 Bankruptcy.. 200
    5. Overview of Chapter 11 Bankruptcy...202

C. Which Bankruptcy Is Right for You? 203

D. Additional Resources... 204

Bankruptcy is a powerful remedy for people who are over their heads in debt. It may also be used to "stay" (temporarily stop) a foreclosure. But for how long depends on a number of factors discussed in this chapter. If you need more information or believe that you want to file for bankruptcy, consult one or more of the additional resources listed in Section D.

For many people, bankruptcy can be a very difficult step to take. It tends to conjure up feelings of failure, shame and guilt. But be assured that bankruptcy is a legitimate and viable strategy if you're in a severe financial crisis. Bankruptcy is about new beginnings, a "fresh start." It is designed to help you resolve your financial problems under the supervision of the bankruptcy court and get a fresh financial start on life.

A. File for Bankruptcy and Stop the Foreclosure

Without question, filing for bankruptcy is your most dramatic option for delaying a foreclosure. This is because the moment you file for bankruptcy, a federal court order automatically goes into effect immediately. Called an Order for

Relief (commonly referred to as the "automatic stay"), the order requires that your foreclosing trustee (non-judicial foreclosure), or the pending state court foreclosure lawsuit (judicial foreclosure), as well as all your other creditors, cease their collection-related activities, including all foreclosure procedures. Once the state court or your foreclosing trustee learns of the bankruptcy filing, the foreclosure is stopped dead in its tracks. The purpose of the automatic stay is to freeze your economic situation until a court-appointed bankruptcy trustee (not be confused with the foreclosing trustee who is a completely different person) can step in and determine the following:

- decide whether or not bankruptcy is appropriate, and if so,

- distribute your property or income (depending on which type of bankruptcy you file; see Section B below) to your creditors to pay what you owe them.

For most people, all it takes to file an "emergency" bankruptcy is a two-page petition, a list of your creditors (including your foreclosing lender) and the filing fee. But if you file no additional documents, the bankruptcy court will allow you only 15 days to file the remainder of bankruptcy papers and schedules, or dismiss your case. If, on the other hand, you file the additional papers needed to keep your bankruptcy case alive and ticking, you may delay the foreclosure for weeks, months or even permanently.

The rest of this chapter provides:

- an overview of how bankruptcy works

- some guidance on which type of bankruptcy is best for you, if any,

- an update on the new bankruptcy laws, and

- resources you can use to handle your own bankruptcy or at least educate yourself before you hire a bankruptcy attorney.

Involuntary bankruptcy note. Creditors have the right to file an involuntary bankruptcy against a debtor (which forces the debtor into bankruptcy). If an involuntary bankruptcy is filed against you, see a lawyer immediately.

B. How Bankruptcy Works

Bankruptcy works in two entirely different ways, depending on the type you file. Liquidation bankruptcy--commonly known as Chapter 7 bankruptcy--requires that you give up (liquidate) nonessential items of property in exchange for cancellation of most of your debts. Chapter 7 bankruptcy is described in more detail in Section B3 below. In contrast, reorganization bankruptcy lets you keep your property but requires that you repay at least some of your debts over a three year period. The specific reorganization bankruptcies are Chapter 13 (for individuals), Chapter 12 (for farmers) and Chapter 11 (for businesses and, occasionally, high net-worth individuals). These types of bankruptcies are described in more detail in Sections B2, B4 and B5 respectively.

If, after reading Chapter 1 Section D, you decide to hold on to your real estate but cannot reinstate your loan before the scheduled foreclosure sale (see Chapter 3 or Chapter 4), a reorganization bankruptcy will give you additional time provided you resume your current payments. On the other hand, if you are willing to part with the real estate--perhaps because it is worth less than you owe on it--Chapter 7 bankruptcy may be your best choice. Unfortunately, it is usually impossible to keep real estate you aren't living in (investment property), and very difficult to keep your home, if you file for Chapter 7 while in foreclosure. We explain why in Section B3 below.

1. How Bankruptcy Treats Debts

To understand how the different types of bankruptcy work, you first need information on how bankruptcy treats your debts. This is because some types of debts are paid before other types, and some types of debts can't be discharged in bankruptcy at all. Without this information, you can't decide whether or not bankruptcy is appropriate for you.

Bankruptcy categorizes every type of debt according to:

- whom the debt is owed (the type of creditor)

- whether a lien on your property secures repayment of the debt (the creditor has a right to get paid out of some or all of your property if you fail to pay the debt), and

- whether or not the debt can be discharged in bankruptcy.

a. Types of Creditors

When filling in the bankruptcy forms, you are asked to separate your debts into three groups: priority, secured and unsecured.

1) *Priority debts*. "Priority" debts, as the name implies, are a payment priority, whether the payment comes from your liquidated property (under Chapter 7) or as part of your repayment plan in a reorganization bankruptcy. Priority debts include the following:

- taxes and other debts owed to the government
- alimony and child support
- wages, salaries and commissions owed employees or independent contractors (up to $4,000 per person) earned within 90 days before you file
- contributions you owe to an employee benefit plan
- money you owe farmers or fishermen (up to $4,000 per person), and
- money you owe someone (up to $1,800 per person) who made a deposit to purchase, lease or rent property or services from you for his personal use.

For most individual debtors, only the tax and support priority categories apply. For debtors who are or were engaged in a business, the other categories often apply as well.

2) *Secured debts*. A debt is secured (and the creditor to whom you owe money is a secured creditor) if the creditor has a written document that states that it can sell your property

(collateral) if you don't make your payments. For example, your foreclosing lender is a secured creditor because their mortgage or deed of trust gives them the right to force the sale of your home to satisfy the debt if you don't pay.

3) *Unsecured debts.* Unsecured debts aren't linked to any specific item of real or personal property. Failure to pay an unsecured debt may get you sued, but the creditor can't take any of your property unless the creditor has sued you and obtained a judgment, and then takes the necessary steps to enforce the judgment.

Most debts that people owe are unsecured, including credit card debts, medical and legal bills, student loans, most court judgments, back utility bills and department store charges. In bankruptcy, unsecured creditors are paid last, after priority creditors and secured creditors.

b. Liens on the Property

Liens are discussed in detail in Chapter 1. To summarize, a lien is a legal claim against property as security for a specific amount of money. The most common types of liens are the mortgage and deed of trust, when you borrowed money against your home--either to purchase it or refinance it. Other types of liens are:

- federal and state income tax liens (which when recorded apply to all the property you own, but typically are enforced only against your real estate)

- mechanic's liens (liens recorded against your property by contractors, subcontractors, or by those who

provided building supplies or repair services), and

- judgment liens (liens that judgment creditors can get against your real estate, personal property and business assets by recording the judgment in the country recorder's office.

The point of understanding liens in the context of how bankruptcy treats your debts is a simple one: all debts that are covered by appropriately recorded liens are considered to be secured, and those to whom these debts are owed are considered secured creditors, and, as mentioned above, are usually paid before unsecured creditors.

c. Debts That Can Survive Bankruptcy

Most types of debts can be discharged in bankruptcy, but some remain ("non-dischargeable") and will have to be paid sooner or later. It is important to know what these debts are, since your decision to file for bankruptcy may be influenced by whether you will be able to discharge your major debts. If, for example, your major debt is a child support arrearage, you may reconsider bankruptcy once you understand that this type of debt is non-dischargeable and survives bankruptcy.

Debts that survive bankruptcy fall into two categories:

<u>Category 1</u>. Debts that will remain at the end of all bankruptcy cases. These debts include child support, alimony, most taxes, recent student loans that first became due fewer than seven years ago (plus the time you received any deferment or forbearance), court-ordered restitution or criminal fines, condominium and cooperative association dues or assessments, and debts for personal injuries or death to someone arising from your intoxicated driving.

Category 2. Debts that will remain at the end of a Chapter 7 bankruptcy case if the creditor files an objection in the bankruptcy court and the court rules the debt cannot be discharged. These debts include the following:

- debts incurred on the basis of fraud

- debts from willful or malicious injury to another

- debts from larceny (theft), breach of trust or embezzlement

- debts of $1,000 or more to any one creditor for luxury items purchased within 60 days of filing and cash advances in excess of $1,000 obtained within 60 days of filing, and

- debts arising from a marital settlement agreement or divorce decree (other than child support or alimony, which are in the first category).

Note: Reorganization bankruptcies have something called the "super discharge." If these Category 2 debts are unsecured, whatever balance remains when you have completed your repayment plan is wiped out.

2. Overview of Chapter 13 Bankruptcy

We explain Chapter 13 bankruptcy first because for most people facing

foreclosure, it is the best (and perhaps the only) bankruptcy remedy.

If property is owned by a business. Chapter 13 can be used to stop a foreclosure, but only if you own the property in your own name. If you own your property as a corporation, partnership or limited liability company, you will need to file Chapter 11. See Section B5.

Chapter 13 allows you to pay personal or business-related debts over time without selling off your assets through liquidation. A Chapter 13 bankruptcy allows you three years (and upon a showing of good cause, five years) to pay off as much of your debt as possible.

a. Who Can File a Chapter 13 Bankruptcy

You may file for Chapter 13 bankruptcy if:

- you are an individual (including a married couple), sole proprietor, or member of a partnership (a corporation, partnership or limited liability company itself cannot file a Chapter 13 bankruptcy)

- your secured debts do not exceed $922,000 and your unsecured debts do not exceed $307,000

- you can establish that your income over the next several years will be somewhat predictable, and

- your future income is likely to be high enough to both pay for your basic needs and pay a sufficient amount each month to satisfy Chapter 13 payment requirements.

b. How Chapter 13 Bankruptcy Works

As part of your Chapter 13 bankruptcy filing, you disclose your property, debts, essential expenses, current income and important financial transactions during the previous two years. You also must propose a plan to repay all or a portion of your debts from your "disposable income" -- your current income less your essential expenses -- over a three year period.

The bankruptcy court appoints a trustee to administer your Chapter 13 case. The Chapter 13 trustee's primary role is to:

- make sure your proposed plan is feasible and meets the requirements of the law

- advise you, other than on legal matters, and help you perform under your plan

- collect payments from you, typically on a monthly basis

- disburse the money to your creditors, after deducting a trustee's fee (which may be as high as 10% of each payment), and

- maintain detailed accounting records that inform the court whether you have fulfilled your obligations under your plan.

As a general rule, your plan payments must be high enough to pay, over the period of your plan:

- 100% of all your priority debts (see Section B1 above)

- 100% of the arrearages (and interest) on your secured debts, such as your mortgage or deed of trust, and

- an amount on your unsecured debts equal to the value of your nonexempt property (see Section B3 below). Be aware that some courts don't enforce this provision, while others won't approve a plan unless you intend to pay a sizeable portion of your unsecured debts.

c. Can Your Lender Foreclose After You File for Chapter 13?

Although the automatic stay initially bars your lender from proceeding with the foreclosure (see Section A, above), your lender may file a written request (called a "motion for relief from the automatic stay") asking the bankruptcy court for permission to continue. The court is likely to grant this motion in these kinds of situations:

- your plan does not provide for payment of the arrearage on your mortgage or deed of trust within a reasonable time (depending on the judge, anywhere from 6 to 36 months)

- you fail to resume the regular monthly payments on your mortgage or deed of trust after filing

- you fail to make your plan payments on time

• you fail to maintain adequate insurance on the property or fail to maintain it in reasonable condition, or

• the judge refuses to confirm your plan and dismisses your case (you can file again, but you won't have the benefit of the automatic stay).

With the help of a bankruptcy attorney, yon should be able to defeat your lender's motion for relief from the automatic stay and fend off the foreclosure if you can immediately cure the problems that led to the filing of their motion in the first place.

If you successfully complete your plan, which may be modified from time to time depending on your circumstances, the remaining unsecured debts will be discharged (except for those identified in Category 1, above).

d. If You Realize Chapter 13 Isn't Right for You After You File

If for some reason you are unable to complete your Chapter 13 plan, you can voluntarily dismiss the case or convert it to another chapter--almost always Chapter 7. If, when you convert to Chapter 7, you've already cured the arrearage through plan payments you have been making, and you've stayed current on your loan payments, you may be able to keep your property. That will depend on how much equity you have in it. (See Section B3d on the next page for help in determining your equity.) If you haven't cured your arrearage or you haven't remained current, then most likely the lender will motion the court to have the automatic stay lifted and proceed with their foreclosure.

3. Overview of Chapter 7 Bankruptcy

A Chapter 7 bankruptcy is the traditional form of bankruptcy, commonly referred to as a "straight" or "liquidation" bankruptcy. As we have emphasized throughout this chapter, Chapter 7 isn't a good remedy if you're trying to hold on to your real estate. But if you are willing to let it go, Chapter 7 may be very helpful in getting your finances in order.

As a general rule, people facing foreclosure are rarely able to hang on to their real estate in a Chapter 7 bankruptcy. This is because if there is equity in your property, the trustee will try to sell it and use the sale proceeds to pay your creditors. On the other hand, if there isn't any equity in your property, the trustee will abandon it and allow your lender to proceed with their foreclosure. So, in either scenario, Chapter 7 is rarely, if ever, a smart strategy to stop foreclosure, except for a brief period of weeks or months.

a. Who Can File a Chapter 7 Bankruptcy

A Chapter 7 bankruptcy may be filed by virtually any person or business organization, such as a sole proprietorship, corporation, partnership or limited liability company. If you file as an individual, you can represent yourself.

b. How Chapter 7 Bankruptcy Works

The basic idea behind a Chapter 7 bankruptcy is that you're entitled to keep certain items of property, which

BANKRUPTCY ABUSE PREVENTION AND CONSUMER PROTECTION ACT OF 2005

In 2005, Congress passed the most far-reaching changes to the U.S. Bankruptcy Code since it was adopted in 1970's. The Act is primarily aimed at consumer cases. Most importantly, it makes it more difficult to file Chapter 7 by putting debtors through a "Means Test."

The first step is to determine whether the debtor's income exceeds a defined state median family income (as reported annually by the U.S. Bureau of the Census). If the debtor's income is below the applicable state's medium family income, the Means Test does not apply, the debtor's is presumed to have filed in good faith, and may proceed with his Chapter 7 bankruptcy. However, if the debtor's income exceeds the state's median family income, then the Means Test applies.

Under the Means Test, the debtor's "current monthly income" is reduced by certain deductions to determine a "Net Amount." If the Net Amount multiplied by 60 months is greater than the lesser of (1) 25% of the debtor's non-priority unsecured claims or $6,000, whichever is greater, or (2) $10,000, then there is presumption of abuse and the case will be dismissed. If, however, the Net Amount is less, then there is a presumption the case was filed in good faith and may proceed.

are legally considered "exempt" from liquidation. (See Section B3e below for more on exempt property.) A Chapter

7 trustee who is appointed by the court to oversee your case assumes control of, and sells, your nonexempt assets for the benefit of your unsecured creditors. (The trustee can "abandon" assets he or she feels are valueless or too expensive or cumbersome to liquidate.) The Chapter 7 trustee distributes the proceeds from the sale of your nonexempt assets to your creditors.

All debts that remain unpaid are no longer your personal responsibility (except for certain debts that survive bankruptcy). In legal jargon, they are "discharged." Your case is normally completed in three to six months with usually just one visit to the federal courthouse or trustee's office. After that, you are not allowed to file another Chapter 7 bankruptcy for six years.

Once you file your bankruptcy papers, you can't sell any nonexempt property without the court's consent. You will, however, be allowed to maintain control of your exempt property and any property and income you acquire after you file bankruptcy.

If you are a partnership, corporation or limited liability company in Chapter 7. If your real or personal property is held in the name of a partnership, corporation or limited liability company, an attorney must represent the entity during the bankruptcy proceedings. All business activity must cease once the bankruptcy is filed and all business assets must be turned over to the Chapter 7 trustee. In rare circumstances, the court may grant permission for the Chapter 7 trustee to continue to operate your business (for example, if it's an apartment building or retail store), until it can be sold. All income derived from the business after filing Chapter 7 will be used by the bankruptcy trustee to pay your creditors.

c. Can You Save Property in Foreclosure by Filing Chapter 7 Bankruptcy?

In most cases, the answer is no. If you file for bankruptcy when in foreclosure, you have to deal with the arrearage that led to the foreclosure in the first place. Chapter 7 bankruptcy has no procedure to handle the repayment of your arrearage--or any other debts--over time. Rather, your nonexempt property is liquidated and your creditors are paid in a particular order required by the Bankruptcy Code--which will probably leave the arrearage unpaid. Even if the arrearage could be paid in your Chapter 7 bankruptcy case, your lender will not want to wait--given that payment is not guaranteed. Therefore, the bankruptcy court will most likely let the foreclosure proceed--unless the bankruptcy trustee decides to sell the property herself.

The bankruptcy trustee is likely to sell the property herself when the property has equity that can be used to pay some of your unsecured creditors. For real estate you don't live in, this decision would depend on whether you have any equity in it. (See subsection d.) If a sale would pay off your lender and other lienholders and still produce a surplus, the trustee will sell the property. Otherwise, the trustee will abandon it (relinquish any control over it), which almost always means the foreclosing lender will get the automatic stay lifted and proceed with the foreclosure.

d. Calculate Your Non-exempt Equity Using Bankruptcy Equity Worksheet

Your equity is the difference between what your property is worth and what you have to pay others before you see a dime. Your non-exempt equity is your equity minus your homestead exemption. If there is anything left over, the trustee will probably sell your home and distribute that amount to your unsecured creditors.

For a rough estimate of the amount of nonexempt equity you have in your home, fill out the Bankruptcy Equity Worksheet below.

Worksheet Instructions:

1. *Estimated sales price of your home.* In a bankruptcy sale, a typical home goes for 20-30% less than it's current market value. The bankruptcy trustee knows this and may take it into account when deciding whether or not to sell your home. However, the trustee is not required to use this discounted value and may use the full market value of your home in deciding whether to take it. To be on the safe side, put your home's full estimated sales price on this line. To get a rough idea of what your home is worth, you might ask a real estate agent, hire an appraiser, or look at comparable properties for sale in your area.

2a. *Costs of sale of your home.* Costs of sale vary, but tend to be about 8% of the sales price. The trustee does not have to subtract the costs of sale in determining whether to take your home, but many do.

2b. *Amount owed on real estate loans.* Enter the amount needed to pay off your loans and any other liens that are secured by your home as collateral. If you can't come up with a reasonably reliable estimate, contact each lender and ask how much you'll need to pay off their loan.

2c. Outstanding liens and taxes and priority debts. Fill in the total of all unpaid liens--claims against your home that have been recorded at the county recorder's office and priority debts. See Section B1 above for more on liens and priority debts. (Incidentally, judgment liens may be removed or subordinated as part of the Chapter 7 bankruptcy process if they prevent you from receiving your homestead allowance.)

If you aren't sure whether there are liens on your home, visit the county recorder's office or contact the customer service department of a local title insurance company for assistance.

3. Subtotal. Add up lines 2a, b and c.

4. Estimated equity. Subtract the subtotal from the estimated sales price of your home. For bankruptcy purposes, this is the equity in your property--that is, the amount your house will sell for, less what must be paid to others from the proceeds before you see anything.

5. Homestead exemption. Fill in the amount of your homestead exemption. You will need to consult your state's laws because exemptions are different in each state.

6. Estimated nonexempt equity. Subtract the homestead exemption from your estimated equity (4 - 5). Here's how to understand your calculations of estimated nonexempt equity:

• If the amount is less than zero: Your estimate shows that all of your equity is exempt. If your estimate is correct, the trustee won't sell your home because the proceeds would go to your foreclosing lender, any junior lienholders, and you (your homestead exemption), with nothing left over to pay your unsecured creditors. In that situation, the trustee will simply file a Notice of Abandonment and allow you to keep your home. Of course, in that event, you will still need to deal with your foreclosing lender and

---

BANKRUPTCY EQUITY WORKSHEET

1. Estimated sales price of your home	$_____
2. Estimated costs of sale	
a. Costs of sale of your home (approximately 8%)	$_____
b. Amount owed on real estate loan(s)	$_____
c. Outstanding liens, taxes and priority debts	$_____
3. Subtotal (add lines 2a, b and c)	$_____
4. Estimated equity (lines 1 - 3)	$_____
5. Homestead exemption (for your state)	$_____
6. Estimated nonexempt equity (lines 4 - 5)	$_____

IF YOU DON'T LIVE IN YOUR PROPERTY

Non-owner occupied real property (investment) is never exempt in Chapter 7, so you'll eventually lose it. If there is equity in the property, the Chapter 7 trustee will certainly sell it to pay off your creditors. On the other hand, if there isn't any equity, the Chapter 7 trustee will file a Notice of Abandonment with the court and allow your lender to proceed with their foreclose.

negotiate a resolution of the default in order to avoid a foreclosure.

- If the amount is greater than zero: You have nonexempt equity in your home and the trustee is likely to sell your home to pay off your unsecured creditors. If you find yourself in this predicament, don't file Chapter 7 bankruptcy. Consider a reorganization bankruptcy instead.

⚠️

The Bankruptcy Equity Worksheet is for estimate purposes only. The bankruptcy trustee may challenge the market value you claim and determine that your residence is worth more than you think. Depending on your homestead amount, this could mean the difference between keeping your home and losing it.

e. Understanding the Homestead Exemption

There are two schemes of property (real and personal) that may be considered exempt when filing bankruptcy, the federal exemptions or your state's exemptions. You must choose exemptions from one scheme or the other--no mixing and matching is allowed. In some cases, the state exemptions are more liberal. In other states, the federal exemptions may be more beneficial for you. You will need to research your state's exemption scheme before deciding whether to use your state's exemption or federal exemption scheme.

f. Can Your Lender Foreclose After You File for Chapter 7?

In Chapter 7 bankruptcy, the automatic stay will keep your lender from foreclosing until:

- the Chapter 7 trustee decides whether to sell or abandon your property

CLAIMING A LOW EXEMPTION

If Chapter 7 is your only bankruptcy option and you have equity in your home, there may be a reason to claim a lower exemption than you are entitled to. The lower the exemption you claim, the more likely there be will be money to pay the unsecured creditors after a sale by the bankruptcy trustee. In other words, by claiming less than you could, you might make it worthwhile for the bankruptcy trustee to sell your home, rather than abandoning it and allowing the lender to foreclose on your home.

If you file for Chapter 7 bankruptcy and opt for this strategy, you most definitely should get some professional help.

- your lender successfully asks the court to terminate the automatic stay

(by filing a document called "motion seeking relief from the automatic stay")

- you receive a bankruptcy discharge (the stay is automatically lifted), or

- your case 1s dismissed (either by the bankruptcy court   court or upon your request).

The most likely scenario is that your lender will file a Motion for Relief from the Automatic Stay shortly after you file Chapter 7. The court will grant the motion unless there is equity in the property that the trustee can capture in a quick sale. Either way, you will probably lose your home. The bottom line is that Chapter 7 is never a good strategy (unless you are only looking for a month or two delay while utilizing one of the other strategies described in this book.)

g. Converting From Chapter 7 to Chapter 13

If you file a Chapter 7 bankruptcy and later discover that Chapter 13 is a better option, you can convert your case to Chapter 13. As discussed in Section B2 above, Chapter 13 will allow you to pay your debts out of your future income. Plus, you will not be required to give up your property as long as you stay current on your mortgage and successfully complete a plan that pays off your arrearage within a reasonable time.

Your right to convert is absolute as long as you did not previously convert from Chapter 13 to Chapter 7. Note, however, that if you missed your regular loan payments on your real property

after you filed Chapter 7, most courts will require that you make the missed payments before your Chapter 13 plan can be approved.

"CHAPTER 20" BANKRUTPCY

A strategy that may seem attractive but isn't likely to work is referred to as "Chapter 20." First, you file for Chapter 7 to get rid of your dischargeable debts and your personal liability for your secured loans. Immediately after you receive a Chapter 7 discharge, you file Chapter 13. You then pay off over time the mortgages or deeds of trust and other liens on your property and any remaining non-dischargeable debt. This approach will not save your house-since the foreclosure will usually be allowed to proceed in the Chapter 7 bankruptcy--but it may improve your overall debt situation if you are willing to let go of the house.

4. Overview of Chapter 12 Bankruptcy

If you are not a family farmer. Skip this section, as Chapter 12 bankruptcy is not an option.

A Chapter 12 bankruptcy is known as the "adjustment of debts of a family farmer with regular income" or, more commonly, the "family farmer bankruptcy." Congress enacted Chapter 12 in 1986 with the hope of slowing the burgeoning number of small farms in the United States being lost through foreclosure. Chapter 12 allows you to keep your farm, reorganize your finances, make payments over three (or five years), and discharge the remaining debts not paid through the bankruptcy--except for debts that automatically survive bankruptcy. (See Section B1 above.)

Chapter 12 bankruptcy is largely modeled on Chapter 13 bankruptcy. (Read Section B2, above, for a detailed discussion of Chapter 13 bankruptcy.)

a. Who Can File a Chapter 12 Bankruptcy?

Chapter 12 bankruptcy has very strict eligibility requirements. If you operate a family farm, you can use Chapter 12 only if:

• your total debts do not exceed $1.5 million

• at least 80% of your debts, excluding the debt associated with your home, arise from farming operations, and

• at least 50% of your income is based on farming operations.

A corporation or partnership (at least half owned by your family) that operates the farm may file Chapter 12 bankruptcy if 50% or more of your family's income is based on farming operations.

There are two key advantages of a Chapter 12 bankruptcy. First, you retain the right to continue operating your farm while in Chapter 12. Second, during your case, you pay your foreclosing lender "the reasonable rent customary in the community where your property is located," regardless of the actual payment amount specified in your loan documents.

b. Debtor-in-Possession in Chapter 12

While you are in Chapter 12 bankruptcy, you are called a "debtor-in-possession" or "DIP," and have full authority to operate your farm on a day-to-day basis. In other words, you do not need special permission from the bankruptcy court to conduct ordinary business or farm your land. Only special activities that fall outside the scope of ordinary farm business, such as selling off your farm or equipment, must be submitted to the bankruptcy court for approval.

The bankruptcy court appoints a trustee to administer every Chapter 12 case. The Chapter 12 trustee's primary role is to collect payments from you, typically on a monthly basis, pursuant to a Chapter 12 Plan. The trustee then disburses the money to your creditors, after deducting a small trustee's fee. The Chapter 12 trustee is also responsible for maintaining detailed accounting records that inform the court whether you are fulfilling your obligations under your plan.

In addition, the bankruptcy court may order a Chapter 12 trustee to look into your farm operations and determine if it is economically worthwhile for you to continue your farming business.

c. When a Creditor Can Foreclose After You File for Chapter 12

Secured Creditors may motion for relief from the automatic stay (covered in Section A, above) anytime after you file Chapter 12. A common reason is because you have no equity in your farm or you don't need the farm to carry out your Chapter 12 plan. With the help of a lawyer, you should be able to defeat your lender's motion--for example, by proving to the bankruptcy court that your farm is also your family residence. Most bankruptcy judges are sympathetic to farmers who also live on their farms.

5. Overview of Chapter 11 Bankruptcy

Chapter 11 bankruptcies are complex and costly and are very difficult to do without a lawyer. It is unlikely to be the remedy of choice for most readers of this book. Nevertheless, you should review this section if it applies to your situation.

a. Who Can File a Chapter 11 Bankruptcy?

Chapter 11 reorganization is the most common bankruptcy chapter used for corporations, limited liability companies, and partnerships. It may also be used by individuals whose secured debts exceed $922,000 and unsecured debts exceed $307,000.

b. What Happens in a Chapter 11 Bankruptcy?

A Chapter 11 bankruptcy can last anywhere from three months to three years, depending on the complexity of the case and how it evolves through the bankruptcy court.

During the Chapter 11, the debtor proposes a "Plan of Reorganization" to pay his creditors. Plans of reorganization vary greatly in length and complexity. In a simple Chapter 11 reorganization, the plan may be only 15 or 20 printed pages. A major bankruptcy may involve a plan of several hundred printed pages. A copy of the proposed plan must be sent to all creditors affected by the plan. In a large bankruptcy, that could be thousands of creditors!

For all practical purposes, you are out of bankruptcy once your Chapter 11 plan of reorganization is confirmed by the court. A confirmed plan constitutes a binding contract and provides a new relationship between you and your creditors. Your payment of debt is limited to the schedule and amounts provided in your plan. If all goes as expected, you emerge from Chapter 11 bankruptcy still owning your real property. After confirmation, the bankruptcy court usually retains jurisdiction (control) of the case only to enforce your compliance with the terms of the plan.

In Chapter 11, you act as your own bankruptcy trustee. You are called a "Debtor-in-Possession" or "DIP" for short. As a DIP, you continue to operate your business and manage your real estate, largely without interference from creditors or the bankruptcy court. You are free from paying all of your pre-petition debts until your plan is approved by the court.

But it is no picnic! You are expected in Chapter 11 to negotiate with your creditors a reorganization (restructure) of your financial affairs. Your negotiations result in an acceptable plan of reorganization to restructure your finances and repay your creditors in full or part.

Some individuals choose not to file Chapter 11 reorganizations because of the complexity and costs involved, including high filing fees and substantial attorney fees. In addition, you must pay a quarterly fee to the U.S. Trustee's Office (a percentage of your post-petition disbursements, often several hundreds or thousands of dollars) until your case is closed.

c. When a Creditor Can Foreclose After You File for Chapter 11

Although your lender is "stayed" from pursuing foreclosure, they may file a Motion for Relief from the Automatic Stay, asking the court to allow them to proceed with their foreclosure. (Automatic stays are covered in more detail in Section B2, above.)

Your lender may argue that they are entitled to relief from stay because you have no equity in your property--that is, your property is worth less than your loan. However, this sole argument is unlikely to convince a judge to allow your lender to foreclose. Even if you have no equity in your property, your property may still be necessary for your reorganization. In other words, you may be able to sell or refinance your property in the future (presumably after it appreciates in value and builds up some equity) and use the proceeds to pay your creditors.

If your lender seeks relief from stay during your bankruptcy because it has not received regular loan payments during the Chapter 11 bankruptcy, relief will not likely be granted. Under most circumstances, a secured creditor is not entitled to loan payments during the Chapter 11 bankruptcy, unless the property is losing value.

Lenders seek relief from an automatic stay if they believe the collateral securing its loan (your property) is not "adequately protected." In other words, your lender could argue that its secured position is deteriorating if your property is decreasing in value,

your property is uninsured, you failed to pay property taxes, or you are not maintaining the property. Under these circumstances, the Court may require you to make adequate protection payments, or worse, terminate the automatic stay and allow your lender to proceed with their foreclosure. So it is crucial that during the pendency of the bankruptcy you maintain your property in good conditions, and pay the taxes and insurance promptly.

If your real estate is your only asset, a Motion for Relief from Automatic Stay may be equivalent to asking the court to short-circuit your reorganization and liquidate your entire estate. Because of this, much of the litigation associated with Chapter 11 centers around whether your property is necessary for your reorganization. Bankruptcy courts are reluctant to grant such a motion until you have had an opportunity to see if your property can be sold or refinanced, or your loan restructured, especially during the first 120 days of your case.

C. Which Bankruptcy Is Right for You?

Now that you have an overview of the different types of bankruptcy, you can consider which chapter might be best for you. The accompanying sidebar lists additional resources to help you make this decision.

If you want to keep your real estate, you should file a reorganization bankruptcy. For just about everyone this will be a Chapter 13 bankruptcy, or for farmers, a Chapter 12 bankruptcy. If you don't qualify for Chapter 13 because your debts are too large, you should speak with an attorney about filing Chapter 11 bankruptcy.

If you don't qualify for a reorganization bankruptcy--because you don't have enough income to make all required payments under the plan--then your only choice will be Chapter 7. This means you will definitely lose real estate you're not living in, and probably your home as well, unless you can negotiate a solution with your lender (see Chapter 5).

If the question of saving your real estate is no longer an issue, there are advantages and drawbacks to bankruptcy.

D. Additional Resources

Although this chapter provides adequate information to help you understand your options, it cannot possibly give all the information you need to actually file for bankruptcy. For that, you should consult the references listed in the accompanying sidebar, and if you wish (or your situation is too complex), a bankruptcy lawyer. Keep in mind that bankruptcy often requires a lot of negotiating with your creditors, the bankruptcy trustee, and the bankruptcy judge.

BANKRUPTCY RESOURCES

If you decide to handle your own bankruptcy, or want more information on the step-by-step process, here are several good books:

How to File for Bankruptcy, by Stephen Elias, Albin Renauer and Robin Leonard (Nolo Press), contains all the information necessary for you (as long as you are not a business entity) to decide whether or not to file for Chapter 7 bankruptcy, and instructions on how to do it yourself.

How to File Your Own Bankruptcy, by Edward A. Haman, Esq. (Sphinx Publishing), contains valuable information and forms for filing bankruptcy and adhering to the rules.

Chapter 13 Bankruptcy: Repay Your Debts, by Robin Leonard (Nolo Press), can help you decide whether or not to file Chapter 13 bankruptcy. It provides step-by-step instructions on how file your own Chapter 13 bankruptcy.

Complete Idiot's Guide to Surviving Bankruptcy, by Carol Costa and James Beaman (Alpha) contains everything you'd ever want to know about bankruptcy and surviving the various hurdles.

Money Troubles: Legal Strategies to Cope With Your Debts, by Robin Leonard (Nolo Press), covers how to negotiate with your creditors, deal with bill collectors, handle lawsuits, assess whether or not to file bankruptcy, handle exempt property, and rebuild your credit.

These resources are available in many libraries, most bookstores, and online at www.amazon.com or www. barnesandnoble.com.

chapter

10

HOW TO SELL YOUR PROPERTY QUICKLY TO STOP FORECLOSURE

A. Deciding Whether to Sell Your Property 206

B. Hire a Real Estate Agent..207

    1. Interview Real Estate Agents 208
    2. Selecting a Listing Agreement... 209
    3. Negotiating the Listing Agreement 210
    4. If You Have Problems With Your Real Estate Agent...212

C. Implement a Plan to Sell Your Property 212

    1. Classified Advertisements..212
    2. "For Sale" Signs 213
    3. Fact Sheets (Flyers) 213
    4. Open Houses..213

D. Prepare Your Property for Sale...214

    1. Make Disclosures Required by Law 214

E. Offers and Counter-Offers 215

    1. Buyer Presents an Offer 215
    2. Making Counter-Offers 215
    3. Accepting an Offer or Counter-Offer...217
    4. Back-up Offers...217

F. Proceeding Through to Closing 217

    1. Working With the Escrow Officer or Settlement Agent 217
    2. Removing Contingencies...218
    3. Closing 218

G. Special Rules for Dealing With Equity Purchasers...218

    1. Laws Regulating Equity Purchasers...219
    2. Special Rules for Equity Purchase Contracts.. 220
    3. If the Equity Purchaser Violates the Law...221

206

H. Arranging a "Short Sale" With Your Lender 222

    1. Will Your Lender Agree to a Short Sale? 223
    2. Income Tax Liabilities With a Short Sale 223
    3. Overview of Short Sale Procedures 224

For some readers, selling your property may be the most efficient strategy for stopping foreclosure and salvaging some of your equity. But selling your property, which can be time-consuming and stressful under normal circumstances, can be downright terrifying while a foreclosure is pending. Nevertheless, this chapter explains how you can sell your property at the best price possible before you lose it at a foreclosure sale.

If you decide to sell your house, we recommend you read *For Sale By Owner* by George Devine (Nolo Press). It explains in detail the ins and outs of selling your home, including disclosures, tax liability, and real estate sale agreements.

A. Deciding Whether to Sell Your Property

There are some definite advantages to selling your property: you get rid of a financial burden, preserve your credit, and salvage some of your equity. On the other hand, there may be much better ways to handle an impending foreclosure. Before you even consider putting your property on the market, carefully read Chapter 1, Section D. There you'll have a chance to assess whether or not to keep your property and to evaluate your options if you decide to give it up.

PROBLEMS SELLING PROPERTY IN FORECLOSURE

If you decide to sell your property during the foreclosure, you will need to be sensitive to the time limitations. Afterall, there's the ticking "clock" to consider. In a normal market, most properties sell within three to four months. Unfortunately, you're likely to have less than 30-60 days to find a buyer and complete the transaction. Most lenders won't give you extra time to sell your property. Be especially cautious of these important issues:

• You may have difficulty getting a sales price high enough to pay your loans. Ideally, you want to receive enough funds to pay off all your underlying loans and have some funds leftover for yourself. Unfortunately, this won't be possible if you have negative equity--if your property is worth less than the balance of your loan. In that situation, you'll need to obtain your lender's approval before selling your property for less than what you owe (called a "short sale"). See Section H for more on short sales.

• Selling may not solve your financial problems. Your financial crisis may require more drastic measures than just selling your home. If this is your situation, read about bankruptcy (in Chapter 9) before deciding whether to sell your property.

• You may need to get your lender's permission. If you are involved in a short sale situation (see Section H) or if the close of escrow will extend out beyond the scheduled foreclosure sale, you will need your lender's permission to delay the foreclosure sale.

• There may be adverse tax consequences. You may face potential tax liability if you sell your property; see Chapter 1, Section D5 for an overview of tax issues involved in selling your house. Here are the rules in a nutshell:

- If you make a profit on the sale, you may have to pay capital gain taxes on the profit. However, you may be able to postpone this tax liability if you sell your primary residence and purchase another one within 24 months or you are over 55 and meet the requirements for this one time exemption.

- If you sell your property for less than the amount due on your loan and your lender accepts that amount in satisfaction of your debt, you may be liable for paying taxes on the amount your lender forgave (see Section H2). If you are considering selling your property, consult with a CPA or tax consultant.

B. Hire a Real Estate Agent

Because of your pending foreclosure, it is always advisable to use a real estate agent. An agent's experience in marketing foreclosure properties, qualifying buyers, handling negotiations, and promptly closing the transaction, will be invaluable to you as time runs out. Your challenge is to find a real estate agent who can help you sell your property at a reasonable price within the limited time left before the foreclosure sale.

If you find an agent who is experienced (or specializes) in properties in foreclosure, they will appreciate the urgency of not just finding a buyer, but closing the sale as quickly as possible. After all, agents understand that the only way they will collect their commission is if the transaction closes before the foreclosure sale. If you know any real estate agents, ask them for a referral to someone with experience in selling properties in foreclosure. Friends, relatives and business acquaintances may also steer you in the right direction. Title companies, local newspapers, and the internet, are also good resources.

If you decide to sell your property without an agent. We suggest you read *For Sale by Owner,* by George Devine (Nolo Press), *For Sale By Owner,* by Piper Nichole (Career Press), *Survival Guide for Selling a Home,* by Sid Davis (American Management Association), and *The Everything Homeselling Guide,* by Ruth Rejnis (Adams Media Corporation). It is the sine qua non of do-it-yourself real estate books.

1. Interview Real Estate Agents

Look for an experienced real estate agent who has successfully sold properties in foreclosure. An experienced agent can also negotiate with your lender over a possible "short sale" or a brief postponement of the foreclosure sale (to allow a pending sale to close), if it becomes necessary.

Even though you're in a hurry, it behooves you to interview several agents rather than hiring the first one who comes your way. Here are several questions you should ask prospective real estate agents:

- *Will the agent place your property in the Multiple Listing Service (MLS)?* The MLS (and related internet services) list and describe properties currently on the market. This is the largest and most frequently used resource for agents looking for properties for sale. The MLS is updated daily and downloaded only to real estate agents. Once you select an agent, she will immediately list your property in the MLS. In that way, the broadest range of agents (and their potential buyers) will learn of your property's availability, price and features.

- *Does the agent have specific experience selling properties in foreclosure?* Ask for references and get specific details on how quickly the agent sold the property and whether it was at, over, or under the asking price. Also, if your loan is larger than the value of your property, find out if the agent has negotiated any "short payoffs" with lenders or extensions of foreclosure sales (to allow a pending transaction to close).

- *How much does the agent think your property will sell for?* Watch out for an agent who gives you an unrealistically inflated estimate to ensure getting the listing. You don't have time to let your property sit on the market before you drop the price. Ask the agent to see a print-out of "comparables" (a list of recently sold properties in your neighborhood).

- *How much will the agent charge?* Most real estate agents set their commissions at approximately 5-6% of the sales price of the property. However, some agents may be willing to negotiate a lower commission rate, especially if you agree on a lesser level of services. You will pay the commission out of the sales price. For example, if your property sells for $400,000, you'd pay your real estate agent $24,000 (at the 6% commission rate). In most cases, your agent will split the commission evenly with the buyer's agent (which is no additional cost to you).

- *How will the agent market your property in the limited time left before the foreclosure sale?* In addition to the usual ways properties are marketed (Section C, below), does your agent have other unique ways to market your property? (For example, posting a sign at a local factory, hospital or school; or perhaps offering a special discount to corporate relocation agencies for a referral. Ask your agent to be creative.)

- *What services will the real estate agent provide?* Will she help you fill out required disclosure forms? Recommend appraisers, inspectors, and contractors, if needed? Negotiate with potential buyers and handle offers and counteroffers? Help pre-qualify buyers for a loan? Open escrow (if your state uses escrows), review escrow instructions, find a title insurance company, help remove contingencies and make sure the sale closes on time? But remember, as pointed out earlier, you may be able to negotiate a lower commission rate if you're willing to take on some of these services yourself.

2. Selecting a Listing Agreement

Once you find an agent, you'll need to enter into what's known as a "listing agreement." There are three types of listing agreements you should consider using:

- exclusive listing agreement

- exclusive agency agreement, or

- open listing agreement (non-exclusive).

As you'll see below, some of these arrangements are better for your real estate agent than for you. Remember that the listing agreement is negotiable. If you can't settle on an agreement that you feel comfortable with, consider finding another agent. Don't hesitate to insist on terms you're comfortable with, and to quickly move on if the agent won't cooperate.

a. Exclusive Listing Agreement

Most people enter into an Exclusive Listing Agreement (formally known as an Exclusive Authorization and Right to Sell). During the listing period-typically 90 days to six months, although it may be shorter if the property is already in foreclosure-your property is listed with only one agent. You agree to pay the full commission on the sales price, usually 6%, if your agent successfully sells the property during the listing period, even if someone other than the agent (including you!) finds a buyer.

Example: Roy owns a $500,000 home in Cleveland, Ohio. Confronting foreclosure, Roy decides to list his home with an agent under an exclusive listing agreement. A month later, Roy's next-door neighbor expresses an interest in buying Roy's home as a rental investment. Even if Roy and his neighbor seal the deal, Roy's agent will get the full commission of approximately $30,000.

b. Exclusive Agency Agreement

An Exclusive Agency Agreement is really a misnomer. The only thing that makes it "exclusive" is that you agree to work with one agent at a time. Under this arrangement, you and your real estate agent simultaneously try to sell your property. You pay a commission only if your agent (not you) finds a buyer.

Most agents are reluctant to enter into this type of relationship, perhaps because of potential disputes over who found the buyer. If you select an agent who agrees to an agency agreement, you and your agent will want to weekly (or even daily) exchange lists of potential buyers each of you found.

c. Open Listing Agreement

An Open Listing Agreement resembles the exclusive agency agreement described in Section B2b, above, but you ask more than one agent to simultaneously market your property. Whichever agent ultimately finds the

USE ADDITIONAL RESOURCES

While this section provides an overview of what you should do to sell your real estate in a hurry, you would be well advised to obtain an additional resource that goes into detail about how to accomplish the tasks discussed here. Although we recommend *For Sale by Owner* by George Devine (Nolo Press) and *For Sale by Owner* by Piper Nichole (Career Press), there are many resources in the libraries, bookstores, and on the internet, designed to provide this type of information to the real estate novice.

buyer will receive the commission. If you find the buyer yourself, you won't pay any commission.

Because real estate agents compete against each other (and you) to find a buyer (and earn a commission), this type of listing is obviously the least popular among agents. Similarly, you may not want an open listing because the agents may not have enough incentive to find a buyer for your property. Remember, unlike a normal sales situation, with a pending foreclosure time is of the essence!

3. Negotiating the Listing Agreement

As with most other kinds of contracts, much of the listing agreement consists of standard clauses (boilerplate) which are seldom if ever modified. But most agents are agreeable to negotiating

changes to the listing agreement. After all, agents survive on obtaining listings and are appreciative of the time-sensitive needs of a property owner confronting foreclosure. However, if your agent balks at your proposed changes, you may be left with a difficult decision. Unless you are convinced that this agent is perfect for your situation, you may simply need to select someone else.

To protect your interests during the foreclosure, you should negotiate the following items:

- *Term of the listing*: Most agents expect terms of four to six months, which is too long given the time limitations of your foreclosure. The listing should be limited to 60 days. Or, if you do not have 60 days, it should terminate no less than five days before the scheduled foreclosure sale. In that way, if no buyer is found in time, you may still engineer one of the other strategies described in this book during the last five days, such as bankruptcy (See Chapter 9), or giving your lender a deed in lieu of foreclosure (See Chapter 11).

- *Commission to agent*: Listing agreements typically contain a standard clause providing that the commission is earned when the agent presents you an offer from a *"ready, willing and able"* buyer. Unfortunately, this means you could be liable for a commission even if the transaction does not close in time to beat the foreclosure sale. To protect yourself, cross out the phrase *"commission earned when agent presents an offer from a ready, willing and able buyer"* and then write in the phrase *"no *commission will be paid unless and until escrow closes prior to the foreclosure sale"* on the blank lines near the end of the listing agreement or along the border of the agreement. Make sure your agent initials your changes. Further, have your agent agree that if the buyer pays you any portion of the sales price in the form of a promissory note or mortgage (rather than cash), your agent will receive a promissory note or mortgage for her proportionate share of the commission. Write the language on the blank lines near the end of the listing agreement or along the border of the agreement. Once again, make sure your agent initials the language.

Consider raising your agent's commission for a quick sale. Keep in mind that you are on a very short fuse with a foreclosure pending. Consider increasing the commission to motivate your agent to sell your property quickly. For example, you can offer a 7% commission if your property sells within the first 30 days and a 6.5% commission if it sells within 60 days (assuming you have 60 days before the sale).

- *Commission based on final sales price*: The listing agreement presented to you by your agent may contain a standard clause providing a 6% commission on the "full sales price," even though you will probably end up negotiating a lower price with the buyer. In order to avoid this problem, state in the listing agreement (on the blank lines at the end or in the margin) that your agent's commission will be based on the final sales price established at the closing.

- *Right to terminate*: To emphasize that you need your agent to be aggressive and market your property actively, specifically state in the listing agreement that: *"Seller has the right to terminate the agreement at any time (subject to five days prior written notice) if Seller determines, in his/her sole discretion, that the agent is not handling the sale of the property properly."*

- *Marketing plan*: You are hiring a real estate agent to take advantage of his professional marketing ability, affiliation with the multiple listing service, and capability for mass advertising. It is a good idea to require that your real estate agent commit to a very specific marketing plan, which you should attach as an addendum to your listing agreement. For example, your lender should commit to a weekly classified ad in the Sunday newspaper, weekly open houses, listing in the MLS and on the Internet, weekly caravans for agents, and a special display advertisement in a local magazine or newspaper. (See Section C.)

- *Additional services*: You'll need help to complete the real estate transaction quickly and correctly. Specifically state in the listing agreement that your agent will *"assist Seller in qualifying buyers, negotiating offers and counter-offers, helping the Buyer find a mortgage broker or lender quickly, removing escrow contingencies, and helping the sale close promptly."*

4. If You Have Problems With Your Real Estate Agent

Your agent stands to make thousands of dollars from selling your property. That alone should motivate him to aggressively market your property. If, however, you're dissatisfied with your agent's performance, immediately meet with him and discuss your specific concerns. A heart-to-heart meeting with your agent will likely resolve most of your concerns. If it doesn't, you may want to change agents quickly so you can still sell your property before time runs out.

If you decide to terminate the services of a real estate agent you no longer want to work with, ask him to cancel the agreement early. If you've signed a listing agreement that terminates on a specific date, ask him to end the listing early, simply on the grounds that there are "irreconcilable differences" between you and your agent (meaning that you can no longer work together harmoniously). The agent may be unwilling to give up the commission, especially if you appear to have a buyer or another agent lined up. As an alternative, consider offering him a partial commission if your property sells by a certain date, a reimbursement for the agent's actual expenses, and/or a payment for hours worked on selling your property.

Address right to terminate in the listing agreement. In Section B2, above, we suggest that your listing agreement give you the right to terminate the agreement if you decide that the agent is not properly handling the sale of the property.

C. Implement a Plan to Sell Your Property

Just because you hire an agent to sell your property doesn't mean you can kick back and wait for buyers to show up. Remember, you are facing foreclosure and don't have the luxury of waiting. You should be prepared to help your agent as much as possible, even though you are paying a commission. Ask your agent how you can help, and be prepared to do some of the legwork yourself. Here are some suggestions.

1. Classified Advertisements

Your goal should be to reach as many potential buyers as possible, with specific and appealing information about your property. You'll need to advertise within the shortest time possible and within your agent's advertising budget. But beware. Some real estate firms place big, splashy newspaper ads that advertise their company rather than the properties. Or they describe your property in a "teaser" ad without listing its address. These ads may generate phone calls or walk-ins for their real estate office, but they won't help you. Instead, request that your agent advertise your property in the real estate classified section of your local newspaper every Sunday. At the very least, your agent should commit to one classified ad every Sunday during the term of the listing agreement. If your agent's budget permits, weekdays should also be included.

If your community has a weekly "shopper" or neighborhood paper that is distributed for free, you may want to advertise there as an excellent compliment to your other advertising. Buyers looking for bargains often peruse papers such as these. If your agent won't commit to advertising in each of the small local papers or shoppers, consider spending your own money to advertise. Remember, you can't stop the foreclosure by just hoping your property will sell.

Your agent will undoubtedly volunteer to write the newspaper ad, but you should go over it before it is published. You want your ad to be clear and understandable, not full of confusing abbreviations, real estate jargon or misleading (often exaggerated) descriptions of your home.

You'll need to decide whether to mention that your property is in foreclosure. This is often a difficult decision for property owners, and there are arguments supporting either choice. Because mentioning the word *"foreclosure"* in an ad tends to bring out speculators who hope to get a bargain at your expense, we suggest you simply state *"immediate sale," "reduced for quick sale," "owner anxious"* or *"all reasonable offers considered"* and then see what happens.

2. "For Sale" Signs

All real estate firms have "for sale" signs and will proudly post them on your property. On open house days, your agent should also post signs throughout your neighborhood announcing an open house at your property. Nevertheless, you should stay on top of your agent and recommend that signs be posted at intersections near your property. If

necessary, you can even help your agent put up the signs.

3. Fact Sheets (Flyers)

A set-up sheet is usually a one-page flyer that shows a picture (preferably color) of your property. It lists the basic facts about your property and highlights its special features. And if your property has a unique design, special financing, or new renovations, be sure your agent points this out in the fact sheet.

Your real estate agent will distribute copies of your property fact sheet to other agents, pass them out at open houses, and post them on the internet. It is in your best interests to also give copies to friends, co-workers, neighbors, and business associates. You may want to leave copies in local stores and businesses (with the owners' permission). Finally, look into sending copies to relocation, housing or personnel departments of local corporations and universities, which often help relocating employees find housing. You may also place your fact sheet on real estate programs on local cable television and radio shows. Some of these services are free while others charge a nominal fee. Your agent should be familiar with which programs or websites are available and their comparative costs.

4. Open Houses

An open house is a special day (typically Saturday or Sunday) in which your home is opened to the public by your agent. Potential buyers are invited to inspect your property without a special appointment. You might think of an open house as a nuisance and a painful reminder of your financial straits. But don't underestimate the value of all those people traipsing through your home. Remember, all you need is just one of those visitors to make an offer to buy the property. If you want to avoid the aggravation of an open house, get the property ready (your agent can give you tips) and let your agent deal with the "lookie-lou's" while you spend the day elsewhere.

D. Prepare Your Property for Sale

One of the most effective ways to sell your property is to make it attractive to buy: mow the lawn, tidy-up the property, and place plants and flowers in strategic locations. Given the pending foreclosure, it does not make sense to spend a lot of money and time on anything but minor improvements, such as a fresh coat of paint.

1. Make Disclosures Required by Law

With the help of your real estate agent, you'll complete several disclosure forms, which must be given to prospective buyers:

- *Real Estate Transfer Disclosure Statement.* You are responsible for disclosing all property defects you personally know about, no matter how insignificant (i.e. the roof leaks, your next door neighbors party loudly on weekends, the basement floor is cracked, there's dry rot around the windows, the refrigerator is on its last legs, or whatever else you can think of). These disclosures effectively protect you from any later claim or lawsuit by the buyer based on failure to disclose. (If in doubt whether to disclose it, error on the side of caution and disclose it!)

- *Flood disclosure.* You must advise prospective buyers in writing if your property is in a flood hazard area. You can tell if your property is in a flood hazard zone if your lender required you to obtain flood insurance when you bought your property. If you aren't sure whether your property is in a flood hazard area, ask your real estate agent to investigate or check with the Federal Emergency Management Agency (FEMA).

- *Seismic disclosures.* In some states, you must disclose in writing to potential buyers whether your property lies within any seismic zones. You must also specify if it has any known earthquake weaknesses. Check with your real estate agent or a local city or county planning department.

- *Fire hazards.* You must disclose in writing to prospective buyers if your property is located in an area that the state has designated fire hazard area. Check with your real estate agent.

If you have any doubts about the condition of your property. Hire a contractor to inspect it. If the contractor finds problems, disclose them to all potential buyers. You can use the contractor's detailed written report to complete your disclosure form and you can also give copies of the inspector's report to potential buyers.

E. Offers and Counter-Offers

Sooner or later, you will receive an offer to purchase your property. You may be relieved and perhaps a little nervous. Fortunately, there are standard methods to deal with offers, and your agent will help you through the process. For starters, make sure your agent pre-qualifies the buyer.

1. Buyer Presents an Offer

The process starts when a prospective purchaser submits a written offer to purchase your property. The offer is contained in a document called, depending on your state, a Purchase Agreement, Real Estate Purchase Contract, Deposit Receipt, or Sales Agreement. The agreement will contain several pages of detailed information, including the price and other financial terms. You should be particularly concerned that the price is sufficient to cover all of your debts and that the proposed closing date is *before* the foreclosure sale.

The offer will also include "contingencies," events that must happen or else the sale won't close. For example, if the offer is contingent upon the buyers qualifying for financing or your property passing certain physical inspections, you should consider strict deadlines for removing those contingencies. On the other hand, if the offer is contingent upon something that will not likely occur before the foreclosure sale, such as the buyers first selling their property, you should reject the contingency. Make sure you review the purchase agreement carefully with your agent, paragraph by paragraph. Most offers give you a strict deadline in which to accept, reject, or propose a counter-offer.

2. Making Counter-Offers

Although you are anxious to sell your property, you may find yourself facing an offer that doesn't quite satisfy your needs as to price, terms, contingencies, and/or closing date. No problem. You have the right to "counter-offer" to the buyer with terms that are acceptable to you. Work with your agent to write a counter-offer and have it presented to the buyers (or their agent) as soon as possible. Although the offer will typically contain a three-day deadline for responding, chances are you will want to respond sooner because of the shortage of time. Do not be nonchalant or casual. Do not wait more than 24 hours to give a counter-offer. Once you have a potential buyer, keep the momentum moving forward.

And don't be surprised if the buyers submit a counter-offer to your counter-offer. In fact, sometimes the process can go on with numerous rounds of offers and counteroffers. But don't be discouraged; a series of counteroffers is a sign that you are moving closer in your negotiations. And with each counter-offer, make it clear how long you're giving the potential buyers to accept or reject it. With a foreclosure pending, you should require that the buyer respond to your counter-offer within 24 hours.

Several important issues in the offer to which you might want to counter-offer are:

• *Price*. Most potential buyers expect you to counter on price, and will bid a little low precisely to see how you will respond. In fact, if your negotiating strategy is to stick with the price you've established, your agent should go out of her way to make this clear to the buyer before the offer is presented.

- *Financing.* If the offer contains financing terms you believe are impractical, or if the buyer wants you to accept a mortgage or deed of trust for a portion of the sales price and you don't want to, the counteroffer is your opportunity to refuse those provisions.

- *Occupancy.* If you're living in the property, the offer should give you a reasonable amount of time to move out after the transaction closes. You may wish to lengthen the time of occupancy in your counter-offer.

- *Contingency of buyer selling property.* As mentioned, a contingency is an event that must happen before the sale closes. Most contingencies are standard conditions in real estate transactions and don't raise a problem. However, other contingencies are problematic and could endanger the timely close of the sale. The worst example of a problematic contingency is where the buyers propose to purchase your property contingent on first selling their home. This contingency is never acceptable in a foreclosure scenario. It would be excruciatingly painful to lose your property at a foreclosure sale because you fruitlessly waited for buyers to sell their property. Refuse to accept this contingency in your counter-offer. Afterall, a buyer who really wants your property can seek

short-term financing to complete the transaction.

- *Inspections.* Frequently, buyers want a detailed inspection of your property before closing, either by themselves or by a licensed property inspector. The purpose of the inspection is to determine whether there are any physical problems that would prohibit them from purchasing the property. If a buyer's offer allows too much time for inspections, shorten the time limits in your counter-offer. For example, the first inspection should be conducted within 5-7 days after acceptance of the counter-offer.

- *Condition of the property.* Reiterate in your counter-offer that your property is being sold in its "as is condition, without any warranties or representations." This claim will eliminate the condition of your property as an excuse for the buyers to delay the closing. It will also protect you from a lawsuit if a buyer purchases your property and subsequently discovers defects. But keep in mind that the "as is" clause does not eliminate your obligation to disclose the physical condition of your property (see Section D on the previous page).

- *Closing (settlement).* Closings typically occur within 30 to 45 days. But you may not have that much time before the foreclosure sale. To avoid this conflict, state in your counter-offer that the settlement or closing must occur no later than a specific date (preferably at least five days before the scheduled foreclosure sale). Also specify that because "time is of the essence," there will be no extensions of that date.

3. Accepting an Offer or Counter-Offer

Carefully review the buyer's offer and counter-offer, if there is one. All terms of the buyer's offer (or counter-offer) will stand unless you counter that they be eliminated or modified.

Be sure that all counter-offers show not only the date, but the exact local time of presentation and expiration. Once you and your agent have determined that all of the terms are acceptable to you (such as price, financing, closing date), you can sign the offer or counter-offer and give it to your agent. Your agent should then deliver the buyer's offer to purchase (deposit receipt) to an escrow company, attorney, or settlement agent, and make sure the transaction proceeds smoothly.

4. Back-up Offers

Sometimes, contingencies are not resolved, and deals are cancelled, leaving you without a buyer, even though the foreclosure sale is lurking around the corner. To avoid having to start all over if a deal falls through, you should accept "back-up" offers.

Example: Tonya accepts a buyer's offer with a contingency that the buyer find acceptable financing within 30 days. Several days later, Tonya also accepts a back-up offer from someone that already has financing. As it turns out, the first buyer can't find financing within 30 days, so Tonya cancels the escrow and pursues the backup offers.

In your counter-offer, you'll need to disclose to the buyers that you will be accepting backup offers from other potential buyers during the escrow period. Make sure that any buyers making a back-up offers understand (in writing) that their offer will not be formally considered unless the pending sale falls through.

F. Proceeding Through to Closing

This section contains an overview of the transaction process, which begins with signing the purchase agreement and ends with transfer of ownership.

1. Working With the Escrow Officer or Settlement Agent

Depending on your state, the sale process consists of steps taken by an escrow officer, attorney or settlement agent (a person responsible for handling the details of the transaction). During this process, the buyer and the seller fulfill the terms and conditions stated in the purchase agreement. For example, you and/or the buyer will execute documents, clear title, inspect the property, pay off existing lienholders, obtain new financing, and exchange documents and money. The terms and conditions of the purchase are described in a document called escrow instructions or settlement rules.

After you've agreed to sell your property, your real estate agent will deliver the offer and any counter-offers to the settlement agent, attorney, or escrow officer depending on which state you are in. Because of the pending foreclosure, you should understand the purchase process and closely monitor its progress. A prompt and timely closing involves detailed, picky, and often overlapping steps.

2. Removing Contingencies

If the sales agreement contains contingencies (such as the buyer obtaining and approving the results of a physical inspection of the property), the settlement agent will make sure you and the buyer, with the help of your agents, remove them. During this period, you should contact the settlement agent at least once a week to make sure that the process is moving forward.

As you and the buyer satisfy or waive each contingency, you will sign a document stating that the contingency has been satisfied. Because of the pending foreclosure, sign a separate statement as each contingency is satisfied or waived. Have your agent monitor the timely removal of each contingency.

Buyers frequently need extra time to satisfy a contingency. Without the extra time, the transaction would end (that is, the deal would fall through) unless buyer and seller agree to extend it. Any agreement to extend the time to meet a contingency (or to change any other term of the transaction) must be in writing and signed. If an extension threatens to extend the transaction beyond the date of the scheduled foreclosure sale--and the foreclosing lender refuses to temporarily postpone the sale date--you have no choice but to refuse the buyer's request for an extension.

If the buyer can't remove a contingency that jeopardizes the entire deal--for example, an inspection turns up a physical problem with the exterior of the property that may need to be repaired before the closing--you should negotiate that the condition will be satisfied after the closing and withhold a portion of the sales proceeds so the repairs can be made without delaying the closing.

If, after trying in good faith, the buyer still can't resolve a contingency, the deal is dead and you should immediately pursue your back-up offers.

3. Closing

The transaction closes when the deed is recorded naming the buyer as the new owner of the property and checks are issued to everyone entitled to be paid from the proceeds (such as your foreclosing lender and any other lienholders). Depending on the custom in your state, you and the buyer--not necessarily together--must go to the settlement agent, escrow officer, or attorney's office, to review and sign the closing documents. Your agent should make sure that the paperwork necessary for closing is completed several days before the anticipated closing date.

G. Special Rules for Dealing With Equity Purchasers

If the buyer is not an equity purchaser. This section does not apply if you receive an offer from a buyer who wants to:

- purchase your non-residential property
- live on the property as her personal residence, or

- purchase the property with a deed in lieu of foreclosure.

If you are selling your own home, you may receive an offer from what's known as an "Equity Purchaser." Equity purchasers are individuals (or occasionally companies) who purchase single-family residences (one-to-four family dwelling units, one of which is owner-occupied) on which a foreclosure is pending. Equity purchasers don't intend to live in the property. Typically, they are interested in purchasing the property as an investment and plan to quickly re-sell or rent it.

Equity purchasers subscribe to publications that publish daily lists of properties in foreclosure. They usually want to purchase properties by offering a couple thousand dollars (for the equity) and promising to take over (and renegotiate) the loan with the foreclosing lender. Some equity purchasers also give the homeowner an option to buy back the property within one year, or allow them to rent the property for several months.

Example: Sam owns a home in Denver, Colorado, that is in foreclosure. Sam estimates that he has approximately $50,000 in equity. A few weeks before the foreclosure sale, Sam is approached by Russell, who offers to purchase Sam's home for $5,000 plus bring the foreclosing lender current. Russell offers Sam the right to rent the home for six months and the right to purchase it back within one year for $50,000. Russell would be an equity purchaser.

Most equity purchasers will contact you directly and avoid your real estate agent. Your agent can help you deal with equity purchasers. But because an equity purchaser's offer typically will not include enough cash to allow your agent to receive a full commission, your agent may be naturally reluctant to negotiate with an equity purchaser. As a result, don't be surprised if your agent dissuades you from considering an offer from an equity purchaser. Keep in mind that there is nothing wrong with selling to an equity purchaser, as long as there is a "level playing field" and negotiations are fair and honest.

1. Laws Regulating Equity Purchasers

Unfortunately, equity purchasers have been known to prey on homeowners in financial distress (especially the poor, elderly, and financially unsophisticated) by inducing them to sell their homes at a fraction of the fair market value. Because of the potential for abuse, an increasing number of states have passed laws to protect homeowners from unethical equity purchasers. California has one of the best equity purchaser laws in the country and other states are quickly following suit. The rules strictly regulate equity purchaser activities and protect unsuspecting property owners in the throes of foreclosure. Check your state's website (see Appendix) to determine whether your state has laws regarding equity purchasers.

In California, for example, the Home Equity Sales Contract Act protects you when selling your home to an equity purchaser. The laws protect you against deceit and misleading representations and prohibit unfair contractual terms. Most important, the laws give you an opportunity to cancel your sales contract within five days if you decide it is a bad deal. (Chapter 12, Section A gives an overview of how to look up the laws yourself.)

2. Special Rules for Equity Purchase Contracts

Let's say you decide to sell to an equity purchaser. He or she must give you a written contract that conforms to numerous technicalities required by law. If your state does not have equity purchaser laws, the following terms should be included in your counter-offer:

• The contract should be in the language you primarily used to negotiate the contract. For example, if you speak Spanish, the contract must be in Spanish (even if your mortgage or deed of trust is in English)

• The contract should include the name, business address and telephone number of the equity purchaser

• The contract should state the address of your residence in foreclosure

• The contract should describe the total amount of money the equity purchaser will pay for your residence and provide a complete description of the terms of payment

• The contract should describe the terms of any proposed rental agreement if the equity purchaser is going to lease your residence back to you

• The contract should state the date and time at which possession will be transferred to the equity purchaser, and

• The contract should be completely filled out, signed, and dated by

both you and the equity purchaser before execution of the mortgage or deed of trust. This prevents an equity purchaser from inserting unreasonable terms in the blank spaces.

In California, even if you sign a contract with an equity purchaser, you still have the right to back out by delivering a signed notice to the buyer. Your right to cancel extends to midnight of the fifth business day following the day you signed the contract or 8:00 a.m. on the day scheduled for the foreclosure sale, whichever occurs first. To protect yourself, the equity purchase contract should contain the following notice, placed near the space reserved for your signature, in at least 12-point bold type:

"YOU MAY CANCEL THIS CONTRACT FOR THE SALE OF YOUR HOUSE WITHOUT PENALTY OF OBLIGATION AT ANY TIME BEFORE [DATE AND TIME OF DAY]. SEE THE ATTACHED NOTICE OF CANCELLATION FORM FOR AN EXPLANATION OF THIS RIGHT."

Make sure your equity purchase contract is accompanied by a fill-in detachable form in duplicate, captioned "Notice of Cancellation" in a size equal to 10-point type if the contract is printed, or capital letters if the contract is typed. A sample follows.

NOTICE OF CANCELLATION

THE CONTRACT WAS SIGNED ON [DATE CONTRACT WAS SIGNED].

YOU MAY CANCEL THIS CONTRACT FOR THE SALE OF YOUR HOUSE, WITHOUT ANY PENALTY OR OBLIGATION, AT ANY TIME BEFORE [DATE THAT IS FIVE (5) BUSINESS DAYS AFTER THE DATE THE CONTRACT WAS SIGNED].

TO CANCEL THIS TRANSACTION, PERSONALLY DELIVER A SIGNED AND DATED COPY OF THIS CANCELLATION NOTICE TO [NAME OF EQUITY PURCHASER] AT [ADDRESS] NOT LATER THAN _____, 200_ [DATE FIVE BUSINESS DAYS AFTER THE DATE CONTRACT WAS SIGNED].

I HEREBY CANCEL THIS TRANSACTION AS OF __, 200_.

_____
Seller's Signature

The equity purchaser should also include the following notice in the contract, in at least 14-point boldface type if the contract is printed, or in capital letters if the contract is typed:

UNTIL YOUR RIGHT TO CANCEL THIS CONTRACT HAS ENDED, [name of equity purchaser] OR ANYONE WORKING FOR HIM/HER CANNOT ASK YOU TO SIGN A DEED OR ANY OTHER DOCUMENT.

Pursuant to equity purchaser laws, until five business days have elapsed from the date you signed the contract, the equity purchaser cannot:

- accept a deed or any interest in the property from you

- record any documents, including the: contract with the equity purchaser, a deed, or any other document of conveyance

- sell or transfer any interest in your property to a third party

- take out a loan against your property, or

- pay you any money.

Note: If your state does not have any equity purchaser laws, you can simply add the requirements described in this Section into your counter-offer and they will automatically become part of your contract.

3. If the Equity Purchaser Violates the Law

Equity purchasers cannot make any untrue or misleading statements about the value of your residence or how much you'd receive after a foreclosure sale. Likewise, they must be truthful about all of the contract terms, your rights or obligations under the contract, and the purpose of all documents you sign.

If an equity purchaser buys your property and gives you an option to repurchase it, he may not place new deeds of trust or mortgages on your property, or transfer title to a third party, without your prior written consent.

Illegal provisions make the equity purchase contract voidable at your option. Under

California law, an equity purchase contract cannot contain provisions that limit the equity purchaser's liability or require arbitration of any dispute. Equity purchasers will be liable for any damages resulting from these illegal provisions.

Pursuant to California law, you have the right to cancel the transaction within two years if the equity purchaser acted improperly (as described in this chapter). But you must give the equity purchaser written notice of the violation and record a Notice of Rescission in the county recorder's office. The equity purchaser then has 20 days in which to deed your property back to you.

If the equity purchaser refuses to cancel the sale after the 20th day, or you subsequently discover that the equity purchaser took unconscionable advantage of you during the foreclosure process, you can file a lawsuit in Court to cancel the contract. If this becomes necessary, find a lawyer to handle the lawsuit.

You may be allowed to recover your actual money damages plus reasonable attorney fees and costs. The court may also award punitive damages if the equity purchaser's conduct was intentional or malicious. If your state does not have laws to protect you from unethical equity purchasers, simply incorporate the requirements described in this section into your contract and they will become enforceable.

H. Arranging a "Short Sale" With Your Lender

The following section contains an overview of the short sale process. Most likely, your agent will handle the details of the transaction. Nevertheless, it will be helpful for you to understand the short sale and the procedures.

If you have equity in your property. A short sale only applies to property owners who don't have equity (or have negative equity) in their property. If you have equity in your property, skip this section.

You may run into a major stumbling block in selling your property if its market value has fallen below the amount you owe your lender. In this case, you have "negative equity." In other words, your property is "under water"; you owe your lender more money than your property is worth! If you were to sell your property to avoid foreclosure, you'd have to add money at the closing because your lender is entitled to full repayment of the loan. Assuming you can't afford to pay the lender the difference between the selling price and the loan balance, what is your alternative?

One of the best solutions is called a "short sale," "short pay," or "short payoff." This procedure allows you to sell your property for as much as the market will bear. All of the net proceeds, minus closing fees and real estate agents' commissions, go to your lender as payment in full. Your lender accepts the discounted amount as payment in full and cancels its mortgage or deed of trust.

Example: Susan purchased a home in Peoria, Illinois, several years ago for $400,000 with a loan for $350,000 from Valley Savings Bank. Susan decided to sell her house to avoid foreclosure and was

shocked to discover that the market value of her property had fallen to about $325,000. Susan found a buyer who would pay $325,000 to purchase the property. After seeing the contract, Valley Savings agreed to a short sale and ultimately accepted $300,000 as payment in full, even though Susan's mortgage still had a balance of approximately $340,000.

A short sale is relatively straightforward if there aren't any junior lienholders encumbering your property. Unfortunately, things get more complicated when junior liens, tax liens, or mechanic's liens encumber property. You have two choices:

- convince all senior and junior lienholders to accept a pro rata (proportionate percentage) share of the sale proceeds, or

- convince the junior lienholders to accept less than a pro rata share or nothing at all.

If the junior lienholder won't cooperate, you won't able to complete a short sale.

1. Will Your Lender Agree to a Short Sale?

If you're wondering why on earth your lender would agree to a short

sale, consider it from your lender's perspective. If your lender takes back your property in foreclosure, they will absorb huge losses. Foreclosing and re-marketing expenses, coupled with the decline in the real estate value, can claim as much as 60% of the market value of the property. In addition, your lender probably won't receive any loan payments during the foreclosure. And if they are a junior lienholder that is foreclosing, they may have to bring the senior lienholder current to protect their junior lien from being wiped out if the senior lienholder forecloses.

Many lenders do not readily admit they will agree to a short sale for fear that the practice might become widespread. However, when confronted with the expense of an imminent foreclosure, lenders will often agree to a short sale that will minimize their losses. But lenders rarely "pre-approve" short sales, so don't bother approaching your lender with hypothetical questions about accepting a short sale. The better approach is to accept a written offer from a buyer that is based upon a short sale, accept the offer subject to your lender's approval, open escrow, and then have your real estate agent submit the sales agreement to your lender for approval.

2. Income Tax Liabilities With a Short Sale

If you go forward with a short sale, keep in mind that you may be liable for income taxes on the amount of your loan you are not paying back. Because your lender releases you from debt, it is called "discharge of debt" and is considered taxable income by the IRS. For example, if your loan balance is $300,000, but your lender accepts $250,000 as a short sale payoff, the $50,000 forgiven by your lender is considered discharge of debt income by the IRS and is taxable.

Two IRS exceptions may relieve you of tax liability:

- *Bankruptcy exception.* If you file for bankruptcy, your debt will be relieved. (IRC § 108(a)(1)(A).)
- *Insolvency exception* (or the "balance sheet test"). If your secured and unsecured debt exceeds the value of your assets at the time of the short sale, the discharge of debt income may not be taxable. (IRC § 108(a)(1)(B).)

If you're interested in pursuing these exclusions, contact a CPA or tax consultant for further advice in this specialized area.

3. Overview of Short Sale Procedures

There are three steps to completing a short sale with your lender. Your real estate agent can help you with the details.

a. Select a Listing Agent and Place Your Property on the Market

Follow the general instructions in Section B to find an agent and list your property. Because your lender is not required to accept a short sale, advise potential buyers that any sale is subject to your lender's approval. Your agent will disclose this information in the Multiple Listing Service:

"The sale terms are subject to the consent of the lender. Please contact the listing agent for details."

The goal of a short sale is to price your property low enough that you can sell it before the foreclosure sale, yet high enough that your lender will accept the short payoff. Your real estate agent will help you get your property appraised and approximately priced.

Have your property appraised. Unlike a regular sale, most lenders require an appraisal for short sales. You'll either need to obtain a formal appraisal, or at the very least, letters from a minimum of three real estate agents, estimating the current market value of your property ("broker's price opinions"). Your failure to get an appraisal could cause a delay in closing.

b. Find a Buyer and Open Escrow

Once you receive an acceptable offer from a potential buyer, you'll need to add language in your counter-offer that protects you in the event your lender will not accept a short payoff:

"This sale is contingent on the lender accepting less than the outstanding balance of their loan."

If the buyer accepts your counter-offer, your agent should immediately open escrow and submit the purchase agreement to your lender for approval.

c. Submit Short Sale Documents to Your Lender

As soon as you receive a fully-executed purchase agreement (and escrow instructions in states where applicable), your real estate agent should contact your lender's office and talk with someone who has authority to approve a short sale. Many institutional lenders now have individuals (or separate departments) specializing in short sales. The department may be called the "Short Payoff Department," "Loan Workout Department," "Loss Mitigation Department" or "Asset Management and Recovery Department."

Your agent will submit the following documents to the appropriate department or individual at your lender's office:

- a cover letter from your agent advising the lender of the buyer's offer to purchase your property and the need for a short payoff

- a copy of the listing agreement

- a letter from you authorizing your agent to negotiate on your behalf

- a copy of the signed offer or counter-offer from the buyer

- a copy of the escrow instructions (in applicable states)

- a list of comparable sales in your neighborhood supporting the listing price (sometimes these can be found in the appraisal and broker's opinion letter)

- your tax returns from the last two years and bank statements from the last two months

- an estimated closing statement, calculating the net proceeds to your lender upon closing, and

- a "hardship letter" from you describing the specific circumstances causing the financial problems leading to the foreclosure. You should explain why you can't afford to pay the shortfall (difference between the loan balance and the sales price) and give a sympathetic plea for compassion and help from your lender.

Now the real negotiations begin! Your agent will need to convince your lender's representative that a short sale will cost the lender less than the costs of foreclosing your property (coupled with the market decline in value and the cost to resell it). If your lender sees a choice of losing upwards of 60% on a foreclosure versus losing only 20% to 30% on a short sale, they will likely be more inclined to make a common-sense business decision in your favor. To prepare for these discussions, you may find it helpful to break down the foreclosure costs.

Example: Charles owns a property in Billings, Montana, encumbered by a $200,000 loan. If his lender, Walnut Bank decides to foreclose, it will incur the following costs (calculated as a percentage of the loan):

Loan balance:	*100%*
Market decline:	*-20%*
Foreclosure costs:	*-05%*
REO discount price:	*-10%*
Repairs:	*-05%*
Holding costs:	*-08%*
Adm & legal costs:	*-03%*
Sales costs:	*-07%*
Total:	*-58%*

NET TO LENDER: *<42%>*

Your lender will probably want to make sure that there is no other viable solution to the problem. You and your real estate agent should emphasize that you have no resources to pay the shortfall and that your property is being sold for its true market value. (For an in-depth discussion of how to negotiate with your lender, see Chapter 5.)

chapter

11

GIVING YOUR LENDER A DEED
IN LIEU OF FORECLOSURE

A. Reasons to Use a Deed in Lieu 228

B. Will Your Lender Accept a Deed in Lieu? 229

    1. Advantages to Your Lender 229
    2. Why Your Lender May Refuse a Deed in Lieu 229
    3. HUD Deed in Lieu Program 230
    4. Department of Veterans Affairs Deed in Lieu Program 230

C. Negotiate Terms of the Deed in Lieu 231

    1. Issues to Address With Your Lender 231
    2. Get Agreement in Writing 232

D. How to Prepare a Deed in Lieu of Foreclosure 232

    1. How to Fill in a Deed in Lieu 233
    2. Deliver the Deed in Lieu to Your Lender 236
    3. Get the Canceled Loan Documents From Your Lender 236
    4. Make Sure the Deed in Lieu Is Recorded 236

After a lot of soul searching, you may come to the difficult conclusion that your property is just not worth keeping. It may become painfully obvious that no matter how much your home means to you and your family, you have no equity in it and you can't afford the monthly payments. Let's say that other strategies described in this book won't work in your personal situation, but you still want to avoid a foreclosure sale and prevent any further damage to your credit.

Fortunately, there is a solution. You can voluntarily give your property to the foreclosing lender. This will automatically stop the foreclosure. However, you must first get the lender's permission to do this. If the lender agrees, you will sign a Deed in Lieu of Foreclosure ("deed in lieu"), a document that transfers the property from you to your lender.

Provided your lender consents, you can give your lender a deed in lieu at any stage in the foreclosure process--from the date you first missed a payment until the day of the foreclosure sale. If your lender accepts the deed in lieu, the trustee or Court must immediately terminate the foreclosure. Your lender will now own the property without completing the lengthy foreclosure process.

A. Reasons to Use a Deed in Lieu

A deed in lieu may be your best strategy if you believe your property is not worth saving and most of the following match your circumstances:

- you either have no equity, or you have negative equity, in your property

- even if you stop the foreclosure, you cannot afford the monthly mortgage payments

- you don't want a foreclosure on your credit report, and

- you've diligently, but unsuccessfully, tried to find a buyer for your property.

Example: Peter owns a duplex in Newark, New Jersey. The property is in foreclosure and there are approximately 15 days left before the foreclosure sale. Peter has no equity in the property, can't afford the monthly payments, and hasn't been able to locate a buyer. Under the circumstances, Peter contacts his lender and negotiates a deed in lieu of foreclosure. Once the lender accepts the deed in lieu from Peter, the foreclosure stops.

You'll derive several benefits by giving your lender a deed in lieu rather than selling your property to a third party:

- *The foreclosure stops immediately.* Regardless of whether your lender is pursuing a judicial or nonjudicial foreclosure, it immediately stops once your lender accepts your deed in lieu. Your property will not be auctioned off at a foreclosure sale.

- *You protect your credit rating.* Although missing payments and having foreclosure proceedings commence will lower your credit score (if reported to the credit reporting agencies), an actual foreclosure sale may effectively ruin your credit for many years. However, a deed in lieu will not appear on your credit report; therefore a foreclosure sale would not appear, which may be crucial to you in the future. You can explain to future creditors that you and your lender resolved the default with no need for a foreclosure sale.

- *Your lender cannot get a deficiency judgment.* If a judicial foreclosure is pending, deeding your property to your lender can give you immunity from any deficiency--the difference between the balance of the loan and the amount the property sells for at a foreclosure sale. (See Chapter 4,

Section B11 for more on deficiency judgments.)

B. Will Your Lender Accept a Deed in Lieu?

Unfortunately, many property owners mistakenly believe they can stop a foreclosure by simply giving a deed in lieu to the lender without their approval or by recording it in the county recorder's office without the lender's consent. However, neither of these actions are legal. For the deed in lieu to be effective, your lender must willingly accept the deed in lieu and have it recorded in the county recorder's office (We cover the step-by-step procedures in Sections C and D, on the following pages.)

1. Advantages to Your Lender

A foreclosing lender that accepts a deed in lieu receives immediate title to your property with no additional costs or delays. Their only alternative is to pay foreclosure fees to a trustee, sheriff, or legal fees to attorneys, then wait 2-3 months (nonjudicial foreclosure) or up to 1-2 years (judicial foreclosure), to get the property.

Your lender also avoids the uncertainty of waiting to see if you're going to file a lawsuit to enjoin the foreclosure sale, file bankruptcy, or use some other strategy to stop the foreclosure.

2. Why Your Lender May Refuse a Deed in Lieu

Despite the many advantages of accepting a deed in lieu, your lender may prefer to proceed with a foreclosure. This is because your lender runs certain risks by accepting a deed in lieu from you. Here are the most common problems:

- Mortgages, deeds of trust, or liens encumbering your property are unaffected by the deed in lieu. In contrast, if your lender forecloses, it will take the property subject to any existing senior liens, which will remain on the property. Nevertheless, any junior liens will be wiped out by the foreclosure sale. But, if your lender accepts a deed in lieu, junior liens will remain on the property. For example, by accepting a deed in lieu, your foreclosing lender will have the obligation to bring junior loans current, resume monthly payments, and pay off lienholders when the loans comes due. Further, your property will be more difficult to sell because of the continuing obligations to junior lienholders. As a result, most lenders will not accept a deed in lieu unless there are no junior liens encumbering the property.

- You could later try to set aside the deed in lieu. Although rare, former owners have had second thoughts and sued their lenders to set aside a deed in lieu, based upon theories of lender fraud or coercion. As a consequence, lenders are sometimes hesitant to accept deeds in lieu.

- Your lender may be concerned about inheriting liability if there are serious property problems. A lender may refuse a deed in lieu if your property has substantial physical problems (beyond general disrepair), such as toxic substances in the soil, structural weaknesses, a collapsing foundation, hillside erosion, or boundary disputes. If the foreclosing lender voluntarily accepts title to your property, they could become liable for correcting those problems. In contrast, if the foreclosure sale occurs, and the property is sold to a third person, they would not be liable for the property's problems.

If your lender won't accept a deed in lieu: Don't panic. Consider selling your property at the best price you can get. (See Chapter 10.) If the proceeds won't cover your outstanding loan, you can approach your lender with a short sale, covered in Chapter 10, Section H.

3. HUD Deed in Lieu Program

If your loan is insured by the Federal Housing Administration ("FHA"), contact the U.S. Department of Housing and Urban Affairs ("HUD") and ask about their deed in lieu program. HUD will encourage your lender to accept a deed in lieu if you meet three requirements:

1. You defaulted due to hardship basically beyond your control, such as illness, job loss, divorce or job transfer.

2. It is unlikely that you will be able to bring and keep your loan current.

3. No junior liens encumber your property or you can pay them off within 20 days of the date of your request for a deed in lieu.

If you don't meet the above criteria, HUD will discourage your lender from accepting a deed in lieu, so you'll have to pursue other options. (For general information on negotiating with HUD, see Chapter 5, Section D.)

4. Department of Veterans Affairs Deed in Lieu Program

If your loan is insured by the U.S. Department of Veteran Affairs ("VA"), contact the local VA office before delivering a deed in lieu to your lender. The VA must approve your deed in lieu before your lender can accept it.

The VA often gives approval if a deed in lieu will save time and money, and collection of the debt appears doubtful. The VA may require you to submit a financial statement along with a letter explaining why the VA should approve a deed in lieu.

According to the VA's Loan Servicing Guide, the VA will approve a deed in lieu under the following circumstances:

• You cannot afford your loan payments and your financial condition is unlikely to improve.

• You haven't succeeded in selling your property after reasonable exposure on the market.

• There are no junior liens, deeds of trust, or mortgages on your property.

• The value of your property is the same or less than the balance of your loan.

• You agree in writing to be liable for any monetary loss the VA suffers by terminating the loan prematurely and re-selling your property. (Although this is a serious commitment on your part, in practice the VA rarely if ever chases veterans for the deficiencies.

So, it does not appear to be a viable reason for avoiding the VA program.)

If the VA disapproves your deed in lieu, it will instruct your lender to proceed with the foreclosure. (For a general discussion on negotiating with the VA, read Chapter 5, Section E.)

C. Negotiate Terms of the Deed in Lieu

Because your lender must consent to a deed in lieu, you will need to contact your lender by telephone (or letter) and request that they accept a deed in lieu rather than proceeding with the foreclosure. Instructions on how to reach and negotiate with the responsible person at your lender's office are in Chapter 5, Section A.

1. Issues to Address With Your Lender

If your lender is willing to accept a deed in lieu, negotiate the following issues together:

- *Will your lender cancel the mortgage or deed of trust*? Your lender should sign the reconveyance (cancellation) on the back of your loan document and give it to you. Although technically unnecessary, it is a better policy to have your lender agree to return your loan documents in exchange for your deed in lieu.

- *How will you deliver the deed*? Determine exactly who is authorized to accept the deed in lieu, and where. Typically, you simply hand your lender's representative the keys to your property along with a signed deed in lieu.

- *When will your lender take possession*? If you live on the property, your lender will probably allow you remain there for several weeks. Be sure to settle in advance the exact date you will voluntarily move out. As a condition of your continuing occupancy, agree to keep the property in good condition, to cooperate with potential buyers that want to inspect the property, and to voluntarily move out on the promised date. Typically, you won't have to pay for insurance, property taxes or rent during this occupancy period. If you don't live on the property, have your lender confirm in writing that they will assume responsibility for the tenant(s) leasing the property and that you will have no further responsibilities.

- *Will your lender correct your credit report*? Have your lender agree to promptly contact the three credit reporting agencies (Experian, Transunion, and Equifax) and request that they remove all references to foreclosure in your credit report, including the Notice of Default and/or Notice of Sale.

- *Will your lender waive a deficiency judgment*? If a judicial foreclosure is pending, you are potentially liable for a deficiency judgment. Ask your lender to agree in writing to relieve you of all financial responsibility under your mortgage, including back payments, attorney fees and foreclosure costs.

2. Get Agreement in Writing

Because the foreclosure clock is ticking, it is important to get your lender's written consent to a deed in lieu. Write a letter to your lender confirming that your lender agrees to accept a deed in lieu. Leave room at the bottom of the letter for your lender to indicate acceptance. A sample letter appears below.

February 23, 200X

Ms. Darlene Smith
Bundy Savings Bank
2323 State Street
Hartford, CN

Re: Loan 65454, Secured by Property at 27 Green Avenue, Hartford, CN

Dear Ms. Smith:

Your bank holds the first mortgage in the amount of $405,000 on the property listed above. On July 10, 200X, you started foreclosure proceedings. The sale is now scheduled for March 10, 200X. This letter confirms that I have agreed to sign, and you have agreed to accept, a deed in lieu of foreclosure on my property. You have also agreed to:

1.   Draft a deed in lieu of foreclosure and have it ready for me to sign no later than Friday, February 27, 200X.

2.   Advise the Sheriff to stop the foreclosure sale as soon as I sign the deed in lieu and deliver it to you.

3.   Promptly inform Experian, Transunion and Equifax to remove any reference to foreclosure on my credit reports.

4.   Permit me to occupy the property through May 15, 200X without paying rent, insurance, or property taxes.

If this letter accurately reflects our agreement, please sign your name on the space provided below and return a copy to me.

Thank you for your anticipated cooperation in this matter.

Very truly yours,

Susan Temple

AGREED AND ACCEPTED TO:

By: _____
Authorized Officer, Bundy Savings Bank

D. How to Prepare a Deed in Lieu of Foreclosure

After you negotiate the terms of the deed in lieu, your lender will probably prepare a deed in lieu for you to sign. If your lender does not have a blank deed in lieu, or you want to expedite the process, you can use the Deed in Lieu of Foreclosure form provided on the next page or in the Appendix.

A quitclaim deed may also be used. Your lender may use a quitclaim deed, rather than a deed in lieu, to accomplish the same result. If your lender uses a quitclaim deed, make sure the words "Deed in Lieu of Foreclosure" are printed or typed across the top of the form, above the words "Quitclaim Deed."

1. How to Fill in a Deed in Lieu

The following instructions are keyed to the sample Deed in Lieu of Foreclosure on the next page. Preparing a deed in lieu isn't difficult, but pay attention to the details. One careless mistake could invalidate the whole document. If at all possible, you should type the information on the form.

a. Recording information

Fill in your lender's correct name and address in the space below "Recording requested by." If you are not sure of the lender's exact legal name and address, contact your lender before you fill in this information.

b. Tax statements

Property tax statements should be mailed to the new owner, which is your foreclosing lender. Again, enter your lender's full legal name and correct address.

c. Documentary transfer tax information

In most states, local transfer taxes are levied when real property is sold and a deed is recorded. In your case, however, the transfer should not be subject to this tax because you're deeding the property back to your lender, not selling it. You don't need to add anything.

d. Location of the Property

Your property is located either in a city or an unincorporated area. Check the appropriate box and give the name of the city, if applicable.

e. Identification of owners (grantors)

Here you fill in your name, along with the names of all owners of the property (who must sign the deed in lieu at the bottom). Use the full legal name for each owner, as listed in the original deed. Here are some guidelines:

- If you are single: It's a good idea to add the words "an unmarried person" after the name to show that a spouse wasn't mistakenly omitted. For example, "John Wong, an unmarried person."

- If any of the property owners are married: If both spouses are owners, list both of their names, followed by "husband and wife"--for example, "Adam Hart and Felicia Hart, husband and wife." If only one spouse owns the property, list the owner's name, followed by the words, "a married person, as his [or her] sole and separate property."

- If you hold title to the property as a business (other than a sole proprietorship): Specify the business

DEED IN LIEU OF FORECLOSURE

Recording requested by
        (a)
and when recorded mail
this deed and tax statement to:
        (b)
Deed in Lieu of Foreclosure

1. This transfer is exempt from the documentary transfer tax. (c)

2. This property is located in_____,
[] an unincorporated area

[] the city of _____   (d)

3. For valuable consideration, receipt of which is hereby acknowledged, _____
_____ (e) hereby deeds (f) to _____ (g) in lieu of
foreclosure, the following real property in the City of
_____, County of _____, State of _____, (h)
commonly known as_____
_____.

Date:_____, 200X   _____ (i)
Date: _____, 200X   _____
Date: _____, 200X   _____

ACKNOWLEDGMENT (i)

State of _____)
County of _____)

On _____, 200_, before me, _____, a notary public,
personally appeared _____, personally known to me
or proved to me on the basis of satisfactory evidence to be the person(s) whose
name is/are subscribed to this instrument, and acknowledged to me that he/she/
they executed the same in his/her/their authorized capacity(ies) and that by his/
her/their signature(s) on the instrument, the person(s) or the entity upon behalf of
which the person(s) acted, executed the instrument.

entity after its name--"a corporation," "a partnership" or "a limited liability company," and the state it was formed. For example, "Sea Shore, a Michigan general partnership."

• If there are two or more owners: After you list all owners' names, designate how the owners hold title, such as "tenants in common," "joint tenants," or "husband and wife." If you aren't sure, look at the original deed for this information. For example, "Donald Martinez and Sonya Thomas, joint tenants."

f. Words of transfer

Note that there are magical words that legally transfer your property to your lender: "hereby deeds to [name] in lieu of foreclosure." (The phrase "hereby quitclaims to" will also do the job.) This phrase establishes your intent to convey your property to your lender. Don't change the wording of this phrase; any changes could invalidate the deed in lieu.

g. Identification of the new owner (grantee)

The deed in lieu must clearly identify the name of your foreclosing lender. Again, fill in your lender's exact legal name.

h. Physical description of your property

The deed in lieu must identify the property being transferred. Start by filling in the city (cross out "city of" if the property is not within the city limits) and the county in which your property is located.

Next, you'll need to fill in the legal description, which includes some pretty strange-sounding terms. The easiest way is to copy the legal description from your old deed. If you can't find your old deed, you should be able to get a copy from your escrow company, a local title insurance company, or your lender. Or you can visit the recorder's office in the county where your property is located to obtain a copy.

Don't make any typographical errors. Double-check what you've filled in by having someone read the legal description from your old deed out loud while you follow along reading the deed in lieu you've prepared.

Although not required, it is helpful to fill in the street address of your property after the words "commonly known as." For example, "2345 State Street, Seattle, Washington."

i. Date, signature and acknowledgment

All owners must sign the deed in lieu in the presence of a notary public. A notary simply confirms that each signature is genuine and that you signed the document in her presence. If you don't know a notary, contact your lender; most lenders have notaries in their offices. Everyone signing should bring a valid picture ID, such as a driver's license or passport.

Enter the date that you are signing the deed in lieu. The deed in lieu is effective from the date of delivery, which is presumed to be the date of execution (signing).

All owners (grantors) of the property, and their spouses (even if not on the deed) must sign the deed in lieu for it to be valid. Each person must sign his or her name exactly as it is listed earlier in the deed in lieu.

2. Deliver the Deed in Lieu to Your Lender

Make a copy of the signed and notarized deed in lieu for your records and deliver the original document to your lender. Ask for a signed receipt for the deed in lieu. Remember, your lender must accept the deed in lieu for it to be effective. Request that the lender advise the trustee or their attorney to stop the foreclosure. You should also telephone the trustee or their attorney the next day and confirm that the foreclosure has been canceled.

3. Get the Canceled Loan Documents From Your Lender

In exchange for delivering the deed in lieu, your lender should return to you your original mortgage or deed of trust. Again, ask for a signed receipt from your lender.

4. Make Sure the Deed in Lieu Is Recorded

Once your lender receives your deed in lieu, they should record it in the county recorder's office. Although it is entirely okay to just deliver the deed without recording it, recordation will make the transfer of title official and give public notice that you have given up all rights, title and interest to your property. We

suggest you follow up with your lender in a couple days to confirm that the deed in lieu was recorded and to request a copy for your files.

12

HELP BEYOND THIS BOOK

A. Real Estate Lawyers 238

    1. How to Find a Real Estate Lawyer 238
    2. What to Look for in a Real Estate Lawyer 239
    3. Hiring a Real Estate Lawyer as a Legal Coach 240

B. Using a Foreclosure Consultant 240

    1. Foreclosure Consultant Laws 241
    2. Foreclosure Consultant Must Provide Written Contract 242

C. The Law Library, Internet, and Legal Research 243

    1. Find a Law Library That's Open to the Public 243
    2. Use a Good Legal Research Resource 243
    3. Find and Read Relevant Statutes 244
    4. Find and Read Relevant Cases 244

This book describes judicial and nonjudicial foreclosures and various strategies for stopping foreclosure, but it doesn't cover everything. At some point you may need more information or assistance this book doesn't provide. You may need to turn to:

- a real estate lawyer who can provide legal information, advice, or legal representation. (See Section A.)

- a foreclosure consultant, who can assist in negotiating with your lender or refinancing your property. (See Section B),

- the law library, an excellent source for additional information on any particular issue raised in the course of your foreclosure (See Section C.), or

- the internet, a convenient source of additional information on legal issues, statutes, and cases. (See Section C).

A. Real Estate Lawyers

Throughout this book, we've suggested that you see an attorney (specializing in real estate) if you find yourself in a complex or difficult situation. While very few lawyers specialize in foreclosure, most real estate attorneys have a working knowledge of foreclosure in your state and will be more helpful than a general practitioner. Here are some of the things a real estate lawyer can do for you:
  - negotiate with your lender

  - help you assess your financial situation, especially in the context of filing for bankruptcy (but you will want to hire an attorney who specializes in bankruptcy if you decide to file.)

  - prepare papers for filing a lawsuit in court to enjoin (stop) a foreclosure

  - represent you in court

  - coach you on how to prepare legal papers

  - coach you on appearing in court, and

  - answer your legal questions.

Real estate lawyers generally charge anywhere from $150 to $400 per hour depending on geographical regions and the lawyer's experience. But keep in mind, real estate attorneys tend to charge more than general practitioners because of their specialized knowledge. So the extra expense is usually worth it.

1. How to Find a Real Estate Lawyer

There are several ways to find a real estate lawyer suited to your particular situation:

- *Personal Referrals*: This is your best approach. If you know someone who was pleased with the services of a real estate lawyer, call that lawyer first. If he or she doesn't handle foreclosure matters, ask for a recommendation of someone else who's experienced and competent.

- *Telephone directory (yellow pages)*: Most telephone directories have a separate listing for real estate attorneys. In addition, many attorneys advertise free consultations in which they will answer questions and help you determine whether they can help you.

- *Internet*. You can use one of the many popular search engines on the internet to find an attorney in your area that specializes in real estate law, and more specifically, foreclosure defense. Google, Yahoo, and MSN all have excellent search engines. Just type in "real estate attorney" and your city and the results will amaze you!

- *Legal clinics*: Many law schools sponsor legal clinics and provide free legal advice to consumers. Some legal clinics offer free services to low-to-moderate income people while others limit their programs to very-low-income people. Make sure that the legal clinic has experienced real estate attorneys available to help you.

- *Group legal plans*: Some unions, employers, and consumer action organizations offer group plans to their members or employees, who can obtain comprehensive legal assistance free or for low rates. If you're a member of such a plan, check with it first to see if they have lawyers on their panel who are experienced with real estate matters.

- *Pre-Paid legal insurance*: Pre-paid "legal insurance" plans offer some services for a low monthly fee and charge more for additional or different work. That means that participating lawyers may use the plan as a way to get clients, who are attracted by the low-cost basic services, and then sell them more expensive services later. If you're considering joining such a plan to get the help you need, make sure the plan has real estate attorneys available and find out if it costs extra to consult with a real estate attorney. If the plan offers extensive free advice with an experienced real estate attorney, your initial membership fee may be worth the consultation you receive, even if you use it only once. You can always join a plan for a specific service and then not renew.

Note: There's no guarantee that the real estate lawyers available through these plans are of the best caliber; sometimes they aren't. As with any consumer transaction, check it out carefully before signing up. Ask about the plan's complaint system, whether you get to choose your lawyer, and whether or not the lawyer will represent you in court.

- *Chain discount law firms*: Local branches of discount law firms routinely offer legal advice on real estate matters. You can call and ask about their basic fees, and probably get an initial consultation for about $50 to $150.

- *Lawyer referral panels*: Most county bar associations will refer you the names of real estate attorneys who practice in your area. But bar associations usually provide only minimal screening for the attorneys listed, which mean those who participate may not be the most experienced or competent. You may find a skilled real estate attorney willing to work for a reasonable fee this way, but take the time to check out the credentials and foreclosure experience of the person to whom you're referred.

2. What to Look for in a Real Estate Lawyer

Once you have the names of a few real estate lawyers, do some screening before you commit yourself to hiring one. It's important that you be as comfortable as possible with any lawyer you hire. When making an appointment, ask to talk directly to the lawyer. If you can't, this may give you your first hint as to how accessible the lawyer will be later. If you're told that a paralegal will be handling the routine aspects of your case under the supervision of a lawyer, you may need to decide if you are satisfied with that arrangement.

If you do talk directly to a prospective lawyer, ask some specific questions about foreclosure. Do you get clear, concise answers? If not, try someone else. If the lawyer says little except to suggest that he or she can handle the problem (for a substantial fee, of course), watch out! You're talking with someone who doesn't know the answer and won't admit it (common), or someone who pulls rank on the basis of professional standing.

Once you find a real estate lawyer you like, make an hour-long appointment to discuss your situation fully. Most attorneys will not charge for this initial consultation. Your goal at the initial conference is to find out what the lawyer recommends and how much it will cost. Go home and think about the lawyer's suggestions. If they don't make complete sense or you have reservations, call someone else. Try to see more than one attorney, compare their strategies, and decide which one you feel most comfortable with.

3. Hiring a Real Estate Lawyer as a Legal Coach

If it does not make economic sense for you to turn your case over to an attorney to fight your foreclosure, you may still want to hire one on an hourly basis as a "legal coach," to give you occasional advice.

Attorneys have traditionally either assumed overall responsibility for a

client's case or declined representation. However, due to a combination of economics, time demands of modern law practice, and increased competition from foreclosure consultants, paralegals (trained attorney assistants), accountants, and other professionals, you may be able to locate a real estate lawyer who is willing to act as your legal coach.

Your legal coach may do legal research if you need it, suggest techniques to resolve problems as they arise, clarify a confusing law, inform you of time deadlines, or suggest ways to make your arguments more persuasive. He or she will not, however, take over your case unless you specifically agree that's what you want.

As you go through the foreclosure process and the different options available to stop the foreclosure, there are many opportunities to consult with a legal coach. But don't consult a coach until you read through all relevant sections of this book. You may find that this book addresses questions you would normally pay a lawyer to answer or points you in a direction to easily find the answers on your own.

B. Using a Foreclosure Consultant

During foreclosure (either judicial or nonjudicial), you may be contacted by someone claiming to be a "foreclosure consultant." A foreclosure consultant is an individual who, for a fee, offers to help you stop the foreclosure.

Some of the services a foreclosure consultant may offer include:

• counseling you on your debt situation

- negotiating with your lender

- arranging for an extension of the period in which you must cure the default or reinstate the loan

- arranging to extend or postpone the foreclosure sale

- providing you general advice while you are in foreclosure

- helping you obtain refinancing of your property

- finding an attorney to handle a lawsuit against your lender, and

- assisting in filing bankruptcy.

Some states have recently passed laws to regulate foreclosure consultants. For example, some states require that a foreclosure consultant must have a current state real estate broker's license, and be bonded in an amount equal to at least twice the fair market value of your property. If you are in one of those states, and approached by a foreclosure consultant you should ask to see his license and bond before proceeding any further. (If your state does not have laws regulating foreclosure consultants, then incorporate the requirements you read in this section into the contract the foreclosure consultant gives.)

A good foreclosure consultant can provide a valuable service when you appear doomed to lose your property in foreclosure. On the other hand, unscrupulous consultants can be a dangerous waste of precious time, cost you money you don't have, and further disrupt your already damaged relationship with your lender.

Unfortunately, some dishonest consultants have been known to use illegal schemes and other unreasonable commercial practices to improperly obtain money or place liens on property. Property owners in financial distress (especially the poor, elderly, and financially unsophisticated) are vulnerable to foreclosure consultants who induce them to pay large sums of money to avoid foreclosure. The purpose of this section is to help you distinguish between honest consultants and crooked ones.

1. Foreclosure Consultant Laws

Several states have adopted laws designed to protect unsuspecting property owners and regulate foreclosure consultants' business conduct. (You will need to refer to your state's laws and website listed in the Appendix.) If your state does not have laws regulating foreclosure consultants, then simply incorporate the following requirements into a written agreement that the foreclosure consultant and you will sign.

A consultant is expected to negotiate with your lender, but he cannot legally:

- demand, charge or collect any fee or compensation from you until after the consultant performs every service he contracted to perform

- charge a fee which exceeds 10% per year of the amount of any loan he makes or obtains for you

- take any wage assignment any type of lien on your property (such as a mortgage or deed of trust) or any

WHO IS NOT A FORECLOSURE CONSULTANT

Of course, not everyone who approaches you is a foreclosure consultant or covered by state laws regulating foreclosure consultants. The following are not considered foreclosure consultants:

- lawyers rendering advice in the course of their practice

- licensed real estate brokers or sales people who, or sell your residence in foreclosure without claiming any interest in the property

- licensed accountants acting in that capacity

- people acting under the express authority of the Department of Housing and Urban Development, or other department of the United States of America, or your state's government

- people who are owed an obligation secured by a mortgage or deed of trust encumbering a residence

- personal property brokers, commercial finance lenders, or anyone else licensed to make loans, and

- any person or entity doing business as a bank, savings bank, trust company, credit union, insurance company, title company or escrow company.

other type of security for payment

- receive any compensation from a third party without first disclosing it in writing to you

- acquire any ownership interest in your property which is in foreclosure

- take a power of attorney, except to inspect documents on your behalf, or

- induce you to enter into any contract that does not comply with or waives any of your state's laws.

If the foreclosure consultant fails to agree with any of these requirements, you can and should immediately fire the consultant.

2. Foreclosure Consultant Must Provide Written Contract

In those states having laws regulating foreclosure consultants, the consultant must give you a written contract before they can perform any service for you. If your contract doesn't meet the letter of the law, you don't have to sign it. If your state doesn't have these laws, have the consultant sign a contract that contains all of these terms.

In the past, some consultants have attempted to circumvent these restrictions by including a waiver of conditions in the contract. However, take heart in knowing that such a waiver in a consultant contract is considered void and unenforceable. Any provision in the contract that attempts to limit the liability of the consultant's representatives or employees is also void.

a. How to Cancel a Contract

Depending on your state, once you sign a contract with a foreclosure consultant, you have three to five days in which to cancel the contract.

The cancellation must be in writing, but it need not be in a particular form. For example, you could simply write a one-sentence letter advising the consultant that you were canceling the contract. Although not required to do so, you should mail a copy of your cancellation notice by certified mail, return receipt requested. Remember to keep a copy for your records.

b. How to Terminate a Contract

If you believe that a foreclosure consultant has violated any of the restrictions described in this section, you have the right to immediately terminate the contract. You may also file a lawsuit against the consultant for all damages resulting from any misrepresentations made or fraudulent act committed during the services he performed on your behalf, along with attorney's fees.

If the consultant's conduct is found to be intentional or malicious, you can also recover punitive damages for as much as three times the compensation received by the consultant. In some states, a consultant who is found to have violated these restrictions also may be punished by a fine and imprisonment.

C. The Law Library, Internet, and Legal Research

Often, you can handle a problem yourself if you're willing to do some research in a law library or on the internet. The trick is to know what kinds of information you can find there. Sometimes, what you need to know isn't written down. For instance, if you want to know whether you can successfully sell or refinance your property before the foreclosure sale, you can't find out by going to the law library or surfing the internet. You'll probably have to talk to a real estate agent or mortgage broker. But if want to explore particular legal arguments, supporting (or opposing) cases, and/or applicable law, a law library or the internet can be your best friends.

Here, briefly, are the basic steps of researching legal questions.

1. Find a Law Library That's Open to the Public

Public law libraries are often found in county courthouses, law schools, and state capitals. If you can't find one, search the internet, ask a public library reference librarian, court clerk, lawyer, or look in the yellow pages of your telephone book.

2. Use a Good Legal Research Resource

To find the answer to a legal question, or look up a statute or case, you need some guidance in basic legal research techniques. Any of the following resources that may be available in your law library will tell you how to do legal research:

- *How to Find the Law,* by Morris Cohen, Robert Berring and Kent Olson (West Publishing)

• *Legal Research: How to Find and Understand the Law,* by Stephen Elias and Susan Levinkind (Nolo Press)

• *The Legal Research Manual: A Game Plan for Legal Research and Analysis,* by Christopher and Jill Wren (A-R Editions), or

• *Introduction to Legal Research: A Layperson's Guide to Finding the Law,* by Al Coco (West Publishing).

To find legal resources online, get a copy of *Law on the Net* by James Evans (Nolo Press).

3. Find and Read Relevant Statutes

After consulting a background resource, you may need to read a particular statute for yourself. In most states, they are called "statutes" or "codes" and are contained in a series of books. West Annotated Codes, published by West Publishing (www.westlaw.com) publishes the statutes or codes for most states.

After you read the statute in the hardcover portion of the book, turn to the very back of the book. There should be an insert pamphlet (called a "pocket part") for the current year that contains recent amendments and supporting cases that have become law since the hardcover volume was first published. Look to see if the statute is in the pocket part as well.

When you first read a statute, you'll probably be totally confused, if not in tears. Relax. No one understands these statutes as they're written. That's why there are usually pages and pages of cases interpreting the statutes. You can

OBTAINING STATUTES FROM THE INTERNET

These and other statutes may be obtained online at the following Web site: www.leginfo.gov, www.reginfo.gov, or look at your state's legislative website (listed in the Appendix).

Even if you download the statutes, however, you will ultimately want to take your research to a law library to avail yourself of the many tools that are available there and not on the Web, including the annotations that follow each statute in the hardcover annotated codes described below.

go to the pages that follow the statute and read its interpretation, or go directly to cases (court opinions) that have interpreted the statute.

4. Find and Read Relevant Cases

To fully understand the statutes, it's usually necessary to read one or more cases (court decisions) that have dealt with how the particular statute applies to situations like yours. These decisions can be found in the following:

FINDING CASES ON THE INTERNET

Cases decided during past years are available on the internet. However, to fully research case authority on your issue, you will also have to visit one of the legal internet websites (and updating tools) that are available online:

* www.findlaw.com
* www.hg.org
* www.Alllaw.com
* www.ipl.org
* www.Lexis.com

- *State Court Reports* contain Supreme Court cases only from that state.

- *Appellate Reports* covers Appellate Court cases only from that state.

Some states publish their Supreme Court and Appellate Court opinions together.

Once you find a relevant case or two, you can also find similar cases by using cross-reference tools known as digests and Shepards (www.shepards.com). These are explained in *Legal Research: How to Find and Understand the Law*, by Stephen Elias and Susan Levinkind (Nolo Press) and other legal research texts.

__APPENDIX__

COMMUNICATIONS CHART

EQUITY WORKSHEET

PROMISSORY NOTE WORKSHEET

DEED OF TRUST WORKSHEET

MORTGAGE WORKSHEET

NOTICE OF DEFAULT WORKSHEET (NONJUDICIAL FORECLOSURE)

NOTICE OF SALE WORKSHEET (NONJUDICIAL FORECLOSURE)

NOTICE OF SALE WORKSHEET (JUDICIAL FORECLOSURE)

LEGAL PLEADING PAPER

DEED IN LIEU OF FORECLOSURE

COMMUNICATIONS CHART

Date of contact: Time:

[] Telephone [] Letter   [] Fax   [] Email   [] Meeting/location

Name of contact person:

Who initiated communication?

What we discussed:

Agreements we reached, if any:

Date of contact: Time:

[] Telephone [] Letter   [] Fax   [] Email [] Meeting/location

Name of contact person:

Who initiated communication?

What we discussed:

Agreements we reached, if any:

Date of contact: Time:

[] Telephone [] Letter   [] Fax   [] Email   [] Meeting/location

Name of contact person:

Who initiated communication?

What we discussed:

Agreements we reached, if any:

EQUITY WORKSHEET

1. Estimated sales price: _____

2. List estimated costs of sale: _____

     _____ a.   Real estate agent's commission (6% of sales price): _____

     _____ b.   Closing costs (2% of estimated sales price): _____

     _____ c.   Balance due on first mortgage or deed of trust: _____

     _____ d.   Balance due on junior lienholders: _____

     _____ e.   Balance due on any other loans: _____

     _____ f.   Missed payments on first loan: _____

     _____ g.   Missed payments and late fees on junior lienholders: _____

     _____ h.   Any other liens: _____

     _____ i.   Unpaid property taxes: _____

     _____ j.   Foreclosure costs: _____

3. Total estimated costs of sale: _____

4. Your equity (1–3): _____

PROMISSORY NOTE WORKSHEET

Date note is signed:

Borrower(s):

Lender:

Principal amount borrowed:

Interest rate:

Term (number of months, years or other arrangement):

Payment frequency (monthly or other arrangement):

Commencement date (date payments begin):

Payment amount:

Is there a reference in the note to the deed of trust?

DEED OF TRUST WORKSHEET

Date signed: _____

Date recorded: _____

Trustor: _____

Trustee: _____

Beneficiary: _____

County in which property is located: _____

Legal description: _____

Principal amount borrowed: _____

Date notarized: _____

Did you sign the deed of trust? _____

MORTGAGE WORKSHEET

Date signed: _____

Date recorded: _____

Mortgagor: _____

Mortgagee: _____

County in which property is located: _____

Legal description: _____

Principal amount borrowed: _____

Date notarized: _____

Did you sign the Mortgage? _____

NOTICE OF DEFAULT WORKSHEET (NONJUDICIAL FORECLOSURE)

ARE THE FOLLOWING CORRECT ON THE NOTICE OF DEFAULT, AND CONSISTENT WITH INFORMATION ON YOUR PROMISSORY NOTE AND/OR DEED OF TRUST?

Name of trustor (you and any co-signers)   ☐ No   ☐ Yes   Name:

Name of beneficiary (lender)?   ☐ No   ☐ Yes   Name:

Name of trustee?   ☐ No   ☐ Yes   Name:

Information about recording
of deed of trust?   ☐ No   ☐ Yes   Date:

Legal description of the property? Document No.: Book/Page No.:

Amount of original indebtedness?

Amount in default?   ☐ No   ☐ Yes   Amount:

RECORDING REQUIREMENTS

Was the Notice of Default recorded in the recorder's
office for the county in which your property is located? ☐ No   ☐ Yes

MAILING REQUIREMENTS

Was a copy of the Notice of Default mailed to you by
certified or registered mail prior to recording?   ☐ No   ☐ Yes   When:

Was a copy of the Notice of Default mailed to you by
first-class mail?   ☐ No   ☐ Yes

Was a copy of the Notice mailed by first-class mail
to everyone entitled to receive the Notice—including
tenants, junior beneficiaries and anyone
who recorded a Request for Notice? (You will need to
call them and ask them if they received the Notice.)   ☐ No   ☐ Yes   When:

PUBLICATION REQUIREMENTS

If the trustee did not have your correct address, was the
Notice of Default published in a newspaper of general
circulation? (You have the right to ask the trustee to see his *Affidavit
of Publication* and copies of the newspapers.)   ☐ No   ☐ Yes

his/her/their authorized capacity(ies) and that by his/her/their signature(s) on the instrument, the person(s) or the entity upon behalf of which the person(s) acted, executed the instrument.

_____
[NOTARY SEAL] Signature of Notary Public

(Ask the trustee for proof.)   ☐ No   ☐ Yes When? _____

RECORDING REQUIREMENTS

Was the Notice of Sale recorded in the county
recorder's office where your property is located
weeks before the scheduled date?   ☐ No   ☐ Yes When? _____

PUBLICATION REQUIREMENTS

Before the sale date, was the Notice of Sale
published in a newspaper of general circulation
in the county where the property is located
several times before the sale?
(As the trustee for proof.)   ☐ No   ☐ Yes

                                                        1st Date:
                                                        2nd Date:
                                                        3rd Date:

POSTING REQUIREMENTS

Was a copy of the Notice of Sale posted in
a public place?   ☐ No   ☐ Yes

Where? _____

Was a copy of the Notice of Sale posted
On your property?   ☐ No   ☐ Yes

NOTICE OF SALE WORKSHEET (NON-JUDICIAL FORECLOSURE)

ARE THE FOLLOWING CORRECT ON THE NOTICE OF TRUSTEE'S SALE, AND
CONSISTENT WITH INFORMATION ON YOUR NOTICE OF DEFAULT, PROMISSORY NOTE
AND DEED OF TRUST?

Name of trustor (you and any co-signers)?   [] No [] Yes   Name:

Name of beneficiary (lender)?   [] No [] Yes   Name:

Name of trustee?   [] No [] Yes   Name:

Information about recording of deed of trust?   [] No [] Yes   Date:
          Document Number:
          Book/Page Number:

Description of the property?   [] No [] Yes

Total amount of outstanding indebtedness?   [] No [] Yes   Amount:

Date, time and location of sale   [] No [] Yes   Date:
          Time:
          Location:

Is the date of sale at least 20 calendar days from
date the Notice of Sale was issued?   [] No [] Yes

MAILING REQUIREMENTS

Did the trustee wait several months
after recording a Notice of Default before
mailing you a Notice of Sale?   [] No [] Yes   When?

Was a copy of the Notice of Sale mailed to you by
registered or certified mail several weeks
before the scheduled sale date?   [] No [] Yes   When?

Was a copy of the Notice of Sale sent to you by
first-class mail before scheduled sale date?   [] No [] Yes   When?

Prior to the scheduled sale date,
was a copy of the Notice of Sale sent by
registered or certified mail to everyone
entitled to receive notice--including tenants,
junior beneficiaries and anyone
who recorded a Request for Notice?
(Ask the trustee for proof.)   [] No [] Yes   When?

Worksheet continued:

RECORDING REQUIREMENTS

Was the Notice of Sale recorded in the county
recorder's office where your property is located
weeks before the scheduled date?   [] No [] Yes When?

PUBLICATION REQUIREMENTS

Before the sale date, was the Notice of Sale
published in a newspaper of general circulation
in the county where the property is located
several times before the sale?
(As the trustee for proof.)   [] No [] Yes
                                                     1st Date:
                                                     2nd Date:
                                                     3rd Date:

POSTING REQUIREMENTS

Was a copy of the Notice of Sale posted in
a public place?   [] No [] Yes

Where?

Was a copy of the Notice of Sale posted
On your property?   [] No [] Yes

NOTICE OF SALE WORKSHEET (JUDICIAL FORECLOSURE)

DID THE NOTICE OF SALE INCLUDE

Date of sale?   ☐ No   ☐ Yes   Date:

Time of sale?   ☐ No   ☐ Yes   Time:

Specific location of sale?   ☐ No   ☐ Yes   Location:

Correct legal description of the property,
including the street address?   ☐ No   ☐ Yes

Correct name and address of lender?   ☐ No   ☐ Yes

SERVICE AND MAILING REQUIREMENTS

How many days was the Notice of Sale mailed
to you by first-class mail before the scheduled
sale date?   ☐ No   ☐ Yes   When?

Was the Notice of Sale personally served on you?   ☐ No   ☐ Yes   When?

Was the Notice of Sale mailed by first-class
mail to everyone entitled to receive notice
(including tenants and junior lienholders)?   ☐ No   ☐ Yes   When?

PUBLICATION REQUIREMENTS

Was the Notice of Sale published once a week
over several weeks before the sale date?   ☐ No   ☐ Yes   1st Date:
                                                                       ☐ No   ☐ Yes   2nd Date:
                            ☐ No   ☐ Yes   3rd Date:

Was the Notice of Sale published in a newspaper
in the county where your property is located?   ☐ No   ☐ Yes

POSTING REQUIREMENTS

Was Notice of Sale posted in a public place?   ☐ No   ☐ Yes   Where?

Was the Notice of Sale posted on your front
door or another conspicuous place?   ☐ No   ☐ Yes   Where?

1
2
3
4
5
6
7
8
9
10
11
12
13
14
15
16
17
18
19
20
21
22
23
24
25
26
27
28

Recording requested by

    (1)

and when recorded mail
this deed and tax statement to:

    (2)

Deed in Lieu of Foreclosure

1. This transfer is exempt from the documentary transfer tax.   (3)

2. This property is located in_____,
            [] an unincorporated area

            [] the city of _____   (4)

3. For valuable consideration, receipt of which is hereby acknowledged,
_____ (5) hereby deeds (6) to _____ (7)
in lieu of foreclosure, the following real property in the City of
_____, County of _____, State of _____, (8)
commonly known as_____.

Date:_____, 200X   _____ (9)

Date: _____, 200X   _____

Date: _____, 200X   _____

ACKNOWLEDGMENT (9)

State of _____)
County of _____)

On _____, 200_, before me, _____, a notary public,
personally appeared _____, personally known to me
or proved to me on the basis of satisfactory evidence to be the
person(s) whose name is/are subscribed to this instrument, and
acknowledged to me that he/she/they executed the same in his/her/their
authorized capacity(ies) and that by his/her/their signature(s) on the
instrument, the person(s) or the entity upon behalf of which the
person(s) acted, executed the instrument.

_____
[NOTARY SEAL] Signature of Notary Public

GLOSSARY

Acceleration. A clause in your promissory note or mortgage that allows the lender to demand the immediate payment of the full balance of your loan (rather than just the amount that is due) because you defaulted on your loan.

Accounting. A cause of action in a lawsuit in which you request that the court order a certified public accountant to audit your lender's books and records to determine the correct amount you owe the lender.

Amortization. Repayment of a loan over regular time intervals (such as monthly, quarterly, or annually) with payments of principal and interest so that at the end of the term, the entire amount of the loan has been paid in full.

Anti-deficiency laws. State statutes providing that you are not liable to your lender for the shortage between the proceeds received at the foreclosure sale and the balance due on your loan. Only a minority of states in the United States have anti-deficiency laws. In anti-deficiency states, if your lender conducts a nonjudicial foreclosure, you are not liable for the deficiency.

Arrearage. The past due balance on your loan, including unpaid interest, principal, late charges, and attorney fees.

Assignment. Where a party to a contract transfers his/her rights and obligations under the contract to a third party.

Assumption. A clause in a mortgage or deed of trust that requires the new owner of the property to become personally liable to the lender for the loan's repayment.

Auction. The final step in a foreclosure in which your property is sold at a public sale to the highest bidder. The person conducting the auction is called the "auctioneer."

Automatic stay. Upon the filing of a bankruptcy petition, a federal injunction automatically arises which stops (stays) all debt collection actions, including foreclosure.

Balloon payment. The final lump-sum payment of principal due at the end of the term of a loan.

Bankruptcy. A proceeding authorized by federal law and carried out in the federal bankruptcy courts, which provide debtors with various kinds of relief from their debts. Chapters 7, 11, 12, and 13 and different types of bankruptcies.

Beneficiary. The company (or individual) named in a deed of trust that lends you money and is entitled to receive the payments. The deed of trust acts as written security that you will repay the promissory note. If the beneficiary (lender) is not repaid, they have the right to start foreclosure proceedings.

Bid. During the auction sale, offers submitted by potential purchasers to pay a designated price for the property which is communicated orally to the auctioneer.

Bona fide purchaser for value ("BFP"). A purchaser of property who pays for it without notice or knowledge that that there may be a problem with title or possession of the property.

Bond. A certificate issued by a bonding company (for a specific amount of money) at the beginning of a lawsuit to guaranty that the successful party will be compensated for losses resulting from the lawsuit if the bonded party eventually loses the lawsuit.

Borrower. The person or entity that borrows money from the lender.

Collateral. Real or personal property pledged as security for repayment of a loan.

Complaint. The initial document filed in the Court and served on the opposing party, which commences a lawsuit. The Complaint consists of pages of allegations ("causes of action") describing how the actions of the defendant has damaged the plaintiff, the party bringing the lawsuit.

Conforming loan. A loan that meets FNMA standards and guidelines. A lender can more readily sell a conforming loan because investors know it meets the guidelines.

Conventional loans. A real estate loan, usually from a bank or mortgage company, that is not insured by the Federal Housing Agency or guaranteed by the Department of Veterans Affairs.

Conveyance. Transferring title of real property from one person to another by deed.

Damages. Monetary compensation recovered in Court by any person who has suffered a loss or injury because of the unlawful acts or negligence of another.

Debtor. In the context of bankruptcy, the individual, partnership, corporation, or limited liability company, that files bankruptcy.

Debtor-in-possession. In a Chapter 11 or 13 bankruptcy case, the debtor remains in control of his/her assets during the case, as opposed to a trustee taking control of the assets.

Declaratory relief. A cause of action in a lawsuit in which the plaintiff(s) requests that the court determine the respective legal rights and obligations of the plaintiff(s) and defendant(s) as to a specific dispute.

Deed. A document in which ownership of real property is conveyed from one party to another.

Deed in Lieu of Foreclosure. A deed in which you convey your property to your lender instead of (in lieu of) your lender continuing the foreclosure.

Deed of trust. A three-party document in which the borrower ("trustor") pledges the property to a neutral third party ("trustee") as security for repayment of the loan to the lender ("beneficiary").

Default. Borrower's failure to comply with any of the terms and conditions of the mortgage, promissory note, and/or deed of trust.

Defendant. The party against whom a lawsuit has been filed.

Deficiency. The shortage between the balance of your unpaid loan and the proceeds received by your lender from the foreclosure sale.

Deficiency judgment. A judgment entered by a court against you for the shortage between the balance of your unpaid loan and the proceeds received by your lender from the foreclosure sale.

Due-on-sale clause. A clause in your mortgage or deed of trust which allows your lender to demand immediate payment of the entire loan upon sale of your property. This clause allows lenders to prevent subsequent purchasers from taking over the existing loan at lower than current market interest rates.

Encumbrance. A lien recorded against real property, such as a deed of trust, mortgage, or judgment lien. Because it is a financial obligation, a lien is said to "burden" or "encumber" the property. When the property is sold or refinanced, the encumbrance must be paid off.

Equity. Your interest in the property after deducting any outstanding liens and encumbrances from the property's current market value.

Equity of redemption. Your right to save your property from foreclosure by paying off the entire debt, including interest and costs.

Equity purchaser. A person who offers to purchase your property while it is in foreclosure, by paying a nominal fee for your equity.

Escrow. A neutral third party responsible for processing the documents and monies in a real estate sales transaction, and handling the closing.

Estate. In a bankruptcy context, the term used to describe the assets and liabilities of the debtor.

Eviction. The legal procedure to have a tenant removed from a property because the tenant has breached the lease, also known as an unlawful detainer lawsuit.

Fair market value. The price that a property would sell for in an open market between a willing buyer and a willing seller in an arms-length transaction. In a judicial foreclosure, a determination by the court as to the value of your property as of the date of the foreclosure sale.

Forbearance. An agreement by your lender to voluntarily refrain from foreclosing your property so that you may have more time to repay your loan. (Also known as a "standstill" or "workout" agreement.)

Foreclosure. The procedure in which your property is sold at a public auction to pay off your defaulted loan. There are two types of foreclosure, judicial and nonjudicial.

Foreclosure Consultant. An individual who assists you while in foreclosure by negotiating with your lender and/or obtaining a refinance of the loan. Some states have laws to regulate the activities of foreclosure consultants.

Guarantor. A person who becomes secondarily liable for another's debt.

Impounds. Additional payments to your lender (over and above your monthly payments of principal and interest), which are held by your lender and then used to make annual (or semi-annual) payments for insurance and taxes on your property.

Interest. The cost of borrowing money from your lender. The interest rate is described in your loan documents as a yearly percentage of the loan.

Irreparable injury. Injury to you or your property that cannot he reasonably recovered in monetary damages, and which therefore must be received in some other form, such as an injunction.

Joint tenancy. Where two or more people (such as husband and wife) hold title to real property equally with rights of survivorship. Upon the death of either joint tenant, the deceased tenant's ownership interest is automatically transferred to the surviving tenant.

Judgment. A final decision by a court resolving the dispute between the plaintiff(s) and defendant(s) in a lawsuit and determining the rights and obligations of the parties.

Judicial foreclosure. The forced sale of real property, handled through a court proceeding.

Junior lienholder. The holder of a mortgage or deed of trust that is subordinate to a senior lienholder (the junior was recorded subsequent to the senor lienholder).

Jurisdiction. The authority of the court to decide a lawsuit with control over the property and the parties. In a foreclosure context, the court in the county in which the property is located has jurisdiction to conduct the lawsuit.

Lease. An agreement between the owner of the property (called "landlord" or "lessor") and the person taking possession of the property (called "tenant" or "lessee") for a specific period of time (months or years), and in exchange for paying a specified amount of money ("rent").

Lender. The individual or entity that loans you money. Also referred to as the "beneficiary" or "mortgagee."

Levy. A seizure of real property by the sheriff for the purpose of conducting a foreclosure sale.

Lien. A document recorded in the county recorder's office indicating that your property is security for the repayment of a debt or obligation. Liens are either voluntary (such as mortgages and deeds of trust) or involuntary (such as mechanic's liens, tax liens, and judgment liens).

Lienholder. The party holding a lien recorded against your property. A lienholder is "senior" if it is the first lien recorded against your property. All other lienholders subsequently recorded against your property are said to be "junior" lienholders.

Liquidation. The process in a Chapter 7 bankruptcy in which the trustee sells the non-exempt assets of the debtor to pay off creditors.

Lis Pendens. The latin phrase for "Notice of Pending Action," which is a document recorded in the county recorder's office warning that a lawsuit has been filed in the county courthouse involving title and/or possession to a particular property.

Listing agreement. Written agreement between a property owner and a real estate agent to sell the property at a certain price and terms in return for a commission.

Mechanic's lien. A lien recorded in the county recorder's office against your property by a contractor, sub-contractor, or supplier, when you fail to pay their bill in connection with your property.

Mortgage. A two-party security document in which the property owner (mortgagor) pledges real property as security for repayment of the loan to the lender (mortgagee).

Mortgagee. The lender who receives the mortgage as security for repayment of the debt.

Mortgagor. The property owner who pledges his/her property as security for repayment of the debt.

Negotiable. The legal right of a holder to sell a mortgage or deed of trust to a third party, who then has the right to collect the payments.

Nonjudicial foreclosure. A procedure (without the involvement of the court), resulting in a trustee conducting a public auction of your property and using the sale proceeds to repay your lender.

Non-recourse. A clause in a mortgage or promissory note stating that the borrower is not personally liable to the lender if the borrower defaults on the loan.

Note. An abbreviation for promissory note.

Notice. Written or oral communication of information directly to a person or entity. Depending on the situation, written notice can be by personal delivery, mailing, posting it on the property, publishing it in a local newspaper, or recording it in the county recorder's office.

Owner-occupied. When you live in the property you have pledged as security for the repayment of your loan.

Permanent injunction. A court order at the conclusion of a trial permanently preventing your lender from foreclosing your property.

Plaintiff. The aggrieved party that files a civil lawsuit.

Plan of reorganization. An agreement between the debtor and creditors, and approved by the bankruptcy court in a Chapter 11 case, for repayment of debts pursuant to a specific schedule.

Posting. Affixing a foreclosure notice to a post or wall on the property being foreclosed.

Power of sale. A right given to the trustee in a deed of trust (and some mortgages) to conduct a nonjudicial foreclosure of the property, rather than going through the lengthy process of a judicial foreclosure in court.

Preliminary injunction. A court order prohibiting your lender from foreclosing during the pendency of the lawsuit--that is, until the court can conduct a trial.

Pre-payment penalty. A clause in your mortgage or promissory note that allows your lender to charge you a penalty fee if you pay off your loan before its due date.

Principal. At any given time, the amount of money you owe your lender, not including interest.

Private mortgage insurance. Insurance obtained by your lender, but paid by you, which protects your lender in the event they foreclose and lose money on the loan.

Private sale. A trustee's sale conducted in a nonjudicial foreclosure.

Promissory note. Your written promise to repay money that has been loaned to you.

Purchase money. Money loaned by the seller, or a third-party lender, used by the buyer to pay all or part of the purchase price of a property.

Receiver. During a judicial foreclosure, the court appoints a person to manage the multi-tenant property (ie. apartment building or commercial building) and collect the rents from the tenants.

Reconveyance. Once your promissory note has been paid in full, the trustee will cancel the deed of trust, return the original document to you, and record a reconveyance in the county recorder's office.

Recording. The procedure of filing documents in the county recorder's office in order to give public notice of real estate transactions. In this way, the recorder's office becomes a clearinghouse of information as to what liens (their amounts and priorities), transfers, deeds, reconveyances, easements, and similar documents are recorded against a particular property.

Recourse. A clause in a mortgage or promissory note stating that the borrower is personally liable for payment of the loan.

Redemption. Your right to pay off the entire loan and have the foreclosure stopped. After the foreclosure sale, the right of the former property owner to buy back his property by paying the amount of the foreclosure sale proceeds.

Redemption period. A time period in which you take back your property by paying off the total balance of your loan. The time period is different in each state.

Refinance. Paying off your existing loan(s) with funds obtained from a new loan on your property.

Reinstatement period. The period between the time the foreclosure started and before the actual sale, in which you can cure the default and stop the foreclosure by simply paying the arrearage on your loan. The time period is different in each state.

Rents and profits clause. A clause in your mortgage or deed of trust that allows your lender to collect the rents directly from your tenants if you default on your loan.

REO (real estate owned). Real property taken back by the lender after a foreclosure sale because no one else bid more than the lender's opening credit bid.

Reorganization. Efforts by a debtor during a chapter 11, 12 or 13 bankruptcy to restructure his/her assets and debts as part of a plan to repay creditors part or all of what is owed.

Rescission. The act of canceling a previously recorded document. In a foreclosure context, the trustee will "rescind" the Notice of Default or Notice of Sale when you pay the arrears and bring your loan current.

Sanctions. A monetary penalty charged by the court against the plaintiff or defendant for failing to follow court rules and regulations.

Secondary market. Informal markets in which lenders sell portfolios of their loans to Fannie Mae, Freddie Mac, Ginnie Mae, investment groups, or other lenders, so that they can recycle the funds into more loans to new borrowers.

Secured. Loans are either secured or unsecured. If your loan is secured by a mortgage or deed of trust, you have pledged your property as security to be sold (foreclosed) in the event you default under the terms of your loan.

Security. Property pledged by you to your lender to assure payment of your loan.

Senior lienholder. The lender with the earliest mortgage or deed of trust recorded against your property, which therefore has priority over all subsequently recorded ("junior") liens.

Short sale. Having your lender agree to accept less than the full balance of the loan when your property is sold. (Also called "short pay".)

Sold-out junior. A lender whose junior mortgage or deed of trust is eliminated when a senior lender completes a foreclosure sale of your property.

Specific performance. An equitable remedy in which the court orders that a defendant perform the terms of a contract because monetary damages would be inadequate.

Standstill agreement. The agreement with your lender to voluntarily refrain from foreclosing your property so that you may have more time to repay your loan. (Also known as a "forbearance" or "workout" agreement.)

Statutory redemption. In a judicial foreclosure, your legal right to take back (redeem) your property after the foreclosure sale by paying the price your property sold for at the foreclosure sale.

Temporary Restraining Order (TRO). A court order prohibiting your lender from foreclosing for a brief period (i.e. two weeks) until the court can conduct a hearing to consider the issues in dispute. In the context of a pending foreclosure, a TRO enjoins your lender (and trustee) from continuing a nonjudicial foreclosure until the court can conduct a formal hearing.

Tenant. A party holding possession (without holding title) of real property for a specific period of time in exchange for paying rent during that period.

Tenants-in-common. A description of parties owning property together. Upon death of a tenant-in-common, the deceased tenant's ownership interest is transferred to his next of kin, as opposed to the surviving tenants-in-common. Each tenant-in-common may encumber only his interest in the property, leaving the interest of the other tenants-in-common unencumbered.

Tender. An offer of money that is due in satisfaction of a claim, but without any stipulation or condition.

Title insurance. Insurance purchased by the seller of property to insure that the buyer will become the actual owner of the property without any interfering liens. Title insurance is also obtained by the lender (and paid by the borrower) that insures that the lender's mortgage

or deed of trust will be recorded in the priority position.

Trustee. In a deed of trust, the party that holds legal title to your property as security for your repayment of the promissory note. The trustee's only responsibilities are to conduct the nonjudicial foreclosure, if necessary, and reconvey the deed of trust when you pay off the loan. In a bankruptcy context, the trustee takes control of the debtor's assets and is responsible for selling them to pay off creditors.

Trustee's Deed Upon Sale. The deed given by the trustee to the successful purchaser at the trustee's sale.

Trustee's sale. A public auction of your property conducted by the trustee (or auctioneer on behalf of the trustee) at the conclusion of a nonjudicial foreclosure.

Trustor. The legal name of the property owner who pledges real property as security for repayment of the loan to the lender. You would be the trustor if you signed a deed of trust pledging your property as security for a loan.

Unlawful detainer. A lawsuit by a landlord against a tenant who fails to pay rent or refuses to relinquish possession of real property upon the termination of the lease. If your property is sold at a trustee's sale, the new owner can file an unlawful detainer action to have you evicted.

Unsecured. Loans are either secured or unsecured. If your loan is unsecured, you have not pledged any of your assets as security for repayment of the note. If your lender wants to recover the unpaid debt, it must file a lawsuit in court against you, rather than foreclosing.

Venue. The proper county to conduct a lawsuit. In a foreclosure context, venue is proper only in the county in which your property is located.

Waste. An abuse or destructive use of your property, including neglect of the land, structures, trees, gardens, and related improvements, in violation of your loan documents. Although seldom used alone, waste of your property is a related cause for your lender conducting a foreclosure.

Workout agreement. The agreement by your lender to voluntarily refrain from foreclosing your property so that you may have more time to repay your loan. (Also known as a "forbearance" or "standstill" agreement.)

Summary of State Foreclosure Laws

Summary of Alabama Foreclosure Law

In Alabama, lenders use either mortgages or deeds of trust to secure real estate loans. If the lender used a mortgage, then the foreclosure will be judicial. If the lender used a deed of trust then the foreclosure will follow non-judicial procedures. Most foreclosures of single-family residences in Alabama are non-judicial.

Judicial Foreclosure Guidelines

If no power of sale is contained in a mortgage, the lender, or any assignee thereof, must, after default of the mortgage, file a lawsuit to foreclose. After obtaining a court order to foreclose, the lender must publish a Notice of Sale. The notice must state the time, place, terms and purpose of the sale, and it must be published for four (4) consecutive weeks in a newspaper published in the county wherein said lands, or a portion thereof,

are situated. The sale must take place at the courthouse door of the county where the property is situated and sold to the highest bidder for cash. After the sale, the borrower has the right of redemption for 12 months and the lender has the right to file for a deficiency judgment.

Non-Judicial Foreclosure Guidelines

Notice of Sale. If the deed of trust contains a power of sale clause and specifies the time, place and terms of sale, then that specified procedure must be followed. However, if the deed of trust does not specify those terms, then the lender must publish a Notice of Sale once a week for four successive weeks in a newspaper published in the county in which the property is located. If the property is located in more than one county, the publication is to be made in all counties where it is located. The Notice of Sale must give the time, place and terms of said sale, together with a description of the property. If no newspaper is published in the county where the property is located, the notice shall be placed in a newspaper published in an adjoining county for four successive weeks.

Foreclosure Sale. The sale must take place at the front or main door of the courthouse of the county where the property located between 11:00 a.m, and 4:00 p.m., and sold for cash to the highest bidder. The sale may not take place until at least 30 days after the Notice of Sale was first published. After the sale, the borrower does not have a right to redemption, but the lender still has the right to file an action for a deficiency judgment.

For more information on Alabama foreclosure law, go to: www.legislature.state.al.us

© 2001. The Real Estate Library.

Summary of Alaska Foreclosure Law

In Alaska, lenders use both mortgages and deeds of trust. If the lender used a mortgage, then the foreclosure will be judicial. If the lender used a deed of trust, the foreclosure will be non-judicial. Most foreclosures of single-family residences in Alaska are non-judicial.

Non-Judicial Foreclosure Guidelines

If the deed of trust contains a power of sale clause and specifies the time, place and terms of sale, then the specified procedure must be followed, provided it meets the minimum protection laws set forth by the State of Alaska. Otherwise, the non-judicial foreclosure is carried out in the following three phases:

Notice of Default. The trustee must record a Notice of Default in the office of the recorder in the district in which the property is located not less than 30 days after the default and not less than three months before the sale. The Notice of Default must state the name of the borrower, the book and page where the deed of trust was recorded, description of the property, the borrower's default, the amount the borrower owes, and the trustee's desire to sell. It must also state the date, time and place of the sale. Within ten days after recording the Notice of Default, the trustee must mail a copy of the Notice by certified mail to the last know address of (1) the borrower, and (2) any person whose claim or lien on the property appears of record or is known to the lender or trustee, and (3) any occupant. The trustee may have the notice delivered personally instead of sending it by certified mail.

Reinstatement Period. Any time before the sale, the borrower may cure the default and stop the sale by paying a sum equal to the missed payments plus attorney's fees. The lender may not require the borrower to pay off the entire remaining principal balance of the loan to cure the default, just the missed payments and attorney's fees. But, if the lender has recorded a Notice of Default two or more times, then the Alaska statutes provide that the lender can refuse to accept the borrower's monies for the missed payments and costs and proceed with the foreclosure sale.

Foreclosure Sale. The sale must be made at a public auction held at the front door of a courthouse of the superior court in the judicial district where the property is located. The trustee must sell to the highest and best bidder and the lender may bid at auction. The trustee may postpone the sale by delivering to the person conducting the sale a written and signed request for the postponement to a stated date and hour. The person conducting the sale shall publicly announce the postponement to the new date and hour at the time and place originally fixed for the sale. This procedure shall be followed in any succeeding postponement.

Deficiency Judgment. With non-judicial foreclosures, the lender is prohibited from obtaining a deficiency judgment, and the borrower does not have any redemption rights.

For more information on Alaska foreclosure law, go to: www.legis.state. ak.us

274

© 2003, The Real Estate Library

Summary of Arizona Foreclosure Laws

In Arizona, lenders mostly use deeds of trust to secure real estate loans. As such, most foreclosures of single family residences follow the non-judicial procedures.

Non-Judicial Foreclosure Guidelines

Notice of Sale. The trustee must record a Notice of Sale in the office of the recorder of the county where the property is located. Within five days after the notice is recorded, the trustee must mail, by certified mail, a copy of the notice to each of the people who are parties to the trust deed. Additionally, the notice must be published in a newspaper in the county where the property is located once a week for four consecutive weeks. The last notice must be published not less than ten days prior to the date of the sale. Optionally, if it can be done without a breach of the peace, the trustee can post the notice at least 20 days prior to the date of the

sale, in some conspicuous place on the property to be sold. Or, the trustee can post the notice at the courthouse or at a specified place at the place of business of the trustee in the county in which the property is located.

Reinstatement Period. The trustor, and any subordinate lienholder, have the right up until 5:00 pm of the day prior to the scheduled sale, to reinstate the loan by curing all defaults.

Foreclosure Sale. The sale must occur at least three months after the Notice of Sale was recorded. The trustee or the trustee's agent must conduct the sale. The sale is conducted as a public auction. The property will be sold for cash to the highest bidder, except that the lender can make a "credit bid" (which means to cancel out all, or some part, of the money the borrower owed the lender), instead of paying cash. Every bid is an irrevocable offer until the sale is completed, which happens when the bidder pays the bid price to the trustee's satisfaction. A successful high bidder must pay the bid price by 5:00 pm of the day after the bid, other than a Saturday or legal holiday. If the high bidder fails to make the payment by 5:00 pm, the day after being notified of the option to buy, the trustee can either continue the sale (and re-open bidding) or offer the property to the second highest bidder.

The trustee may postpone the sale to another time, or another place, by giving notice of the new date, time and place by public declaration at the last place and time the property was offered for sale. No other notice is required. A trustee may also, by written agreement, extend the time for a buyer to come up with the payment.

Once the sale is complete, the proceeds will go to the payment of the obligations secured by the deed of trust that was foreclosed, then to junior lienholders in order of their priority. The successful bidder gets a Trustee's Deed, which provides conclusive evidence that the trustee conducted the foreclosure sale property. After the sale, the borrower is not entitled to redeem the property.

Deficiency Judgments. A lender may not bring a deficiency suit against a person who lost a property that is 2.5 acres or less at a foreclosure sale, provided the property was a single one-family or a single two-family dwelling. This is so even if the high bid at foreclosure was less that the balance due on the loan. However, in foreclosures against other types of property, a deficiency suit is allowed, but is limited to the difference between the balance owed and the fair market value of the property, and then only if the suit is brought within 90 days of the foreclosure sale.

For more information on Arizona Foreclosure Law, go to: www.azleg.state.az.us

Summary of Arkansas Foreclosure Law

In Arkansas, lenders use both mortgages and deeds of trusts. If the lender used a mortgage, then the foreclosure will be judicial. If the lender used a deed of trust (with a power-of-sale clause), then the foreclosure will be non-judicial. Both types of foreclosures are used equally in Arkansas.

In a foreclosure under a mortgage or deed of trust in Arkansas, the property must sell for not less than two-thirds of its appraised value. If it does not, then the property may be offered for sale again within 12 months. The second sale may be to the highest bidder without reference to the previous appraisal.

Judicial Foreclosure Guidelines

In judicial foreclosure, a court decrees the amount of the borrower's debt and gives him or her a short time to pay. If the borrower fails to pay within that time, then the clerk of the court, as commissioner, advertises the property for sale.

The lender may bid at the sale by crediting a portion (or all) of the amount the court found was owed to the lender against the sales price of the property. If the real estate does not sell for an amount equal to what's due on the mortgage loan (deficiency), then the lender may seize other property from the borrower as in an ordinary judgment.

The borrower has one year from the date of the sale to redeem the property by paying the amount for which the property was sold, plus interest.

Non-Judicial Foreclosure Guidelines

<u>Notice of Default and Intention to Sell</u>. The non-judicial process begins with the trustee recording a Notice of Default in the county recorder's office where the property is located. The notice shall be mailed within 30 days of recording, by certified mail, to the borrower. This includes any borrower of record or of whom the lender has actual notice. The notice must also be mailed to anyone who records a Request for Notice that specifically described the mortgagee including its recording information.

Within five days after the notice is recorded, the trustee must mail, by certified mail, a copy of the Notice of Default to each of the people who are parties to the trust deed. Additionally, the notice must appear in a newspaper in the county where the property is located once a week for four consecutive weeks, with the last notice being published no more than ten days prior to the date of the sale.

The Notice must contain the names of the parties to the deed of trust, a legal description of the trust property and, if applicable, the street address of the property, the book and page numbers where the deed of trust is recorded or the recorder's document number, the default for which foreclosure is made, the trustee's intention to sell the trust property to satisfy the obligation, including, in conspicuous type, a warning as follows: "YOU MAY LOSE YOUR PROPERTY IF YOU DO NOT TAKE IMMEDIATE ACTION" and the time, date, and place of sale.

<u>Foreclosure Sale</u>. The sale is conducted as a public auction on a weekday between the hours of 9:00 am and 4:00 at the property or the courthouse. Any person including the lender may bid at the sale, except the trustee, who may bid on the behalf of the beneficiary (lender). The lender may bid by canceling out what it is owed on the loan, including unpaid taxes, insurance, costs or sale and maintenance, but for cash for any higher price. The high bidder must pay the price bid at the time of sale, or within ten days.

The trustee may postpone the sale by public proclamation at the time, place and date last appointed for sale, up to seven days past the original date, but if for a longer time, then the whole notice procedure must be performed a second time, including the 60-day wait.

Once the sale is complete, the proceeds will go to the pay for the expenses of the foreclosure sale, then toward the obligations secured by the trust deed that was foreclosed and then to junior lienholders in order of their priority. The original borrower is entitled to receive any remaining funds. The successful bidder receives a Trustee's Deed within ten days after the sale. Thereafter, the borrower does not have any redemption rights.

The lender may sue the borrower for a deficiency within 12 months of a non-judicial foreclosure. The lender must sue for (1) the difference between the foreclosure sale price and the balance due on the loan, or (2) the balance due on the loan minus the fair market value of the property, whichever is less.

For more information on Arkansas Foreclosure Laws, go to:_ www.arkleg.state.ar.us

Summary of California Foreclosure Law

In California, lenders only use deeds of trusts to secure loans. However, lenders have the option of foreclosing using either judicial or non-judicial procedures. Nevertheless, nearly all foreclosures of single-family residences are non-judicial and take approximately four months.

Non-Judicial Foreclosure Guidelines

Notice of Default. The non-judicial process begins with the trustee recording a Notice of Default and Election to Sell in the county where the property is located. The trustee must also mail the Notice, by certified mail, return receipt requested, to the borrower within ten days, post the Notice on the property itself, and post the Notice in a public place in the county where the property is located.

Reinstatement Period. The reinstatement period runs from the date the Notice of

Default is issued until five dates before the foreclosure sale. During this period, the borrower can stop the foreclosure by simply bringing the loan current and paying all of the trustee's fees.

Notice of Trustee's Sale. No sooner than three months after issuing the Notice of Default, the trustee must issue a Notice of Trustee's Sale. The Notice must be: 1) recorded in the county where the property is located at least 14 days prior to the sale; 2) mailed by certified, return receipt requested, to the borrower at least 20 days before the sale; 3) posted on the property itself at least 20 days before the sale; 4) posted in a public place in the county where the property is to be sold, and 5) published at least once a week for three weeks in a newspaper of general circulation within the county. The Notice must contain the time and location of the trustee's sale, as well as the property address, the trustee's name, address and phone number and a statement that the property will be sold at auction.

Redemption Period. During the final five days before the trustee's sale, the borrower has the right to stop the foreclosure by paying the total amount of the loan, plus all arrears and fees.

Trustee's Sale. The sale may be held on any business day between the hours of 9:00 am and 5:00 pm and must take place at the location specified in the notice of sale, but typically on the courthouse steps. The trustee may require proof of the bidders ability to pay their full bid amount. Anyone may bid at the sale, which must be made at public auction to the highest bidder. If necessary, the sale may be postponed by announcement at the time and location

of the original foreclosure sale. The winning bidder receive a Trustee's Deed Upon Sale.

In California, lenders may not seek a deficiency judgment after a non-judicial foreclosure sale and the borrower has no rights of redemption.

For more information on California foreclosure laws, go to: www.leginfo. ca.gov

Summary of Colorado Foreclosure Law

In Colorado, lenders use mostly deeds of trusts, and occasionally mortgages. If the lender used a mortgage, then the foreclosure will be judicial. If the lender used a deed of trust, the foreclosure will be non-judicial. Most foreclosures of single-family residences in Colorado are non-judicial.

Non-Judicial Foreclosure Guidelines

In Colorado, the governor appoints a "Public Trustee" for each county in the state. The public trustee must act as an impartial party when handling a power of sale foreclosure.

Notice of Election and Demand For Sale. The process begins when the lender files the required documents with the Office of the Public Trustee of the county where the property is located. The Public Trustee then files a "Notice of Election and Demand" with the county clerk and recorder of the county. Once recorded, the notice must be published in a newspaper of general circulation within the county where the property is located for a period of five

consecutive weeks. In addition, the lender still needs to obtain a court order authorizing the sale.

Notice of Right to Cure and Right to Redeem. The Public Trustee must mail, within 21 days after the publication of the Notice of Election, a Notice of Right to Cure to the borrower and any owner or claimant of record, at the address given in the recorded instrument. The Public Trustee must also mail, at lease 21 days before the foreclosure sale, a notice to the borrower describing how to redeem the property. The Public Trustee often combines these two notices.

Intent to Cure. The owner of the property may stop the foreclosure proceedings by filing an "Intent to Cure" with the Public Trustee's office at least 15 days prior to the foreclosure sale and then paying the necessary amount to bring the loan current by noon the day
before the foreclosure sale is scheduled.

Foreclosure Sale. The foreclosure sale must take place between 45 and 60 days after the recording of the Notice of Election and Demand. The Public Trustee typically conducts the sale at the entrance to the courthouse, unless other provisions were made in the deed of trust. The highest bidder, including the lender, receives a Certificate of Purchase to the property.

Thereafter, the lender has the option to file a suit for deficiency in Colorado and the borrower has up to 75 days after the sale to redeem the property by paying the foreclosure sale amount, plus interest.

For more information on Colorado
Foreclosure Laws, go to: www.state.co.us

Summary of Connecticut Foreclosure Law

In Connecticut, lenders only use
mortgages to secure real estate loans.
As such, all foreclosures use the judicial
process.

Judicial Foreclosure Guidelines

The judicial foreclosure process in
Connecticut begins with the lender
serving a complaint for foreclosure on
the borrower and all parties claiming
an interest in the property at least 12
days before the complaint is filed in the
county courthouse. A Lis Pendens is
also recorded in the county recorder's
office. The borrower then has two
days to file an "Appearance" while an
out of state borrowers have 90 days to
respond. Once there is an appearance
by the borrower, the lender will file a
"Demand for Disclosure of Defense." If
the defendant is without an attorney, he
has 15 days to respond to the Demand.
If the borrower is represented by
counsel, he has only five days to file a
"Disclosure of Defense." Thereafter, the
Court will consider the positions of the
parties and render a judgment.

Strict Foreclosure. In a judgment of strict
foreclosure, the Court has determined
that the borrower has no equity in the
property. So no actual foreclosure

sale is held. Instead, the court sets a specific date ("Law Date") by which deadline the borrower must pay off the debt ("Redemption Period") or lose the property. If the borrower fails to do so, the title automatically vests in the lender as of the next date ("Vesting Date"). Thereafter, the borrower no longer has any claim to the property. The lender then has 30 days to record a Certificate of Foreclosure, which must contain a description of the property, the mortgage in default, the foreclosure proceedings and the date the title became absolute.

<u>Judgment of Foreclosure By Sale</u>. In a judgment of Foreclosure By Sale, the court has determined that there is equity in the property in excess of the debt being foreclosed (or there is a federal lien). In the judgment, the court will: 1) establish the time and manner of the sale; 2) appoints three appraisers to determine the value of the property; and (3) then appoints a committee to sell the property. The borrower may stop the foreclosure proceedings at any time before the sale by paying the balance due on the mortgage. If no such payment is made, the committee will go forward with the sale.

<u>Unemployed Borrower Exception</u>. If the borrower is unemployed, or underemployed, the Court will consider special circumstances. During this period (not to exceed six months), the foreclosure stops and the loan will be restructured to fit the borrower's budget.

The lender may sue to obtain a deficiency judgment in Connecticut, for the difference between total debt and the appraised value of the property (Strict Foreclosure) or the difference between total debt and the net proceeds of the sale (Judgment of Foreclosure By Sale). The lender must file the motion seeking a deficiency within 30 days after the vesting date.

For more information on Connecticut Foreclosure Law, go to: www.cga.ct.gov

© 2003 The Real Estate Library

Summary of Delaware Foreclosure Law

In Delaware, lenders only use mortgages to secure real estate loans. As such, all foreclosures use the judicial process and take approximately 5-6 months.

Judicial Foreclosure Guidelines

Notice of Default. Although Delaware law does not require it, the mortgage will probably require the lender to send the borrower a Notice of Default and a Notice of Acceleration to the borrower when there is a default. The notices warn the borrower of a default and that the entire amount of the loan is now due.

Writ of Scire Facias. Lenders in Delaware typically use the "Scire Facias" process to conduct a judicial foreclosures. The proceeding begins when the lender files a summons and complaint with the court and a writ of scire facias is issued. The lender must send by certified mail a copy of the complaint and "Notice to Lien Holders and Tenants of Filing of Action" to the borrower, property owner (if different), junior lienholders, tenants, and any

other interested parties. The borrower must file an answer within 20 days of being served, together with an "Affidavit of Defenses," which is evidence as why the foreclosure should not take place. This procedure is quite different than other judicial foreclosures because instead of the lender having to prove the borrower in default of the mortgage, the borrower has the burden to prove he isn't in default. Once the borrower has answered, the court will issue a "Case Scheduling Order." At this hearings, the court will consider the merits of the case. Unless the court is satisfied with the borrower's explanation and evidence, it will authorize a foreclosure sale. Eleven days after the court rules the borrower in default, the lender will submit a request to the county sheriff to conduct a sale of the property.

Notice of Sale. The sheriff must deliver a Notice of Sale to the borrower at least ten days before the sale date. . The notice must be posted on the property and other public places at least 14 days before the sale date. The notice must be published in two local newspapers appearing at least three times per week for the two weeks prior to the sale date. The notice must include the date, time, location of the sale, property description, and location of the property

Sheriff's Sale. The sale must be conducted by the sheriff and held at either the local courthouse or at the property at least 14 days after the Notice of Sale was posted. The property sold to the highest bidder.

Redemption Period. The borrower has the right to redeem the property at any time before the court confirms the sale.

The borrower must pay off the entire balance of the loan plus the lender's foreclosure fees and costs.

Confirmation Hearing. Approximately 30 days after the sale, the court will schedule a hearing to confirm the sale. If there are no objections to confirmation, the sale will be confirmed by the court and the sheriff will transfer title to the property to the winning bidder. The borrower has no right of redemption once the court has confirmed the sale.

Deficiency Judgment. If the sale proceeds are insufficient to pay off the foreclosing mortgage plus fees and costs, the lender must file a separate lawsuit on the note to obtain a deficiency judgment.

For more information on Delaware foreclosure law, go to: _www.legis.state. de.us

Summary of Florida Foreclosure Law

In Florida, lenders only use mortgages to secure real estate loans. As such, all foreclosures use the judicial process, which takes approximately five months.

Judicial Foreclosure

Court of Equity. All mortgages are foreclosed in equity, which means the court severs, for separate trial, all counterclaims against the foreclosing lender. The foreclosure claim shall, if tried, be tried to the court without a jury. Under Florida law, the lender is not required to notify the borrower of the foreclosure lawsuit, but most mortgages provide for notice, in person, by mail, or publication. Once the court enters a judgment, it will order how the foreclosure must take place, and the foreclosure must take place on those terms.

Notice of Sale. The clerk of the court issues the Notice of Sale, containing the location, date, and time of the sale. The notice is published once a week for two

284

weeks, with the second notice appearing at least five days before the sale date. The sale typically takes place 20-35 days after the court ruling and judgment.

<u>Foreclosure Sale</u>. The clerk oversees the sale, which typically occurs at the county courthouse at 11:00 a.m. on the scheduled sale date. The borrower's equitable right of redemption ends at the foreclosure sale. The sale is conducted as an auction. The winning bidder must provide a 5% deposit and pay the remaining balance by the end of the same day. If the winning bidder fails to do so, a new sale will be scheduled at least 20 days later.

<u>Confirmation Period</u>. There is a period of time after the sale that "the court reviews the sale to ensure a fair price has been paid." Basically, this period of time allows the borrower to object to the sale on the basis that, for example, proper procedures were not followed, or collusion existed between the bidders. This period is usually ten days after which the court will confirm the sale, and a Certificate of Sale will be filed passing title to the winning bidder. If the sale is not confirmed, another sale will be ordered. After the confirmed sale, the lender may sue to obtain a deficiency judgment against the borrower.

For more information on Florida Foreclosure Law, go to: www.flsenate.gov/statutes

Summary of Georgia Foreclosure Law

In Georgia, lenders use both mortgages and security deeds. If the lender used a mortgage, then the foreclosure will be judicial. If the lender used a security deed, the foreclosure will be non-judicial. Most foreclosures of single-family residences in Georgia are non-judicial. A non-judicial foreclosure can be completed in less than two months.

Judicial Foreclosure Guidelines

The proceeding starts when the lender files a petition, stating the name of the borrower, the mortgage, the property, the defaulted amount and request for a sale of the property to satisfy the default. The borrower receives a 30-day written notice in which the defaulted amount must be paid to the court. If the default amount is not paid within the time limit, a foreclosure sale is scheduled.

The sale procedures are the same as described below. After the sale, a confirmation hearing is scheduled and the borrower is notified within five days of the hearing. Provided the sales price of the property was comparable to its market value, the court will confirm the sale. Thereafter, lenders may seek a deficiency judgment if still needed.

Non-Judicial Foreclosure Guidelines

Demand Letter. First, the lender issues a demand letter, advising the borrower that the loan is in default. The letter advises that unless the loan is brought current within 30 days, the loan will be accelerated and foreclosure proceedings will commence.

Notice of Sale. A Notice of Sale must be mailed by certified mail, return receipt requested to the borrower no later than 15 days prior to the date of the foreclosure sale. The time period begins the day the letter is postmarked. The notice must state the date, time, and location of the sale, a description of the property, mortgage information, and the borrower's name. The notice must be mailed to the address given to the lender by written notice from the borrower. No waiver or release of the rights to notice are valid if it was signed at the same time as the original documents. The notice must be published in a newspaper of general circulation in the county where the sale will be held once a week for four consecutive weeks prior to the date of the sale.

Reinstatement Period. If the security deed specifically provides it, the borrower can stop the foreclosure by paying-off the default amount plus applicable fees. Of course, the borrower can always stop the foreclosure by paying off the total loan balance.

Foreclosure Sale. The sale must be made by public auction on the first Tuesday of the month between 10:00 am and 4:00 p.m. at the county courthouse. If that Tuesday is a holiday, the sale will be the next day. The winning bidder, if other than the lender, is required to pay the full bid amount immediately following the sale. If the sale is cancelled, the foreclosure process starts all over again.

For more information on Georgia Foreclosure Law, go to: www.legis.state.ga.us

286

© 2003. The Real Estate Library.

Summary of Hawaii Foreclosure Law

Hawaii is a lien theory mortgage state. Deed's of trust, while similar to a mortgage are not recognized in Hawaii. Foreclosures in Hawaii are either by judicial process, or where the mortgage contains a "power of sale" clause, the mortgagee may elect to proceed by non-judicial process. About half of the foreclosures in Hawaii are non-judicial; but with continuous attacks on the legality of the process, many title insurers are beginning to once again require judicial foreclosure.

Judicial Foreclosure Guidelines

The judicial process of foreclosure, which involves filing a lawsuit to obtain a court order to foreclose, is used either when no power of sale is present in the mortgage or where the lender (or title insurer) wants judicial oversight of the process. Judicial foreclosures are more expensive and more time consuming, however there is assured finality with judicial supervision. After service of the complaint, the borrower has 21 days to respond. After the borrower has answered the, or if no answer is filed, the lender will seek an

interlocutory decree of foreclosure and a commissioner will be appointed to conduct the sale. The commissioner will then advertise the property for sale in a newspaper of general circulation for 4 weeks, and hold at least one open house. The property will be auctioned off to the highest bidder, but other bidders are still allowed to bid higher at the confirmation hearing. Once the court finds the sales price fair, it will confirm the sale and convey the property to the buyer by deed. Thereafter, the lender can request a deficiency judgment.

Non-Judicial Foreclosure Guidelines

If the mortgage contains a power of sale clause, a private foreclosure sale (non-judicial foreclosure) may be carried out. Presently, there are two different legal types of non-judicial foreclosures in Hawaii: the traditional (HRS § 667-5) non-judicial foreclosure, and the "alternative power of sale foreclosure process" (HRS § 667-21). Generally, the traditional non-judicial power of sale foreclosure is more commonly employed because the alternative process requires the cooperation and consent of the borrower which is unlikely.

Notice of Intent to Foreclose. The Notice must be published once a week for three successive weeks in a newspaper having general circulation in the county where the property is located. The last publication to be not less than 14 days before the day of sale. Copies of the notice must be mailed or delivered to the borrower, any junior lienholders, the state director of taxation, and any other person entitled to receive notice. Additionally, the notice must be posted on the property not less than 21 days before the date of sale.

The notice must state: 1) The date, time, and place of the public sale; 2) The dates and times of the two open houses of the property, or if there will not be any open houses, the public notice shall so state; 3) The unpaid balance of the moneys owed to the lender under the loan; 4) A description of the property, including the address and its tax map key number; 5) The name of the borrower(s); 6) the name of the lender; 7) The name of any prior or junior lienholders on the property; 8) The name, the address, and the telephone number of the person in the State conducting the public sale; and 9) The terms and conditions of the public sale.

Reinstatement Period. Up until three days before the sale, the borrower may cure the default and stop the sale by paying the lien debt, costs and reasonable attorney's fees, unless otherwise agreed to between the lender and the borrower.

Foreclosure Sale. The sale, which may be held no earlier than 14 days after the last notice is published, is conducted as a public auction and sold to the highest bidder. The sale may be postponed from time to time by public announcement made by the lender or their representative. There are no statutory rights of redemption in Hawaii.

For more information on Hawaii Foreclosure Laws, go to: www.capitol.hawaii.gov

Summary of Idaho Foreclosure Law

In Idaho, lenders only use deeds of trust to secure real estate loans. As such, all foreclosures in Idaho use the non-judicial procedures and takes approximately five months.

Non-Judicial Foreclosure Guidelines

Notice of Default. The non-judicial process begins when the lender mails a Notice of Default to the borrower. The Notice is also recorded in the recorder's office for the county where the property is located. The borrower has at least 115 days to resolve the default and stop the foreclosure. The borrower can do this by paying the lender the full amount due, including costs.

Notice of Sale. At least 120 days before the date of the sale, a Notice of Sale must be mailed, registered or certified, return receipt requested, to the borrower and the occupants of the property (if not the borrower). The borrower must also be personally served at least 30 days prior to the sale. The lender must also record the Notice in the county recorder's office where the property is located. The notice must be published in a newspaper in the county where the property is located at least once a week for four consecutive weeks. The final publication must be no less than 30 days in advance of the foreclosure sale. Finally, the Notice must be posted on the property in a conspicuous place. The notice must describe the nature of the default, a legal description of the property, its street address, the lender's name, the date, time, and place of the sale, and the name and phone number of the person conducting the sale. An affidavit of mailing, posting, and publishing must be recorded at least 20 days prior to the sale date.

Foreclosure Sale. The foreclosure sale must take place on the date, at the time and at the place specified in the notice. The trustee's attorney typically conducts the sale as an auctioneer. Any person may bid, including the lender. At the conclusion of the sale, the trustee will transfer ownership of the property to the winning bidder after receiving full payment. The winning bidder receives a Trustee's Deed and is entitled to possession of the property ten days after the sale. The trustee may postpone the sale up to 30 days by public announcement at the originally scheduled sale. The trustee may also reschedule the sale, but a new notice must be published and mailed to all of the parties involved.

Redemption Period. If the property consists of more than 20 acres, the buyer has a period of one year after the sale to redeem it. If it is less than 20 acres, the period of time is only six months.

For more information on Idaho Foreclosure Law, go to: www.legislature.idaho.gov

Summary of Illinois Foreclosure Law

In Illinois, lenders only use mortgages to secure real estate loans. As such, all foreclosures in Illinois are judicial.

Judicial Foreclosure Guidelines

Pursuant to the Illinois Mortgage Foreclosure Act, the lender begins the process by filing a lawsuit against the borrower in the circuit court in the county where the property is located. The summons and complaint are then served on the borrower, and any other person entitled by Illinois statutes to receive notice. All parties then have 30 days to respond to the court action. Once the borrower responds (or If the borrower does not respond within the 30 days), the lender will request that the court rule on the pending matter. If the court rules against the borrower and orders a sale of the property, it will enter a judgment terminating the borrower's interest in the property, including the last dates for the borrower to exercise the right of reinstatement and redemption, and set the date and time of the foreclosure sale.

Reinstatement Period. A borrower has the right to stop the foreclosure within 90 days of being notified of the court action by paying the default amount plus all fees and costs.

Notice of Sale. A Notice of Sale must be sent to all affected parties, including the borrower and any junior lienholders. The notice must state property address, legal description, times the property can be inspected before the sale, the date, time, and location of the sale, terms of the sale, the case title, number, court handling the lawsuit, and a contact person. The notice must be published in the legal notice and real estate sections of a local newspaper once a week for three weeks. The first publication must be not more than 45 days before the sale date with the last publication no less than seven days before the sale date.

Redemption Period. 210 days after served with the summons, or 90 days after the court enters a judgment of foreclosure, which occurs last, the borrower can redeem the property by paying the total amount of the loan plus all costs and expenses. The borrower must give the lender 15 days notice of his/her intent to redeem by filing a "Certificate of Notice to Redeem" with the court and mailing a copy to the lender at least three days before the date of redemption. The redemption period can be shortened to 90 days after served or 60 days after judgment, whichever is later, if the value of the property is less than 90% of the full amount owed and the lender gives up all rights to a deficiency judgment.

290

Foreclosure Sale. The sale must occur at least 45 days after the first publication of the Notice of Sale. The sale must be conducted pursuant to the terms and conditions specified in the notice of sale, provided they meet the minimum standards provided in the <u>Illinois Statutes</u>. The sheriff, or a person selected by the judge, will conduct the sale. If the sale is postponed for any reason, the person conducting the sale must announce the details of the new sale date. But, if the sale is postponed for more than 60 days from the originally scheduled sale date, a new notice must be published.   Anyone may bid, including the lender, and the property will be sold to the highest bidder. Once the bidder has paid the full bid price, the sheriff will give the bidder a Certificate of Sale, which is subject to confirmation by the court. Upon court confirmation, the winning bidder will receive a deed and ownership of the property. If the property is still occupied, the winning bidder will not receive possession for 30 days. The borrower has no rights of redemption after the foreclosure sale.

Deficiency Judgment. The lender is entitled to a deficiency judgment for the difference between the sales price and the balance of the mortgage plus all of the lender's costs.   The amount of the deficiency will be determined by the court at the sale confirmation hearing.

For more information on Illinois Foreclosure Law, go to: www.ilga.gov

© 2003, The Real Estate Library.

Summary of Indiana Foreclosure Law

In Indiana, lenders only use mortgages to secure real estate loans. As such, all foreclosures in Indiana use the judicial procedures.

Judicial Foreclosure Guidelines

Pre-Foreclosure Period. The judicial process involves the lender filing a lawsuit to obtain a court order to foreclose. However, there is a waiting period between the date the lawsuit is filed and the day the property is sold. In Indiana, the date the mortgage was signed determines the length of time a lender must wait between filing the lawsuit and conducting with the foreclosure sale. The wait time is anywhere from three to 12 months depending on the age of the mortgage. The borrower may file a waiver of the time limit, which allows the sale to proceed without delay. But when this occurs, the lender loses the right to pursue a deficiency judgment.
After the pre-foreclosure period expires, the court will issue an order of sale and judgment. The clerk will certify the order and forward it to the sheriff

Notice of Sale. The sheriff must publish the Notice of Sale once a week for three weeks in a newspaper in the county where the property is located. The first publication must occur at least 30 days before the sale. At the time the first notice runs, the borrower, and each owner of the property, must be served with the notice by the sheriff. The sheriff must also post the notice in at least three public places as well as the county courthouse.

Redemption Period. At anytime before the foreclosure sale, the borrower can satisfy the judgment by paying the debt and all applicable costs, and the judgment will be dismissed.

Sheriff's Sale. The sheriff appoints an auctioneer to conduct the foreclosure sale. The sale must be conducted between 10:00 am and 4:00 pm on any day except Sunday. The property will be sold to the highest bidder. The sheriff will convey title by a deed given immediately to the winning bidder after the sale. If the lender postpones the sale, a new Notice of Sale is required, and it must be re-served and re-published. The owner may continue to reside in the property, rent free, until the foreclosure sale, provided the owner is not committing waste. But the borrower does not have any redemption rights after the sale.

For more information on Indiana Foreclosure Law, go to: www.ai.org/legislature

Summary of Iowa Foreclosure Law

In Iowa, lenders only use mortgages to secure real estate loans. As such, all foreclosures are judicial. A typical foreclosure takes 4-6 months.

Judicial Foreclosure Guidelines

Pre-Foreclosure Period. The judicial foreclosure process begins when the lender mails a written Notice of Default to the borrower 30 days before filing a lawsuit. The notice states the amount owed and an exact date when that amount must be paid.

Lawsuit. If the borrower does not rectify the default within the 30 days, the lender will file a complaint for foreclosure in the county courthouse where the property is located. The borrower has 21 days to respond. Generally, if the court finds the borrower in default, they will give them a set period of time to pay the delinquent amount, plus costs (Reinstatement Period). If the borrower does not pay within the set period of time, the court will render a judgment for the amount due, and order the property to be sold to satisfy the judgment.

Notice of Sale. Notice of the sale must be posted in at least three public places in the county where the property is located, one of which must be at the county courthouse. In addition, there shall be two weekly publications of the Notice in a newspaper printed in the county, with the first publication at least four weeks before the date of sale, and the second at a later time before the date of sale. If the borrower is in actual possession of the property, the notice must be served on them at least 20 days prior to the date of the sale. The Notice must contain the date, time, and place of the sale.

Foreclosure Sale. Most sales occur within two months, but if the lender is pursuing a foreclosure without redemption, the borrower can demand that the sale be delayed for 12 months. The sale must be at public auction, between 9:00 am and 4:00 pm. The sheriff can receive sealed written bids prior to the public auction. The sheriff may require all sealed written bids to be accompanied by a refundable payment (of any fees estimated to be paid at the public auction by the purchaser), to be returned if the person is not the purchaser. The sheriff must keep all written bids sealed until the commencement of the public auction, at which time the sheriff will open and announce the written bids as though made in person. The highest bidder will receive title to the property. The sale may be postponed, but if it postponed for more than three days, notice of the new sale date must be publicly announced at the time the sale was to have been made.

Redemption. If the lender chooses foreclosure without redemption, the winning bidder receives a deed immediately. If the court allows a redemption period, the period can last from six months up to one year, depending on the lender's situation. If the lender wants to pursue a deficiency judgment, the borrower has a one-year redemption period. If the lender surrenders its deficiency rights, the redemption period is reduced to six months.

For more information on Iowa Foreclosure Law, go to: www.legis.state.ia.us

© 2003. The Real Estate Library.

Summary of Kansas Foreclosure Law

In Kansas, lenders only use mortgages to secure real estate loans. As such, all foreclosures in Kansas are judicial.

Judicial Foreclosure Guidelines

The judicial foreclosure begins by the lender filing a lawsuit asking that court to foreclose on the property because the borrower is in default. The lawsuit is served on the borrower by the sheriff or by mail. If the borrower cannot be located, a notice of the lawsuit is published in a local newspaper. The borrower has 20 days to respond. If the borrower fails to respond, or the court determines that there is a default, it will order the Sheriff to sell the property. The borrower then has 10 days to reinstate the loan.

Notice of Sale. If the borrower fails to reinstate, a Notice of Sale will be published in a newspaper once a week for three weeks. The last publication of the notice must be no more than 14 and no less than seven days before the scheduled date of sale. Notice of the sale must also be sent to the borrower within five days of the first advertisement. The notice must state the date, time, and location of the sale.

Sheriff's Sale. Unless otherwise ordered by the court, the sale is typically held at the courthouse of the county in which the property is located. The sale is by public auction and the property sold to the highest bidder. The winning bidder will receive a Certificate of Purchase. The sale is then confirmed by the court.

Redemption Period. The redemption period for the borrower begins on the sale date, but the length of time varies. If more than one-third of the principal was paid by the borrower before the foreclosure, the redemption period is 12 months. Conversely, if less than one-third of the principal was paid, the redemption period is only three months. In order to redeem, the borrower has to pay the amount of the winning bid, plus all unpaid interest and fees. Once the borrower's right of redemption expires, the winning bidder exchanges the Certificate of Purchase for a Sheriff's Deed, which vests perfected title in the winning bidder.

Deficiency Judgment. The lender may sue to obtain a deficiency judgment for the difference between the foreclosure sale price and the amount due on the original mortgage.

For more information on Kansas Foreclosure Law, go to: www.kslegislature.org

Summary of Kentucky Foreclosure Law

In Kentucky, lenders only use mortgages to secure real estate loans. As such, all foreclosures in Kentucky are judicial.

Judicial Foreclosure Guidelines

The foreclosure starts when the lender files a complaint in the circuit court in the county where the property is located. The lender will also records Notice of Pending Action ("Lis Pendens") in the country recorder's office. The Sheriff will then serve a copy of the complaint and lis pendens on the borrower. The borrower has 21 days to respond. After the borrower responds, or 21 days after the borrower fails to respond, the lender will request a ruling from the court. If the court rules against the borrower, it will set a foreclosure sale date. The court will also decree the amount of the debt and give the borrower a short period of time to pay the loan. If the borrower fails to pay within that period, the clerk of the court will start advertising the property for sale.

Notice of Sale. The clerk of the court must publish a Notice of Sale once a week for three weeks in a local newspaper. The notice must contain the date, location, amount of default, and terms of the sale.

Appraisal. At some point prior to the scheduled sale date, an appraisal of the property must be made.

Foreclosure Sale. The sale usually occurs at least one month after the court rules against the borrower. The sale, conducted by a court official called a "Master Commissioner," occurs at the courthouse. The highest bidder purchases the property. The purchaser may pay in cash or post a bond in order to pay in installments. Any postponement of the sale must occur through court order. After the sale, a motion to confirm is filed with the court. The clerk holds the deed until the sale is confirmed.

Redemption Period. If the foreclosure sale price is less than two-thirds of the appraised value, the borrower has a period of one year from the date of the sale to redeem the property by paying the amount for which the property was sold, plus interest. If the sales price was more than two-thirds of the appraised value, the borrower does not have redemption rights.

Deficiency Judgment. The lender has the right to obtain a deficiency judgment against the borrower but only if the borrower was personally served with the lawsuit and failed to answer. The amount of the deficiency will be the difference between the amount the borrower owed on the original loan and the foreclosure sale price,

For more information on Kentucky Foreclosure Law, go to: www.lrc.state.ky.us

Summary of Louisiana Foreclosure Law

In Louisiana, lenders only use mortgages to secure real estate loans. As such, all foreclosures in Louisiana are judicial and typically take 3-5 months.

Judicial Foreclosure Guidelines

<u>Executory Process</u>. The executory process takes place when the lender uses a mortgage that includes an "authentic act that imparts a confession of judgment," as provided in the Louisiana statutes. Essentially this means that the borrower signed and acknowledged the obligations of the mortgage in the presence of a notary public and two witnesses. This type of mortgage makes the foreclosure process easier for the lender because once the suit has been filed, the borrower has a brief period to respond. If the borrower does not answer, a default judgment will be taken. If the borrower does respond, the lender will move for summary judgment. If the court rules that there is a default, it will issue an order for the foreclosure to begin.

Writ of Seizure and Sale. Once ordered, the borrower is served with a demand for the delinquent payments. The borrower then has three days to submit the delinquent payments or the court will order a Writ of Seizure and Sale. The court clerk will deliver the writ to the sheriff.

Notice of Sale. The sheriff will personally serve the borrower with the Notice of the writ and of the sale. Notice of the writ must be advertised for 30 days, including published at least two times in a newspaper in the parish where the property is located.

Foreclosure Sale. The sheriff will conduct the sale as an auction. Anyone may bid, including the borrower. The winning bidder must pay the sale price in cash on the day of the sale, or if arrangements are made, within 30 days if a 10 percent deposit is made. Once the sales price has been paid, the sheriff will issue a deed to the winning bidder.

Deficiency Judgments. The borrower does not have redemption rights after the sale, but the lender may still sue to obtain a deficiency judgment.
For more information on Louisiana Foreclosure Law, go to: www.louisiana. gov

© 2003, The Real Estate Library

Summary of Maine Foreclosure Law

In Maine, lenders only use mortgages to secure real estate loans. As such, all foreclosures in Maine are judicial or strict foreclosure.

Judicial Foreclosure Guidelines

Pre-Foreclosure Period. Before the foreclosure can begin, the lender must deliver a default notice to the borrower. If the borrower does not pay the full amount in default plus interest and fees within 30 days, the lender will start the formal foreclosure proceedings by filing a lawsuit in court and having the borrower served. A copy of the complaint will also be recorded in the county's Registry of Deeds. If the borrower opposes the foreclosure, the court will conduct a hearing. If there is no opposition to the lawsuit by the borrower, a default judgment will be entered. If the Court determines that a breach has occurred, it will enter a judgment of foreclosure, establish a redemption period, and order the sale of the property.

Redemption Period. If the court rules in favor of the lender, the borrower will have 90 days from the date of judgment to stop the foreclosure by paying off all amounts due.

Notice of Public Sale. After the redemption period expires, the lender will publish a Notice of Sale once a week for three weeks in a local newspaper. The notice must also be mailed to all parties appearing in the lawsuit, and their attorneys of record, no less than 30 days prior to the sale date. The notice must contain the property description, and the date, time, and location of the sale.

Foreclosure Sale. The sale is often conducted at the office of the lender's attorney (who also conducts the sale), or at the local courthouse. The sale may be postponed for no more than seven days at a time and the postponement must be announced at the originally scheduled sale. At the sale, anyone can bid, including the lender. The property will be sold to the highest bidder. Usually, the bidders are required to bring a pre-designated deposit, and must pay-off the balance within 30 days. After the sale and payment of the balance, the lender will transfer the property to the winning bidder.

Although Maine allows lenders to pursue foreclosure by judicial methods, the other method of foreclosure is called "strict foreclosure."

Strict Foreclosure Guidelines

The strict foreclosure process is based on Maine's foreclosure doctrine that the lender owns the property until the mortgage has been paid in full. Thus, if any of the conditions established in the mortgage are breached, the borrower will lose any right to the property and the lender will either take possession of the property or arrange for it's sale.

Redemption Period. In either case, the borrower has a 12-months redemption period. If the lender has taken possession of the property, they must hold possession for the entire redemption period to finalize the foreclosure. If the lender chooses to sell the property (without taking possession of it first), they must file a lawsuit. The lender must wait until the redemption period has expired and then sell the property by special procedures established by the court.

Deficiency Judgment. The lender may file for a deficiency judgment, but it is limited to the difference between the fair market value (as of date of sale), as determined by an appraisal, and the balance of the loan in default.

For more information on Maine Foreclosure Laws, go to: www.maine.gov

Summary of Maryland Foreclosure Law

In Maryland, lenders only use mortgages to secure real estate loans. As such, foreclosures will be judicial.

Judicial Foreclosure Guidelines

Complaint Filed. The foreclosure begins when the lender files a summons and complaint in the county courthouse against the borrower seeking foreclosure of the property to satisfy the debt. But unlike most states, the lender is not required to notify the borrower of the pending lawsuit. The court will then conduct a hearing to determine whether a default has occurred. However, if there is an "Accent to Decree" in the mortgage, there is no need for the hearing prior to the court ordering a sale of the property.

Redemption Period. If the court finds that a default has occurred it shall: 1) fix the amount of the debt, interest, and costs then due; and 2) provide the borrower with a reasonable time within which payment may be made. The court will order that if payment is not made within the time fixed in the order, the property will be sold to satisfy the debt.

Notice of Sale. A Notice of Sale must be published in a newspaper of general circulation in the county where the property is located at least once a week for three successive weeks, with the first publication to be not less than 15 days prior to sale. The last publication of the notice must be no more than one week prior to the sale. The Notice must also be sent by certified and registered mail, not more than 30 days and not less than ten days before the sale date, to the borrower at their last known address, and the property owner (if different). If the sale is postponed for any reason, a new Notice of Sale with the new sale date must be published in the manner the original Notice of Sale was published.

Sheriff's Sale. The sale must be conducted by the person authorized to make the sale (i.e. sheriff) and take place immediately outside the courthouse entrance, at the property itself, or at another location advertised in the Notice of Sale. The terms of the sale vary by process. The property will be sold to the highest bidder. Within 30 days after the sale, the person authorized to make the sale must file a complete report of the sale with the court for ratification.

Ratification Notice. The clerk of the court will then issue a notice containing a brief description identifying the property and stating that the sale will be ratified unless cause to the contrary is shown within 30 days after the date of the notice. A copy of the notice shall be published at least once a week in each of three successive weeks before the expiration of the 30-day period in one or more newspapers of general circulation in the county in which the report of sale was filed. If no objections are filed, the sale will be confirmed by the court and the ownership of the property will transfer to the winning bidder.

<u>Deficiency Judgment</u>. Lenders have a period of three years after the sale date to file for a deficiency judgment. However, the amount of the deficiency is limited to the remaining balance of the loan in default after the foreclosure sale proceeds have been applied.

For more information on Maryland Foreclosure Law, go to: <u>www.mlis.state.md.us</u>

Summary of Massachusetts Foreclosure Law

In Massachusetts, lenders typically use mortgages to secure real estate loans. Nevertheless, lenders are given the right to use non-judicial foreclosure procedures as long as there is a power-of-sale clause in the mortgage.

Non-Judicial Foreclosure Guidelines

<u>Notice of Intention to Foreclose</u>. The lender will not be entitled to a deficiency judgment unless they mail a Notice of Intent to Foreclose, postage prepaid, by registered mail with return receipt requested, to the borrower, no less than 21 days before the date of sale. The notice must give a warning to the borrower of liability for a deficiency if the proceeds from the foreclosure sale are insufficient to cover the amount of the debt.

<u>Notice of Sale</u>. The lender must record a Notice of Sale in the county where the property is located. The notice must also: 1) be sent, by registered mail, to the borrower at his last known address at least 14 days prior to the foreclosure sale, and all junior lienholders; 2) published once a week for three weeks, in a newspaper of general circulation within the town where the property is located.

The first publication must be at least 21 days before the sale date. The notice must contain the place, time and date of the foreclosure sale, the date the loan document was recorded, the borrowers name, the amount of the default, and the terms of the sale.

Foreclosure Sale. The sale must be conducted at public auction on the date, time and place specified in the Notice of Sale. A licensed auctioneer will conduct the sale. The property will be sold to the highest bidder, who must make a deposit and pay the balance within 30 days. The lender Is not entitled to any deficiency judgment.

Redemption Rights. The borrower has no rights of redemption after a non-judicial foreclosure, but can receive any surplus of the sale proceeds.

For more information on Massachusetts Foreclosure Law, go to: www.mass.gov/legis

Summary of Michigan Foreclosure Law

In Michigan, lenders use both deeds of trusts and mortgages to secure real estate loans. If a mortgage (without a power-of-sale clause) was used, the lender will typically conduct a judicial foreclosure. If a deed of trust or mortgages (with a power-of-sale clause) was used, the lender will typically utilize non-judicial procedures. Most foreclosures in Michigan are non-judicial.

Non-Judicial Foreclosure Guidelines

Notice of Sale. The foreclosure begins with the lender publishing a Notice of Sale once a week for four successive weeks in a newspaper of general circulation in the county where the property is located. The notice must also be posted on the property at least 15 days after the Notice of Sale was first published. The notice must contain the borrower(s) and lender's name, a description of the property, the date and amount of the mortgage, the terms of the sale, and the time, place and date of the sale, and the length of the redemption period.

Foreclosure Sale. The sale must occur no less than 28 days after the first publication of the Notice of Sale. The sale will be conducted as a public auction and everyone may bid, including the lender. The property will be sold to the highest bidder. The trustee must conduct the sale between the hours of 9:00 am and 4:00 pm on the date specified in the notice. The sale may be postponed by posting a notice at the time and place where the sale was originally scheduled. If the postponement is for more than one week, the notice of postponement must be published in the manner as the original Notice of Sale. After the sale, the trustee completes the necessary documents to transfer the property to the winning bidder, which states the borrower's redemption rights.

Redemption Period. The length of the borrower's redemption period varies under Michigan law. If the property is four units or less and not more than three acres in size, and the amount claimed by the lender is not more than 2/3 of the original indebtedness, the redemption period is six months. If the property is abandoned, the redemption period is shortened to only 30 days. In all other cases, the redemption period is one year from the date of sale. During this period, the borrower can redeem the property by paying the winning bid amount plus all applicable costs.

For more information on Michigan Foreclosure Law, go to: www.legislature.mi.gov

Summary of Minnesota Foreclosure Law

In Minnesota, lenders use both deeds of trust and mortgages to secure real estate loans. If a mortgage was used, then the judicial foreclosure will typically be used. If a deed of trust or a mortgage (with a power-of-sale clause) was used, then the non-judicial process will most likely be used, and take approximately three months.

Judicial Foreclosure Guidelines

A judicial foreclosure begins when the lender formally notifies the borrower of the default. If the borrower fails to cure the default, the lender will then file a court action for foreclosure against the borrower. If the court determines that the borrower is in default, it will order the property be sold. The borrower has the right to stop the foreclosure at anytime prior to the scheduled sale date by paying the default amount, plus all fees and applicable costs. Lenders may pursue a deficiency judgment, but it is limited to the difference between the fair marker value of the property and the unpaid balance of the original loan, regardless of the foreclosure sale price. Borrowers have from six months to one year to redeem the property by paying the past due amount on the loan and applicable fees.

Non-Judicial Foreclosure Guidelines

In Minnesota, a non-judicial foreclosure may only occur if: 1) no lawsuit to collect on the deed of trust is already underway; 2) the deed of trust and any assignments to new lenders have been recorded; and 3) a notice has been given eight weeks before the foreclosure on a homestead.

If all of these conditions have been met, then the foreclosure may proceed as follows:

Demand Letter. The lender is required to sent the borrower a demand letter at least 30 days before commencing the foreclosure. The letter demands that the borrower begin the loan current or it will be accelerated.

Notice of Sale. The lender will cause a Notice of Sale to be recorded in the county where the property is located. The occupants of the property must be personally served with the notice at least four weeks prior to the sale. All other lienholders and parties in interest will receive a copy of the notice by mail. The notice must be published for six weeks in a local newspaper. The notice must contain the borrower(s) and lender's names, the original loan amount, the current amount of default, the date of the deed of trust, a description of the property, and the date, time, and place of the sale

Sheriff's Sale. The sheriff of the county in which the property is located must conduct the sale on the date specified in the Notice of Sale. At some point during the sale, the sheriff must read an itemized statement, which has been filed by the lender, of the amount due at the time of the sale. The property will be sold to the highest bidder, who will receive a Certificate of Sale. The Certificate effectively transfers ownership and possession to the winning bidder after the redemption period has expired.

For more on Minnesota Foreclosure Law, go to: www.leg.state.mn.us/leg/statutes.asp

© 2003 The Real Estate Library

Summary of Mississippi Foreclosure Law

In Mississippi, lenders may use either deeds of trust or mortgages to secure real estate loans. If a mortgage was used, the foreclosure will be judicial. If a deed of trust was used, the foreclosure will use non-judicial procedures. Most foreclosures of single-family residences are non-judicial.

Non-Judicial Foreclosure Guidelines

Notice of Sale. The trustee must record a Notice of Sale containing, at a minimum, the borrowers name and the date, time and place of the sale, in the county where the property is located. The notice must also be posted at the courthouse door in the county where the property is located. Finally, the notice must be published in a newspaper of general circulation in the county for a period of three consecutive weeks before the date of the sale.

Reinstatement Period. The borrower may cure the default and stop the foreclosure process at any time before the foreclosure sale by paying the delinquent payments, plus costs and fees.

Foreclosure Sale. The trustee must conduct the sale between the hours of 10:00 a.m. and 4:00 p.m. The sale must be held in the county where the property is located, or, if different, in the county where the borrower resides. In either case, the sale must be conducted at the normal location for foreclosure sales within the given county. The sale must be made at public auction for cash to the highest bidder. The lender is permitted to bid. The winning bidder, if other than the lender, must supply the sales amount usually in the form of cash or certified funds at sale. If not, then the sale must be re-scheduled and re-published. The trustee can postpone the sale to the next day by announcing the postponement at the originally scheduled sale. After the sale, the trustee prepares a deed conveying ownership to the winning bidder. If there is a surplus, it is dispersed to the junior lienholders. However, if the sales proceeds are insufficient to satisfy the borrower's debt, the lender is not entitled to a deficiency judgment.

Redemption. Borrowers who lose their property as the result of a non-judicial foreclosure have no rights of redemption in Mississippi.

For more information on Mississippi Foreclosure Law, go to: www.ls.state.ms.us

© 2003, The Real Estate Library

Summary of Missouri Foreclosure Law

In Missouri, lenders use both mortgages and deeds of trusts to secure real estate loans. If a mortgage was used, then the foreclosure will be judicial. If a deed of trust or a mortgage (with a power-of-sale clause) was used, then the non-judicial foreclosure procedures will be followed. Most foreclosures of single-family residences are non-judicial.

Non-Judicial Foreclosure Guidelines

Upon a borrower's default, the lender must follow the procedures set out in the deed of trust. At the very least, the lender must provide the borrower will an unambiguous warning that the foreclosure process is about to begin. Once the lender provides the required warning, the foreclosure can proceed.

Notice of Sale. The trustee must mail a Notice of Sale to the borrower, at his last known address, at least 20 days prior to the scheduled day of sale. The Notice must also be published in a newspaper within the county. In a county with a city with a population over 50,000, the trustee must publish the notice daily starting 20 days before the sale and ending on the day of the sale. In all other counties, the trustee must publish the notice once a week for four weeks, with the last publication no more than one week prior to the sale. A copy of the notice must be mailed to the borrower, and all other affected parties, at least 20 days before the sale date. The notice must include information regarding the date, time, place, and terms of sale, and a description of the property.

Trustee's Sale. The sale will be conducted by the trustee at public auction at the county courthouse between the hours of 9:00 a.m. and 5:00 p.m. If the sale is postponed for more than seven days, the trustee must re-issue and re-publish a new Notice of Sale. The property will be sold for cash to the highest bidder. Anyone may bid, including the lender. The winning bidder will receive a Certificate of Sale. Once the redemption period has expired, the winning bidder will exchange the Certificate for a deed of conveyance.

Redemption Procedures. If the property is sold to a third party, the borrower does not have any redemption rights. But if the lender is the winning bidder, the borrower has the right to redeem the property. However, redemption is complex and difficult to achieve. First, the borrower must give advance notice within ten days prior to the sale of his intent to redeem. Second, the borrower must post a bond within 20 days after the sale, equal to the mortgage interest, any secondary loan interest, taxes that will accrue during the redemption period, foreclosure expenses, legal fees, damages, plus six percent interest. If the borrower can meet these requirements, the borrower can redeem the property within one year by paying those amounts due.

For more information on Missouri Foreclosure Law, go to: www.moga.state. mo.us

Summary of Montana Foreclosure Law

In Montana, lenders use either mortgages or deeds of trust (also called "trust indenture") to secure real estate loans. If a mortgage was used, the foreclosure will be judicial. If a trust indenture was used, the foreclosure will follow non-judicial procedures. Most foreclosures of single-family residences follow the non-judicial procedures, and typically take 5-6 months.

Non-Judicial Foreclosure Guidelines

Notice of Sale. The non-judicial foreclosure begins with the recording of a Notice of Sale in the county where the property is located and then: 1) mailed, by registered or certified mail, to the borrower at his last known address, and all lienholders and parties requesting notice, at least 120 days before the foreclosure sale; 2) published once a week for three successive weeks in a newspaper of general circulation in the county where the property is located; and 3) posted on the property at least 20 days before the foreclosure sale. The notice must contain the time, date and place of sale, the borrower's, lender's and trustee's names, a description of both the property and the default, and the book and page where the trust indenture is recorded.

Reinstatement Period. At any time before the trustee's sale, the borrower may satisfy the debt by paying the default, plus costs and attorney's fees, which will stop the foreclosure proceedings and reinstate the loan.

Trustee's Sale. The trustee must conduct the sale between the hours of 9:00 am and 4:00 pm at the courthouse in the county where the property is located, or the property, of the trustee's office (if within in the county). The property must be sold at public auction to the highest bidder. The sale may be postponed for up to 15 days by posting a notice at the time and place where the sale was originally scheduled. The winning bidder receives a Trustee's Deed transferring ownership and can take possession of the property after ten days. After the sale, the borrower does not have any redemption rights, nor can the lender obtain a deficiency judgment against the borrower.

For more information on Montana Foreclosure Law, go to: www.leg.state.mt.us

© 2003. The Real Estate Library.

Summary of Nebraska Foreclosure Law

In Nebraska, lenders only use mortgages to secure real estate loans. As such, all foreclosures are judicial and take 4-6 months.

Judicial Foreclosure Guidelines

The foreclosure begins with the lender filing a complaint to foreclose at the court in the county where the property is located. State law does not require the lender to send notice to the borrower, but the mortgage may require it. Regardless, the borrower has 30 days to respond. If the borrower does not respond (or if the borrower responds and a hearing is held), the court will rule whether a default has occurred. If a judgment of foreclosure is entered, the court will order the entire property to be sold, or just some part of it. But the order of sale must be delayed for up to nine months if the borrower files a written request for a delay with the clerk of the court within 20 days after the judgment is rendered. Otherwise, the order commanding the sale of the mortgaged property will be given 20 days after the judgment.

Reinstatement Period. The borrower has the right to cure the default at any time while the suit is still pending by paying the delinquent amount owed on the mortgage, as well as any interest and costs that have accrued. However, the court may still enter a decree of foreclosure and sale, which may be enforced if the buyer goes into default on the mortgage again in the future.

Notice of Sale. The sheriff must give public notice of the time and place of the sale by: 1) posting the notice on the courthouse door; 2) posting the notice in at least five other public places in the county where the property is located; and 3) by advertising the property for sale once a week for four weeks in a newspaper published in the county where the property is located.

Sheriff's Sale. Either the sheriff, or a court official called a "Master Commissioner," will conduct the foreclosure sale. It will be a public auction with the property sold to the highest bidder. Anyone, including the lender, may bid. Thereafter, the court must confirm the sale. Upon confirmation, all redemption rights are extinguished.

Deficiency Judgment. At any time after the sale, the lender can file for a deficiency judgment for the difference between the unpaid balance of the mortgage and fair market value of the property as of the date of sale, regardless of the sale's price.

For more information on Nebraska foreclosure law, go to: www.statutes.unicam.state.ne.us

© 2003. The Real Estate Library.

Summary of Nevada Foreclosure Law

In Nevada, lenders typically use deeds of trust, and occasionally mortgages, to secure real estate loans. If a mortgage was used, the foreclosure will be judicial. If a deed of trust was used, the foreclosure will follow non-judicial procedures. Most foreclosures of single-family residences follow the non-judicial procedures and take approximately four months.

Non-Judicial Foreclosure Guidelines

Notice of Default and Election to Sell. The non-judicial foreclosure starts with the trustee mailing a Notice of Default and Election to Sell by certified mail, return receipt requested, to the borrower, at their last known address. Simultaneously, the notice must also be recorded in the county where the property is located. Any additional postings and advertisements must be done in the same manner as for an execution sale in Nevada. The notice must state that the loan is default, that the loan balance is being accelerated, and that the borrower needs to cure the default or the property will be sold.

Reinstatement Period. Beginning on the day after the Notice of Default was recorded with the county and mailed to the borrower, the borrower has 35 days to cure the default by paying the delinquent amount on the loan. The owner of the property may stop the foreclosure proceedings by filing an "Intent to Cure" with the Public Trustee's office at least 15 days prior to the foreclosure sale. Then the borrower must pay the necessary amount to bring the loan current by noon on the day before the foreclosure sale is scheduled.

Notice of Sale. No less than three months after recording the Notice of Default, the trustee can issue the Notice of Sale. The sale date must be scheduled at least 21 days after the Notice of Sale is issued. The notice must be posted in three public places in the county and published in a local newspaper once a week for three weeks. The notice must also be mailed to all of the affected parties, including the borrower, and all junior lienholders.

Trustee's Sale. The sale will be held at the place (often trustee's office), the time and on the date stated in the Notice of Sale. The sale will be conducted as a public auction, with the highest bidder having the right to purchase the property. Except for the lender, the winning bidder has to pay the full bid amount in cash or cashier's check to the trustee. If the sale is postponed, a public announcement is made at the time and place of the sale. After the sale, the trustee transfers ownership to the winning bidder. Once the sale is completed, the borrower has no rights of redemption.

Deficiency Judgment. Lenders have three months after the sale to try and obtain a deficiency judgment.

For more information on Nevada foreclosure law, go to: www.leg.state. nv.us/nrs

© 2003. The Real Estate Library.

Summary of New Hampshire Foreclosure Law

In New Hampshire, lenders use mostly mortgages (and occasionally deeds of trust) to secure real estate loans. If a mortgage was used, the foreclosure will be judicial. If the mortgage or deed of trust had a power of sale clause, or a deed of trust was used, the foreclosure will follow non-judicial procedures, or one of several special methods: Entry under Process, Entry and Publication, or Possession and Publication.

Judicial Foreclosure Guidelines

In New Hampshire, the judicial process of foreclosure is very similar to that of the strict foreclosure process used in other New England states. The lender must file a complaint against the borrower in the Court having jurisdiction in the county where the property is located. The lender must then obtain a Decree of Sale from the court. Generally, if the court finds the borrower in default, they will give them a set period of time to pay the delinquent amount, plus costs. If the

borrower does not pay within that period of time, the court will order the property to be sold. Anyone may bid at the foreclosure sale, including the lender.

Non-Judicial Foreclosure Guidelines

Notice of Default. If the mortgage or deed of trust contains a power of sale clause, the foreclosure is initiated when a Notice of Default is sent to the borrower. The default notice must detail the default amount, provide a 30-day grace period in which to pay the default, and a warning that failure to do so will result in foreclosure of the property.

Reinstatement Period. The borrower has until the foreclosure sale date to pay off the default amount, damages and costs, and thereby stop the foreclosure.

Notice of Sale The Notice of Sale is recorded in the county where the property is located. The notice is then: 1) mailed to the borrower at least 25 days before the sale; and 2) published once a week for three weeks, with the first publication appearing not less than 20 days before the sale, in a newspaper of general circulation in the county where the property is located. The trustee must also post the notice in three public places in the county. The notice must contain the time, date and place of sale, a description of the property and the default, as well as a "warning" to the borrower, informing him the property is going to be sold and what rights he has to stop the procedure.

Trustee's Sale. The foreclosure sale must be held on the property itself, unless the power of sale clause specifies a different location.

Special Methods of Foreclosure

1.   Entry under Process - The lender may foreclose by entering the property under process of law and maintaining actual possession of the property for one year.

2.   Entry and Publication - By peaceable entry onto the property and continued, actual, peaceable possession for a period of one year, and by a publishing a notice stating the time of possession, the lender and borrowers name, the date of the mortgage and a description of the property in a newspaper of general circulation in the county where the property is located. The notice must be published for three successive weeks, with the first publication appearing at least six months before the borrowers right to redeem has expired.

3.   Possession and Publication - By the lender in possession of the property publishing a notice stating that from and after a certain day, the property will be held for default of the mortgage and the borrowers rights to the property will be foreclosed. The notice must be published in a newspaper printed in the county where the property is located for three successive weeks and must give the borrower(s) and lender's names, the date of the mortgage, a description of the property, and the lender's intention to hold possession of the property for at least one year.

Borrowers have no rights of redemption when any of the non-judicial or special methods of foreclosure are used.

For more information on New Hampshire Foreclosure Law, go to: www.state.nh.us

Summary of New Jersey Foreclosure Law

In New Jersey, lenders only use mortgages to secure real estate loans. As such, all foreclosures are judicial.

Judicial Foreclosure Guidelines

Pre-foreclosure Period. At least 30 days before starting the foreclosure process, the lender must send the borrower a letter warning of the impending foreclosure. During this pre-foreclosure period, the borrower can prevent the foreclosure and reinstate the loan by simply paying off the amount in default.

Lawsuit for Foreclosure. The lender formally initiates the judicial foreclosure by filing a complaint for foreclosure in the court and recording a Notice of Pending Action ("Lis Pendens") in the county recorder's office. The lender has the option of suing for either the default payments or the entire unpaid principal balance of the loan. The borrower must be personally served with a copy of the lawsuit within 45 days. If the borrower can't be timely

served, a notice of the lawsuit must be published. The borrower then has 35 days to file an answer to the complaint. If the borrower fails to respond, the lender will file a Notice of Intent to Enter Foreclosure Judgment, giving the borrower a final opportunity to cure the default. If the borrower does not cure within 45 days, the lender can ask the court to enter the judgment. Once the court enters a judgment in favor of the lender, it will schedule a sale date. Nevertheless, the court decree will still give the borrower a short time to pay. If the borrower still fails to pay within that time, the clerk of the court will issue a writ of execution to the Sheriff to sell the property. The Sheriff is required to schedule a sale of the property within six months.

Notice of Sale. The Notice of Sale must be: 1) posted in the recorder's office of the county where the property is located; 2) posted on the property; and 3) published in two newspapers in the county. One of these publications must be in either the largest municipality in the county or the county seat. The lender must also notify the borrower at least ten days prior to the foreclosure sale.

Foreclosure Sale. The sale is conducted as a public auction, overseen by the sheriff or another officer of the county. The property is awarded to the highest bidder. The sheriff must transfer ownership to the purchaser within ten days following the sale, subject to the court confirming the sale. The sale can be postponed twice by the trustee and twice by the borrower. Any other postponements will require a court order. If needed, the lender can seek a deficiency judgment against the borrower after the sale.

Redemption Period. In one of the shortest redemption periods in the United States, the borrower has only ten days in which to object to the court and/or redeem the property.

For more information on New Jersey Foreclosure Law, go to: www.njleg.state.nj.us

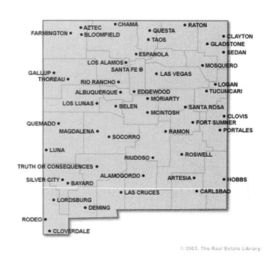

© 2003, The Real Estate Library.

Summary of New Mexico Foreclosure Law

In New Mexico, lenders only use mortgages to secure real estate loans. As such, all foreclosures use the judicial process, which typically takes 6 months.

Judicial Foreclosure Guidelines

First the lender will file a complaint in the court in the county where the property is located.
Once the complaint has been filed, a Lis Pendens (notice of pending action) will be recorded in the country recorder's office. Then the lender will serve the borrower with a copy of the complaint. The borrower has 30 days to respond. If the borrower can not be personally served, the lender must publish a notice of the pending lawsuit once a week for four consecutive weeks in a local newspaper. In that case, the borrower has 20 days to respond from the date of the last publication. If the time limit for the borrower to respond has expired, the court will enter a ruling.

Reinstatement Period. Generally, the court decrees the amount of the borrower's debt and gives him or her a short time to pay. If the borrower fails to pay within that time, the court then issues a notice of sale.

<u>Notice of Sale</u>. The Notice of Sale must contain a legal description of the property, and state the place, the time and the date of sale, which must be at least 30 days after the notice was first issued. The notice must be published once a week for four consecutive weeks in a local newspaper. The final publication of the notice must occur at least three days before the date of sale.

<u>Judicial Sale</u>. The property will be sold to the highest bidder on the date specified in the notice. An acceptable bid must be at least 80 percent of the fair market value of the property at the time of the sale. Once the property is sold a deed will be recorded, giving ownership of the property to the winning bidder. The sale is subject to approval of the court.

<u>Redemption Period</u>. After the sale is approved by the court, the borrower has from one to nine months to redeem the property. First, he must file a Notice to Redeem. Then, he must pay the amount of the winning bid, plus costs and interest.

<u>Deficiency Judgment</u>. After the sale, the lender can continue the lawsuit and seek a deficiency judgment against the borrower for the difference between the sales price and the unpaid balance of the loan.

For more information on New Mexico Foreclosure Law, go to: www.legis.state. nm.us

Summary of New York Foreclosure Law

In New York, lenders use mortgages almost exclusively to secure real estate loans. As such, almost all foreclosures follow judicial procedures.

Judicial Foreclosure Guidelines

<u>Filing Complaint</u>. The judicial foreclosure process begins with the lender filing a complaint against the borrower in the court having jurisdiction in the county where the property is located. A Lis Pendens (notice of pending action) is then recorded in the county recorder's office. The borrower is notified and given 20 days to respond. If the borrower responds, the court will schedule a hearing to determine whether there has been a default and order the sale of the property. Once a judgment has been entered, the court will appoint a Referee who will determine the amount owed and recommend how the property will be sold. After the court has confirmed the Referee's Report, it will issue an order directing the sale of the property to satisfy the lender's loan.

Reinstatement Period. If the court finds the borrower in default, they will give them a set period of time to pay the delinquent amount, plus costs. If the borrower does not pay within that period, the court will enter a decree ordering the property to be sold by the sheriff or a referee.

Notice of Sale. The Notice of Sale must published in a newspaper of general circulation within the county once a week for at least four weeks before the scheduled sale date. The notice must give the date, time, and location of the sale.

Sheriff's Sale. The sale is usually scheduled at least four months after the court's decree. The foreclosure sale will be conducted as a public auction at the county courthouse. The property will be sold to the highest bidder. Anyone may bid, including the lender. The winning bidder typically has to pay at least ten percent of the purchase price at the sale, and the balance within 30 days. After the property has been paid in full, the officer conducting the sale must execute a deed to the purchaser. The Sheriff must also pay, out of the proceeds, the amount of the debt, including interest and costs, to the lender and obtain a receipt for the payment from the lender. Within 30 days after the completing the sale and executing the deed to the purchaser, the Sheriff must file a report of sale with the clerk of the court, including a receipt from the lender. Unless otherwise ordered by the court, the sale can't be confirmed until three months after the filing of the report of sale. Once the sale is confirmed, the borrower has no right of redemption.

Deficiency Judgment. If proceeds from the sale are insufficient, the lender can pursue a deficiency judgment against the borrower. But the motion for a deficiency judgment must be made within 90 days after the sale or the lender loses that right.

For more information on New York Foreclosure Law, go to: www.assembly. state.ny.us

Summary of North Carolina Foreclosure Law

In North Carolina, lenders use either mortgages or deeds of trust to secure real estate loans. If a mortgage was used, the foreclosure will be judicial. If a deed of trust or a mortgage (with a power-of-sale clause) was used, the foreclosure will follow non-judicial procedures. Most foreclosures of single-family residences follow the non-judicial procedures.

Judicial Foreclosure Guidelines

The judicial process of foreclosure, which involves filing a lawsuit to obtain a court order to foreclose, is used when no power of sale is present in the mortgage. Generally, after the court declares a foreclosure, the property will be auctioned off to the highest bidder.

Non-Judicial Guidelines

Preliminary Hearing. First, a preliminary hearing in court must be held before a non-judicial foreclosure can take place. Preliminary notices will be mailed to all of the parties involved at least ten days before the hearing, or 20 days if the notice is published and posted. The court will then conduct a hearing to determine whether a default has occurred and whether a foreclosure sale of the property should be conducted.

Notice of Sale. The clerk issues a Notice of Sale and mails it first class mail to the borrower, and all other parties entitled to receive notice, at least 20 days before the sale. The notice is also published in a newspaper of general circulation in the county where the property is located once a week for two successive weeks, with the last notice being published no more than ten days before the sale. Finally, the notice is posted at the courthouse for 20 days prior to the foreclosure sale. The notice of sale must name the borrower(s), the lender, provide a description of the property, and state the date, time and location of the sale.

Foreclosure Sale. The sale must be conducted at the courthouse in the county where the property is located. It will occur between the hours of 10:00 am and 4:00 pm on any day except Sundays or legal holidays. If the sale is postponed for any reason, a notice stating the new date and time of sale is posted at the courthouse. The property will be sold to the highest bidder. Upset bids may be filed with the court clerk for a period of ten days after the foreclosure sale, by submitting a deposit of at least five percent of the bid to the county clerk. The winning bidder has 30 days to pay the balance of the purchase price. After the sale, the lender can still seek a deficiency judgment against the borrower in court.

Redemption Rights. The borrower retains a short ten-day right of redemption after the sale by paying what is owed the lender plus all foreclosure costs.

For more information on North Carolina Foreclosure Law, go to: www.ncga.state.nc.us

316

Summary of North Dakota Foreclosure Law

In North Dakota, lenders only use mortgages to secure real estate loans. As such, all foreclosures are judicial.

Judicial Foreclosure Guidelines

Notice of Intent to Foreclose. In North Dakota, the lender is required to give the borrower no less than 30 days advance notice of their intent to foreclose. The notice must be sent by registered or certified mail no later than 90 days before the suit is filed. If the borrower cannot be found, the notice must be published in a newspaper within the county where the property is located. The notice must contain: 1) a description of the real estate; 2) the date and amount of the mortgage; 3) the specific amounts due for principal, interest and taxes paid by the lender; and 4) a statement that a lawsuit will be filed if the amount is not paid within 30 days from the date the notice was mailed.

Filing Complaint. After the 30-day period has expired, the lender will file a lawsuit in the District Court in the county where the property is located. The complaint will determine whether the lender will seek a deficiency judgment if needed. The borrower must be personally served with the summons and complaint. All other defendants will be served by mail. After a hearing, the court will determine whether there is a default and whether the property should be sold. Once the court decrees the amount of the borrower's debt, it will give the borrower a short time to pay. If the borrower fails to pay within that time, the clerk of the court will then advertise the property for sale.

Renstatement Period. The borrower may stop the foreclosure process by paying the delinquent amount, plus foreclosure costs, at any time prior to the time the sale is confirmed by the court.

Notice of Sale. The Notice of Sale will be mailed to the borrower and published in a newspaper within the county. The last publication must occur at least ten days before the sale date.

Sheriff's Sale. All foreclosure sales must be conducted by the sheriff (or his deputy) in the county where the property is located. The property will be sold to the highest bidder, who will be issued a Certificate of Sale. After the borrower's redemption period has ended, the Certificate will exchanged for a deed.

Post-sale Redemption Period. Borrowers typically have a period of one year to redeem the property by paying the balance due on the loan, plus costs. But if the mortgage includes short-term redemption rights, then the redemption period will be limited to only six months.

Deficiency Judgment. After the sale, the lender can seek a deficiency judgment against the borrower for the difference between the sale's price and the total amount of the loan plus costs.

For more information on North Dakota foreclosure laws, go to: www.nd.gov

Summary of Ohio Foreclosure Law

In Ohio, lenders only use mortgages to secure real estate loans. As such, all foreclosures are judicial, and can take anywhere from five to seven months.

Judicial Foreclosure Guidelines

Lawsuit Filed. The foreclosure begins with the lender filing a summons and complaint in the county court where the property is located. The borrower is named as a defendant, as well as all parties having an ownership interest, lien or encumbrance on the property. The borrower and all of the defendants are served with copies of the summons and complaint and given 28 days to respond. If the borrower cannot be found, the lender must publish notice of the lawsuit in a local newspaper. After the court renders its decision, the borrower will be given a brief period to pay the debt. If the borrower fails to pay within that time, the case will proceed based upon the lender's motion for summary judgment or trial. If the court rules in favor of the lender, it will issue an order of sale and deliver it to the Sheriff.

318

Appraisal. At some point prior to the scheduled date of foreclosure, an appraisal of the property must be made by three disinterested "freeholders" of the county. Copies of the three appraisals will be filed with the court clerk.

Notice of Sale. The Sheriff must publish the notice once a week for three consecutive weeks in a newspaper of general circulation in the county in which the property is located. The notice must state the date, time, and location of the sale.

Sheriff's Sale. The sheriff will conduct the sale at the courthouse and the property will be sold to the highest bidder. The property must be sold at a price not less than two-thirds of the average value of the three appraisals. The court will then review the sale, and file an order confirming the sale. The sheriff then prepares and issues a deed transferring ownership to the winning bidder.

Redemption Rights. The borrower may redeem the property at any time before the court confirms the foreclosure sale by paying the amount of the judgment, plus costs and interest.

Deficiency Judgment. The Lender may obtain a deficiency judgment after the sale is confirmed, for difference between the amount the lender lost and the proceeds from the sale. But the statute of limitations is two years in the event the judgment was rendered prior to confirmation of the sale and the property was a dwelling with two units or less.

For more on Ohio Foreclosure Laws, go to: www.legislature.state.oh.us

Summary of Oklahoma Foreclosure Law

In Oklahoma, lenders use either mortgages or deeds of trust to secure real estate loans. If a mortgage was used, the foreclosure will most likely be judicial. If a deed of trust was used, the foreclosure will follow non-judicial procedures. The majority of foreclosures in Oklahoma are judicial.

Judicial Foreclosure Guidelines

Lawsuit filed. The process starts with the lender filing a lawsuit for foreclosure in the courthouse in the county where the property is located, and a Lis Pendens (Notice of Pending Action) recorded in the county recorder's office. A copy of the summons and complaint are personally delivered to the borrower, after which the borrower has 20 days to respond. If the borrower does not respond, or the court rules that there has been a default, the court will issue a judgment and order that the county sheriff sell the property to payoff the default.

Notice of Sale. The Sheriff will record a Notice of Sale in the recorder's office in the county where the property is located. The notice must also be published in a local newspaper once a day for four consecutive weeks. The first publishing date must be at least 30 days prior to the sale date. Copies of the notice will also be mailed to the borrower, property owners (if different), and all other parties in interest.

Sheriff's Sale. Prior to the sale, the Sheriff will arrange for the property to be appraised. The sheriff will conduct the sale as a public auction. The opening bid must be no less than 2/3 of the property's appraised value. The property will be auctioned off to the highest bidder. The winning bidder must provide cash or certified funds equal to ten percent of the bid amount. If for any reason the sale is cancelled, the entire process starts all over again. After the sale, it takes approximately 15 days for the court to confirm the sale. The borrower has those 15 days to redeem the property by paying off the full amount owed to the lender. But once the court confirms the sale, the borrower's redemption rights are terminated.

Deficiency Judgment. A lender may sue to obtain a deficiency judgment, but the action must be taken within 90 days after the date of sale.

For more information on Oklahoma Foreclosure Laws, go to: www.lsb.state.ok.us

320

Summary of Oregon Foreclosure Law

In Oregon, lenders mostly use deeds of trust, and occasionally mortgages, to secure real estate loans. If a mortgage was used, the foreclosure will be judicial. If a deed of trust was used, the foreclosure will follow the non-judicial procedures. Most foreclosures of single-family residences in Oregon follow the non-judicial procedures, and takes approximately 130 days.

Non-Judicial Guidelines

Notice of Default. The lender records a Notice of Default in the recorder's office in the county where the property is located. The notice is published in a local newspaper once a week for four consecutive weeks. The notice must also be served on the borrower and any occupants in the property at least 120 days before the scheduled sale date. The notice must contain a property description, recording information on the trust deed, a description of the default, the sum owing on the loan, the lender's election to sell if the default is not cured.

Reinstatement Period. The borrower may cure the default at any time up to five days prior to the sale date by paying all past due amounts, plus costs.

Notice of Sale. The trustee records a Notice of Sale in the recorder's office where the property is located. The notice must also be published once a week for four successive weeks in a local newspaper, with the last notice being published at least 20 days prior to the foreclosure sale. The notice must contain a property description, recording information on the trust deed, a description of the default, the sum owing on the loan, the lender's election to sell, and the date, time and place of sale.

Trustee's Sale. The sale must be set at least 120 days after the Notice of Default was issued. The sale will be a public auction to the highest bidder for cash. Any person, except the trustee, may bid at the sale, which will take place between 9:00 am and 4:00 pm at the location stated in the Notice of Sale. The winning bidder must pay in full cash at the time of the auction. The trustee transfers ownership of the property to the winning bidder within ten days of the sale. The property owner has those ten days to vacate the property. The sale may be postponed for up to 180 days from the original sale date if at least 20 days advance notice is given, by mail, to the original recipients of the notices. A deficiency judgment cannot be obtained through a non-judicial foreclosure.

For more information on Oregon Foreclosure Laws, go to: www.leg.state.or.us

Summary of Pennsylvania Foreclosure Law

In Pennsylvania, lenders exclusively use mortgages to secure real estate loans. As such, all foreclosures are judicial.

Judicial Foreclosure Guidelines

Notice of Intent to Foreclose. To begin the process, the lender must send a Notice of Intent to Foreclose to the borrower before any foreclosure proceedings may begin. The notice must be sent, by first class mail, to the borrower, at their last known address and if different, to the property. The notice is not normally sent until the borrower is at least 60 days behind in their mortgage payments. In the notice, the lender must make the borrower aware that the mortgage is in default and that the lender intents to accelerate the mortgage payments if the borrower does not cure the default within 30 days.

Lawsuit Filed. If the borrower does not cure the default by paying the past due amount, plus any late charges that have accrued, within the 30 days, the lender will file a lawsuit to foreclose. The borrower will be served with the summons and complaint. The sheriff has 30 days to serve the documents, or they will expire and need to be reissued. If the borrower cannot be found, service will be by mail or publication. The borrower then has one month to respond. If the borrower does not respond, the lender will issue a 10-Day Notice to the defendants that if they don't respond within ten days, a default judgment will be taken against them. Thereafter, if the court determines there has been a default, it will enter a judgment in favor of the lender and order that the property be sold.

Notice of Sheriff's Sale. At least 30 days before the sale, the Sheriff must give notice of the sale by posting a copy of the notice on the property as well as delivering a copy to the borrower (if they are at a different location). Copies must also be mailed to all of the lienholders at least 30 days before the sale. The notice is then published at least once a week for three consecutive weeks in both a local general-interest newspaper and a local legal newspaper.

Sheriff's Sale. The property will be sold at a public auction under the guidelines established by the court. The property will be sold to the highest bidder. Payment of the purchase price and all settlement charges must be made within 30 days of the sale, or the sale will declared null and void. The sale may be postponed once up to 100 days by an announcement at the sale. The court must approve any further postponements. The borrower has the right to cure the default and prevent the sale at any time up to one hour before the Sheriff's foreclosure sale. Borrowers have no rights of redemption once the foreclosure sale is complete and have 20 days to vacate the property.

<u>Deficiency Judgment</u>. Lenders have up to six months after the foreclosure sale to file for a deficiency judgment.

For more information on Pennsylvania Foreclosure Laws, go to: <u>www.pacode.com</u>

© 2003. The Real Estate Library.

Summary of Rhode Island Foreclosure Law

In Rhode Island, lenders use mortgages (with or without power-of-sale clause) to secure real estate loans. If the mortgage did not have a power-of-sale clause, then the foreclosure will be judicial. If the mortgage had a power-of-sale clause, then the foreclosure will follow non-judicial procedures. Most foreclosures of single-family residences in Rhode Island are non-judicial and take no more than two months.

Non-Judicial Foreclosure Guidelines

<u>Notice of Sale</u>. The lender must mail a Notice of Sale by certified mail, return receipt requested, to the borrower at his or her last known address. The notice must be sent at least 20 days prior to the sale date if the borrower is other than a individual consumer mortgagor, and 30 days prior to the sale for individual consumer mortgagors. The lender must also publish the notice in a public newspaper at least once a week for three successive weeks before the sale date, with the first publication at least 21 days before the sale date. The notice must contain the names of the borrower(s) and lender, the amount

due, a description of the property, or the book and page of the mortgage, and the date, time, and place of sale.

Foreclosure Sale. A licensed auctioneer, will conduct the sale at the property as a public auction, between the hours of 9:00 am and 5:00 pm. Any person may bid at the sale, including the lender. The highest bidder will execute a purchase agreement on the date of the auction and must tender the entire sales price. Upon full payment, a deed is recorded transferring ownership. Any surplus in sale proceeds is paid to the junior lienholders. After the sale, there are no redemption rights or deficiency judgments allowed.

For more information on Rhode Island Foreclosure Laws, go to: www.rilin.state.ri.us

Summary of South Carolina Foreclosure Law

In South Carolina, lenders only use mortgages to secure real estate loans. As such, all foreclosures are judicial and take approximately six months.

Judicial Foreclosure Guidelines

Lawsuit Filed. The lender starts the process by filing a complaint against the borrower for foreclosure. The action is filed in the court having jurisdiction in the county where the property is located. A Lis Pendens (aka Notice of Pending Action) is recorded in the office of Registry of Deeds. The borrower is personally served with the summons and complaint. If the borrower cannot be located, the lender must publish notice of the lawsuit in a local newspaper for three weeks. The borrower has 30 days to respond. If the borrower does not respond, or the parties cannot resolve the foreclosure, the case will be referred to a hearing officer. It the hearing officer determines that there was a default, the borrower will be given a set period of time to reinstate loan by paying the delinquent amount, plus costs. If the borrower does not pay within the reinstatement period, the court will then order the property to be sold.

Notice of Sale. A Notice of Sale must be posted at the courthouse door and two other public places at least three weeks prior to the date of sale. The notice must also be published in a newspaper of general circulation within the county where the property is located for three consecutive weeks. The notice must contain a description of the property, the, date, time and place of sale, the borrower(s) name and the lender's name.

Sheriff's Sale. Unless otherwise ordered by the court, the sale will be conducted at the courthouse where the property is located by the sheriff of that county. The sale must be held on the first Monday of each month, unless it is a holiday, and then the sale may take place on the following Tuesday. The sale must occur between the hours of 11:00 am and 5:00 pm, but the sheriff may close the bidding prior to that time.

Upset Bidding. Despite the fact that the bidding at the public sale will end, in South Carolina, the auction actually continues for an additional 30 days. During this 30-day time period, anyone may place a bid higher than the last bid amount. The successful purchaser will be the one with the highest bid at the end of the 30 days. Anyone, other than the successful purchaser, who has placed a bid during this time, will be entitled to a refund of any deposit made in good faith and they will have no further interest in the property. During this period, the borrower also has the right to redeem the property. The borrower can also request an appraisal of the property during the 30-day

period. If the value is higher than the closing bid, it will lower the amount of the deficiency.

Sale Confirmation. If no objection to the sales price of the property has been filed with the sheriff's office within three months after the date of sale, the sale will be considered confirmed and the sheriff will make any necessary deed endorsements.

Deficiency Judgment: After the 30-day period has expired, lenders in South Carolina may file for a deficiency judgment against the borrower for the difference between the amount owed the lender and the amount received at the Sheriff's sale. But if the lender waives the right to a deficiency judgment, then there is no 30-day waiting period, and the borrower has no right to redeem the property after the sale.

For more information on South Carolina Foreclosure Laws, go to: www. scstatehouse.net/code

Summary of South Dakota Foreclosure Law

In South Dakota, lenders use mortgages, and occasionally deeds of trust, to secure real estate loans. If a mortgage was used, the foreclosure will be judicial. If a deed of trust was used, then the foreclosure will follow non-judicial procedures. In South Dakota, foreclosures of single-family residences are typically judicial.

Judicial Foreclosure Guidelines

Complaint filed. The judicial process begins with the lender filing a lawsuit to obtain a court order to foreclose in the courthouse in the county where the property is located. The borrower, and all interested parties, are given notice and have 30 days to respond. If the borrower does not respond, or does respond, and the court determines there is a default, it will declare a foreclosure and order the property sold. After the order is entered, there is a 30-day waiting period to allow the borrower to bring the loan current (reinstatement period).

Notice of Sale. At the expiration of the 30-day waiting period, the Sheriff will start advertising the foreclosure sale. The Sheriff will publish the notice once a week for four successive weeks in a newspaper of general circulation in the county where the property is located. At least 21 days prior to the sale date, the lender must serve a written copy of the notice on the borrower and any lienholders whose interest in the property would be affected by the foreclosure. The notice must contain the names of the borrower(s) and lender, the mortgage date, the amount due, a description of the premises, and the date, time, and place of sale.

Sheriff's Sale. The sale must be conducted by the sheriff of the county, or his deputy, between the hours of 9:00 am and 5:00 pm. The sale will be conducted as a public auction and sold to the highest bidder. Any person, including the lender, may bid at the sale. The winning bidder will receive a Certificate of Sale, and is entitled to the deed once the borrower's redemption period has expired (see below). The sale may be postponed, from time to time, by inserting a notice of such postponement, as soon as possible, in the newspaper in which the original advertisement was published, and continuing publication until the time when the postponed sale occurs.

Redemption Period. Generally, the borrower has one year from the date of sale to redeem the property. But if the property is 40 acres or less, and the mortgage contains a power of sale clause, there is only a six-month redemption period. If the property is abandoned, the time period is reduced to 60 days.

326

For more information on South Dakota Foreclosure Laws, go to: www.legis.state.sd.us

© 2003, The Real Estate Library

Tennessee Foreclosure Law

In Tennessee, lenders use either deeds of trust or mortgages to secure real estate loans. If a mortgage is used, the foreclosure will be judicial. If a deed of trust was used, the foreclosure will follow non-judicial procedures. In Tennessee, the vast majority of single-family residences are foreclosed non-judicially, and take approximately two months.

Non-Judicial Foreclosure Guidelines

Notice of Sale. The foreclosure starts with a Notice of Sale published in a newspaper in the county where the property is located, at least three different times with the first publication appearing at least 20 days prior to the sale. If no newspaper is published in said county, the notice must be posted at least 30 days in advance of the sale in at least five public places within the county. At least one of the notices must be placed at the courthouse door and another in the neighborhood of the property. The notice must also be served upon the borrower at least 20 days prior to the date of sale if the borrower is in possession of the property. The notice must give the names of the parties, describe the property and street address (if available), and state the date, time, and place of the sale.

Redemption Period. The borrower has the right at any time prior to the sale to stop the foreclosure by paying the total amount owed to the lender plus all applicable fees.

Foreclosure Sale. The sale must be conducted as a public auction between the hours of 10:00 am and 4:00 pm. The property will be sold for cash to the highest bidder. The sheriff may set a minimum acceptable price for the property as long as the price is equal to or greater than 50% of its fair market value. The successful bidder at the foreclosure sale will receive a Certificate of Sale and will only be entitled to receive a deed after the borrower's right of redemption has expired.

Deficiency judgments. Deficiency judgments are allowed in Tennessee and the borrower has a period of two years to redeem the property. However, if the borrower waived the right of redemption in the original deed of trust, which frequently occurs, the lender does not have a right to a deficiency judgment.

For more information on Tennessee Foreclosure Law, go to: www.legislature. state.tn.us

Summary of Texas Foreclosure Law

In Texas, lenders use deeds of trust, and occasionally mortgages, to secure real estate loans. If a mortgage was used, the foreclosure will be judicial. If a deed of trust was used, the foreclosure will follow non-judicial procedures. Most foreclosures of single-family residences in Texas are non-judicial and take approximately two to three months.

Non-Judicial Guidelines

Letter of Demand. Prior to proceeding with a foreclosure, Texas law requires that the lender mail the borrower by certified mail a Letter of Demand declaring the loan in default and informing the borrower that he has 20 days to pay the delinquent payments or foreclosure proceedings will begin.

Notice of Sale. After the expiration of the 20-day reinstatement period, but at least 21 days before the scheduled sale date, the lender must: 1) file a Notice of Sale with the county clerk; 2) mail the notice to the borrower at their last known address by certified mail; and 3) post the notice on the county courthouse door.

Trustee's Sale. The foreclosure sale must take place between the hours of 10:00 am and 4:00 pm, on the first Tuesday of the month, even if that Tuesday falls on a legal holiday. The sale will be conducted at the courthouse by auction and the property will be sold to the highest bidder for cash. Anyone may bid, including the lender, who can bid by canceling out the balance due on the note, or some part of it. If the bid amount is higher than the amount owed to the lender, any surplus will go to junior lienholders. After the sale, the borrower has no right of redemption.

Deficiency Judgment. Lenders may obtain deficiency judgments, but they are limited to the difference between the fair market value of the property at the time of sale and the balance of the loan in default.

For more information on Texas Foreclosure Laws, go to: www.capitol. state.tx.us

© 2001, The Real Estate Library

Summary of Utah Foreclosure Law

In Utah, lenders use deeds of trust, and occasionally mortgages, to secure real estate loans. If a mortgage was used, the foreclosure will be judicial. If a deed of trust was used, the foreclosure will most likely follow the non-judicial procedures. Most foreclosures of single-family residences in Utah are non-judicial and take between 4-5 months.

Judicial Foreclosure

The judicial foreclosure begins with the lender filing a complaint against the borrower in the county courthouse where the property is located. In the lawsuit, the lender will seek a Decree of Sale to have the property sold. If the court finds the borrower in default, it will enter a decree of foreclosure and order of sale, directing the sheriff to conduct a foreclosure sale of the property.

Non-Judicial Guidelines

Notice of Default. The non-judicial procedures begin with the lender recording a Notice of Default in the county recorder's office. A copy of the Notice is also mailed to the borrower and all parties with recorded interests in the property, within ten days of recording. The notice states that the borrower has three months to cure the default or the property will be sold at a foreclosure sale. During this period, the borrower can reinstate the loan by simply paying the amount in default plus all of the lender's costs.

Notice of Trustee's Sale. After the expiration of the three months, the lender must publish a Notice of Trustee's Sale once a week for three consecutive weeks in a newspaper of general circulation in the county where the property is to be sold. The last publication must be at least ten days but not more than 30 days before the date of sale is scheduled. The notice must be mailed to the borrower (and property owner if different), and all other interested parties with recorded interests by certified mail. The notice must also be posted in some conspicuous place on the property and at the office of the county recorder of the county in which the property is located, at least 20 days before the scheduled sale. The date, time, and place of sale must be clearly advertised in the Notice of Sale.

Trustee's Sale. The sale will be scheduled approximately five weeks after the Reinstatement Period ends. The sale must be held between the hours of 8:00 am and 5:00 pm at the county courthouse. The sale will be conducted as a public auction with the highest bidder purchasing the property. Most trustees require that the winning bidder pay $5,000 down and the remaining balance of the purchase price within 24 hours. The winning bidder will receive a Trustee's Deed. If the sale price is greater than the amount owed to the foreclosing lender, the surplus will be paid to junior lienholders, and then the borrower. After the sale, the borrower does not have a right of redemption, nor does the lender have a right to a deficiency judgment.

For more information on Utah Foreclosure Laws, go to: www.le.state.ut.us

330

© 2003. The Real Estate Library.

Summary of Vermont Foreclosure Law

In Vermont, lenders use mortgages, and occasionally deeds of trust, to secure real estate loans. If a mortgage was used, the foreclosure will follow the strict foreclosure process. If a deed of trust was used, the foreclosure will follow non-judicial procedures.

Strict Foreclosure Guidelines

The strict foreclosure process is based on the premise that the lender owns the property until the mortgage has been paid in full. If the borrower breaks any of the conditions contained in the mortgage prior to the time the loan is paid in full, the borrower will lose any right to the property.
Strict foreclosure begins with the lender filing a lawsuit against the borrower in the county where the property is located. The borrower will be served a summons to appear before the court and informed of his rights. Once the borrower answers, the lender will typically file a motion for summary judgment, in order to avoid trial. If the

court finds in favor of the lender, it will issue a decree to sell the property. The defendants have five days to object to the decree.

Notice of Intent to Foreclose. Once a decree has been issued by the court, the lender will send a Notice of Intent to Foreclose to the borrower by registered or certified mail at his or her last known address. The notice must include information on the mortgage to be foreclosed, state the condition(s) breached, the lender's right to accelerate the loan, and the total amount necessary to cure the default. The notice must also inform that the borrower is entitled to receive a Notice of Sale at least 60 days prior to the date of sale.

Redemption Period. The borrower may redeem the property at any time prior to the foreclosure sale by paying the full amount due on the loan, plus costs.

Notice of Sale. 30 days after the Notice of Intent was issued, the Notice of Sale must be mailed to the borrower. The notice must be mailed no less than 60 days prior to the sale date. The notice must also be published once a week for three weeks in a local newspaper, with the first publication appearing no less than 21 days before the sale date.

Public Auction. The sale must be held on the property itself, and the property must be sold to the highest bidder. Anyone may bid at the sale, including the lender. The borrower is entitled to receive any surplus from the sale, but they may also be sued for deficiency if the sale price is not enough to cover the amount of the mortgage in default.

After the sale, the borrower has six months to redeem the property.

Deficiency Judgment. The lender is entitled to a deficiency judgment. However, if the lender buys the property at the sale, the borrower can force the lender to credit the fair market value of the property against the amount owed.

For more information on Vermont Foreclosure Laws, go to: www.leg.state.vt.us

Summary of Virginia Foreclosure Law

In Virginia, lenders use either mortgages or deeds of trusts to secure real estate loans. If a mortgage was used, the foreclosure will be judicial. If a deed of trust was used, the foreclosure will follow the non-judicial procedures. Foreclosures of single-family residences are commonly non-judicial and take two-three months.

Non-Judicial Foreclosure Guidelines

Notice of Default. Virginia Statutes require that the Notice of Default be published in a local newspaper in the county where the property is located. These requirements are in addition to whatever publication terms are stipulated in the deed of trust. If the deed of trust does not provide for publication, then the notice shall be published once a week for four successive weeks. The notice must give the borrower 30 days to pay the default and reinstatement the loan.

Notice of Sale. After expiration of the 30-day period, a copy of the Notice of Sale must be mailed to the borrower at least 14 days before the foreclosure sale. The notice must be published once a week for four consecutive weeks. The notice must include anything required by the deed of trust and includes a legal description of the property, a street address, and a tax map identification or general information about the property's location. The notice must include the time, place and terms of sale. It must give the name of the trustee and the address and phone number of a person who will be able to respond to inquiries about the foreclosure sale.

Redemption Period. Any time before the sale, the borrower may cure the default and stop the sale by paying the total lien debt, costs and reasonable attorney's fees.

Trustee's Sale. The sale, which may be held no earlier than eight days after the first notice was published and no more than 30 days after the last notice is published, is to be made at auction to the highest bidder. Any person, other than the trustee, may bid at the foreclosure sale, including a person who has submitted a written one-price bid. Written one-price bids will be received by the trustee for entry by announcement at the sale. Any bidder in attendance may inspect these written bids. Additionally, the trustee may require bidders to place a cash deposit of up to ten percent of the sale price, unless the deed of trust specifies a higher or lower amount. In the event of postponement of sale, which may be done at the discretion of the trustee, advertisement of such postponed sale shall be in the same manner as the original advertisement of sale. Once the sale is complete, the proceeds will go to: 1) the expenses of executing the sale; 2) to discharge all taxes, levies, and assessments, with costs and

interest if they have priority over the foreclosing deed of trust; 3) to discharge in the order of their priority, if any, the remaining debts and obligations secured by the deed of trust, and any liens of record junior to the foreclosing deed of trust; and 4) any remaining proceeds go to the borrower.

Deficiency Judgment. Lenders may obtain deficiency judgments, without limits, in Virginia, but the borrower has no redemption rights.

For more information on Virginia Foreclosures Laws, go to: www.leg1.state.va.us

Summary of Washington Foreclosure Law

In Washington, lenders use either deeds of trust or mortgages to secure real estate loans. If a deed of trust was used, the foreclosure will follow non-judicial procedures. If a mortgage was used, the foreclosure will be judicial. Foreclosures of single-family residences in Washington are typically non-judicial and take approximately four-five months.

Judicial Foreclosure Guidelines

A judicial foreclosure involves filing a lawsuit to obtain a court order to foreclose. It is utilized by lenders when a mortgages was used or the lender is foreclosing on commercial or multi-residential property. After the court declares a foreclosure, the property will be auctioned off to the highest bidder. After the sale, the borrower can be sued for a deficiency, unless the property is found to be abandoned for six months before the Decree of Foreclosure. Unless redemption rights have been precluded, the borrower may, within one year after the date of the sale, redeem the property by paying the amount of the highest bid at the foreclosure, plus interest.

Non-Judicial Foreclosure Guidelines

Notice of Sale. The process begins with the lender recording the Notice of Sale in the county recorder's office at least 90 days before the scheduled sale date. The lender is also required to send the Notice by both regular mail and certified mail, return receipt requested, to the borrower at their last known address, and by regular mail to the attorney of record for the borrower, if any, not less than 30 days prior to the day of sale. The sheriff must publish the notice once a week, consecutively, for four weeks, in a daily or weekly legal newspaper of general circulation in the county in which the property is located. Additionally, the sheriff must also post the notice in two public places, one of which must be the courthouse door, in the county where the sale is to take place for a period of not less than four weeks prior to the day of sale. The notice must contain the time and place of the foreclosure sale, the names of the parties to the deed, the date of the deed, recording information, a property description, the terms of the sale, and the borrowers rights (or lack of) of redemption.

Reinstatement Period. The borrower has up to 11 days before the sale to stop the foreclosure process by paying the past due payments, plus expenses, including trustee and attorney fees.

Foreclosure Sale. The sale must be conducted as a auction between 9:00 am in the morning and 4:00 am in the afternoon at the courthouse door on a Friday. If Friday falls on a legal holiday, the sale is then held on the next following regular business day. The sale may not be conducted less than 190 days from the date of default. The highest bidder will receive a Certificate of Sale and is entitled to possession 20 days thereafter. The trustee may postpone the sale by giving notice at the sale, and by posting written notices of the postponement under the Notices of Sale originally posted. The borrower has no right to redeem the property after the sale.

Deficiency Judgment. If the non-judicial foreclosure process is used by the lender, it cannot sue for a deficiency judgment.

For more information on Washington Foreclosure Law, go to: www.leg.wa.gov

Summary of West Virginia Foreclosure Law

In West Virginia, lenders use either mortgages or deeds of trust to secure real estate loans. If a mortgage is used, the foreclosure will be judicial. If a deed of trust was used, the foreclosure will follow non-judicial procedures. Foreclosures of single-family residences are commonly non-judicial in West Virginia.

Judicial Foreclosure Guidelines

The judicial process of foreclosure, which involves filing a lawsuit to obtain a court order to foreclose, is used when a mortgage was used. Generally, after the court declares a foreclosure, the property will be auctioned off to the highest bidder.

Non-Judicial Foreclosure Guidelines

Letter of Default. The non-judicial process begins when the Lender send the borrower a Letter of Default advising of the impending foreclosure. The letter also advises the borrower that the foreclosure can be stopped by paying off the default and reinstating the loan.

Reinstatement Period. The borrower is then given ten days to cure the default or the lender can accelerate the loan and take action to possess the property. But, if the borrower has already been notified of a default more than three times, the borrower can no longer simply reinstate the loan by bringing the loan current. Instead, the borrower must pay-off the entire loan balance plus all applicable fees up until the date of sale.

Notice of Sale. The Notice of Sale must be posted on the front door of the courthouse in the county in which the property is located. The Notice must also be posted at three other public places in the county, one of which must be the property itself, at least 20 days prior to sale. The notice must also be mailed to the borrower and all junior lienholders at least 20 days prior to the foreclosure sale. Additionally, the Notice must be published as a Class III legal advertisement in the county where the property is located once a week for four weeks. The Notice must contain the time and place of the foreclosure sale, the names of the parties to the deed, the date of the deed, recording information, a property description, and the terms of the sale.

Foreclosure Sale. The sale must be held at the time and place stated in the Notice of Sale and conducted as a public auction. The property is sold to the highest bidder. Unless the deed of trust specifies the terms of sale, the buyer must pay at least one-third of the bid amount in cash at the sale, and the balance due within 30 days. Upon full payment, a Trustee's Deed is recorded giving ownership to the buyer. After a non-judicial foreclosure sale, deficiency actions are not permitted and there are no rights of redemption.

For more information on West Virginia Foreclosure Laws, go to: www.legis.state. wv.us

© 2003. The Real Estate Library

Summary of Wisconsin Foreclosure Law

In Wisconsin, lenders use mortgages, and occasionally deeds of trust, to secure real estate loans. If a mortgage was used, the foreclosure will be judicial. If a deed of trust was used, the foreclosure will follow non-judicial procedures. The majority of foreclosure of single-family residences are judicial.

Judicial Foreclosure Guidelines

Lawsuit Filed. The judicial process begins when the lender files a summons and complaint with the court in the county where the property is located. The lender must deliver a copy of the documents to the borrower and other interested parties. If the Court determines that a default has occurred, the court will declare a foreclosure and order the property sold to payoff the lender.

Reinstatement Period. No sale can be made for one year from the date the judgment is entered unless the lender waives the right to a deficiency, in which case the delay is six months. If the property is abandoned, the sale will

only be delayed for two months. During this period, the borrower is given the right to pay the default and reinstate the loan.

Notice of Sale. The local Sheriff records the Notice of Sale in the county where the property is located. The Notice must also be published once a week for six consecutive weeks in a local newspaper. The last publication must be completed at least one week prior to the date of sale. The notice must be served upon the borrower in the same manner that civil process in a lawsuit is served. In instances where the borrower can't be found, then the notice shall be posted in a conspicuous spot on the property and three conspicuous public places, and served on any occupants. The notice must specify the names of the borrower(s) and lender, the date the mortgage was recorded, the amount due at the date of the notice, a property description, and the time and place of sale.

Sheriff's Sale. The sale cannot be conducted until after the borrower's reinstatement period has expired, regardless of whether it is 12 months, six months, or two months. The sale must be held at the time and place stated in the notice. The Sheriff conducts the sale as a public auction. Any party may bid provided they pay at least ten percent of their bid amount. The winning bidder will receive a Certificate of Purchase. If necessary, the sale may be postponed. Within ten days, the Sheriff must file a report of the sale and post the sale proceeds with the clerk of the court. Upon confirmation of the sale, the clerk will pay the parties entitled to the proceeds and deliver the deed to the purchaser. If the buyer fails to pay the balance of the loan within the 10-day period, the deposit is forfeited, and a resale is held. If the court does not confirm the sale for any reason, the clerk refunds the deposit and a resale occurs.

Redemption Period. Unless the foreclosure sale has been confirmed by court order, the borrower has one year to redeem the property by paying the amount of the highest bid at the foreclosure sale, plus interest.

Deficiency Judgment. Wisconsin law requires that the sale to be confirmed by court order. If the lender states their intentions in the application for sales confirmation, then they may file a deficiency suit. Otherwise, deficiency suits are not allowed.

For more information on Wisconsin Foreclosure Laws, go to: www.legis.state.wi.us

Summary of Wyoming Foreclosure Law

In Wyoming, lenders use either deeds of trust or mortgages to secure real estate loans. If a mortgage was used, the foreclosure will be judicial. If a deed of trust was used, the foreclosure will follow non-judicial procedures. Foreclosures of single-family residences are commonly non-judicial and take approximately three months.

Judicial Foreclosure

The judicial process of foreclosure, which involves filing a lawsuit to obtain a court order to foreclose, is used when the defaulted loan is secured by a mortgage. Generally, after the court declares a foreclosure, the property will be auctioned off to the highest bidder.

Non-Judicial Foreclosure Guidelines

Notice of Intent to Foreclose. The non-judicial process begins when the lender serves a Notice of Intent to Foreclose upon the record owner, and any persons in possession of the property (if different than the record owner), by certified mail, return-receipt requested, at least ten days before the first publication of the Notice of Sale.

Notice of Sale. The Notice of Sale must be published at least once a week for four consecutive weeks in a newspaper printed in the county where the property is located. The Notice must specify the name of the borrower(s), the lender and the lender's representative, the date of the deed of trust, when it was recorded, the amount of the default, a description of the property, and the time and place of sale.

Foreclosure Sale. The sale must be held at the front door of the courthouse of the county in which the property is located, between the hours of 9:00 am and 5:00 pm. It must be conducted by the person appointed for that purpose in the deed of trust, or by the sheriff of the county. Anyone may bid, including the lender. The highest bidder will receive a Certificate of Purchase and then a deed (after the borrower's redemption period expires).

Such sale may be postponed from time to time by inserting a notice as soon as possible in the newspaper in which the original advertisement was published and continuing such publication until the time to which the sale shall be postponed, at the expense of the party requesting such postponement. Lenders may obtain deficiency judgments in Wyoming.

Redemption Period. The borrower has three months after the date of sale to redeem the property by paying the amount of the purchase price together with interest at the rate of ten percent from the date of sale, plus the amount of any assessments or taxes, and the amount due on any prior lien which the purchaser paid after the purchase, with interest.

For more information on Wyoming Foreclosure Laws, go to: www.legisweb.state.wy.us

AMACOM Books
a division of the American Management Association
1601 Broadway
New York, NY 10019

Dear Reader:

I'd like to thank you for reading *Stop Foreclosure Now*. I realize thousands of books are available and I am indebted to you for taking the time to read mine. I sincerely appreciate the encouragement you've given me and hope *Stop Foreclosure Now* helped stop your foreclosure or avoid it altogether.

I'd like to further express my sincere thanks to you for your support. As someone who grew up reading everything I could get my hands on, I always found myself wishing I could talk to the authors about their books. Of course, I never could, but I promised myself that someday, if a book of mine was ever published, I'd make myself available to my readers as best I could. In short, I'd try to give readers the experience and continuing education I had wanted but never received.

So, if you have an investors' group or book club that is interested in my book, please let me know. I'd be delighted to speak to your group or club in person. Or, you can call me over a speakerphone, and we can chat about foreclosure in your state and strategies to stop foreclosure. I'd like to hear what members of your group think about it - such feedback and interaction is quite valuable and enjoyable to me. If you're not in an investor's group or book club, but would like to drop me a line, please do so. Either way, I can be reached at lloydsegal@msn.com.

I truly wish you the best in all your endeavors.

Sincerely,

Lloyd Segal

About the Author

Trained as an attorney, Lloyd Segal is a mortgage banker, author, real estate investor, and public speaker. Now located in Santa Monica, California, Mr. Segal was born in Pittsburgh, Pennsylvania. He graduated Boston University and Southwestern University Law School, and studied at the University of Innsbruck, Austria. Author of *Everything You Wanted to Know About Chapter 11 Bankruptcy . . . but Were Afraid to Ask*, and *Stop Foreclosure Now in California*, Lloyd Segal is a public speaker, sharing experiences of more than 25 years in real estate as a mortgage banker and real estate attorney. He is a frequent guest speaker at various universities, boards of realtors, Coldwell Banker national conventions, and numerous other real estate and service organizations throughout the United States. He is also the founder of the California Foreclosure Institute, which provides in-depth educational services with respect to all aspects of foreclosure.

Look for These Exciting Real Estate Titles at
www.amacombooks.org/go/realestate

A Survival Guide for Buying a Home by Sid Davis $17.95

A Survival Guide for Selling a Home by Sid Davis $15.00

An Insider's Guide to Refinancing Your Mortgage by David Reed $16.95

Are You Dumb Enough to Be Rich?, Second Edition by G. William Barnett II $18.95

Everything You Need to Know Before Buying a Co-op, Condo, or Townhouse
   by Ken Roth $18.95

Mortgages 101, Second Edition by David Reed $16.95

Mortgage Confidential by David Reed $16.95

Real Estate Investing Made Simple by M. Anthony Carr $17.95

Stop Foreclosure Now by Lloyd Segal $19.95

The Complete Guide to Investing in Foreclosures by Steve Berges $17.95

The First-Time Homeowner's Survival Guide by Sid Davis $16.00

The Home Buyer's Question and Answer Book by Bridget McCrea $16.95

The Landlord's Financial Tool Kit by Michael C. Thomsett $18.95

The Property Management Tool Kit by Mike Beirne $19.95

The Real Estate Investor's Pocket Calculator by Michael C. Thomsett $17.95

The Successful Landlord by Ken Roth $19.95

Who Says You Can't Buy a Home! by David Reed $17.95

Your Eco-Friendly Home by Sid Davis $17.95

Your Guide to VA Loans by David Reed $17.95

Available at your local bookstore, online, or call 800-250-5308.

Savings start at 40% on bulk orders of 5 copies or more!
Save up to 55%!
Prices are subject to change.
For details, contact AMACOM Special Sales
Phone: 212-903-8316   E-Mail: SpecialSls@amanet.org